The Good
FRANCHISE GUIDE

PICTURE YOURSELF IN YOUR OWN BUSINESS

Fastframe is one of the most exciting new retail Franchises to be launched in recent years.

It combines an expert picture framing service with an attractive shop layout. We are looking for sales orientated individuals who are keen to build a successful business backed by the Marketing, Group Purchasing and Central Services of an experienced Franchisor.

Minimum Capital £15,000 – Total Capital £34,000

⅔rds Finance available

FASTFRAME
expert picture framing

For full details contact:
Margaret Hewison, Franchise Director
Fastframe Franchises Ltd, 28 Blandford Street, Sunderland, SR1 3JH
Telephone: (091) 565 2233

Fourth Edition

Taking Up a Franchise

The *Daily Telegraph* Guide

Colin Barrow and Godfrey Golzen

'an excellent book which must be an essential tool for people running or wanting to run a business'
THE GUARDIAN

▶ ▶ ▶ ▶ Taking up a franchise? Now in its fourth edition, this best-selling book will provide you with the necessary facts and figures you need to make the *right* decision.

The information it provides includes:

- What franchising is
- How it operates
- Evaluating and financing a franchise
- A checklist for franchises
- Financial and marketing data on around 100 franchisors
- Lists of useful organisations and publications

£7.95 paperback
ISBN 1 85091 342 0   336 pages 216x138mm

KOGAN PAGE

The Good FRANCHISE GUIDE

An independent survey of over 400 franchises in the UK

Tony Attwood and Len Hough

KOGAN PAGE

The Authors

Tony Attwood has recently launched a licensed employment agency which will soon be franchised. He is the author of **Buying for Business** and **Business Rip-Offs and How to Avoid Them**, also published by Kogan Page.

*Len Hou*gh worked with a large manufacturing company to set up a national network of franchise outlets. During this work he undertook a study of franchising in this country.

Copyright© Tony Attwood and Len Hough 1988

All rights reserved. No reproduction, copy or transmission of this publication may be made without written permission.

No paragraph of this publication may be reproduced, copied or transmitted save with written permission or in accordance with the provisions of the Copyright Act 1956 (as amended), or under the terms of any licence permitting limited copying issued by the Copyright Licensing Agency, 7 Ridgmount Street, London WC1E 7AE

Any person who does any unauthorised act in relation to this publication may be liable to criminal prosecution and civil claims for damages.

First published in Great Britain in 1988 by Kogan Page Limited, 120 Pentonville Road, London N1 9JN

British Library Cataloguing in Publication Data

Attwood, Tony, *1947* -
   The good franchise guide.
   1. Great Britain. Franchising
   I. Title II. Hough, Len
   658.8'708'0941

   ISBN 1-85091-511-3

Typeset by Sovereign Printing Group, Sidmouth, Devon
Printed and bound in Great Britain by Biddles Ltd, Guildford

EUROCLEAN

Euroclean is the UK's largest drycleaning franchise, a member of the Black Arrow Group Plc.

Euroclean operates shops successfully all over the country, with areas available throughout the UK.

We offer full marketing and advertising support, shop site selection and the provision of on-site training.

The minimum investment is £15-£20,000, with up to 70% financing available, subject to status. We operate a method of flat license fees, and not a percentage of your sales.

We are full members of the British Franchise Association, and have regional offices in Scotland and Northern Ireland.

For more information call us on:

01-595 4234 - England   031-228 4535 - Scotland

EUROCLEAN
Europe's most fashionable drycleaner

Fourth Edition

Taking Up a Franchise

The *Daily Telegraph* Guide

Colin Barrow and Godfrey Golzen

'an excellent book which must be an essential tool for people running or wanting to run a business'
THE GUARDIAN

▶ ▶ ▶ ▶ Taking up a franchise? Now in its fourth edition, this best-selling book will provide you with the necessary facts and figures you need to make the *right* decision.

The information it provides includes:

- What franchising is
- How it operates
- Evaluating and financing a franchise
- A checklist for franchises
- Financial and marketing data on around 100 franchisors
- Lists of useful organisations and publications

£7.95 paperback
ISBN 1 85091 342 0   336 pages 216x138mm

KOGAN PAGE

Share in the multi-million pound overnight market

Run your own business, under license as part of a nationwide, express parcel organisation.

Receive regular monthly commissions on every parcel handled, leaving us to collect customer cash.

Full sales and management support is available and up to 70% of your initial investment could be funded from leading banks.

Investment required is from £8,500 depending on area, and you'll need a light commercial vehicle.

Individuals, partners or husband and wife teams with enthusiasm, dedication and success in their sights, should write NOW for an information pack.

Complete the coupon and return to:
Amtrak Express Parcels Limited, Company House, Tower Hill, Bristol BS2 0EQ.

PLEASE RUSH ME A FRANCHISE INFORMATION PACK.

Name

Address

Postcode

AMTRAK

Contents

Index of Advertisers	viii
Editors' Report	xi
Researching *The Good Franchise Guide*	xix
Directory of Franchisors	1
Broadcasting Franchises	322
Postscript	324
Index of Franchisors	325
Franchises by Trade Category	331

Index of Advertisers

Amtrak Express Parcels Ltd	vi
Banaman	xvi
Barclays Bank plc	xix
Commercial Devices	x
Daytello	86
Department of Employment	*Inside front cover*
Euroclean	v
Exchange Travel	xiii
Fastframe Franchises Ltd	ii
Fersina International	*Inside back cover*
Kall-Kwik Printing (UK) Ltd	ix
Perfect Pizza	xiii
Snap On Tools Ltd	ix
Swinton Insurance Brokers Ltd	*Back cover*
TNT Parcel Office	x

ENJOY A CAREER WITH
Snap-on

OPERATE YOUR OWN BUSINESS As a Snap-on Dealer you will have the opportunity to build a business that you will profit from for many years. You will have the finest tools in the world to sell and the backing of the Snap-on reputation which professional mechanics have come to depend on.

COMPLETE PRODUCT LINE As a Snap-on Dealer you will have over 9,200 products available to sell to professional mechanics. From gleaming Snap-on spanners to a complete line of tool boxes and roll cabs. You will be able to offer your customers the tools they need.

PRODUCT GUARANTEE The Snap-on product guarantee protects Dealers and Customers by backing up tools with a policy which has become the standard of the industry.

IMMEDIATE EARNINGS Your first sale in your territory means money in your pocket. With training and experience there is no limit to what you can earn.

INCOME POTENTIAL Top Snap-on Dealers are in the upper 10% of national income brackets. You can earn that comfortable income while being able to provide for a college education for your children, a new home or a retirement income. Sales management positions are always filled by successful Snap-on Dealers.

TRAINING AND ASSISTANCE A company employed Field Manager, once a successful Dealer himself, provides guidance in record keeping, a training in sales techniques and product information. Your Field Manager will hold regular meetings with you and other Dealers in your area to introduce new tools and exchange ideas to help your business become more successful. He will also ride with you for the first few weeks as you learn where and who your customers are.

SUCCESS COUNTS!

And we *are* successful! Over 140 *quality* UK quick-printing Centres speak for themselves!

So if you want…
- A franchise that *works*.
- With a great *future*.
- And the highest *earning potential* in its field.

And if *you* have…
- The Determination to succeed.
- Proven business skills.
- Capital of £28-30,000

Call Anne Wright, Franchise Sales Manager, on Freephone 0800 289700, or write to her at:

Kall-Kwik Printing (UK) Ltd
Kall-Kwik House
106 Pembroke Rd, Ruislip,
Middlesex HA4 8NW
Phone: (0895) 632700

Kall-Kwik PRINTING
Just a quick call away

|T|N|T| Parcel Office
The UK's Fastest Growing Franchise Network
A Business Of Your Own

TNT is the market leader in the express parcels delivery sector. We are currently able to offer franchise opportunities to selected applicants in various locations throughout the U.K.

If you are self motivated, prepared to promote and sell our services and have the determination to succeed and make money, this could be your first step towards being in business FOR yourself – but not BY yourself.

INVESTMENT £5000 – £10000.

For further details of this exciting business opportunity please telephone the
FRANCHISE SALES MANAGER on 0827–715311 Ext 235

SC Consultancy Services Ltd

BUILDING A SUCCESSFUL FRANCHISE

Whatever your line of business, SCCS can help you. We will determine whether franchising represents the optimum direction for expanding your business. We will develop and franchise your concept only if franchising is appropriate. If it isn't, we will identify and develop an alternative marketing and business plan.

SCCS offers you a professional approach to managing inevitable change using proven problem-solving techniques, identifying opportunities for you to exploit.

Why not contact us for a FREE copy of our leaflet entitled 'Franchising — The down side'!

For further details contact **Derek Ayling** MBA, C.Eng.
Saffery Champness Consultancy Services Ltd.

MANAGEMENT CONSULTANTS
Orchard Court, Whaddon Lane, Owslesbury, Winchester
Hants. SO21 1JJ Telephone: (0962) 74544

Editors' Report

A Poor Image Often Deserved

The Good Franchise Guide is a snapshot of British franchising. As such it reveals a set of attitudes and feelings which can be seen both from the actual information supplied to us, and from the way franchisees and franchisors have reacted to the questions we have asked.

For the most part the answers to our questions speak for themselves and are to be found in the body of the book itself.

And yet, having completed our research we find that there are a few issues which raise themselves time and again, and which need to be highlighted apart from the individual entries.

Secrecy is a dominant feature. It is apparent in the refusal of franchisors to divulge the addresses of franchisees, and in their failure to give basic information on the financial structure of the franchise. Indeed so fanatically secret are some franchisors that they will put nothing whatsoever in writing, responding to requests from potential franchisees by telephoning and demanding an immediate meeting.

The Problem of Consultants

Some financial consultants perform very useful functions, and a number of consultants have written to us giving information on their clients, and ensuring that we have every scrap of information that we need to make a fair assessment of their clients in *The Good Franchise Guide*.

But the majority work in the reverse manner; their prime aim apparently being to stop rival consultancies getting information about their clients.

Some of the franchises which appear on the books of consultants are not the fully fledged, well-researched and prepared businesses that they claim to be. Rather a businessman has a neat idea; the consultant recognises it as a possible franchise and puts out some basic publicity material to prospective franchisees to see what sort of response is gained. If there is a flood of serious enquiries the franchise is quickly put together and the first territories sold. If there is no interest then the idea is dropped, and the 'franchise' disappears from the lists.

Ideas Dressed up as Franchises

Many franchises are little more than ideas. Many franchises listed in this publication could be set up as independent operations by anyone with a spot of basic business experience. Of course even the most basic franchises do contain something of value to franchisees – but this may be little more than help with preparation of the company accounts and VAT records.

Sometimes the supply of materials and items for re-sale is presented as a major advantage for a franchisee. Yet we have seen situations in which such supplies are provided at prices which are higher than those which the franchisee could expect to pay on the open market. This is particularly galling for a franchisee who has just paid out thousands of pounds for the franchise and is tied in to the franchisor for the purchase of materials for the next ten years.

Unjustified Claims

The profit one might make as a franchisee must be of central concern to a potential purchaser of a franchise. The majority of the franchisees we contacted were in fact doing as well as, or better than predicted by the franchise prospectus. But we worry about the franchisees we were not given permission to contact, for some of the projections that we saw looked so unlikely that we cannot believe they will be borne out in practice.

Time and again we have seen franchises which state that while only 20 percent of non-franchised businesses survive their first year, 98 percent of franchises survive three years. Only a couple of franchises using this information quote their sources (the British Franchise Association – BFA – and Dun and Bradstreet for example), and none of them qualifies it by explaining the nature of the research undertaken. In fact the BFA research concludes that 98 percent of franchisees working with *established* franchises are successful – many franchises that quote this figure cannot possibly be called *established* operations.

PERFECT PIZZA
The Franchise that Delivers

We are looking for franchisees to share in our success.

Perfect Pizza is the UK's leading pizza delivery and takeaway franchise, and are currently growing rapidly, particularly in Greater London, the South of England and the Midlands.

Perfect Pizza is backed by the United Biscuits Group, one of the country's most successful food and restaurant/catering companies.

An investment of £80,000 is required and bank financing is available.

If you think that you have the right qualities and commitment contact:—

Franchise Sales Department,
Perfect Pizza, 65 Staines Road, Hounslow, Middlesex TW3 3HW
Tel: 01-577 1711

Exchange Travel Franchise

Already considered to be one of the fastest growing franchise networks in the UK, Exchange Travel the largest privately owned travel group in the country, offers a unique and proven retail travel agency franchise opportunity.

Our annual management fee funds the provision of all central services, computerised accounting and area management support.

The cost of site selection, surveys, cash flows, sales forecasts, staff recruitment, training and local launch all being incorporated in the initial franchise fee.

In a growing industry where personal service counts, we offer a
GUARANTEED MINIMUM BUSINESS VALUE OF 7½% OF ANNUAL SALES. Previous travel experience is not required — but you will need:—

★ The ability to manage staff and inspire them with your own enthusiasm.
★ To enjoy working with the general public.
★ A minimum of £30,000 liquid capital and the ability to borrow a further £35,000 — £65,000 depending on location for the first few years.

Call us for a brochure now, on **(0424) 443684** (24 hour service).
Franchise Department, Exchange Travel Agency Ltd., Exchange House, Parker Road, Hastings, East Sussex. TN34 3UB

Management Potential

We asked franchisors to let us know how viable their franchise was for a person wishing to set up a business and then operate it as a manager, rather than as a person working 'in the shop'. A worryingly large number of franchisors who were clearly offering businesses best described as 'one-man-band' operations, tried to claim that these offered great potential for managers.

Working from Home

A substantial number of franchises stress that franchisees could set up their business from home. Virtually none of them pointed out that this might involve seeking planning permission from the local authority – permission which is by no means automatically granted. This could mean a franchisor setting up in business, only to find himself served with an order to cease trading from home, having already spent a lot of money buying into the franchise.

Almost a Pyramid

We would not suggest that any franchise listed in this book operates a form of pyramid selling, but some firms do operate in a way which does require a lot of stocking up by the franchisee before any real sales to the public are made. At the top is the franchisor who buys in goods from manufacturers. The franchisor then insists that each franchisee stocks up with £5,000 worth of these goods (or more) before he starts trading. The franchisee then has to find retail outlets to buy up some of this stock, and the retailer then sells on to the public. The result is undoubtedly good news for the franchisor who moves a lot of stock and gets paid for it long, long before it gets anywhere near the ultimate user. It is less good for the franchisee who may also have to pay out £ 4,000 or more in franchise fees for the privilege of buying the stock. Our view is that the Fair Trading Act should apply in as much that should the franchisee wish to get out of such an arrangement at *any* time the franchisor will be obliged to buy back the items sold to the franchisee at 90 percent of the price paid.

No Pilot

We find the number of franchises that have been set up without first running pilot operations startling and frightening. We urge caution in such cases.

Poor Prospectuses

No company is immune from the typing error, but when a firm puts out a promotional leaflet which is so badly written that its meaning is obscure, one begins to wonder what sort of company one is dealing with. This is not an isolated factor – in our opinion the standard of writing in documents put out by franchisors is worse than in any other sector of business in the UK.

Bad PR

A number of franchisors did not reply to our questionnaires. We make no complaint about that – filling in forms takes time, and no researcher ever achieves 100 percent coverage of his target. Unfortunately it appears that many franchisors do not even bother to reply to would-be franchisees. We think this is just plain bad management. Even if a franchisor has no franchises available in a specific part of the country, he should still reply to letters. By failing to reply he is not only damaging the good name of the franchise, but the good name of each and every branch of his franchise opened up around the country.

Change of Address

Companies move, normally for very good reasons. What we can't understand is why when franchisors move so many of them do not bother to arrange to have their mail forwarded. It is a small detail, but it is typical of the slipshod way in which some franchises conduct their business. For a cost of a few pounds they could ensure that would-be franchisees who still had their old address would have their mail forwarded, but they just don't bother. It is because we suspect that many of the franchises whose letters are now returned marked 'gone away' are still in operation elsewhere that we have listed them at their last known address.

GET UP AND

GO

TO ONE OF THE FASTEST GROWING FRANCHISES

BANNERS, SIGNS, PROMOTIONAL ITEMS
ARE A LARGELY UNTAPPED MARKET
NOBODY SHOULD WASTE THEIR TIME IF THEY
ARE NOT ORGANISED, HARD WORKING AND
MOTIVATED BY EXCITING PRODUCTS AND PROFIT
  MARGINS
ANYONE WANTING TO START THEIR OWN BUSINESS
  KNOWS
NOTHING VENTURED, NOTHING GAINED.

INITIAL FRANCHISE DETAILS FROM
BANAMAN, BANAMAN HOUSE, 78 NEWMAN STREET.
LONDON W1P 3LA TEL: 01-636 7777
CONTACT:- JOHN REES.

BANAMAN
THE ONE STOP PROMOTION SHOP

78 Newman Street, London W1P 3OA
Telephone: 01-636 7777

contact John Rees at our London showroom

One of the most Exciting Franchises available

SOME OF THE HIGH QUALITY HIGH PROFIT PROMOTIONAL ITEMS YOU CAN PRODUCE WITH OUR UNIQUE SYSTEM

BanaMan
THE ONE STOP PROMOTION SHOP

78 Newman Street, London W1P 3OA
Telephone: 01-636 7777

contact John Rees at our London showroom

The Good Bits

Of course it is not all this bad. There are some excellent franchises around – none represents a licence to print money, but many offer a good way of earning a living. Some franchises are household names. Some are less well known but as the franchisee reports show, are doing very well. One has only to look at the comments from the franchisees in our reports to see where the success comes. We must reiterate – the majority of franchisees we contacted were doing as well, or better, than predicted by their franchisor. Most were very happy with their lot and thought their investment had been worthwhile. But on the fringes we suspect things are not so good.

How can the image of franchising be improved? In our estimation the following improvements would help:

1. Better franchisors

You need only read entries in *The Good Franchise Guide* about franchises where information has been promised and not sent, where franchisors have disappeared without trace, etc, to realise that some of the people offering franchises are not doing the name of franchising much good.

2. Better consultants

In our estimation some consultants are spending as much time fighting each other as they are looking after their clients' interests. This cannot be good for franchising.

3. Better franchisees

Too many franchisees are being taken on who will struggle to make a success of the franchise. The good franchisors are turning such people down. These would-be franchisees then turn to less desirable operations, and are signed up either by consultants who are paid a commission on every name they forward, or by franchisors who pursue franchisees with a form of pressurised telephone selling that only the very strong can stand up to.

To all franchisees we can only say, take care. Many of the franchises listed in this publication are excellent – we hope that this book helps you find them.

Tony Attwood and Len Hough *March 1988*

OUR FRANCHISE LOANS WILL SATISFY EVEN THE BIGGEST APPETITE FOR SUCCESS.

At Barclays we're as keen to see your franchise grow as you are.

That's why we set up a Franchise Unit, which offers a special Barclays Franchise Loan.

If you need capital to buy or develop any kind of franchise, we can lend you up to two thirds of your expenditure, from £2,000 to £500,000.

Interest at competitive rates is fixed for the whole term for loans of up to £15,000, or at 3 yearly intervals for larger sums.

For a fast, flexible Franchise Loan, contact your Barclays branch manager or the Franchise Unit.

They'll look forward to hearing from you, with relish.

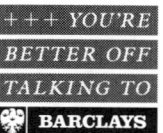

Contact John Perkins, Franchise Unit, 168 Fenchurch Street, London EC3P 3HP. Tel: 01-283 8989 Ext. 3581.

+++ YOU'RE BETTER OFF TALKING TO BARCLAYS

Researching *The Good Franchise Guide*

Research for this publication was undertaken in the latter half of 1987, with final amendments made up to February 1988. All franchises that we could locate were sent questionnaires. Where no reply was received further copies of the questionnaire were mailed up to a maximum of four times. Franchisors were invited to supply lists of franchisees – where no list was supplied we wrote up to twice more asking for the list.

Franchisees were only contacted where a list of the franchisees was supplied by the franchisor in response to our request. We also contacted a number of private individuals who were interested in locating a franchise and asked them to write for details of various franchises. Where we have obtained no information from the franchisor we have turned to the information supplied to the would-be franchisees.

Most of the data presented in the book is self-evident, but clarification is given for the following specific headings:

1988 Franchise target
We have asked franchisors to estimate the number of franchises they will have established by the *end* of 1988.

Bank rating
We have asked franchisees how easy they found it to obtain finance from banks and from other financial institutions.

Territory
Franchisors have told us how the territories are allocated; franchisees have told us if they find the areas too small or too large.

Training
Details of training are given by the franchisor. Franchisees were asked to evaluate the training, and the brief comment given is an average of their responses.

Support
We asked franchisees to evaluate the level of support given by the franchisor.

Operating manual
As with 'Support' we asked franchisees for their opinion.

Profit
Profits can be calculated in so many ways that we felt that the best way to evaluate the profit potential was to invite franchisees to let us know how they were getting on in relation to the predictions made by the franchisor. Where this was not possible we give the first year net profit figure as predicted by the franchisor, and failing that we give whatever figures we can find in the literature.

Risk
This is our estimation of the risk potential in entering this particular industry.

Management only
Many would-be franchisees are interested in setting up a franchise which they can then run as a manager, employing staff to work 'in the shop'. We asked franchisors to evaluate their franchises in relation to the opportunity offered to anyone wanting to act as a manager.

Size and reach
The entry 'BFA' against 'Trade bodies' indicates that the franchisor is a member of the British Franchise Association.

Franchisor's formula for success
Franchisors were invited to supply us with a statement about their own franchise. Where no information was provided we have taken what appears to be the most relevant statement from the brochure sent to would-be franchisees.

Inside story from the franchisees
Where the actual words of franchisees are used we have used quotation marks, and these quotations represent feelings which broadly reflect the view of all franchisees who gave us information for that franchise.

Good Franchise Guide comment
Only added where we feel that the information provided by franchisors and franchisees leaves a gap which we must fill.

Directory of Franchisors

⇨ A1 Damproofing (UK) Ltd

New Side Mill, Charnley Fold Lane, Bamber Bridge, Preston, Lancs PR5 6AA
Phone: 0772 35228

A low cost woodworm, woodrot and rising damp franchise which can be run from home with minimum overheads

Outlets
Number of outlets
Company owned outlets: 00
Franchised: 21
Pilot: 01 started 1983
1988 franchise target: 42
Current reach:

South	03	South west	01	South east	04
Midlands	02	East Anglia	00	North east	00
North west	09	Scotland	00	Wales	00
N Ireland	02	Rep Ireland	00	I of Man/CI	00

Costs
Total: £11,000
Franchise fee: £5,000
Other charges: 10% management fee
Min cash excluding bank: Nil
Min overdraft required: £2,000
Normal bank advance: Total amount required
Working capital first 2 months: £2,000
Associated banks: Nat West
Capital items required: Van provided on a rental basis
Associated leasing co: No

Royalties

Total
- 10.0% of turnover
- 0.0% accounts service
- 0.0% for advertising fund
- 10.0% monthly sales

No standing royalty independent of turnover

Bank rating All institutions considered helpful. 'Most forthcoming'
Territory Post codes – approx 250,000 population
Franchisees report: Adequate territories
Strings Company sells its own chemicals
Training 6 days practical training
4 days management training
Cost: £1,000 included in franchise fee
Training value: Adequate
Support Good
Operating Manual Fair. 'Didn't cover everything'
Profit Variable, but none reported seriously underachieving targets
Risk Lots of competition in this field
Management only Proven franchise with good return on investment

The Accounting Centre

Size and reach
Original company launched:	1985
Overseas connections:	None
UK connections:	Associated with Industrial Chemical Co (Preston Ltd) chemical manufacturers who produce chemicals required.
Viable for whole UK?	Yes
Trade bodies	Building Employers Confederation

Franchisor's formula for success
Independent training is given by one of the country's leading colleges of building technology; continuous field support and on-going training, and chemicals provided by associated company.
The franchise can be developed so that the franchisee can move into a management role with teams working under supervisor's control.

Inside story from the franchisees
Yellow Pages and Thompsons advertising needs to be available as soon as possible after start up. Ideally the franchisee needs a 'husband and wife partnership to cope with paperwork'.

Insider tips
Technician's background and management skills helpful.

Moans and groans
Targets given are hard to realise in first year.

Number of franchisee addresses provided by franchisor: 19

⇨ **The Accounting Centre**
Elscot House, Arcadia Avenue, Finchley, London N3 2JE
Phone: 01-349 3191

Accounting service to small businesses. The franchisor provides computer support while the franchisee (a qualified accountant) looks after individual clients and oversees the bookkeeping and gives advice.

Outlets
Number of outlets
Company owned outlets:	01
Franchised:	17
Pilot:	01 started 1983
1988 franchise target:	20

Current reach:
South	*08	South west	00	South east	00
Midlands	01	East Anglia	00	North east	**04
North west	02	Scotland	00	Wales	02
N Ireland	00	Rep Ireland	00	I of Man/CI	00

* Includes south, south east and East Anglia
** Includes north and north east

Costs
Total	£7,500
Franchise fee:	No information supplied
Other charges:	No information supplied
Min cash excluding bank:	No information supplied
Min overdraft required:	£7,500
Normal bank advance:	No information supplied
Working capital first 2 months:	£2,500
Associated banks:	None
Capital items required:	None
Associated leasing co:	None

AIR-serv

Royalties	10.0% of turnover
	0.0% accounts service
	0.0% for advertising fund
Total	10.0% monthly sales
	No standing royalty independent of turnover
Bank rating	No information supplied
Territory	Allocated according to business population
Strings	None
Training	Variable amount of practical training
	No management training – franchisee must be a qualified accountant
	Cost: Included in franchise fee
	Training value: No information supplied
Support	No information supplied
Operating Manual	No information supplied
Profit	No information supplied
Risk	No information supplied
Management only	The franchise can only be operated by a qualified accountant.
Size and reach	
Original company launched:	1972
Overseas connections:	Licensed with Accounting Corporation of America
UK connections:	The operating division of Inspectorate UK Ltd
Viable for whole UK?	Yes
Trade bodies	Chartered, certified and management accounting Institutes

Franchisor's formula for success.
The implementation of the service requires of the franchisee a substantial level of skill in accounting methodology. The operation of a franchise requires the establishment of credibility with firms of accountants, banks and other funding agencies, for which a formal qualification has proven necessary.

Good Franchise Guide comment: We trust that qualified accountants will have enough insight and skill to be able to evaluate the franchise. The reluctance of the franchisor to supply either a brochure or a list of franchisees left us lacking in information.

Number of franchisee addresses provided by franchisor: 00

⇨ AIR-serv

Unit 11, Woking Business Park, Albert Drive, Sheerwater, Woking, Surrey GU21 5JY
Phone: 048 62 30801

Air lines and vacuum machines in garage forecourts

Outlets
Number of outlets	No information supplied

Costs
Total	No information supplied
Franchise fee:	£16,800 minimum

Royalties
No information supplied

Franchisor's formula for success
There is a genuine requirement for reliable air lines on Britain's garage forecourts. Currently only about one-third of the nation's 21,000 petrol outlets provide accurate free air. This free air in fact costs a garage up to £1,000 per annum in repairs and maintenance.

Alfred Marks Ltd

Good Franchise Guide comment: These machines check tyre pressures for 10p – a service that has been traditionally free in UK garages, and remains so in the majority. How many people will pay for a previously free service remains to be seen (a quick survey of 8 people in our office revealed a zero take-up but maybe we are not typical). £16,800 buys 20 machines and a protected territory. No other information is available from the franchisor – and we feel there should be to convince potential franchisees of the validity of this operation.

Number of franchisee addresses provided by franchisor: 00

⇨ Alfred Marks Ltd

PO Box 1AL, 84/86 Regent Street, London W1A 1AL
Phone: 01-437 7855

Employment agency

Outlets
Number of outlets Company owned and Franchised outlets:	100
Pilot:	No information supplied
1988 franchise target:	100 (see *Good Franchise Guide* comment)

Costs
Total	£35,000
Franchise fee:	£15,000
Other charges:	£4,000 launch costs (inc in £35,000)
Min cash excluding bank:	£10,000
Min overdraft required:	No information supplied
Normal bank advance:	£20,000
Working capital first 2 months:	£4,000
Associated banks:	No information supplied
Capital items required:	Premises £7,000, refurbishment £9,000
Associated leasing co:	None

Royalties
We can find no mention in the literature supplied but reports elsewhere suggest over 10%.

Bank rating	No information supplied
Territory	No information supplied
Strings	No information supplied
Training	4 weeks practical and management training plus 2 weeks staff training Cost: No information supplied Training value: No information supplied
Support	No information supplied
Operating Manual	No information supplied
Profit	£15,000 to £35,000 profit before drawing in first year.
Risk	Slight with such a well known operation
Management only	Could be run by manager but with limited profit

Size and reach
Original company launched:	1919 – became public company in 1960s
Overseas connections:	Subsidiary of Adia, a worldwide organisation with a turnover of $400 million.
UK connections:	None
Viable for whole UK?	Yes
Trade bodies	None

Allied Dunbar

Franchisor's formula for success
One of the pioneers of the UK private employment agency industry was Alfred Marks, founded in 1919 to help cope with the major staff shortages caused by the massive casualties of the First World War. Alfred Marks is the only survivor from those early days and has grown into the country's largest and most successful recruitment organisation.

Good Franchise Guide comment: No locations are available at present, but some may be available in 1988/9.

Number of franchisee addresses provided by franchisor: 00

⇨ Allied Dunbar
Parliament House, North Row, London W1R 1DL
Phone: 01-734 7244

Allied Dunbar Assurance is the world's largest unit-linked assurance company. The company is expanding its number of financial management consultants and practices by offering 'franchises' which are in fact contracts enabling individuals to create what is, essentially their own practice, representing Allied Dunbar in the marketing of its financial management services. Each practice consists of the consultant, a secretary, an administrator and a salesman. Allied Dunbar provide the interest-free finance.

Outlets
Number of outlets   4,000

Costs
Total   'No cost'
Min overdraft required: £2,000 to £3,000 suggested
Normal bank advance: Depends on circumstances
Working capital first 2 months: Depends on circumstances
Associated banks: Connections with all banks
Capital items required: None save a reliable car
Associated leasing co: None

Royalties
                                 No royalties

Territory   No territory

Training   2 weeks residential practical and management training followed by a further 9 weeks ongoing training
                                 Cost: Nil

Size and reach
Original company launched: 1971
Overseas connections: Two Spanish branches
UK connections: Owned by BAT Industries
Viable for whole UK?   Yes
Trade bodies   None

Franchisor's formula for success
No startup capital, no fees, no royalties, no risk capital, no premises. Plus an optional practice buy-out scheme for successful practices.

Insider tips
This is clearly not a franchise in the normal sense of the word. However, it is called a franchise by Allied Dunbar, and for those who are interested in selling life assurance, pensions, unit trusts, saving schemes, school fees schemes etc it looks to be a highly viable proposition given the lack of up-front fees to be paid.

Good Franchise Guide comment: Despite having a large number of agents the company has refrained from supplying us with names and addresses for us to contact.

Number of franchisee addresses provided by franchisor: 00

Alpine

⇨ Alpine

Richmond Way, Chelmsley Wood, Birmingham B37 7TT
Phone: 021-770 6816

Soft drink supplies

Outlets	No information supplied
Costs	
Total	£5,300
Franchise fee:	£3,000
Other charges:	Nil
Min cash excluding bank:	No information supplied
Min overdraft required:	No information supplied
Normal bank advance:	No information supplied
Working capital first 2 months:	£2,300
Associated banks:	No information supplied
Capital items required:	No information supplied
Associated leasing co:	The van is leased through an associated company
Royalties	
	0.0% of turnover
	0.0% accounts service
	0.0% for advertising fund
Total	0.0% monthly sales (except first year)
	No standing royalty independent of turnover
	There is a first year only management charge of 10% over £5,000 per 3 month period
	There is an annual insurance premium of £46
	The franchisor provides all the products and earns his own commission through sales to the franchisee.
Bank rating	No information supplied
Territory	No information supplied
Strings	The franchisor insists that everything is purchased through him
Training	No information supplied
Support	No information supplied
Operating Manual	No information supplied
Profit	Between £10,000 and £18,000 after all expenses
Risk	We are not sure
Management only	No information supplied
Size and reach	
Original company launched:	1965
Overseas connections:	None
UK connections:	None
Viable for whole UK?	Yes
Trade bodies	None

Franchisor's formula for success
Alpine manufacture and bottle a full range of carbonated drinks, squashes, cordials under the Alpine, Drifter and Big Apple trade marks – we also market a range of mixer drinks and breakfast orange.

Good Franchise Guide comment: A classic distributorship – you pay for the rights to distribute the Alpine product.

Number of franchisee addresses provided by franchisor: 00

⇨ Amtrak Express Parcels Ltd
Company House, Tower Hill, Bristol BS2 0EQ
Phone: 0272 272002

Parcel delivery

Outlets
Number of outlets
Company owned outlets:	No information supplied
Franchised:	No information supplied
Pilot:	No information supplied
1988 franchise target:	No information supplied

Costs
Total	No information supplied
Franchise fee:	£7,500 upwards
Other charges:	No information supplied
Min cash excluding bank:	No information supplied
Min overdraft required:	No information supplied
Normal bank advance:	70%
Working capital first 2 months:	No information supplied
Associated banks:	None
Capital items required:	Van, lock-up premises
Associated leasing co:	None

Royalties
None

Bank rating	No information supplied
Territory	No information supplied, but size of territory affects costs
Strings	No information supplied
Training	Brochure states there is a full training given but no further information provided.
Support	No information supplied
Operating Manual	No information supplied
Profit	No information supplied
Risk	Highly competitive area
Management only	One-man-band operation

Size and reach
Original company launched:	No information supplied
Overseas connections:	None
UK connections:	Amtrak Holdings Ltd
Viable for whole UK?	Yes
Trade bodies	None

Franchisor's formula for success
Amtrak knows that by giving a top quality service at very economical prices it can, within the next five years secure for itself a significant permanent share of the lucrative UK parcels market.

Good Franchise Guide comment: A very glossy brochure, but very, very few hard facts for the franchisee (or us) to go on. As there are no royalties we presume the franchisor pays a commission to the franchisee for each job.

Number of franchisee addresses provided by franchisor: 00

Anaco Ltd

⇨ Anaco Ltd
Shenstone, Lichfield, Staffs WS14 0DH
Phone: 0543 481599

Industrial maintenance chemicals

Outlets
Number of outlets	
Company owned outlets:	No information supplied
Franchised:	130
Pilot:	No information supplied
1988 franchise target:	No information supplied

Costs
Total	£5,600
Franchise fee:	£3,250
Other charges:	Nil
Min cash excluding bank:	£1,680
Min overdraft required:	£12,000
Normal bank advance:	70%
Working capital first 2 months:	Covered by overdraft
Associated banks:	None
Capital items required:	None
Associated leasing co:	None

Royalties
No information supplied

Bank rating	No information supplied
Territory	No information supplied
Strings	Tied totally to Anaco products
Training	No information supplied
Support	No information supplied
Operating Manual	No information supplied
Profit	First year operating profit of around £4,000
Risk	Main risk is of being tied to one range of products
Management only	Little salary to spare for a manager at first

Size and reach
Original company launched:	1987
Overseas connections:	None
UK connections:	Autosmart Group
Viable for whole UK?	Yes
Trade bodies	None

Franchisor's formula for success
Anaco are not packers of other people's products – we develop and manufacture our own range in our 100,000 square feet laboratory, research and manufacturing complex at Shenstone near Lichfield. Products fall into the following areas: engineering production, mechanical maintenance, electrical maintenance, electronics and computers, food processing, construction, institutional and leisure, janitorial.

Good Franchise Guide comment: Very professional presentation which actually gives the franchisee a fair amount of information although the franchisor refrained from replying to our requests for information.

Number of franchisee addresses provided by franchisor: 00

⇨ ANC – The British Parcel Service
1 Park Avenue, Wolstanton, Newcastle, Staffs ST5 8RT
Phone: 0782 712221

Parcel delivery

Outlets
Number of outlets   No information supplied save that no franchises are available at present

Costs
Total	£45,000
Franchise fee:	No information supplied
Other charges:	No information supplied
Min cash excluding bank:	£25,000

No further information supplied, but see franchisor's report below

Franchisor's formula for success
We operate a nationwide parcel distribution service based upon regional collection and delivery depots operated by franchisees and a trunking and central sorting operation supplied by the franchisor. The franchisees sell the total service to their local customers and are billed by us for the trunking and delivery service.

Good Franchise Guide comment: Very little information but we often see their vans around, so it is presumably flourishing.

Number of franchisee addresses provided by franchisor: 00

⇨ Anicare Group Services (Veterinary) Ltd
23 Buckingham Road, Shoreham-by-Sea BN4 5UA
Phone: 0273 463022

Group veterinary practices in which all franchisees are graduate veterinary surgeons and members of the Royal College of Veterinary Surgeons

Outlets
Number of outlets
Company owned outlets:	00
Franchised:	08
Pilot:	01
1988 franchise target:	10

Current reach:

South	02	South west	00	South east	06
Midlands	00	East Anglia	00	North east	00
North west	00	Scotland	00	Wales	00
N Ireland	00	Rep Ireland	00	I of Man/CI	00

Costs
Total	£15,000
Franchise fee:	£3,750
Other charges:	No information supplied
Min cash excluding bank:	No information supplied
Min overdraft required:	No information supplied
Normal bank advance:	60%
Working capital first 2 months:	No information supplied
Associated banks:	No information supplied
Capital items required:	No information supplied
Associated leasing co:	No information supplied

Anicare Group Services (Veterinary) Ltd

Royalties

	8.0% of turnover
	0.0% accounts service
	0.0% for advertising fund
Total	8.0% monthly sales
	No standing royalty independent of turnover

Bank rating   Banks helpful
Territory   Franchisee view: 'adequate'
Strings   Lots of ties

Training   No details supplied by franchisor
Cost: No information supplied
Training value: One franchisee found training adequate, another said there was none

Support   Moderate
Operating Manual   Satisfactory
Profit   Variable experience
Risk   Far less risk here than in setting up your own practice in an area where you are unknown
Management only   The vet is the manager

Size and reach

Original company launched:	No information supplied
Overseas connections:	No information supplied
UK connections:	No information supplied
Viable for whole UK?	Presumably yes
Trade bodies	No information supplied

Franchisor's formula for success
No information supplied

Inside story from the franchisees
Useful support at first, but once the franchise is set up the fees seem excessive.

Moans and groans
Franchisor is reported by one franchisee as being unwilling to sell the practice to the franchisee even after many years trading.

Good Franchise Guide comment: Should be of interest to many vets who wish to set up their own practice but who have limited capital available.

Number of franchisee addresses provided by franchisor: 9

⇨ AP Autela

Regal House, Birmingham Road, Stratford-on-Avon CV37 0BN
Phone: 0789 414545

Motor factors

Outlets
Number of outlets	—
Company owned outlets:	'Over 50'
Franchised:	'Over 50'

Costs
Total	£50,000
Franchise fee:	No information supplied
Other charges:	No information supplied
Min cash excluding bank:	£15,000
Min overdraft required:	No information supplied
Normal bank advance:	No information supplied
Working capital first 2 months:	No information supplied
Associated banks:	No information supplied
Capital items required:	No information supplied
Associated leasing co:	No information supplied

Size and reach
Original company launched:	George Angus and Co – around 1920. Autela Components Ltd formed 1967.
Overseas connections:	None
UK connections:	Division of Automotive Products plc
Viable for whole UK?	Yes
Trade bodies	BFA, Motor Factors Assn

Franchisor's formula for success

'The parts aftermarket potential is considerable and the AP Autela product range meets a large part of this potential, particularly with the exclusive sought-after Lockheed brand. Competition in this highly competitive market is fierce, and brings success for only the most professional and determined businessman.'

Good Franchise Guide comment: Very large company (1984 turnover over £25 million) but very little solid information for would-be franchisees.

Number of franchisee addresses provided by franchisor: 00

⇨ Apex Interiors

12 Stephens Brae, Inverness
Phone: 0463 225186

Interior design service

Outlets
Number of outlets	
Company owned outlets:	01
Franchised:	01
Pilot:	01 started 1987
1988 franchise target:	06

Current reach:

South	00	South west	00	South east	00
Midlands	00	East Anglia	00	North east	00
North west	00	Scotland	02	Wales	00
N Ireland	00	Rep Ireland	00	I of Man/CI	00

Apollo Window Blinds Ltd

Costs
Total	£7,500
Franchise fee:	£2,500
Other charges:	£1,000
Min cash excluding bank:	£4,000
Min overdraft required:	£1,500
Normal bank advance:	n/a
Working capital first 2 months:	£1,500
Associated banks:	None
Capital items required:	Motor car
Associated leasing co:	No

Royalties
	5.0% of turnover
	0.0% accounts service
	0.0% for advertising fund
Total	5.0% monthly sales
	No standing royalty independent of turnover

Bank rating	No information supplied
Territory	Based upon towns having a population catchment of 10,000 plus
Strings	No information supplied
Training	No information supplied
Support	No information supplied
Operating Manual	No information supplied
Profit	No information supplied
Risk	No information supplied
Management only	No information supplied

Size and reach
Original company launched:	1986
Overseas connections:	None
UK connections:	None
Viable for whole UK?	Scotland initially
Trade bodies	None

Franchisor's formula for success
In a letter to our would-be franchisee Apex stated 'we have appointed consultants to handle all enquiries from England and Wales . . .' No further information has been received.

Good Franchise Guide comment: A newly developed franchise being concentrated on limited geographical area. Applicants are dealt with individually, and no general brochure is available, which inevitably means a distinct lack of information.

Number of franchisee addresses provided by franchisor: 00

⇨ Apollo Window Blinds Ltd

Johnstone Avenue, Glasgow G52 4YH
Phone: 041-810 3021

High street based fashion window blind outlet with local service backup

Outlets
Number of outlets
Company owned outlets:	00
Franchised:	104
Pilot:	03 started 1973
Total franchise target:	130

Apollo Window Blinds Ltd

Current reach:

South	07	South west	04	South east	13		
Midlands	01	East Anglia	02	North east	09		
North west	18	Scotland	37	Wales	02		
N Ireland	13	Rep Ireland	01	I of Man/CI	00		

Costs
Total	£20,000
Franchise fee:	£4,000
Other charges:	See below
Min cash excluding bank:	£7,500
Min overdraft required:	£2,000
Normal bank advance:	Two-thirds of total
Working capital first 2 months:	£2,000
Associated banks:	Lloyds, Nat West, Royal Bank of Scotland, Barclays
Capital items required:	Shopfitting, vehicle, machinery and stock – total about £16,000
Associated leasing co:	No

Royalties

	3.0% of turnover
	0.0% accounts service
	2.0% for advertising fund
Total	5.0% (See note below)
	No standing royalty independent of turnover

Note: the royalty payments are levied on purchases and the percentages are equivalents, not direct royalties.

Bank rating	No information supplied
Territory	Shopping centre and population
Strings	Very strong ties for materials
Training	10 days practical and management training
	Cost: Included in franchise fee
	Training value: No information supplied
Support	No information supplied
Operating Manual	No information supplied
Profit	No information supplied
Risk	Ever increasing number of franchises in this field makes it a high risk business
Management only	Reasonable return for owner with management ability

Size and reach

Original company launched:	1972
Overseas connections:	None at present
UK connections:	None at present
Viable for whole UK?	Possibly yes
Trade bodies	BBSA, BFA, IFA

Franchisor's formula for success

Apollo has 25% of the window blind market, a market that is estimated to reach £500 million by 1992. Apollo's share has surged through the company's total commitment to a partnership with a series of individuals throughout the country.

Good Franchise Guide comment: A well known, successful, high profile franchise.

Number of franchisee addresses provided by franchisor: 00

Applied Fastenings and Components Ltd

⇨ Applied Fastenings and Components Ltd
Unit 2a/2, St Francis Way, Shefford Industrial Park, High Street, Shefford, Beds SG17 5DZ
Phone: 0462 811767

Retailing applied fastening range of sheet metal working fasteners

Outlets
Number of outlets
Company owned outlets: 01
Franchised: 00
Pilot: 00
1988 franchise target: 05
Current reach: See *Good Franchise Guide* comment below

South	03	South west	03	South east	10
Midlands	12	East Anglia	09	North east	04
North west	05	Scotland	05	Wales	04
N Ireland	01	Rep Ireland	00	I of Man/CI	01

Costs
Total £12,500
Franchise fee: £12,500
Other charges: Legal fees, price not specified
Min cash excluding bank: No information supplied
Min overdraft required: No information supplied
Normal bank advance: Subject to security
Working capital first 2 months: £1,000
Associated banks: Barclays
Capital items required: Delivery vehicle, office furniture, typewriter, calculators, warehouse benches

Associated leasing co: No

Royalties

    10.0% of turnover
    0.0% accounts service
    0.0% for advertising fund
Total   10.0% monthly sales

No standing royalty independent of turnover

Bank rating No information supplied
Territory Reflects the anticipated sales potential together with good road links within territories
Strings Strong ties for materials
Training 1 day or as required practical training
2 days management training
Cost: Included in franchise fee
Training value: No information supplied

Support No information supplied
Operating Manual No information supplied
Profit No information supplied
Risk No information supplied
Management only Reasonable return for owner with management ability

Size and reach
Original company launched: 1980
Overseas connections: None
UK connections: No direct relationship but directors do have interests in other businesses, which are available to offer specialised facilities such as photography, centralised purchasing and sales training

Viable for whole UK? Yes
Trade bodies No

Athena

Franchisor's formula for success
Our franchise is unique in the UK by virtue of offering a wide range of engineering products, none offered by other frachisors. Extensive stocks are held at Shefford, allowing franchisees to trade, without commiting theselves to holding stock. The royalties are only payable after receipt of payment from the franchisees' customers to minimise any cash flow problems. Existing customers within the territories are passed to franchisees.

Good Franchise Guide comments: This franchise appears to have a range of distributors (as listed in 'Current Reach') above – as opposed to the five franchisees.

Number of franchisee addresses provided by franchisor: 00

⇨ Ashcombe Distributors Ltd
New Inn Farm, St Neots Road, Knapwell, Cambs CB3 8LB
Phone: 09544 459

This franchise has been listed in some reference books and magazines. The company has informed us that it is not a franchise, but is in fact a distributorship as stated in the company name.

⇨ At Computer World
Previously at 43 Calthorpe Road, Edgbaston, Birmingham B15 1TS

A franchise at this name and address has been listed in some reference books and magazines. Mail sent to this address is now being returned by the Post Office marked 'Gone Away'. The telephone number quoted is now a dead line. Enquiries have revealed that no forwarding address has been left, although it is possible that the franchise may have been set up once more in another part of the country. In the light of this experience we suggest a certain amount of caution may be in order.

⇨ Athena
Berwick House, 35 Livery Street, Birmingham B3 2PB
Phone: 021-236 6886

Retailer of prints, posters, cards and stationery

Outlets
Number of outlets
Company owned outlets: 60
Franchised: 06
Pilot: 80 over 22 years
Total franchise target: 90
Current reach:

South	12	South west	10	South east	15
Midlands	06	East Anglia	03	North east	04
North west	06	Scotland	02	Wales	02
N Ireland	00	Rep Ireland	00	I of Man/CI	00

Current reach totals refer to company owned outlets only.

Athena

Costs
Total	£72,000
Franchise fee:	£7,500
Other charges:	None
Min cash excluding bank:	£25,000
Min overdraft required:	£50,000
Normal bank advance:	£50,000
Working capital first 2 months:	None
Associated banks:	Nat West, Royal Bank of Scotland, Lloyds, Midland
Capital items required:	Shopfitting, merchandise (about £50,000)
Associated leasing co:	None

Royalties

Total
    7.5% of turnover
    1.5% accounts service
    0.0% for advertising fund
    9.0% monthly sales
No standing royalty independent of turnover

Bank rating   No information available
Territory   Population of 200,000 plus
Strings   Strong ties for stock
Training   3 week practical training
    1 week management training
    Cost: included in franchise fee
    Training value: No information available

Support   No information available
Operating Manual   No information available
Profit   No information available
Risk   Risk reduced by the fact that this is a very well known name in the high street.
Management only   Reasonable return for owner with management ability

Size and reach
Original company launched:	1964
Overseas connections:	20 shops in USA, Canada, Holland
UK connections:	Wholly owned subsiduary of Petnos plc
Viable for whole UK?	Yes
Trade bodies	No

Franchisor's formula for success
Two types of franchise are available. The 'Individual Unit Franchise' is for business people seeking independence by owning and operating their own Athena Gallery. After achieving success in one unit franchisees are encouraged to expand by establishing additional galleries.
The 'Conversion Franchise' is designed for the existing retailer seeking to convert his present trading format to the successful Athena concept. Only premises that fulfil the strict Athena criteria will be considered; secondary locations are not suitable.

Good Franchise Guide comment: Athena has supplied us with a list of shops, but with no indication of which are company owned outlets and which are the 6 franchisees. Although we have therefore not been able to reach the franchisees, the existence of such a large company owned base augurs very well for franchisees

Number of franchisee addresses provided by franchisor: Not known – see above

Autosheen Car Valeting Services (UK) Ltd

⇨ Auto-Smart Ltd
Previously at Basin Lane, Glascote, Tamworth, Staffs B77 2AH

A franchise at this name and address has been listed in some reference books and magazines. Mail sent to this address is now being returned by the Post Office marked 'Gone Away'. Enquiries have revealed that no forwarding address has been left, although it is possible that the franchise may have been set up once more in another part of the country. In the light of this experience we suggest a certain amount of caution may be in order.

⇨ Autosheen Car Valeting Services (UK) Ltd
37 Billing Road, Northampton NN1 5DU
Phone: 0604 232244

Mobile car valeting service

Outlets
Number of outlets
Company owned outlets: 00
Franchised: 74
Pilot: 00
1988 franchise target: 250
Current reach:

South	10	South west	10	South east	16
Midlands	23	East Anglia	06	North east	05
North west	09	Scotland	06	Wales	01
N Ireland	02	Rep Ireland	00	I of Man/CI	00

Current reach analysis also includes franchises licensed but not yet operative.

Costs
Total   £5,200
Franchise fee: £4,950
Other charges: £250
Min cash excluding bank: Nil
Min overdraft required: £7,000
Normal bank advance: £7,000
Working capital first 2 months: £1,000
Associated banks: Lloyds and Midland
Capital items required: None
Associated leasing co: No

Royalties
                    0.0% of turnover
                    0.0% accounts service
                    0.0% for advertising fund
Total   0.0% monthly sales
                    £3,950 initital fee plus £385 per month vehicle and business rental plus £250 pa advertising fee independent of turnover

Bank rating   Banks not helpful; finance houses very helpful
Territory   Post codes related to car population of each area.
                   Some franchisees feel 2 territories may be needed
Strings   Strong ties for vehicle, materials etc
Training   2 days (and refreshers on site) practical training, management training included in practical training.
                   Cost: £500 included in franchise fee
                   Training value: Adequate for chemicals used.
                   'Practical side of valeting woefully inadequate'

Avis Rent a Car Ltd

Support	Good
Operating Manual	Very good. 'Explicit'
Profit	Better than expected
Risk	No failures yet; but there are many competitors in the field. As long as the franchisor keeps advertising the company name then all should be well. A risk might arise if the company's resources become too stretched in taking on too many new franchisees.
Management only	Could be run by manager but with limited profit

Size and reach

Original company launched:	1985
Overseas connections:	None
UK connections:	None
Viable for whole UK?	Yes
Trade bodies	None

Franchisor's formula for success
'The demand for the service from the motoring public is proving to be as intense as predicted. Virtually all of the Autosheen operators are reporting steady growth in business generally.' (from *Autosheen UK News*)

Inside story from the franchisees
Hard work brings its rewards. 'National advertising campaign paid real dividends'

Insider tips
Ensure your area is big enough. One franchisee got help under the Enterprise Allowance Scheme.

Moans and groans
More practical experience or training would be helpful. Support is patchy, but 'they are still feeling their way'.

Number of franchisee addresses provided by franchisor: 9

⇨ **Avis Rent a Car Ltd**
Trident House, Station Road, Hayes, Middx UB3 4DJ
Phone: 01-848 8765

Car rental

Outlets

Number of outlets	No information supplied

Costs

Total	£50,000
Franchise fee:	Depends on market size

Royalties

	10.0% of turnover
	0.0% accounts service
	0.0% for advertising fund
Total	10.0 % monthly sales
	No standing royalty independent of turnover

Franchisor's formula for success
Avis is the the number 1 car rental company in Europe, Africa and the Middle East. In the local markets our share varies from 5% to 75% and it is in this area that we anticipate our greatest growth. We have more vehicles than any of our competitors. We have more rental locations than any of our other competitors.

Good Franchise Guide comment: Obviously a leading franchise, but it is a shame that their brochure should spend so much time talking about the company and so little about the nitty gritty of the franchise. No reply to our requests for information, either. We wonder, could the cut price used car rental people be about to take a slice of the action?

Number of franchisee addresses provided by franchisor: 00

Badgeman Ltd

⇨ Badenoch and Clark
16-18 New Bridge Street, London EC4V 6AU

This recruitment franchise failed to reply to our questionnaire. Our would-be franchisee received a note asking him to telephone. No other information was forthcoming, and the prospective franchisee felt unwilling to proceed without seeing something on the table.

⇨ Badgeman Ltd
Sketchley Business Services Group, Rugby Road, Hinckley, Leics, LE10 2NE
Phone: 01-994 0826

Badgeman Recognition Express is the internationally known leader in the recognition industry. Through a network of franchise owners Badgeman provides a service to companies and other organisations for high quality name badges, name plates and engraved signs.

Outlets
Number of outlets
Company owned outlets: 01
Franchised: 12
Pilot: 01 started 1979
1988 franchise target: 17
Current reach:

South	00	South west	00	South east	07
Midlands	01	East Anglia	00	North east	01
North west	02	Scotland	02	Wales	00
N Ireland	00	Rep Ireland	00	I of Man/CI	00

Costs
Total   £19,000
Franchise fee: £7,500
Other charges: £11,500
Min cash excluding bank: £25,000 required in total if no bank borrowing
Min overdraft required: No prescribed minima for overdraft
Normal bank advance: 70%
Working capital first 2 months: £5,000
Associated banks: Nat West
Capital items required: Printing and engraving machines
Associated leasing co: Not at present

Royalties

	10.0% of turnover
	0.0% accounts service
	2.5% for advertising fund
Total	12.5% monthly sales
	No standing royalty independent of turnover

Bank rating   No information supplied
Territory   By post codes
Strings   No information supplied

Training   7 days practical training
                         3 days management training
                         Cost: £2,000; included in franchise fee
                         Training value: No information supplied

Support   No information supplied
Operating Manual   No information supplied
Profit   First year net profit calculated at £11,950
Risk   No information supplied
Management only   Proven franchise with good return on investment

Balloon Paris

Size and reach
Original company launched:	1972 in USA 1979 in UK
Overseas connections:	Worldwide franchise
UK connections:	Part of Sketchley Business Services Group
Viable for whole UK?	Yes
Trade bodies	BFA

Franchisor's formula for success
Badgeman offers customers their company logo printed onto their badge using high quality print to enhance the image of their company. They can also have the name of staff engraved onto the badge, with customers choosing from a wide range of fastenings. All operations are carried out very quickly – repeat orders within one hour.

Inside story from the franchisees
We understand the franchise package is currently being re-written.

Number of franchisee addresses provided by franchisor: 00

➪ Balloon Paris
77 Walton Street, London SW3
Phone: 01-593 3121

Balloon inform us that the company has changed its policy of expansion and franchises are no longer available in the UK.

➪ Bally Group (UK) Ltd
79 Wells House, 79 Wells Street, London W1P 4JL
Phone: 01-631 4222

The shoes retail group wrote to our would-be franchisee stating that due to a reorganisation across the world the board has decided not to recruit new franchisees. It was one of the most polite, honest and clear letters turning down an application that we saw, and it says a lot for the group should they ever move back into franchising.

➪ Balmforth and Partners (Franchises)
St Mary's House, Duke Street, Norwich NR3 1QA
Phone: 0603 660555 (ext 27)

Complete house sales and purchase service established in 1969

Outlets
Number of outlets
Company owned outlets:	01
Franchised:	16
Pilot:	04 started 1979
1988 franchise target:	28

Current reach:
South	00	South west	00	South east	00
Midlands	00	East Anglia	17	North east	00
North west	00	Scotland	00	Wales	00
N Ireland	00	Rep Ireland	00	I of Man/CI	00

Balmforth and Partners (Franchises)

Costs
Total	£20,000-£25,000 plus working capital
Franchise fee:	£6,000
Other charges:	Nil
Min cash excluding bank:	£18,500
Min overdraft required:	£18,500
Normal bank advance:	£18,500
Working capital first 2 months:	£17,000
Associated banks:	All major clearing banks
Capital items required:	None
Associated leasing co:	Not applicable

Royalties
	7.5% of turnover
	0.0% accounts service
	0.0% for advertising fund
Total	7.5% monthly sales
	No standing royalty independent of turnover

Bank rating	Good – no problems encountered
Territory	Individually ascertained
	Franchisees report boundaries in wrong places for customer base
Strings	Lots of ties but some freedom
Training	4 weeks practical and management training
	Cost: Personal expenses only
	Training value: 'More training needed'
Support	More support wanted
Operating Manual	Generally good but some found it too long, others reported inadequate coverage in certain fields.
Profit	Reasonable – up to expectations
Risk	Results are very much up to the individual – some do not do as well as they felt they were promised.
Management only	Proven franchise with good return on investment

Size and reach
Original company launched:	1969
Overseas connections:	None
UK connections:	None
Viable for whole UK?	East and central England
Trade bodies	National Association of Estate Agents; BFA

Franchisor's formula for success
The Balmforth package has been specially designed to establish the franchise owner in his own business with the minimum of delay. Experience has illustrated the fact that experience in the sphere of estate agency is not required in order to qualify for a Balmforth franchise. The combination of your general business experience and management expertise coupled with the specialist knowledge transferred during the intensive initial training course will need only the catalyst of your commitment in order to ensure success.

Inside story from the franchisees
'A good franchise with an enthusiastic and helpful franchisor'

Insider tips
Ensure your territory is correct.

Moans and groans
Lack of support due to new offices opening and taking priority over existing franchises.

Number of franchisee addresses provided by franchisor: 10

Banaman

⇨ Banaman

Banaman House, 78 Newman Street, London W1P 3OA
Phone: 01-636 7777

Printing and supply of promotional products, tee shirts, badges etc

Outlets
Number of outlets
Company owned outlets:	01
Franchised:	27
Pilot:	00
1988 franchise target:	55

Current reach:

South	05	South west	06	South east	00
Midlands	02	East Anglia	03	North east	02
North west	04	Scotland	02	Wales	01
N Ireland	01	Rep Ireland	01	I of Man/CI	00

Costs
Total	£42,750
Franchise fee:	£9,750
Other charges:	£33,000
Min cash excluding bank:	33%
Min overdraft required:	66%
Normal bank advance:	66%
Working capital first 2 months:	£55,000*
Associated banks:	None
Capital items required:	Shopfittings
Associated leasing co:	None

*£50,000 includes franchise fee, shopfittings, and starting working capital

Royalties
	9.5% of turnover
	0.0% accounts service
	0.0% for advertising fund
Total	9.5% monthly sales

No standing royalty independent of turnover

Bank rating	No information supplied
Territory	Post codes in most cases
Strings	No informatioin supplied
Training	5 days practical training
	5 days management training
	Cost: £3,000 – included in franchise fee
	Training value: No information supplied
Support	No information supplied
Operating Manual	No information supplied
Profit	£22,289 net profit projected for year 1
Risk	The company claim zero direct competition
Management only	Proven franchise with good return on investment

Size and reach
Original company launched:	1984
Overseas connections:	USA over 250 franchises, France 2, Israel 1, Borneo 1
UK connections:	Le Monde Services, trading as Banaman
Viable for whole UK?	Yes
Trade bodies	BFA, BMPA

Baskin-Robbins International Company

Franchisor's formula for success
Our unique concept gives our franchisees the opportunity of supplying signs and banners and a whole range of promotional products and items to their customers. You don't have to have design, art or technical skills to operate any of the systems used in our franchise package. The computer driven signwriting system is really child's play and is available only to our franchisees.

Good Franchise Guide comment: With the promise of such outstanding profits we would have welcomed the chance to talk with franchisees about their achievements, and their view of the uniqueness of the franchisor's claims.

Number of franchisee addresses provided by franchisor: 00

➪ Baskin-Robbins International Company
Bridge Park, Oldfield Lane, Greenford, Middx UB6 0BA
Phone: 01-575 2004

Ice cream franchise

Outlets
Number of outlets	30 approx
Company owned outlets:	No information supplied
Franchised:	No information supplied
Pilot:	No information supplied
1988 franchise target:	No information supplied

Costs
Total	£25,000
Franchise fee:	No information supplied
Other charges:	No information supplied
Min cash excluding bank:	No information supplied
Min overdraft required:	No information supplied
Normal bank advance:	No information supplied
Working capital first 2 months:	No information supplied
Associated banks:	None specified
Capital items required:	Shopfitting – from £25,000 to £50,000
Associated leasing co:	None

Original company launched:	1945
Overseas connections:	None
UK connections:	Wholly owned British company in the food group of Allied Lyons plc, one of Europe's largest brewing and food businesses.
Viable for whole UK?	Yes
Trade bodies	None

Franchisor's formula for success
Baskin-Robbins is the world's largest chain of ice cream parlours, with more than 3400 shops in 17 countries and a turnover of $400 million a year. It offers a choice of full franchise or joint in-store operation.

Good Franchise Guide comment: A classic case of what is clearly a major franchise (anything from Allied Lyons must be) which doesn't reveal too much about itself. The 12 pages of promotional literature sent to would-be franchisees is excellent in terms of company and product background, but gives precious little away about the franchise itself. Sad.

Number of franchisee addresses provided by franchisor: 00

The Bath Doctor

➪ The Bath Doctor

Denbigh House, Denbigh Road, Bletchley, Milton Keynes MK1 1YP
Phone: 0908 270007

Renovating bathroom suites

Outlets
Number of outlets
Company owned outlets:	00
Franchised:	Over 50
Pilot:	No information supplied
1988 franchise target:	No information supplied

Costs
Total	£2,500 to £11,000
Franchise fee:	No information supplied
Other charges:	Nil
Min cash excluding bank:	£625
Min overdraft required:	No information supplied
Normal bank advance:	75%
Working capital first 2 months:	No information supplied
Associated banks:	No information supplied
Capital items required:	No information supplied
Associated leasing co:	None

Royalties
Total	0.0% of turnover
	0.0% accounts service
	0.0% for advertising fund
	0.0% monthly sales
	£25 to £100 per month standing royalty independent of turnover

Bank rating	No information supplied
Territory	No information supplied
Strings	No information supplied
Training	No information supplied
Support	No information supplied
Operating Manual	No information supplied
Profit	See franchisor's statement below
Risk	Some competition, although all firms in this field claim to be the only ones
Management only	One-man-band operation

Size and reach
Original company launched:	1986
Overseas connections:	None
UK connections:	None
Viable for whole UK?	Yes
Trade bodies	BFA

Franchisor's formula for success
Renovating bathroom suites is very profitable, you buy the kit from us at from £38.50 to £50 and recover at least £200 from your client.

Good Franchise Guide comment: Competition seems to be growing, although the presentation of this franchise to potential franchisees is good, although slightly lacking in financial detail.

Number of franchisee addresses provided by franchisor: 00

BDP Ltd

➪ Bath Transformations Ltd

Victory House, Somers Road North, Portsmouth, Hants PO1 1PJ
Phone: 0705 753719 (Franchise literature also quotes 0304 830609)

Repair of bathroom suites in situ

Costs
TotalNo information supplied
Franchise fee:£10,000 ('complete')

Franchisor's formula for success
Every year in the UK between 500,000 and 1,000,000 bathroom suites are ripped out and replaced. 99% of all bathroom suites are probably still usable. Now using ultra modern materials and methods, The Bath Wizard can repair complete bathroom suites in any colour, any type, any age from Victorian to modern GRP.

Good Franchise Guide comment: Sounds like a good idea, although there are rivals in the field. The brochure claims that government, hospitals, restaurants, pubs, police stations, schools and even the QE2 are among the customers. Why did they not send any information to our would-be franchisee?

Number of franchisee addresses provided by franchisor: 00

➪ BDP Ltd

Trading as British Damp Proofing

The Old School, Fleetwood Road, Esprick, Preston
Phone: 039 136 441

Timber remedial and rising damp specialists

Outlets
Number of outlets
Company owned outlets:00
Franchised:54
Pilot:01 started 1982
Total franchise target:120
Current reach:

South	11	South west	03	South east	05
Midlands	06	East Anglia	05	North east	02
North west	16	Scotland	05	Wales	00
N Ireland	01	Rep Ireland	00	I of Man/CI	00

Costs
Total:£11,750 + VATor £25,000 + VAT
Franchise fee:£4,000or £8,000
Other charges:£7,750or £17,000
Min cash excluding bank:£11,750 + VAT
Min overdraft required:£2,000
Normal bank advance:60 to 70% subject to status
Working capital first 2 months:£2,000 – £3,000 approx
Associated banks:Nat West, Lloyds, Royal Bank of Scotland, Midland
Capital items required:Franchise fee includes all items required – eg van on lease or hire purchase
Associated leasing co:North West Securities

Royalties
Total10.0% of turnover
0.0% accounts service
£30 per month (not to exceed 2.5% of turnover) for advertising fund
12.5% monthly sales maximum
£150 month min after 3 months standing royalty independent of turnover

Beardsley Theobalds Businesses

Bank rating	Banks – 'give assistance'
Territory	Min population 300,000 radius from franchisee
	Franchisees report: 'Just right'
Strings	Lots of ties but lots of freedom
Training	10 days practical training
	10 days management training
	Cost: £1,950 + accommodation (inc in franchise fee)
	Training value: Adequate
Support	Good
Operating Manual	Good
Profit	Better than expected but it can take up to two years to reach a healthy position
Risk	A lot of competition in damp proofing including other franchises
Management only	Reasonable return for owner with management ability

Size and reach

Original company launched:	1984
Overseas connections:	None
UK connections:	None
Viable for whole UK?	Yes with European potential
Trade bodies	BFA, Timber Research and Development Assn, Federation of Master Builders, and pending registration with British Standards Institution

Franchisor's formula for success

'We feel we are now established as the largest franchising company in this particular field. Over the years we have come to realise that applicants should be able to market their own areas – we can teach them all the technical/practical requirements necessary on our training courses and also cover marketing/sales etc.'

Inside story from the franchisees

Training has been greatly improved and new franchisees will benefit from this.

Moans and groans

The manual is hard to use until the franchise is fully operational.

Number of franchisee addresses provided by franchisor: 30

⇨ **Beardsley Theobalds Businesses**
Leygore Manor, Northleach, Cheltenham GL54 3NY
Phone: 0451 60667

Business transfer agent

Outlets
Number of outlets

Company owned outlets:	05
Franchised:	11
Pilot:	No information supplied
1988 franchise target:	No information supplied

Costs
Total	£30,000
Franchise fee:	£11,000
Other charges:	No information supplied
Min cash excluding bank:	£15,000
Min overdraft required:	No information supplied
Normal bank advance:	50%
Working capital first 2 months:	No information supplied
Associated banks:	None
Capital items required:	No information supplied
Associated leasing co:	None

Royalties

Total
10.0% of turnover
0.0% accounts service
0.0% for advertising fund
10.0% monthly sales

No standing royalty independent of turnover

Bank rating   No information supplied
Territory   No information supplied
Strings   No information supplied

Training   No information supplied
Support   No information supplied
Operating Manual   No information supplied
Profit   No information supplied
Risk   Business transfer agencies seem to be springing up everywhere – which is bad news for a franchise that won't give out information.

Management only   No information supplied

Size and reach
Original company launched:	1982
Overseas connections:	None
UK connections:	London and Manchester Group owns 40% of ordinary shares
Viable for whole UK?	Yes
Trade bodies	None

Franchisor's formula for success

Taking up a Franchise reports that 'The network which is connected by Prestel to a central computer in London now has over 1000 varied businesses for sale and more than 9000 prospective buyers looking for businesses through the UK.'

Good Franchise Guide comment: Neither the *Guide* nor our would-be franchisees received any information from this company in response to repeated requests.

Number of franchisee addresses provided by franchisor: 00

⇨ Beck and Call

8 Park Road, Chesham, Bucks HP5 2JE

This franchise offering a tutorial agency service has been listed in some reference books and magazines, and at least one franchise magazine was running advertisements for the firm through 1987. Mail sent to this address is accepted, but we have been unable to obtain information either in response to general requests from would-be franchisees or specifically for this publication. In the light of this experience we suggest a certain amount of caution may be in order if the franchise does eventually reappear.

Belgian Chocolates

⇨ Belgian Chocolates
(also known as Bellina Belgian Chocolates)
Bellina Ltd, Knightsdale Road, Ipswich IP1 4JJ
Phone: 0473 47444

This company changed its address some time ago. Mail sent to the old address was returned rather than forwarded; we found the new address through a colleague enquiring in one of the Bellina shops. No reply has been received to enquiries made to the franchisor's new address either by ourselves or our would-be franchisee. However the shops do continue to operate and so the franchise clearly is there.

⇨ Benetton (UK) Ltd
Suite 3 and 4, Pembroke House, Hawthorn Street, Wilmslow, Cheshire
Phone: 0625 535969

A franchise exists at this address. Unfortunately the franchisor has declined to supply information either to ourselves or a would-be franchisee. When the would-be franchisee telephoned she was told that the firm would not send detailed information through the post. They did promise to send a circular, but so far it has not arrived.

⇨ The Better Business Agents
18 Walsworth Road, Hitchin, Herts SG4 9SP

This franchise has been listed in some reference books and magazines. Mail sent to this address is accepted, but we have been unable to obtain information either in response to general requests from would-be franchisees or specifically for this publication. In the light of this experience we suggest a certain amount of caution may be in order if the franchise does eventually reappear.

⇨ Big Apple Health Studios Ltd
15 – 18 Great Newport Street, London WC2H 7NS

This franchise has been listed in some reference books and magazines. Mail sent to this address is accepted, but we have been unable to obtain information either in response to general requests from would-be franchisees or specifically for this publication. In the light of this experience we suggest a certain amount of caution may be in order if the franchise does eventually reappear.

⇨ Big Orange Promotions Ltd
Previously at: New Covent Garden, London SW8

A franchise at this address has been listed in some reference books and magazines. Mail sent to this address is now being returned by the Post Office marked 'Gone Away'. Enquiries have revealed that no forwarding address has been left, although it is possible that the franchise may have been set up once more in another part of the country. In the light of this experience we suggest a certain amount of caution may be in order.

The Bread Roll Company

⇨ A F Blakemore and Sons Ltd
Long Acres Industrial Estate, Rosehill, Willenhall, West Midlands

This franchise has been listed in some reference books and magazines. Mail sent to this address is accepted, but we have been unable to obtain information either in response to general requests from would-be franchisees or specifically for this publication. In the light of this experience we suggest a certain amount of caution may be in order if the franchise does eventually reappear.

⇨ Bob's Tiles
Unit 4a Shand Kydd Industrial Estate, Somerford Road, Christchurch, Dorset BH23 3PH
Phone: 0202 474222

This franchise clearly exists, but they have failed to reply to our questionnaire, and to the written enquiries of our would-be franchisees. When, in desparation, one would-be franchisee telephoned he was told that no information could be given there and then, nor was anything sent through the post. If he would like to phone back later the person who dealt with franchising might be in and would be able to help . . .

⇨ The Body Shop International plc
Hawthorn Road, Wick, Littlehampton, West Sussex BN17 7LR
Phone: 0903 717107

Described by *Taking up a Franchise* as a conspicuous success in 1986 having been promoted to a full Stock Exchange listing – the first UK franchise to gain this recognition. Not surprisingly Body Shop franchises cannot now be had, and would-be franchisees are receiving letters stating that the demand for franchises has been so great that the application file has been closed.

⇨ Bolos Sobre Cesped SA
11 The Boulevard, Worthing, West Sussex

This franchise has been listed in some reference books and magazines, offering according to the *UK Franchise Directory*, a 'Complete complex of lawn bowling in South Spain including living accommodation, management, infrastructure and clientele.'   In response to a letter from a would-be franchisee the franchsor stated that he was unable to proceed with the franchise due to family commitments. The franchisor added that he was looking for someone to take over the project for a very small sum and was interested in talking to anyone who fancied taking the franchise on.

⇨ The Bread Roll Company
Unit 6, 224 London Road, St Albans, Herts
Phone: 0727 35291

The Bread Roll Company manufactures bread rolls and sells these to the public packaged in units retailing at £1. The frachisee buys from the company and sells to the general public and catering establishments.

Outlets
Number of outlets
Company owned outlets: 01
Franchised: 14
Pilot: 'Pilot completed'. No other information available.
1988 franchise target: 35

29

The Bread Roll Company

Current reach:

South	00	South west	00	South east	14
Midlands	00	East Anglia	00	North east	00
North west	00	Scotland	00	Wales	00
N Ireland	00	Rep Ireland	00	I of Man/CI	00

Costs

Total	£18,000
Franchise fee:	£18,000
Other charges:	No information supplied
Min cash excluding bank:	£8,000
Min overdraft required:	No information supplied
Normal bank advance:	60%
Working capital first 2 months:	£1,000
Associated banks:	Barclays
Capital items required:	Two vehicles
Associated leasing co:	Association exists, but details not given

Royalties

5.0% of turnover
0.0% accounts service
0.0% for advertising fund

Total 5.0% monthly sales

Note: the company states that no royalties are payable. However a 5% fee is shown in their projected budget in the prospectus.

No standing royalty independent of turnover

Bank rating — No information supplied
Territory — Population and radius
Strings — Franchisees are required to buy bread and stationery from the franchisor

Training
30 days practical training
30 days management training
Cost: Included in franchise fee
Training value: No information supplied

Size and reach

Original company launched:	1983
Overseas connections:	None
UK connections:	None
Viable for whole UK?	UK only
Trade bodies	National Association of Master Bakers

Franchisor's formula for success
The strengths of this franchise are regular turnover, low overheads, simple systems, large potential market plus a starting turnover of £2,000 per week supplied by our company thus ensuring profit from the early stages.

Inside story from the franchisees
The company supplied us with the names and addresses of three franchisees, but none has responded to our requests for information.

Good Franchise Guide comment: From the information provided we conclude this is more of a distributorship than a franchise in the normal sense.

Number of franchisee addresses provided by franchisor: 03

⇨ Brewer & Turnbull Ltd

Holme Road, Off Cuerdon Way, Bamber Bridge, Preston PR5 6ER
Phone: 0772 626555

Removal and storage operation throughout the UK, via a national network with overseas links also

Outlets
Number of outlets
Company owned outlets: 01
Franchised: 17
Pilot: 07 started 1984
Total franchise target: 27
Current reach:

South	03	South west	01	South east	04		
Midlands	06	East Anglia	01	North east	02		
North west	06	Scotland	04	Wales	00		
N Ireland	00	Rep Ireland	00	I of Man/CI	00		

Costs
Total   £12,000-£15,000
Franchise fee: £2,000-£5,000
Other charges: £10,000
Min cash excluding bank: £5,000
Min overdraft required: £10,000
Normal bank advance: No information supplied
Working capital first 2 months: £5,000
Associated banks: Nat West
Capital items required: Minimum – 1 vehicle £5,000 to £10,000
Associated leasing co: Yes – details not available

Royalties
                                 3.0% of turnover
                                 2.0% advertising fund
                                 0.0% for advertising fund
Total   5.0% monthly sales
                                 No standing royalty independent of turnover

Bank rating   Franchisees needing support shopped around for money; financial institutions not considered very helpful
Territory   Yellow Page areas
                      Franchisees found it 'just right'
Strings   Lots of ties but lots of freedom too
Training   2 to 5 days practical training
                      1 to 2 days management training
                      Cost: Accommodation charged only
                      Note all franchisees are experienced in the industry
                      Training value: Adequate
Support   Opinions vary from poor to good
Operating Manual Opinions vary from poor to good
Profit   Franchisees either doing as expected, or worse than expected
Risk   Franchisees come from within the business and know the risks
Management only   Reasonable return for owner with management ability

Brick-Tie Services Ltd

Size and reach
Original company launched: 1932
Overseas connections: Extensive – worldwide
UK connections: Co-operative arrangements with Whittle International Movers
Viable for whole UK? All UK
Trade bodies: ERC of CBI

Franchisor's formula for success
A well established franchise with a name known nationally and internationally; unique in this industry.

Inside story from the franchisees
'B & T have done everything we expected of them'

Insider tips
'Would encourage others to join'

Moans and groans
More national advertising needed

Number of franchisee addresses provided by franchisor: 04

➪ Brick-Tie Services Ltd
Yorkshire House, East Rd., Leeds, West Yorkshire LS9 8SQ
Phone: 0532 487387

Remedial work in relation to wall tie corrosion

Outlets
Number of outlets
Company owned outlets: 01
Franchised: 00
Pilot: 02 started 1986
1988 franchise target: 10
Current reach:

South	00	South west	00	South east	00
Midlands	00	East Anglia	00	North east	03
North west	00	Scotland	00	Wales	00
N Ireland	00	Rep Ireland	00	I of Man/CI	00

Costs
Total: £9,810
Franchise fee: £3,150
Other charges: Nil
Min cash excluding bank: £3,000
Min overdraft required: £1,800
Normal bank advance: 66%
Working capital first 2 months: £1,800
Associated banks: Barclays
Capital items required: Vehicle
Associated leasing co: None

Royalties
10.0% of turnover
0.0% accounts service
0.0% for advertising fund
Total 10.0% monthly sales
No standing royalty independent of turnover

Bank rating No information supplied
Territory Population plus business potential
Strings No information supplied

Britannic Corporation

Training	10 days practical training 2 days management training Cost: £750 included in franchise fee Training value: No information supplied
Support	No information supplied
Operating Manual	No information supplied
Profit	Net profit for first year quoted as £15,000
Risk	If the number of houses with problems is as high as suggested franchisees should be on to a good thing.
Management only	Reasonable return for owner with management ability

Size and reach

Original company launched:	1986
Overseas connections:	None
UK connections:	Yorkshire Dampcourse Group
Viable for whole UK?	North, North West, North East England
Trade bodies	BCDA, BWPA

Franchisor's formula for success

It is only in recent years that corrosion in cavity wall ties has come to be recognised as a major problem for individual householders and for those responsible for the upkeep and maintenance of multiple domestic and commercial properties. It is estimated that there are now some 10 million properties through the UK constructed with a cavity wall, and it is now known that an extremely high proportion are or will be affected by wall tie corrosion.

Good Franchise Guide comment: This is a new franchise, and as such it is difficult to evaluate.

Number of franchisee addresses provided by franchisor: 00

⇨ Britannia Business Sales Ltd

Skyline Chambers, 14 Manor Row, Bradford, West Yorkshire BD1 4NL
Phone: 0274 722977

Britannia Business Sales operates as a specialist business transfer agency operating solely within the licensed trade. It is currently (December 1987) writing to would-be franchisees who enquire as to its franchise that 'due to the tremendous response we have received from our recent campaign we are unable to accept any further applications'. We have been unable to obtain any further information; but at least the franchisor has the courtesy to reply to potential franchisees.

⇨ Britannia Towing Centre

c/o The Franchise Shop Ltd., 26 High Street, Merstham, Surrey RH1 3EA

This franchise has been advertised in a leaflet distributed by The Franchise Shop. The leaflet describes the franchisor as 'specialising in the supply and distribution of vehicle and caravan towing equipment', and lists nine cities and towns which have Towing Centres. Gross margins are described as over 50%, set up cost is shows as £20,000. No other factual information is given, and the agent has declined to reply to our enquiries.

⇨ Britannic Corporation

77a Aldwick Road, Bognor Regis, West Sussex PO12 2NW

This franchise has been listed in some reference books and magazines. Mail sent to this address is accepted, but we have been unable to obtain information either in response to general requests from would-be franchisees or specifically for this publication. In the light of this experience we suggest a certain amount of caution may be in order if the franchise does eventually reappear.

⇨ British Business Consultants

Cedar Lodge, Tasburgh, Norwich NR15 1NS
Phone: 0508 47068

Management consultants

Outlets
Number of outlets
Company owned outlets: 01
Franchised: 03
Pilot: 01 started 1985
1988 franchise target: 07
Current reach:

South	00	South west	00	South east	00
Midlands	01	East Anglia	01	North east	00
North west	01	Scotland	00	Wales	00
N Ireland	01	Rep Ireland	00	I of Man/CI	00

Costs
Total: No information supplied
Franchise fee: £25,000
Other charges: No information supplied
Min cash excluding bank: No information supplied
Min overdraft required: No information supplied
Normal bank advance: No information supplied
Working capital first 2 months: No information supplied
Associated banks: None
Capital items required: None
Associated leasing co: None

Royalties

  50.0% of turnover
  0.0% accounts service
  0.0% for advertising fund
Total: 50.0% monthly sales

No standing royalty independent of turnover

Bank rating No information supplied
Territory 'Confidential information'
Strings See comment about franchisor secrecy
Training All training matters are described as 'confidential information' by franchisor
Support No information supplied
Operating Manual No information supplied
Profit No information supplied
Risk See comment about franchisor secrecy
Management only 'Proven franchise with good return on investment' (franchisor comment)

Size and reach
Original company launched: 1983
Overseas connections: Four overseas operations
UK connections: None
Viable for whole UK? Yes
Trade bodies: None

Franchisor's formula for success
No information supplied

Bruce and Company

Good Franchise Guide comment: British Business Consultants were kind enough to complete certain parts of our questionnaire, but upon our requesting a list of franchisees and a prospectus they stated that *both* were confidential, along with such matters as training. What we don't understand is how can you recruit franchisees with a confidential prospectus? How can anyone decide how good a franchise is without knowing about the training or costs? Our feeling is that the risk and possibility of strong ties are increased when dealing with a firm that is so strongly entrenched in secrecy.

Number of franchisee addresses provided by franchisor: 00

⇨ British Damp Proofing
(see BDP Ltd)

⇨ British School of Motoring
81-87 Hartfield Road, London SW19 3TJ

This well known driving school has not sent back information on its franchise. Our would-be franchisees were sent a little photocopied note giving the time and place of an information seminar, but no other information was supplied.

⇨ Bruce and Company
45 Bridge Street, Leatherhead, Surrey KT22 8BN
Phone: 0372 375161

Business transfer specialists, finance consultants, auctioneers, valuers

Outlets
Number of outlets
Company owned outlets: 01
Franchised: 12
Pilot: 01 started 1981
Total franchise target: 15 or 16
Current reach:

South	01	South west	02	South east	03
Midlands	03	East Anglia	02	North east	01
North west	01	Scotland	00	Wales	00
N Ireland	00	Rep Ireland	00	I of Man/CI	00

Costs
Total   £5,000
Franchise fee: £5,000
Other charges: Nil
Min cash excluding bank: £10,000 to £12,000
Min overdraft required: No information supplied
Normal bank advance: £5,000 depending on security
Working capital first 2 months: £5,000
Associated banks: No information supplied
Capital items required: Office lease and equipment
Associated leasing co: None

Royalties
   5.0% of turnover
   0.0% other services
   0.0% for advertising fund
Total   5.0% monthly sales
   £500 standing royalty pa independent of turnover

Budget Rent A Car International Inc

Bank rating	Banks very helpful
Territory	Two, three or four counties per franchisee
	Franchisees report: 'Just right'
Strings	'Once you start you are on your own'
Training	10 working days practical training
	Liaison visits for management training
	Cost: included in franchise fee
	Training value: 'Some training but not enough'
Support	Variable responses, but several felt the support was not as good as it should be.
Operating Manual	Variable responses from 'poor' to 'excellent'
Profit	As anticipated
Risk	There is competition in the field, and the need for constant support is central. One franchisee reported being in 'real trouble'.
Management only	Reasonable return for owner with management ability

Size and reach
Original company launched: 1973
Overseas connections: None
UK connections: No
Viable for whole UK?   No information
Trade bodies   None

Franchisor's formula for success
The business transfer market is geographically diverse. A potential buyer may well be a nearby resident to a business for sale but will more often come from a considerable distance. It is this inherent geographical factor in the nature of the market which helps to make the company's plans particularly suitable for a franchise operation.

Inside story from the franchisees
The franchise is sound, but is not highly supportive.

Insider tips
Ensure you have sufficient capital and feel able to run the show yourself.

Moans and groans
Most complaints relate to the manual and training given. However one franchisee did say, 'We have failed to get a foothold in the market and are heavily in debt.'

Number of franchisee addresses provided by franchisor: 14

➪ Budget Rent A Car International Inc
41 Marlowes, Hemel Hempstead, Herts HP1 1LD
Phone: 0442 232555

Car and van hire franchise with strong corporate image operating in well defined locality

Outlets
Number of outlets
Company owned outlets: 00
Franchised: 123
Pilot: 00
1988 franchise target: 125
Current reach:

South	39	South west	07	South east	08
Midlands	12	East Anglia	06	North east	13
North west	08	Scotland	14	Wales	02
N Ireland	01	Rep Ireland	07	I of Man/CI	04

Budget Rent A Car International Inc

Costs
Total	£20,000 to £25,000
Franchise fee:	No information supplied
Other charges:	No information supplied
Min cash excluding bank:	£75,000
Min overdraft required:	No information supplied
Normal bank advance:	No information supplied
Working capital first 2 months:	£75,000
Associated banks:	All main banks have details of the franchise
Capital items required:	Vehicles for which arrangements are made with finance houses
Associated leasing co:	None

Royalties
	7.5% of turnover
	0.0% accounts service
	2.5% for advertising fund
Total	10.0% monthly sales
	No standing royalty independent of turnover

Bank rating No information supplied, but we imagine there would be no trouble with such a well known company

Territory Post codes in London, city boundaries elsewhere.

Strings No information supplied

Training 5 days practical training } then on-going
3 days management training }
Cost: Only charge is for accommodation
Training value: No information supplied

Support No information supplied
Operating Manual No information supplied
Profit No information supplied
Risk Competitive, but Budget are one of the market leaders worldwide

Management only Proven franchise with good return on investment

Size and reach
Original company launched:	1966
Overseas connections:	3000 offices in over 100 countries
UK connections:	None in UK but owned by Gibbon, Green, Van Amerongen
Viable for whole UK?	Only small number of areas available
Trade bodies	BFA

Franchisor's formula for success
Budget's pioneering approach spans all areas of car rental. The leisure market is expanding all the time. Holidaymakers are becoming more independent and look to car rental to provide them with the freedom to explore on their own beyond the package tour. For businessmen, the more frequent the traveller the more he expects the familiarity of the Budget name wherever he goes.

Good Franchise Guide comment: We weren't supplied with any addresses of franchisees, but Budget is Budget, one of the big five in the car rental world. The only query we have (and we suspect the likes of Budget might laugh at us for even mentioning it) is whether the recent arrival of the secondhand car hire business (such as Practical Used Car Rental) will start to eat into the edge of their profits.

Number of franchisee addresses provided by franchisor: 00

Bumpsadaisy

⇨ **Bumpsadaisy**
43 The Market, Covent Garden, London WC2E 8HA
Phone: 01-836 1105

Maternity wear hire business run from home

Outlets
Number of outlets
Company owned outlets:	No information supplied
Franchised:	80
Pilot:	No information supplied
1988 franchise target:	No information supplied

Costs
Total	No information supplied
Franchise fee:	£3,000

No other information supplied

Royalties
	0.0% of turnover
	0.0% accounts service
	0.0% for advertising fund
Total	0.0% monthly sales
	£34.50 per month standing royalty independent of turnover

Bank rating	No information supplied
Territory	No information supplied
Strings	Very strong commitment to buying in Bumpsadaisy stock
Training	No information supplied
Support	No information supplied
Operating Manual	No information supplied
Profit	Most branches average about £300 a month
Risk	Main risk is through the agreement to buy 15 new garments for the following season, irrespective of your success or failure.
Management only	One-woman-band operation

Franchisor's formula for success
Your branch is your home. You work at least one morning and one evening a week. If you have more time, so much the better. We provide a complete franchise package.

Good Franchise Guide comment: The payments and commitments from franchisees appear totally unrelated to success or failure of the venture. Why?

Number of franchisee addresses provided by franchisor: 00

⇨ **Burger King UK Ltd**
20 Kew Road, Richmond, Surrey TW9 2NA
Phone: 01-940 6046

Hamburger restaurants

Outlets
Number of outlets
Company owned outlets:	No information supplied
Franchised:	15 approx. 5000 worldwide
Pilot:	No information supplied
1988 franchise target:	No information supplied

Burgerhouse

Costs
Total	£500,000
Franchise fee:	£15,000 approx
Other charges:	No information supplied
Min cash excluding bank:	£500,000
Min overdraft required:	No information supplied
Normal bank advance:	Nil
Working capital first 2 months:	No information supplied
Associated banks:	None
Capital items required:	No information supplied
Associated leasing co:	None

Royalties
	4.0% of turnover
	0.0% accounts service
	0.0% for advertising fund
Total	4.0% monthly sales
	No standing royalty independent of turnover

Bank rating   No information supplied
Territory   No information supplied
Strings   Probably strong tie for all foods

Training   No information supplied

Support   No information supplied
Operating Manual   No information supplied
Profit   No information supplied
Risk   We begin to wonder just how many burger franchises the UK can take

Management only   Reasonable return for owner with management ability

Size and reach
Original company launched:	No information supplied
Overseas connections:	Parent company: Pillsbury Company USA
UK connections:	None
Viable for whole UK?	Yes
Trade bodies	BFA

Franchisor's formula for success
No information supplied

Good Franchise Guide comment: The American burger giant started franchising in the UK in 1987; our would-be franchisees did not get a reply. It's obviously a sound franchise, (but see our risk comment above), but moving at its own speed and not willing to divulge information.

Number of franchisee addresses provided by franchisor: 00

⇨ **Burgerhouse**
Wrights Office Suite, Redcliffe Street, Sutton in Ashfield, Notts NG17 1DE

This franchise has been listed in some reference books and magazines. Mail sent to this address is now being returned by the Post Office marked 'Gone Away'. Enquiries have revealed that no forwarding address has been left, although it is possible that the franchise may have been set up once more in another part of the country. In the light of this experience we suggest a certain amount of caution may be in order.

Burgerpark

⇨ Burgerpark
13 Bath Street, Leamington Spa, Warwicks

This franchise has been listed in some reference books and magazines. Mail sent to this address is accepted, but we have been unable to obtain information either in response to general requests from would-be franchisees or specifically for this publication. In the light of this experience we suggest a certain amount of caution may be in order if the franchise does eventually reappear.

⇨ Business Transfer Consultants (Franchise) Ltd
Key House, 712 Green Lane, Dagenham, Essex RM13 1YX
Phone: 01-597 2302

Selling a range of businesses, empty premises, factories and other commercial propositions

Outlets
Number of outlets
Company owned outlets: 01
Franchised: 13
Pilot: 01 started 1983
Total franchise target: 26
Current reach:

South	04	South west	01	South east	05
Midlands	02	East Anglia	04	North east	00
North west	02	Scotland	03	Wales	02
N Ireland	01	Rep Ireland	02	I of Man/CI	00

Costs
Total	£15,000
Franchise fee:	£15,000
Other charges:	None
Min cash excluding bank:	£15,000
Min overdraft required:	£15,000
Normal bank advance:	£15,000
Working capital first 2 months:	No information supplied
Associated banks:	None
Capital items required:	Not specified
Associated leasing co:	None

Royalties
	10.0% of turnover
	0.0% accounts service
	0.0% for advertising fund
Total	10.0% monthly sales
	No standing royalty independent of turnover

Bank rating	All banks helpful
Territory	By county
	Franchisees report: Just right
Strings	Strong ties in some areas, but others uncontrolled
Training	21 days practical training
	160 hours management training
	Cost: £5,000, included in franchise fee
	Training value: Adequate

Calligraphics Ltd

Support	Very good
Operating Manual	Very good
Profit	Worse than expected in some cases, although all franchisees were confident of the future.
Risk	The high level of competition makes this a risky area; the risk is alleviated only by a constant high level of support from the franchisor
Management only	Variable depending on franchisee

Size and reach

Original company launched:	1983
Overseas connections:	'International'
UK connections:	None
Viable for whole UK?	Tes
Trade bodies	FID, FPES, MIBM, FNABA, FISM

Franchisor's formula for success
We are unrivalled on the market place with our corporate image and identity, close monitoring of performance and the unique opportunity for franchisees to be able to sell their franchise should they not be suitable to this profession.

Inside story from the franchisees
'The personal involvement of the franchisor makes the training particularly good.'
'I have encouraged others to take up the franchise'

Insider tips
Everyone reports strong support from the franchisor.

Moans and groans
None

Number of franchisee addresses provided by franchisor: 12

⇨ **Buyers World Ltd**
221 Lower Addiscombe Road, Croydon, Surrey CR0 6RB

This franchise has been listed in some reference books and magazines. Mail sent to this address is now being returned by the Post Office marked 'Gone Away'. Enquiries have revealed that no forwarding address has been left, although it is possible that the franchise may have been set up once more in another part of the country.
In the light of this experience we suggest a certain amount of caution may be in order.

⇨ **Calligraphics Ltd**
(trading as Tioli Glass Engraving)

2 Royal Building, The Parade, Liskeard, Cornwall PL14 6AF
Phone: 0579 44029

Manufacturers of the Calligraph PBM-9a Glass Engraving System

Calligraphics is listed under the Tioli name in various magazines and reference books as a while-you-wait glass engraving business, with half a dozen franchisees, and franchise investment costs of around £10,000.
Individuals now enquiring of the company for franchises are being told that instead of a franchise the company is selling its engraving system along with advice on setting up a glass engraving business. They also point out that there is a waiting list for the machines. No price for the machines is quoted in the literature presented to applicants.

Good Franchise Guide comment: We wonder what happened to anyone who actually paid £10,000 for a franchise and now finds a competitor opening up next door.

Number of franchisee addresses provided by franchisor: 00

Can Can Computers (Franchising) Ltd

➪ Can Can Computers (Franchising) Ltd
Can Can House, Station Approach, Trent Valley, Lichfield, Staffs WS13 6HE
Phone: 0543 262090/257008
Business computer systems

Outlets
Number of outlets
Company owned outlets: 01
Franchised: 08
Pilot: 01 started 1985
1988 franchise target: 20
Current reach:

South	06	South west	00	South east	01
Midlands	02	East Anglia	00	North east	00
North west	00	Scotland	00	Wales	00
N Ireland	00	Rep Ireland	00	I of Man/CI	00

Costs
Total	£10,000
Franchise fee:	£10,000
Other charges:	Nil
Min cash excluding bank:	£5,000
Min overdraft required:	No information supplied
Normal bank advance:	£10,000
Working capital first 2 months:	£3,000
Associated banks:	Bank of Scotland
Capital items required:	Motor vehicles
Associated leasing co:	Yes, but name not given

Royalties
	5.0% of turnover
	0.0% accounts service
	3.0% for advertising fund
Total	8.0% monthly sales
	No standing royalty independent of turnover

Bank rating	No information supplied
Territory	By individual negotiation
Strings	Very few – CCCF state 'there is no obligation to stock the complete range of products nor any restrictions from selling products from other sources. Franchisees need stock only those items which they are confident of selling successfully.'
Training	6 weeks per year minimum practical training 4 weeks per year minimum management training Cost: Nil – included in franchise fee Training value: No information supplied
Support	No information supplied
Operating Manual	No information supplied
Profit	Net profit for first year quoted as £34,800
Risk	The computer industry has gained a reputation of being a very high risk business indeed.
Management only	Reasonable return for owner with management ability

Size and reach
Original company launched:	1986
Overseas connections:	None
UK connections:	None
Viable for whole UK?	Yes
Trade bodies	No

Franchisor's formula for success
CCCF will develop a strong corporate image in the business computing marketplace. This image will be based on providing a complete solution to the business system sale. Even though this image will be assisted by national advertising it will be developed by direct and continual marketing in local areas by the group.

Good Franchise Guide comment: Franchisor supplied two names and addresses – neither replied to our questions. We hear of so many horror stories of computer companies going bust on all sides of the industry. This one could be fine, but we suggest it might be best judged by people with a lot of experience in the industry.

Number of franchisee addresses provided by franchisor: 02

⇨ Canterbury of New Zealand (UK) Ltd
101 Marylebone High Street, London W1M 3DB
Phone: 01-486 0702

Co-ordinated activewear for men, women and children

Outlets
Number of outlets
Company owned outlets: No information supplied
Franchised: 22 New Zealand, 17 Australia, 3 USA, 2 Japan
Pilot: No information supplied
1988 franchise target: No information supplied

Costs
Total	£45,000
Franchise fee:	£5,000
Other charges:	£20,000 stock
Min cash excluding bank:	No information supplied
Min overdraft required:	No information supplied
Normal bank advance:	No information supplied
Working capital first 2 months:	No information supplied
Associated banks:	None
Capital items required:	Shopfitting £15,000 to £20,000
Associated leasing co:	None

Royalties
	4.0% of turnover
	0.0% accounts service
	0.0% for advertising fund
Total	4.0% monthly sales
	No standing royalty independent of turnover

Bank rating	No information supplied
Territory	No information supplied
Strings	Total tie to one range of product
Training	No information supplied
Support	No information supplied
Operating Manual	No information supplied
Profit	40% gross profit quoted
Risk	The risk relates to the public's desire to purchase the specific Canterbury range
Management only	Only in later years is there likely to be finance to spare for a manager removed from the store

Capstan Careers Centres

Size and reach
Original company launched: 1904 in New Zealand; 1985 UK
Overseas connections: New Zealand company with licences in Japan, Canada, Sweden, Italy.
UK connections: None
Viable for whole UK? Yes
Trade bodies None

Franchisor's formula for success
Canterbury is the international brand name of New Zealand's largest textile company and has evolved from the world famous 'All Black' rugby jersey.

Good Franchise Guide comment: A single product shop which could turn out to be a great success or a flop – only time (and more information) will tell.

Number of franchisee addresses provided by franchisor: 00

➪ Capstan Careers Centres
Wellington House, Ashford Road, Maidstone, Kent ME15 5BH
Phone: 0622 813561

A franchise at this name and address has been listed in some reference books and magazines. Mail sent to this address is accepted, but we have been unable to obtain information either in response to general requests from would-be franchisees or specifically for this publication. The telephone number quoted rings, but we were unable to obtain a reply. In the light of this experience we suggest a certain amount of caution may be in order if the franchise does eventually reappear.

➪ Car Brokers
Cheapside Chambers, Bradford BD1 4HP
Phone: 0274 370512

A Bradford based company engaged in the sale of new vehicles at discounted prices

Outlets
Number of outlets
Company owned outlets: 03
Franchised: 11
Pilot: 03 started 1986
1988 franchise target: 25
Current reach:
South	02	South west	01	South east	04
Midlands	02	East Anglia	02	North east	00
North west	02	Scotland	00	Wales	01
N Ireland	00	Rep Ireland	00	I of Man/CI	00

Costs
Total £1,250
Franchise fee: £1,250
Other charges: Nil
Min cash excluding bank: Nil
Min overdraft required: Nil
Normal bank advance: Nil
Working capital first 2 months: £500
Associated banks: No information supplied
Capital items required: None
Associated leasing co: No information supplied

Car Market Holdings

Royalties	0.0% of turnover
	0.0% accounts service
	£100 per annum for advertising fund
Total	0.0% monthly sales
	Standing royalty independent of turnover – see advertising fund above
Bank rating	No information supplied
Territory	Minimum of 10 square miles
Strings	No information supplied
Training	14 practical training
	14 management training
	Cost: No charge
	Training value: No information supplied
Support	No information supplied
Operating Manual	No information supplied
Profit	Totally dependent upon number of vehicles sold
Risk	Anyone else could start up a similar operation next door. They might not be as good, but they could still cream off some of your trade.
Management only	Reasonable return for owner with management ability

Size and reach

Original company launched:	1980
Overseas connections:	None
UK connections:	None
Viable for whole UK?	All areas
Trade bodies	None

Franchisor's formula for success
With the help of our computer we can give a discounted price instantly. We know this is the best price your customer will find. Our motto speaks for itself, 'If you can find a vehicle cheaper, take our advice . . . buy it.'

Good Franchise Guide comment: From what we can see this looks more like an agency operation than a franchise, although it is included in some books on franchising. There are no royalties payable.

Number of franchisee addresses provided by franchisor: 00

⇨ Car Market Holdings
Previously at Hilton House, The Downs, Altrincham, Cheshire WA14 2QD

A franchise at this name and address has been listed in some reference books and magazines. Mail sent to this address is now being returned by the Post Office marked 'Gone Away'. The telephone number quoted is now a dead line. Enquiries have revealed that no forwarding address has been left, although it is possible that the franchise may have been set up once more in another part of the country. In the light of this experience we suggest a certain amount of caution may be in order.

Carpet Master Ltd

⇨ Carpet Master Ltd

Shop Unit 36, Bradford Road, Buckingham Avenue Trading Estate, Slough, Berks SL1 4PG
Phone: 0753 691584

Retail carpets

Outlets
Number of outlets
Company owned outlets:	No information supplied
Franchised:	03
Pilot:	No information supplied
1988 franchise target:	No information supplied

Costs
Total	No information supplied
Franchise fee:	£3,721
Other charges:	No information supplied
Min cash excluding bank:	Nil
Min overdraft required:	No information supplied
Normal bank advance:	100%
Working capital first 2 months:	No information supplied
Associated banks:	None
Capital items required:	None
Associated leasing co:	None

Royalties
	0.0% of turnover
	0.0% accounts service
	0.0% for advertising fund
Total	0.0% monthly sales
	No standing royalty independent of turnover

No other information provided on profit, risk, etc

Size and reach
Original company launched:	1987
Overseas connections:	None
UK connections:	None
Viable for whole UK?	Yes
Trade bodies	None

Franchisor's formula for success

Taking up a Franchise describes this firm as 'a young and energetic company quickly reshaping the retail carpet market. Carpet Master offers all its franchisees total support and back-up, every mobile carpet showroom being equipped with the very best carpets and curtains from all of the leading manufacturers.'

Good Franchise Guide comment: Neither we nor the would-be franchisee who wrote, were able to get any information at all on this company. Information comes from a separately obtained leaflet. Franchisee is given a discount on the carpets.

Number of franchisee addresses provided by franchisor: 00

⇨ Carryfast Ltd

Mill Street East, Dewsbury, West Yorks WF12 9AP
Phone: 0924 463184

Previously the parcels division of Unilever. Developed after a management buy-out. Carryfast has nine depots and a turnover of £15 million.

Outlets
Number of outlets
Company owned outlets: 09
Franchised: 02
Pilot: 01 started 1987
1988 franchise target: 06
Current reach:

South	01	South west	01	South east	02
Midlands	02	East Anglia	01	North east	02
North west	00	Scotland	01	Wales	01
N Ireland	00	Rep Ireland	00	I of Man/CI	00

Costs
Total: £22,000 upwards
Franchise fee: £22,000 upwards
Other charges: Nil
Min cash excluding bank: £1,000
Min overdraft required: 66%
Normal bank advance: No information supplied
Working capital first 2 months: £1,000 to £2,000
Associated banks: Nat West
Capital items required: Vehicles – normally 1 or 2 initially
Associated leasing co: No

Royalties
Total:
0.0% of turnover
0.0% accounts service
1.0% for advertising fund
1.0% monthly sales

No standing royalty independent of turnover

Bank rating One franchisee had to shop around; the other got finance at once

Territory By county
Franchisee report: One said 'Not large enough' the other said 'Just right'

Strings Some ties but lots of freedom too

Training Up to 5 days practical training
Up to 5 days management training
Cost: nil
Training value: 'Not enough'

Support 'Very poor' from one, 'good' from the other
Operating Manual 'Very poor' from one, 'good' from the other
Profit One franchisee said 'as expected' while the other said 'Better than projected'

Risk Parcel delivery is very competitive, but the market appears to be growing continuously

Management only Reasonable return for owner with management ability

Size and reach
Original company launched: 1948
Overseas connections: None
UK connections: None
Viable for whole UK? Yes – UK mainland
Trade bodies: Road Haulage Assn; Confederation of British Industry

Cartons Boulangeries

Franchisor's formula for success
Since the total parcels market probably represents some £1,000 million annually in the UK the opportunities for the future growth of successful parcels carriers is enormous and Carryfast and its future franchise partners will be better placed than many to take full advantage of these opportunities.

Inside story from the franchisees
Both existing franchisees' addresses were willing to take time to give views and opinions. Both had criticisms, but the franchisee who was most critical throughout stated that the profit level of the franchisee was better than projected by the franchise prospectus. In other words, if success comes with what this franchisee perceives as weak back-up, what will it be like when the franchisor gets his act together? But against this the less critical franchisee who found support good was only doing 'as expected'.

Insider tips
Make sure you can survive without much help from above.
'I had done this work before; without previous insight the training would have been inadequate. My wife is left with the administration with no training given.'

Moans and groans
'No help or co-operation from franchisor'
'We feel the return is insufficient for the capital invested at this stage'
'It is far harder work than anticipated'.

Good Franchise Guide comment: We were grateful to Carryfast for supplying the addresses of both their franchisees – more than many franchisors would do at the start of a new operation – and it is obvious that a sample of two cannot be taken as revealing the total truth about the franchise. Complaints about new franchisors not having their act together are numerous – perhaps everyone should beware of new franchises. Even if the franchisee's views are correct at this stage we feel that this franchisor will not be long in mending its ways.

Number of franchisee addresses provided by franchisor: 02

⇨ Cartons Boulangeries
Unit 2, Telegraph Hill Estate, Laundry Road, Minster, Ramsgate, Kent CT12 4HJ
Phone: 0843 821940

Quality bakers in French style

Outlets
Number of outlets
Company owned outlets:	01
Franchised:	05
Pilot:	No information supplied

Costs
Total	£38,000 to £65,100
Franchise fee:	£5,000
Other charges:	Shopfitting £20,000
Min cash excluding bank:	£19,000
Min overdraft required:	No information supplied
Normal bank advance:	50%
Working capital first 2 months:	£4,000 plus £1,000 opening stock
Associated banks:	None
Capital items required:	Equipment on lease (quarterly premiums quoted between £1,200 and £2,500)
Associated leasing co:	None

Royalties

'Our licensed operation does not charge a weekly management fee. The agreement is for the supply of our own quality frozen products, and the complete business system.'

Castle Fairs Ltd

Bank rating	No information supplied
Territory	No information supplied
Strings	Tied for franchisor for product
Training	4 days practical training
	3 days management training
	Cost: £600 – not included in franchise fee
	Training value: No information supplied
Support	No information supplied
Operating Manual	No information supplied
Profit	First year net profit quoted within range of £19,370 to £33,750
Risk	Should be low, although there may be regional variations in success
Management only	No information supplied

Size and reach

Original company launched:	No information supplied
Overseas connections:	None
UK connections:	None
Viable for whole UK?	No information supplied
Trade bodies	None

Franchisor's formula for success

Cartons aims to recreate the image of travelling through France and sampling crusty bread, croissants, rolls, patisseries 'eaten with gay abandon at breakfast over coffee and jam, at lunch with wine, cheese and fruit, or to supplement an evening meal.'

Good Franchise Guide comment: We would particularly like to talk to franchisees to see how they are doing. (We would also like to take up an offer of a free tasting, but no one offered.)

Number of franchisee addresses provided by franchisor: 00

⇨ Castle Fairs Ltd

Bowcliffe Road, Bramham, Wetherby, West Yorks LS23 9JS
Phone: 0937 845829

Organisers of exhibitions on a national basis aimed at the retail and leisure markets

Outlets
Number of outlets
Company owned outlets:		02			
Franchised:		06			
Pilot:		02 started 1977			
1988 franchise target:		10			
Current reach:					
South	00	South west	01	South east	01
Midlands	00	East Anglia	00	North east	01
North west	01	Scotland	01	Wales	00
N Ireland	01	Rep Ireland	00	I of Man/CI	00

Costs

Total	£7,500
Franchise fee:	£7,500
Other charges:	Nil
Min cash excluding bank:	£2,500
Min overdraft required:	£7,500
Normal bank advance:	No real limit
Working capital first 2 months:	Varies according to circumstance
Associated banks:	None
Capital items required:	A car
Associated leasing co:	None

Ceil Clean

Royalties
　　　　　　　　　　　　　　　　10.0% of turnover
　　　　　　　　　　　　　　　　0.0% accounts service
　　　　　　　　　　　　　　　　2.0% for advertising fund (approx)
Total　　　　　　　　　　　　　12.0% monthly sales (approx)
　　　　　　　　　　　　　　　　No standing royalty independent of turnover

Bank rating　　　　　　　　No information supplied
Territory　　　　　　　　　Maximum of 12 areas of Britain
Strings　　　　　　　　　　No information supplied
Training　　　　　　　　　 Combined practical and management training totalling one year.
　　　　　　　　　　　　　　　　Cost: Nil – included in franchise fee
　　　　　　　　　　　　　　　　Training value: No information supplied

Support　　　　　　　　　　No information supplied
Operating Manual　　　　　No information supplied
Profit　　　　　　　　　　 Franchisor predicts that with four or five smaller events plus 'a couple of big ones' a year net profits will be over £60,000 per annum.
Risk　　　　　　　　　　　 No information supplied
Management only　　　　　 Reasonable return for owner with management ability

Size and reach
Original company launched:　　1977
Overseas connections:　　　　 None
UK connections:　　　　　　　 None
Viable for whole UK?　　　　　Yes and worldwide
Trade bodies　　　　　　　　　None

Franchisor's formula for success
The attraction is that our franchisees have a large area working from home to develop first class exhibitions. They are not tied to a desk and there is no upper limit to what they can earn. Total head office back up is given in all aspects of the business.

Good Franchise Guide comment: Although the franchisor has six areas assigned he states that it does take about nine months before the first event is organised, and therefore none of the franchisees is in a position to answer questions on the way the franchise is going; which by and large seems fair enough; but will they really make the predicted profit?

Number of franchisee addresses provided by franchisor: 00

⇨ Ceil Clean

Information only available from The Franchise Shop Ltd, 26 High Street, Merstham, Surrey RH1 3EA
Phone: 073 74 4211

Cleaning company specialising in restoration of acoustic ceiling tiles

Outlets
Number of outlets
Company owned outlets:　　　　01
Franchised:　　　　　　　　　 No information supplied
Pilot:　　　　　　　　　　　　01 started 1985
1988 franchise target:　　　　No information supplied

Central Office of Publishing

Costs
Total	No information supplied
Franchise fee:	£9,947
Other charges:	No information supplied
Min cash excluding bank:	No information supplied
Min overdraft required:	No information supplied
Normal bank advance:	No information supplied
Working capital first 2 months:	£2,000
Associated banks:	Lloyds
Capital items required:	Van (about £4,500)
Associated leasing co:	None

Royalties No information supplied
Bank rating No information supplied
Territory No information supplied
Strings No information supplied

Training Described in the leaflet as 'excellent' but no further information supplied
Support No information supplied
Operating Manual No information supplied
Profit Promotional leaflet states 'Earning potential - £15,000 to £40,000'
Risk No information supplied
Management only No information supplied

Size and reach
Original company launched:	No information supplied
Overseas connections:	None
UK connections:	None
Viable for whole UK?	No information supplied
Trade bodies	None

Franchisor's formula for success
'The acceptance of the Ceil Clean method has been so rapid that Ceil Clean is now obtaining orders with major companies and corporates (sic) in many areas of the country which its pilot operation, based in London, is unable to service.

Good Franchise Guide comment: The leaflet claims Marks and Spencer, Abbey National, Ladbrokes, Commercial Union and others among its clients. We really can't understand what the franchise has to hide with such a strong client profile.

Number of franchisee addresses provided by franchisor: 00

⇨ Central Office of Publishing
8, The Green, Heaton Norris, Stockport, Cheshire SK4 2NP
Phone: 061-432 8384

Free community newspaper

Outlets
Number of outlets
Company owned outlets:	No information supplied
Franchised:	No information supplied
Pilot:	No information supplied
1988 franchise target:	No information supplied

Chapter and Verse Bookshop

Costs
No information supplied
Royalties
No information supplied
Bank rating   No information supplied
Territory   Enough to give away 5000 + newspapers
Support   No information supplied
Operating Manual   No information supplied
Profit   'Initial income' projected as £10,000 +
Risk   You are up against major operators. They should not mind at all as the paper is community based, but if you became too successful in selling adverts you could find yourself in trouble.
Management only   One-man-band operation run from home
Size and reach
Original company launched: 1982
Overseas connections: None
UK connections: None
Viable for whole UK?   Yes
Trade bodies   None

Franchisor's formula for success
'In the present economic climate, there is an increasing trend for people to participate in local and community events. These people are requiring a vehicle in which they can freely express their opinions and braodcast their activities. This is where the Digest scores so successfully. Experience has shown that a community responds very positively once a Digest is produced, and by regarding it as their own newspaper rapidly starts contributing to, and assisting with, all aspects of publication'.

Good Franchise Guide comment: A neat idea for the franchisee to write and gather articles and adverts, which are typeset and printed by the franchisor. Must be a lot of frustrated journalists who would love it if it works, but the lack of financial detail given make us wonder. More information please.

Number of franchisee addresses provided by franchisor: 00

➪ Chapter and Verse Bookshop
226 North Street, Bedminster, Bristol BS3 1JD
Phone: 0272 214670

Bookselling

Outlets
Number of outlets
Company owned outlets: 08
Franchised: 00 – new franchise
Pilot: No information supplied
1988 franchise target: No information supplied

Costs
Total   £75,000
Franchise fee: £4,500
Other charges: £40,000 stock
Min cash excluding bank: £37,500
Min overdraft required: No information supplied
Normal bank advance: 50%
Working capital first 2 months: No information supplied
Associated banks: None
Capital items required: £25,000 shopfitting
Associated leasing co: None

Chemical Express Ltd

Royalties	2.5% of turnover
	0.0% accounts service
	0.0% for advertising fund
Total	2.5% monthly sales
	No standing royalty independent of turnover
Bank rating	No information supplied
Territory	No information supplied
Strings	We presume that all stock has to be purchased through franchisor leaving franchisee unable to negotiate discounts.
Training	No information supplied
Support	No information supplied
Operating Manual	No information supplied
Profit	£17,250 first year net profit
Risk	High risk in our opinion. Each year the trade magazine of book selling reveals a very low level of net profitability in the industry.
Management only	Little salary to spare for a manager

Size and reach

Original company launched:	1971
Overseas connections:	None
UK connections:	None
Viable for whole UK?	Yes
Trade bodies	None

Franchisor's formula for success

The success of Chapter and Verse in becoming a business with a turnover of £2,000,000 since first opening its doors in 1971 is based on providing excellent service to its customers. In the same way the success of the Chapter and Verse franchise operation is based on providing excellent long-term service to its franchisees.

Good Franchise Guide comment: We don't think anyone else franchises bookshops, and we are not quite sure if a franchise is necessary in a business which anyone with enthusiasm can enter. More information required to convince us.

Number of franchisee addresses provided by franchisor: 00

➡ **Chemical Express Ltd** — 0121 525 4040   NI Paul Lewis Derry. (01504) 424830
Ninian Way, Tame Valley Industrial Estate, Wilnecote, Tamworth, Staffs B77 5DZ   0370 424830
Phone: 0827 251431

Fully fitted mobile showroom selling over 80 specialist products from graffiti remover to diesel oil additives, beer pipe cleaner, specialist cleaners, cutting fluids etc

Outlets
Number of outlets
Company owned outlets: Information not supplied
Franchised: 22
Pilot: 01 started 1985
1988 franchise target: 80
Current reach:

South	04	South west	01	South east	07
Midlands	02	East Anglia	02	North east	02
North west	03	Scotland	00	Wales	01
N Ireland	00	Rep Ireland	00	I of Man/CI	00

Chemical Express Ltd

Costs

Total	£9,750
Franchise fee:	£6,900
Other charges:	£2,850 stock
Min cash excluding bank:	£2,000
Min overdraft required:	Nil
Normal bank advance:	£9,000
Working capital first 2 months:	No information supplied
Associated banks:	Lloyds
Capital items required:	All supplied as part of package
Associated leasing co:	No

Royalties

	5.0% of turnover
	0.0% accounts service
	2.5% for advertising fund
Total	7.5% monthly sales
	No standing royalty independent of turnover

Bank rating	No information supplied
Territory	By business population in area
Strings	No information supplied
Training	7 days residential and 7 days practical field training, plus on-going training
	Cost: included in franchise fee
	Training value: No information supplied
Support	No information supplied
Operating Manual	No information supplied
Profit	Net profits quoted over a series of examples ranging from £13,200 to £36,360 depending on size of firm.
Risk	No information supplied
Management only	Reasonable return for owner with management ability

Size and reach

Original company launched:	1982
Overseas connections:	None
UK connections:	Sister company – Forward Circuits plc
Viable for whole UK?	Yes
Trade bodies	None

Franchisor's formula for success

We will supply everything the franchisee needs to get started – 'and we mean everything'. And we even offer the unique Chemical Express Guarantee: 'If at the end of your first three months you are not happy with your Chemical Express franchise we will repurchase your stock and take back your mobile showroom for disposal – without quibble.'

Inside story from the franchisees

In response to our request for addresses of franchisees, the franchisor stated that such information was highly confidential. What we don't understand is if the addresses of franchisees are that confidential how customers are going to find out about them.

Good Franchise Guide comment: The guarantee is a bonus – if only more firms would offer it.

Number of franchisee addresses provided by franchisor: 00

Cico Chimney Linings

⇨ Churchtown
20 Houghton Street, Southport, Merseyside

This franchise has been listed in some reference books and magazines. Mail sent to this address is accepted, but we have been unable to obtain information either in response to general requests from would-be franchisees or specifically for this publication. In the light of this experience we suggest a certain amount of caution may be in order if the franchise does eventually reappear.

⇨ Cico Chimney Linings
Westleton, Saxmundham, Suffolk IP17 3BS
Phone: 072 873 608

Restoration of chimneys

Outlets
Number of outlets	
Company owned outlets:	01
Franchised:	Over 20
Pilot:	01 started 1982
1988 franchise target:	No information supplied

Costs
Total	£11,000
Franchise fee:	£6,500
Other charges:	No information supplied
Min cash excluding bank:	£4,000
Min overdraft required:	No information supplied
Normal bank advance:	66%
Working capital first 2 months:	No information supplied
Associated banks:	None
Capital items required:	None
Associated leasing co:	None

Royalties
	10.0% of turnover
	0.0% accounts service
	0.0% for advertising fund
Total	10.0% monthly sales
	No standing royalty independent of turnover

Bank rating	No information supplied
Territory	No information supplied
Strings	No information supplied
Training	No information supplied

Size and reach
Original company launched:	1982
Overseas connections:	None
UK connections:	None
Viable for whole UK?	Yes
Trade bodies	BFA

Franchisor's formula for success
No information supplied

Good Franchise Guide comment: Franchisor refuses to supply information in writing to possible franchisees until they have spoken on the telephone about background etc. So beware if you write – they will seek out your phone number and call you. (Is that really necessary?)

Number of franchisee addresses provided by franchisor: 00

Circle C Stores Ltd

⇨ Circle C Stores Ltd

24 Fitzalan Road, Roffey, Horsham, West Sussex RH13 6AA
Phone: 0403 61698

Circle C Cornerhood Convenience Centres operate on the peripheral areas of large towns, on estates, in villages and small towns. Centres vary from 1000 to 3000 sq ft selling a range of groceries, frozen foods, fruit and veg, toiletry, chemistry, household, confectionery, cigarettes, off licence and video hire, seven days a week from 7.30am to 9pm.

Outlets
Number of outlets
Company owned outlets: 10
Franchised: 15
Pilot: 03 started 1982
1988 franchise target: 40
Current reach:

South	00	South west	00	South east	25
Midlands	00	East Anglia	00	North east	00
North west	00	Scotland	00	Wales	00
N Ireland	00	Rep Ireland	00	I of Man/CI	00

Costs
Total: £70,000 to £95,000
Franchise fee: £6,000
Other charges: Nil
Min cash excluding bank: £30,000
Min overdraft required: £5,000 (arranged by franchisee)
Normal bank advance: £60,000
Working capital first 2 months: £30,000
Associated banks: All major clearers
Capital items required: None
Associated leasing co: No

Royalties
Total:
3.0% of turnover
0.0% accounts service
0.5% for advertising fund
3.5% monthly sales

No standing royalty independent of turnover

Bank rating Very good – no problems
Territory Based on trading area
Franchisees report: 'Just right'
Strings Lots of ties, but plenty of freedom too
Training 2 weeks practical training
4 weeks and on going management training
Cost: included in franchise fee
Training value: Rated as excellent, including the on-going training

Support Excellent
Operating Manual Very good
Profit Good – normally better than expected
Risk Growing competition – see Late Late Supershop for example
Management only Little salary to spare for a manager for small ventures; reasonable return for owner with management ability in larger stores

Size and reach
Original company launched: 1975
Overseas connections: None
UK connections: J 'N' K Markets Ltd
Viable for whole UK? Yes
Trade bodies: None

City Link Transport Holdings Ltd

Franchisor's formula for success
The franchise could be run under management; higher investment in larger units for higher volume of trade brings a good return. Owner occupiers get good returns.

Inside story from the franchisees
Responses from franchisees are all very enthusiastic. Support from the franchisor is particularly highly rated.
'Three of my staff have now left to take up Circle C franchises elsewhere'
'With this franchisor just one phone call will bring an answer to any query.'

Insider tips
'Must give 100% to reap the potential rewards'

Moans and groans
Manual should be updated regularly.
'Extremely hard work'

Number of franchisee addresses provided by franchisor: 13

⇨ City Link Transport Holdings Ltd
Batavia Road, Sunbury-on-Thames, Middx TW16 5LR
Phone: 0932 788799

(Note the company previously operated from Feltham in Middlesex and are still listed under this address in some reference books)

Same day delivery service

Outlets
Number of outlets
Company owned outlets: 16
Franchised: 22
Pilot: 06 started 1972
1988 franchise target: Franchise network already complete
Current reach:

South	13	South west	02	South east	01
Midlands	04	East Anglia	02	North east	04
North west	06	Scotland	03	Wales	01
N Ireland	01	Rep Ireland	01	I of Man/CI	00

Costs
Total — No information provided by the franchisor.
Franchise fee: The network is already complete and further franchises which become available will be charged according to the size of the territory.

Associated banks: Lloyds
Capital items required: At least 1 fully liveried Transit-type van
Associated leasing co: None

Royalties

8.5% of turnover
0.0% accounts service
1.5% for advertising fund
Total — 10.0% monthly sales
No standing royalty independent of turnover

Bank rating — No information supplied
Territory — Ordnance survey grid lines and post codes.
Strings — No information supplied

Clarks Shoes

Training	Combined practical and management training lasting 2 to 3 weeks depending on previous experience. Full ongoing support also given. Cost: £250 plus expenses. Training value: No information supplied
Support	No information supplied
Operating Manual	No information supplied
Profit	No information supplied
Risk	Very competitive area – be prepared for an industry shake out
Management only	Proven franchise with good return on investment

Size and reach

Original company launched:	1969
Overseas connections:	None
UK connections:	None
Viable for whole UK?	Yes
Trade bodies	BFA full member, Franchise agreement also registered with Office of Fair Trading.

Franchisor's formula for success
No information supplied

Good Franchise Guide comment: Any franchise that has allocated all its areas and kept its franchisees is, presumably, doing well. If an area comes on the market be sure to enquire exactly how the previous incumbent did and why it is for sale.

Number of franchisee addresses provided by franchisor: 00

⇨ **Clarks Shoes**
40 High Street, Street, Somerset BA16 0YA
Phone: 0458 43131

Footwear retailing

Outlets
Number of outlets

Company owned outlets:	70 approx
Franchised:	30 approx
Pilot:	No information supplied
1988 franchise target:	No information supplied

Costs

Total	£80,000
Franchise fee:	£5,000
Other charges:	No information supplied
Min cash excluding bank:	£25,000
Min overdraft required:	No information supplied
Normal bank advance:	66%
Working capital first 2 months:	No information supplied
Associated banks:	None
Capital items required:	No information supplied
Associated leasing co:	Yes – but no information given

Royalties

	None
Bank rating	No information supplied
Territory	No information supplied
Strings	You are tied to Clarks shoes – but that is probably an advantage.
Training	None

Cobblestone Paving (UK) Ltd

Size and reach
Original company launched: 1825 (Torlink 1965)
Overseas connections: None
UK connections: This opportunity is organised by Torlink Ltd, a wholly owned subsidiary of C & J Clark Ltd, selling shoes under the Clarks, K Shoes and Levi's names.
Viable for whole UK? Yes
Trade bodies No information supplied

Franchisor's formula for success
It will be of great benefit to you if you have already had some good commercial experience, although not necessarily in the footwear or retail trade.

Good Franchise Guide comment: This franchisor offers a total package, including finding the premises, loan finance, shop design, marketing etc, etc. It is of course a highly respected company – we just wish they had been willing to tell us more and let us talk to franchisees.

Number of franchisee addresses provided by franchisor: 00

⇨ Clubsun Ltd
22a Fish Street, Northampton

This franchise offering sun bed rental has been listed in some reference books and magazines. Mail sent to this address is accepted, but we have been unable to obtain information either in response to general requests from would-be franchisees or specifically for this publication. In the light of this experience we suggest a certain amount of caution may be in order if the franchise does eventually reappear.

⇨ Cobblestone Paving (UK) Ltd
Unit 12, Wheatear Estate, Perry Road, Witham, Essex CM8 1VD
Phone: 0376 517766 (4 lines)

System for colouring and imprinting concrete to give different effects

Outlets
Number of outlets
Company owned outlets: 00
Franchised: 37
Pilot: 01 started 1985
1988 franchise target: 70
Current reach:

South	05	South west	03	South east	08
Midlands	05	East Anglia	08	North east	02
North west	02	Scotland	01	Wales	01
N Ireland	01	Rep Ireland	01	I of Man/CI	00

Costs
Total £15,000
Franchise fee: No information supplied
Other charges: No information supplied
Min cash excluding bank: 100%
Min overdraft required: £2,000
Normal bank advance: Varies
Working capital first 2 months: £2,000
Associated banks: Nat West
Capital items required: Vehicle only
Associated leasing co: None

Coffeeman Management Ltd

Royalties

	6.25% of turnover
	0.0% accounts service
	0.75% for advertising fund
Total	7.0% monthly sales
	No standing royalty independent of turnover

Bank rating	No information supplied
Territory	Approx 200,000 population
Strings	No information supplied
Training	21 days practical and management training
	Cost: £1,000 – included in franchise fee
	Training value: No information supplied
Support	No information supplied
Operating Manual	No information supplied
Profit	No information supplied
Risk	No information supplied
Management only	Reasonable return for owner with management ability

Size and reach

Original company launched:	1974 New Zealand
Overseas connections:	Licensees in other areas
UK connections:	None
Viable for whole UK?	Yes
Trade bodies	None

Franchisor's formula for success

The Creteprint paving system is competitive with more traditional types of paving. Our market is the discerning home-owner/developer, who is prepared to pay for quality and professionalism. This ensures that our franchisees do not get involved in 'discounting' exercises which reduce profitability.

Inside story from the franchisees

The company have informed us that they 'do not supply mailing lists of franchisees as a matter of company policy'. We have asked them why, but they have declined to expand on this policy decision.

Number of franchisee addresses provided by franchisor: 00

⇨ Coffeeman Management Ltd

73 Woolsbridge Industrial Park, Wimborne, Dorset BH21 6SU
Phone: 0202 823501

Supplier of ground coffee, tea, sugar, creamer etc to a variety of firms who are loaned Coffeeman equipment

Outlets
Number of outlets
Company owned outlets: 02
Franchised: 46
Pilot: 00
1988 franchise target: 75
Current reach:

South	07	South west	08	South east	05
Midlands	14	East Anglia	03	North east	03
North west	03	Scotland	00	Wales	01
N Ireland	01	Rep Ireland	00	I of Man/CI	03

Coffeeman Management Ltd

Costs
Total	£9,150 (if optional van supplied add a further £3,800)
Franchise fee:	£4,750
Other charges:	£4,400 (Inc £2,480 machines)
Min cash excluding bank:	£5,000
Min overdraft required:	£5,000
Normal bank advance:	Variable
Working capital first 2 months:	£1,000
Associated banks:	Lloyds and Royal Bank of Scotland
Capital items required:	Coffee machines
Associated leasing co:	Yes – details not provided.

Royalties
	0.0% of turnover
	0.0% accounts service
	0.0% for advertising fund
Total	0.0% monthly sales
	No standing royalty independent of turnover
	NB: Franchisor makes its income from coffee sales

Bank rating	All banks helpful with finance
Territory	Areas are allotted according to individual geographical placing, size, density of population etc.
	Most franchisees happy with territory
Strings	Strong ties for coffee and other supplies
Training	5 days practical and management training plus a further 5 days refresher after 6 months
	Cost: £1,000 included in 'other charges' above
	Training value: Adequate
Support	Very good
Operating Manual	No manual as such
Profit	As expected
Risk	Lot of competition; most firms are regularly telephoned by firms offering coffee machines on site.
Management only	'Proven franchise with good return on investment' (franchisor's comment)

Size and reach
Original company launched:	1978
Overseas connections:	None
UK connections:	None
Viable for whole UK?	Yes
Trade bodies	None

Franchisor's formula for success
The franchise can be run from home, no royalties are due and there is no capital outlay for equipment save coffee machines. No premises are necessary; there is a guaranteed monthly repeat business. No previous selling experience is needed, and it is almost impossible to lose money. The business can be sold as a going concern for invariably higher than paid. The raw product is imported, roasted and packed in our own factory and sent direct to the franchisee, thus there are no middle men. Guaranteed franchise fee refund in first year.

Inside story from the franchisees
Large response which was very enthusiastic.

Insider tips
You must be able to sell as 'cold calling' is the main way of getting customers.

Moans and groans
No manual. More training for cold calling required.

Good Franchise Guide comment: A good guarantee, worth having

Number of franchisee addresses provided by franchisor: 45

Coffilta Coffee Services Ltd

⇨ Coffilta Coffee Services Ltd

Eagle Close, Chandlers Ford Industrial Estate, Chandlers Ford, Eastleigh, Hants SO5 3NF
Phone: 0703 255122

Supply coffee machine on free loan, deliver ingredients and make service calls

Outlets
Number of outlets
Company owned outlets: 04
Franchised: 36
Pilot: 00
1988 franchise target: 50
Current reach:

South	05	South west	05	South east	05
Midlands	10	East Anglia	04	North east	03
North west	03	Scotland	03	Wales	01
N Ireland	00	Rep Ireland	01	I of Man/CI	00

Costs
Total — No charges – the company makes its money from the coffee consumed
Working capital first 2 months: £1,000
Associated banks: None
Capital items required: Car or estate car
Associated leasing co: None

Royalties
Total
0.0% of turnover
0.0% accounts service
0.0% for advertising fund
0.0% monthly sales

No standing royalty independent of turnover

Bank rating — No information supplied
Territory — Radius from franchisees base
Franchisees report: 'Just right'
Strings — Total tie to the product
Training — Practical and management training given as required
Cost: Free on appointment
Training value: Opinions vary from 'No training' to 'Adequate training'
Support — 'Not too good'
Operating Manual — 'None' said one franchisee; 'good' said another
Profit — 35p per cup. (How many cups will your clients drink in a month?) Franchisees report they are doing 'as expected'
Risk — Hardly a month goes by without someone offering us a day's free trial of their coffee machine. It is hard to believe that the market can stand this level of competition.
Management only — Reasonable return for owner with management ability

Size and reach
Original company launched: 1975
Overseas connections: None
UK connections: None
Viable for whole UK? Yes
Trade bodies Local Chamber of Commerce

Colour Counsellors

Franchisor's formula for success
We manufacture our own coffee machines and enjoy an established reputation for the quality of machines, coffee and service. Administrative and sales training is given with full promotional backup. Exclusive areas provide outlets from the commercial and catering sectors and offer a chance of becoming established with a repeat business without incurring large capital investment. Besides manufacturing our own coffee machines, we enjoy an established reputation for the quality of our coffees and service.

Inside story from the franchisees
'I would give every encouragement to anyone wishing to run their own company, and in fact have done so to three separate people.'

Insider tips
Demand national advertising for the product

Moans and groans
The manual is based too much on theory and not written by someone with field experience.

Number of franchisee addresses provided by franchisor: 14

➪ Colour Counsellors
187 New Kings Road, London SW6 4SW
Phone: 01-736 8326

Interior decoration

Outlets
Number of outlets	
Company owned outlets:	65
Franchised:	01
Pilot:	No information supplied
1988 franchise target:	No information supplied

Costs
Total	£4,500
Franchise fee:	£3,500
Other charges:	No information supplied
Min cash excluding bank:	£2,250
Min overdraft required:	No information supplied
Normal bank advance:	50%
Working capital first 2 months:	No information supplied
Associated banks:	None
Capital items required:	None
Associated leasing co:	None

Royalties
	0.0% of turnover
	0.0% accounts service
	0.0% for advertising fund
Total	0.0% monthly sales
	£1,750 pa standing royalty independent of turnover

Bank rating	No information supplied
Territory	No information supplied
Strings	No information supplied
Training	No information supplied
Support	No information supplied
Operating Manual	No information supplied
Profit	No information supplied
Risk	No information supplied
Management only	No information supplied

Command Performance International

Size and reach
Original company launched: 1977
Overseas connections: None
UK connections: None
Viable for whole UK? Yes
Trade bodies BFA

Franchisor's formula for success
No information supplied

Good Franchise Guide comment: It doesn't take much imagination to realise that we haven't been able to get this franchisor to answer our questions. Neither have they replied to letters from a would-be franchisee. The fact that they are still with only one franchisee may indicate that they are awaiting financial information on the success of that venture before proceeding. We note there are no royalties – but where does the money come from for the franchisor?

Number of franchisee addresses provided by franchisor: 00

⇨ Command Performance International
256 High Street, Slough, Berks SL1 1JU
Phone: 0753 822645

Modern hairstyle salon aimed at 18 to 40 year olds, with beauty department, health centre etc; mostly based in the high street.

Outlets
Number of outlets
Company owned outlets: 02
Franchised: 15
Pilot: 05 started 1983
1988 franchise target: 38
Current reach:

South	05	South west	01	South east	02
Midlands	01	East Anglia	01	North east	03
North west	02	Scotland	00	Wales	00
N Ireland	00	Rep Ireland	00	I of Man/CI	00

Costs
Total: £50,000 minimum
Franchise fee: £5,000
Other charges: Nil
Min cash excluding bank: £15,000 minimum
Min overdraft required: Nil
Normal bank advance: 66% of total investment
Working capital first 2 months: No information given
Associated banks: Nat West
Capital items required: Hairdressing equipment, fixtures and fittings, furniture
Associated leasing co: None

Royalties
Total:
5.0% of turnover
0.0% accounts service
5.0% for advertising fund
10.0% monthly sales
No standing royalty independent of turnover

Bank rating Very helpful
Territory Radius from franchisee's base, which is found 'hard to cover at start'
Strings Strong ties for materials etc

Compleat Cookshop

Training	Continuous daily practical training
	10 days management training per annum
	Cost: Nil – included in franchise fee
	Training value: Adequate
Support	Very good
Operating Manual	Excellent
Profit	Better than expected
Risk	Lot of local competition; watch out for other franchises entering this field. The American links should give strong advantages.
Management only	Reasonable return for owner with management ability

Size and reach
Original company launched: 1976 USA (1983 UK)
Overseas connections: USA – 320 outlets; equally owned with
                             Command Performance USA
UK connections: None
Viable for whole UK?   Yes
Trade bodies   BFA (full member). Founder member British
                             Assn of Professional Hairdressers

Franchisor's formula for success
This company is the only one professionally experienced in the UK to franchise haircare salons.

Inside story from the franchisees
Only one franchisee responded, but the report was glowing. The franchisee had been operating for one year and was very confident of success and indeed stated they were exceeding expectations.

Insider tips
Very hard work for one person. Consider a partnership. You must be able to handle staff.

Moans and groans
None

Number of franchisee addresses provided by franchisor: UK – 15; over 1000 USA

➪ Compleat Cookshop

Enterprise House, Buckingham Road, Aylesbury, Bucks HP19 3QQ
Phone: 0296 431296

Retail outlets of fashion houseware and unusual gift items with inventive package and upmarket image but competitive pricing

Outlets
Number of outlets
Company owned outlets: 06
Franchised: 14
Pilot: 00
1988 franchise target: 30
Current reach:

South	01	South west	01	South east	01
Midlands	02	East Anglia	00	North east	00
North west	00	Scotland	03	Wales	00
N Ireland	00	Rep Ireland	00	I of Man/CI	00

65

Compleat Cookshop

Costs
Total	circa £60,000
Franchise fee:	£7,000
Other charges:	No information supplied
Min cash excluding bank:	£15,000
Min overdraft required:	£6,000
Normal bank advance:	70%
Working capital first 2 months:	£6,000
Associated banks:	Lloyds, Barclays, Nat West, Midland
Capital items required:	None
Associated leasing co:	None

Royalties
	0.0% of turnover
	0.0% accounts service
	0.0% for advertising fund
Total	0.0% monthly sales
	No standing royalty independent of turnover

Bank rating	No problems getting finance
Territory	Each franchise is granted for trading town – eg Guildford
	Franchisee view: No problems
Strings	Strong ties for products
Training	Practical and management training is described as 'not limited'
	Cost: Nil – included in franchise fee
	Training value: Adequate
Support	Good
Operating Manual	Not too good at present, but being re-written
Profit	Good
Risk	Not a high risk but a lot of competition
Management only	Proven franchise with good return on investment

Size and reach
Original company launched:	1982
Overseas connections:	None
UK connections:	None
Viable for whole UK?	Yes
Trade bodies	None

Franchisor's formula for success
This is an excellent franchise for those individuals with an ability in retailing. It offers excellent returns in an exciting and growing industry, encompasing fashion houseware, cookware and fitware items.

Inside story from the franchisees
Good concept with good franchisee/franchisor relationship

Insider tips
Town size and stock levels are main factors

Moans and groans
More training would be useful

Number of franchisee addresses provided by franchisor: 20

⇨ Complete Weed Control Ltd
Langston Priory Mews, Station Road, Kingham, Oxon OX7 6UW
Phone: 060 871 8851

A specialist treatment service for parks, amenity areas, sports grounds, local authorities, industrial sites and public houses. This franchise is advertised through The Franchise Shop, Mertsham, Surrey.

Outlets
Number of outlets
Company owned outlets: 01
Franchised: 12
Pilot: 03 started 1981
1988 franchise target: 16
Current reach:

South	01	South west	01	South east	01
Midlands	02	East Anglia	01	North east	01
North west	01	Scotland	01	Wales	02
N Ireland	00	Rep Ireland	00	I of Man/CI	00

Costs
Total   £12,000
Franchise fee: £6,000
Other charges: £6,000
Min cash excluding bank: £4,000
Min overdraft required: £4,000
Normal bank advance: 66%
Working capital first 2 months: £1,500
Associated banks: Barclays
Capital items required: Vehicle (VW Caddy Pick Up) plus spraying equipment
Associated leasing co: None

Royalties
                                   10.0% of turnover
                                   0.0% accounts service
                                   0.0% for advertising fund
Total   10.0% monthly sales
                                   No standing royalty independent of turnover

Bank rating   No problems from banks with finance
Territory   Based on Yellow Pages areas, which are felt to be too large in most cases
Strings   Strong ties for chemicals etc
Training   3 days practical training
                     5 days management training
                     Cost: Nil – included in franchise fee
                     Training value: 'Not enough training'
Support   Very good
Operating Manual Technically good, more marketing help needed
Profit   Not as good as projected in most cases
Risk   Little competition – highly specialist field
Management only 'Proven franchise with good return on investment'

Size and reach
Original company launched: 1972
Overseas connections: None
UK connections: None
Viable for whole UK?   Yes
Trade bodies   National Assn of Agricultural Contractors

Computa Tune

Franchisor's formula for success
If you like an open air life, managing your own business with your own fully trained staff, you can do so with Complete Weed Control. Special features include superb corporate image and identity, no special premises required, limited overheads, professional credibility. Earnings should be £13,000 to £26,000 per annum.

Inside story from the franchisees
Very good response which was very enthusiastic about the franchisee and franchisor relationship

Insider tips
A technical or scientific background is useful and liking for the outside life.

Moans and groans
Manual needs updating more often as new chemicals are being introduced.

Number of franchisee addresses provided by franchisor: 12

⇨ Computa Tune

Unit 3, Richmond Industrial Estate, Brown Street, Accrington, Lancs
Phone: 0254 391792/385891

Engine tuning and fixed price engine service from fully equipped vans

Outlets
Number of outlets
Company owned outlets: 03
Franchised: 11
Pilot: 01 started 1980
1988 franchise target: 25
Current reach:

South	01	South west	00	South east	00
Midlands	00	East Anglia	00	North east	02
North west	07	Scotland	00	Wales	01
N Ireland	00	Rep Ireland	00	I of Man/CI	00

Costs
Total	£12,990
Franchise fee:	£2,500
Other charges:	No information supplied
Min cash excluding bank:	£4,000
Min overdraft required:	£2,000
Normal bank advance:	£9,000 to £10,000
Working capital first 2 months:	£500
Associated banks:	Nat West
Capital items required:	Van, tuning machine, tools
Associated leasing co:	Lombards

Royalties
	10.0% of turnover
	0.0% accounts service
	0.0% for advertising fund
Total	10.0% monthly sales
	No standing royalty independent of turnover

Bank rating	All responses 'very helpful' save one
Territory	Flexible area – around franchisee's home base
	Franchisee view: 'Just right'
Strings	Some ties but not too many
Training	14 days practical training
	7 days management training
	Cost: £1,500 – included in franchise fee
	Training value: 'Excellent'

ComputerLand

Support	Very good
Operating Manual	Very good on the whole
Profit	As projected
Risk	Lot of similar franchises in this field
Management only	One-man-band operation

Size and reach

Original company launched:	1980
Overseas connections:	None
UK connections:	None
Viable for whole UK?	Yes
Trade bodies	BFA

Franchisor's formula for success
Our business concept has been firmly established and our tuning knowledge and business experience is available to all our franchisees. We operate three vans directly from our head office in Accrington, so we are always in contact with the grass roots of the business.

Inside story from the franchisees
Very good support from franchisor and training is considered excellent.

Insider tips
Takes about six months to build up, so ensure enough capital available.

Moans and groans
Manual needs more information on the paperwork side of the business.

Number of franchisee addresses provided by franchisor: 11

⇨ ComputerLand

518 Elder House, Elder Gate, Milton Keynes MK9 1LR
Phone: 0908 664244

Computer Business Centres

Outlets
Number of outlets

Company owned outlets:	00
Franchised:	17 (3 Scotland, 6 Midlands/North, 5 London 3 South)
Pilot:	No information supplied
1988 franchise target:	No information supplied

Costs

Total	£300,000 to £360,000
Franchise fee:	£20,000 (approx)
Other charges:	£55,000 to £70,000 initial inventory
Min cash excluding bank:	No information supplied
Min overdraft required:	No information supplied
Normal bank advance:	No information supplied
Working capital first 2 months:	£60,000 to £80,000
Associated banks:	None
Capital items required:	Fixtures, furniture etc £100,000
Associated leasing co:	None

Royalties

	3.5% of turnover
	0.0% accounts service
	1.0% for advertising fund
Total	4.5% monthly sales
	No standing royalty independent of turnover

Concorde One Hour Photo Labs

Bank rating	No information supplied
Territory	No information supplied
Strings	Franchise operates a central purchasing policy
Training	No information supplied
	Cost: £50,000 not included in franchise fee
	Training value: No information supplied
Support	No information supplied
Operating Manual	No information supplied
Profit	No information supplied
Risk	Computer centres have been notorious for coming unstuck, but this company has an aura of solidity
Management only	Proven franchise with good return on investment

Size and reach

Original company launched:	1976 America – Europe 1979
Overseas connections:	HQ in California – Europe HQ Luxembourg
UK connections:	None
Viable for whole UK?	Yes
Trade bodies	None

Franchisor's formula for success

ComputerLand is the largest computing franchising network in the world with over 800 centres in the USA and 23 other countries. ComputerLand Europe was founded in 1979 to support operations in 18 countries, and is based in Luxembourg. There are now over 100 stores in Europe.

Good Franchise Guide comment: ComputerLand would not respond to requests for information from *The Good Franchise Guide*. However, information sent to prospective franchisees is comprehensive, clear, and includes a full list of ComputerLand centres in the UK. (We did not contact franchisees, as the list went to a would-be franchisee not in response to our request, which was ignored.) If only others would follow this example of openly revealing franchisee addresses (even when they won't talk directly to us).

Number of franchisee addresses provided by franchisor: 00

⇨ Concorde One Hour Photo Labs

46 Church Street, Enfield, Middx EN2 6AZ
Phone: 01-367 4762

One hour photo developing

Outlets
Number of outlets

Company owned outlets:	02
Franchised:	01
Pilot:	No information supplied
1988 franchise target:	No information supplied

Costs

Total	£20,000
Franchise fee:	£5,000
Other charges:	No information supplied
Min cash excluding bank:	No information supplied
Min overdraft required:	No information supplied
Normal bank advance:	75%
Working capital first 2 months:	No information supplied
Associated banks:	None
Capital items required:	No information supplied
Associated leasing co:	None

Contemporary Aluminium Ltd

Royalties	5.0% of turnover
	0.0% accounts service
	0.0% for advertising fund
Total	5.0% monthly sales
	No standing royalty independent of turnover
Bank rating	No information supplied
Territory	No information supplied
Strings	No information supplied
Training	No information supplied
Support	No information supplied
Operating Manual	No information supplied
Profit	No information supplied
Risk	Competition growing almost daily both from franchises and from in-store operations
Management only	Little salary to spare for a manager
Size and reach	
Original company launched:	No information supplied
Overseas connections:	None
UK connections:	None
Viable for whole UK?	Yes
Trade bodies	None

Franchisor's formula for success
According to *Taking up a Franchise* the company 'emphasises business financing and management, based on an intimate knowledge of mini-lab operations over seven years' direct involvement.'

Good Franchise Guide comment: No replies to our requests for information. If you are tempted remember you will be up against a wide range of other franchises just starting up in the same line.

Number of franchisee addresses provided by franchisor: 00

⇨ Conder Products

Abbotts Barton House, Worthy Road, Winchester, Hants SO23 7SH
Phone: 0962 63577

Conder Products (also known as Conder Clentech) inform us that the company is not offering any franchises at present. The company has declined to give any further information.

⇨ Contemporary Aluminium Ltd

Calmark House, Brunel Road, Manor Trading Estate, Thundersley, Essex SS7 4PS

This franchise has been listed in some reference books and magazines. Mail sent to this address is accepted, but we have been unable to obtain information either in response to general requests from would-be franchisees or specifically for this publication. In the light of this experience we suggest a certain amount of caution may be in order if the franchise does eventually reappear.

Cookie Coach Company (UK) Ltd

⇨ Cookie Coach Company (UK) Ltd
Previous address: 11 Banbury Avenue, Slough, Berks

This franchise has been wound up at the request of the Department of Trade and Industry. Peat Marwick have been appointed Receiver. Some 46 franchisees were in operation at the time of the closure, and the Receiver's job is to sell the business, with the franchisee connection as a going concern.

The collapse of this company, which was on the BFA Register, is a timely warning to us all. According to *Taking up a Franchise* the Receiver is likely to find a deficiency of over £500,000.

⇨ Country Properties
6 Brand Street, Hitchin, Herts
Phone: 0462 54040

Estate agency specialising in properties in areas outside large towns

Outlets
Number of outlets
Company owned outlets: 03
Franchised: 10
Pilot: 02 started 1983
1988 franchise target: 18
Current reach:

South	00	South west	00	South east	17
Midlands	00	East Anglia	01	North east	00
North west	00	Scotland	00	Wales	00
N Ireland	00	Rep Ireland	00	I of Man/CI	00

Reach total is shown for franchises due to be opened by end 1988

Costs
Total	£25,000
Franchise fee:	£3,000
Other charges:	Tuition – see below
Min cash excluding bank:	About 20%
Min overdraft required:	£20,000
Normal bank advance:	About 70%
Working capital first 2 months:	£8,000
Associated banks:	'All major banks'
Capital items required:	Car
Associated leasing co:	None

Royalties
	7.5% of turnover
	0.0% accounts service
	0.5% for advertising fund
Total	8.0% monthly sales
	No standing royalty independent of turnover

Bank rating   Banks not too helpful in some cases
Territory   Population
   Franchisees report: Just right
Strings   Some ties but a lot of freedom
Training   200 hours practical training (part in situ)
   30 days management training
   NB Training is for inexperienced franchisees only
   Cost: £5,000 – not included in franchise fee
   Training value: Good

Countrywide Business Transfer Consultants

Support	Good
Operating Manual	Very good
Profit	On target
Risk	Estate agency is obviously a highly competitive field, although this franchise claims a unique niche in specialising in out-of-town properties.
Management only	'Possible management-only potential, but not recommended'

Size and reach

Original company launched:	1982
Overseas connections:	None
UK connections:	None
Viable for whole UK?	Yes – but in groupings
Trade bodies	BFA, National Assn of Estate Agents

Franchisor's formula for success
A very successful, professional estate agency franchise offering an outstanding opportunity for both inexperienced and experienced alike to enter a highly competitive but lucrative world. Full support and encouragement for individuality within the proven framework.

Inside story from the franchisees
Felt to be a good franchise with good backup available from franchisor. 'I have just applied for a second area, so it can't be that bad.'

Insider tips
Estate agency is a way of life rather than just a job. You must have the right attitude and aptitude to be an estate agent.

Moans and groans
None

Number of franchisee addresses provided by franchisor: 10

⇨ Countrywide Business Transfer Consultants

Prospect House, 10 New Street, Braintree, Essex CM7 7ER
Phone: 0376 28080

Business transfer consultants operating a system of regional offices linked to a head office which enables potential purchasers of businesses to obtain the benefits of access to all areas of the UK

Outlets
Number of outlets

Company owned outlets:	01
Franchised:	12
Pilot:	No information supplied
1988 franchise target:	20

Current reach:

South	01	South west	02	South east	03
Midlands	02	East Anglia	02	North east	00
North west	01	Scotland	00	Wales	01
N Ireland	00	Rep Ireland	00	I of Man/CI	00

Costs

Total	£9,750
Franchise fee:	£9,750
Other charges:	Nil
Min cash excluding bank:	£9,750
Min overdraft required:	No information supplied
Normal bank advance:	No information supplied
Working capital first 2 months:	No figure given for 2 months – £15,000 for 6 months
Associated banks:	None
Capital items required:	None
Associated leasing co:	None

Countrywide Garden Maintenance Services

Royalties
                   10.0% of turnover
                   0.0% accounts service
                   0.0% for advertising fund
Total   10.0% monthly sales
                   No standing royalty independent of turnover

Bank rating   No information supplied
Territory   Counties subject to business level activity within area
Strings   No information supplied
Training   One week initial practical training at head office
                   One week on site management training with follow up.
                   The franchisor states 'We do not operate a policy of a fixed training period due to the fact that some franchisees need more training in some aspects of the work than others. It is therefore our policy to identify the franchisees' weak points and concentrate on these at our regular visits to their office.'
                   Cost: Nil – included in franchise fee
                   Training value: No information supplied
Support   No information supplied
Operating Manual No information supplied
Profit   'The earning capacity of each Regional Office will vary according to the type of area and the commitment of the individual concerned. However it is anticipated that the average turnover would project figures as follows: 1st year full trading . . . £40k'
Risk   Growing number of rivals in this field
Management only Reasonable return for owner with management ability

Size and reach
Original company launched: 1983
Overseas connections: None
UK connections: None
Viable for whole UK?   Yes
Trade bodies   None

Franchisor's formula for success
The business transfer market is sometimes complex, geographically diverse but most rewarding both in financial and job satisfaction. Countrywide operate a system of Regional Offices closely linked via the main head office thus enabling potential purchasers to obtain the benefits of access to all areas of the UK.

Good Franchise Guide comment: An increasingly competitive field – but there is an infinite number of estate agents, and they all seem to be able to survive, and make a fair profit.

Number of franchisee addresses provided by franchisor: 00

⇨ Countrywide Garden Maintenance Services
164-200 Stockport Road, Cheadle, Cheshire SK8 2DP
Phone: 061-428 4444

Supplies private, industrial and public sectors a garden maintenance service on a fixed price contract every week, 52 weeks a year, plus interior plant rental and maintenance for offices and hotels

Outlets
Number of outlets
Company owned outlets: 01
Franchised: 02
Pilot: 01 started 1983
1988 franchise target: 15

Countrywide Garden Maintenance Services

Current reach:
South	01	South west	01	South east	00
Midlands	00	East Anglia	00	North east	00
North west	01	Scotland	00	Wales	00
N Ireland	00	Rep Ireland	00	I of Man/CI	00

Costs
Total	£9,750
Franchise fee:	£3,000
Other charges:	£6,750
Min cash excluding bank:	£9,750
Min overdraft required:	£4,000
Normal bank advance:	70%
Working capital first 2 months:	£2,000 to £4,000
Associated banks:	None
Capital items required:	None
Associated leasing co:	None

Royalties

	8.0% of turnover
	0.0% accounts service
	2.0% for advertising fund
Total	10.0% monthly sales
	No standing royalty independent of turnover

Bank rating	No information supplied
Territory	Post codes and population
Strings	Mowers, tools and other equipment all supplied by the franchisor
Training	2 weeks plus ongoing practical training
	3 days plus ongoing management training
	Cost: £800 – not included in franchise fee
	Training value: No information supplied
Support	No information supplied
Operating Manual	No information supplied
Profit	Year 1 net profit quoted as £12,152
Risk	This franchise is deliberately taking on the local competition – the risk is that 'the locals' may not always be as ramshackle as the franchisor suggests in his comments.
Management only	Could be run by manager but with limited profit

Size and reach
Original company launched:	1983
Overseas connections:	None
UK connections:	None
Viable for whole UK?	Yes
Trade bodies	None

Franchisor's formula for success
The concept of the franchise is to provide to both the private and industrial sectors a first class garden maintenance service on a regular weekly basis, all the year round, on a fixed yearly contract. This type of service is normally carried out by a part or full-time employee usually performing a poor, irregular and unreliable service requiring constant supervision. We approach each contract with a very professional, smart, well trained and supervised team, properly equipped, who arrive on-site and quickly and effectively carry out a planned programme of work to maintain the garden and grounds.

Good Franchise Guide comment: One of those ideas that could be just what everyone needs. One to watch for the future.

Number of franchisee addresses provided by franchisor: 00

Cover Rite

⇨ Cover Rite
The Orient Trading Estate, Martock, Somerset
Phone: 0935 824866

Supply of seamless wall and floor systems

Outlets
Number of outlets   No information supplied

Costs
Total   £10,000
No other information on costs supplied

Royalties   No information supplied
Bank rating   No information supplied
Territory   No information supplied
Strings   No information supplied
Training   5 days practical and management training
                             Cost: Nil – included in franchise fee
                             Training value: No information supplied
Support   No information supplied
Operating Manual   No information supplied
Profit   Net profit in first year quoted as £12,504
Risk   Difficult to say on limited information supplied
Management only   No information supplied

Franchisor's formula for success
Coverite seamless wall and floor systems have been specifically designed to provide a durable, easy to clean finish with excellent acid and chemical resistance.

Good Franchise Guide comment: Information supplied is limited. Even our attempt to find out more via a telephone call was thwarted: they had an answering machine on. In our estimation prospective franchisees should not fill in the application form provided with the colour brochure etc without getting a lot more information first.

Number of franchisee addresses provided by franchisor: 00

⇨ Coversure Insurance Services
4 Longstaff Way, Hartford, Huntingdon, Cambs PE18 7XT
Phone: 0480 413858

Motor, commercial and life assurance franchise only available to those with at least three years' insurance experience.

Outlets
Number of outlets
Company owned outlets: 02
Franchised: 02
Pilot: 01 started 1986
1988 franchise target: 05 to 08
Current reach:

South	00	South west	00	South east	00
Midlands	00	East Anglia	04	North east	00
North west	00	Scotland	00	Wales	00
N Ireland	00	Rep Ireland	00	I of Man/CI	00

Coversure Insurance Services

Costs
Total   £5,000
Franchise fee: £5,000
Other charges: Nil
Min cash excluding bank: £5,000
Min overdraft required: No information supplied
Normal bank advance: No information supplied
Working capital first 2 months: £2,000
Associated banks: Midland
Capital items required: Computer – included in the £5,000
Associated leasing co: Lombard North Central

Royalties
                                     0.0% of turnover
                                     0.0% accounts service
                                     0.0% for advertising fund
Total   0.0% monthly sales

                                     No standing royalty independent of turnover

Bank rating   No information supplied
Territory   Variable by population
Strings   No information supplied

Training   7 days general and 9 days on site practical and management training
                                     Cost: Nil – included in franchise fee
                                     Training value: No information supplied

Support   No information supplied
Operating Manual   No information supplied
Profit   No information supplied
Risk   Insurance consultants normally need to be well-briefed and good salesmen. If you are not the risk will be high.

Management only   Reasonable return for owner with management ability

Size and reach
Original company launched: 1986
Overseas connections: None
UK connections: Insurance Management Services
Viable for whole UK?   Britain only – not N Ireland
Trade bodies   None

Franchisor's formula for success
No information supplied

Good Franchise Guide comment: The franchisor informed us that there were no royalties. However the authoritative *Taking up a Franchise* quoted royalties in the range of 1.5 to 2 per cent. We have twice asked for a brochure, but without success, and our conclusion for the moment is that the franchisor takes a commission on sales.

Number of franchisee addresses provided by franchisor: 00

Cranford Conservatories

⇨ Cranford Conservatories

Unit 8 Sankey Bridges Industrial Estate, Liverpool Road, Warrington, Cheshire

This franchise has been listed in some reference books and magazines. Mail sent to this address is accepted, but we have been unable to obtain information either in response to general requests from would-be franchisees or specifically for this publication. In the light of this experience we suggest a certain amount of caution may be in order if the franchise does eventually reappear.

⇨ Crimecure/30 Ltd

Darley House, Cow Lane, Garston, Watford, Herts WD2 6PH
Phone: 0923 223842; 663322; 241514

Installation of alarms, locks and security systems to all types of property

Outlets
Number of outlets
Company owned outlets: 00
Franchised: 25
Pilot: 00
1988 franchise target: 100
Current reach:
England	22	Scotland	01	Wales	02
N Ireland	00	Rep Ireland	00	I of Man/CI	00

Costs
Total £7,500
Franchise fee: £7,500
Other charges: Nil
Min cash excluding bank: According to applicant
Min overdraft required: £3,000
Normal bank advance: 'Variable'
Working capital first 2 months: £3,000
Associated banks: All banks
Capital items required: Vehicle
Associated leasing co: None

Royalties

Total
15.0% of turnover
0.0% accounts service
0.0% for advertising fund
15.0% monthly sales
No standing royalty independent of turnover

Bank rating No information supplied
Territory 80,000 households per territory
Strings No information supplied

Training
8 days practical training
2 days management training
Cost: Nil – included in franchise fee
Training value: No information supplied

Support No information supplied
Operating Manual No information supplied
Profit No information supplied
Risk Lot of competition, but this is a well known operator
Management only Could be run by manager but with limited profit

Crown Eyeglass plc

Size and reach
Original company launched: 1959 (Dampcure-Woodcure Group)
Overseas connections: None
UK connections: Dampcure-Woodcure/30 Ltd
Viable for whole UK? Yes
Trade bodies: IAAI

Franchisor's formula for success
Part of the Dampure-Woodcure/30 group which has been established since 1959. We issue maintenance contracts for all work carried out. Where Dampcure-Woodcure/30 is also established in the same area, this is of great benefit for the Crimecure/30 branch in motivation, referrals etc. We now have one Crimecure/30 and Dampcure/30 franchisee sharing the same office, which we believe to be the first of its kind in the country.

Insider tips

This is part of the Cure/30 Group of Companies Ltd comprising Dampcure/30, Woodcure/30 and Crimecure/30. A listing under Cure/30 does appear in some reference books, although there is no franchise as such under that general title.

Good Franchise Guide comment: One of the few franchises to follow up enquiries from would-be franchisees with a polite letter asking if there was still an interest. No phone calls, no salesmen at the door – all very civilised.

Number of franchisee addresses provided by franchisor: 00

⇨ Crown Electrical Appliances
6 Railway Approach, East Grinstead, Sussex
Phone: 0342 25273

This franchise dealing in the repair of domestic electrical appliances has been listed in some reference books and magazines. Mail sent to this address is accepted, but we have been unable to obtain information either in response to general requests from would-be franchisees or specifically for this publication.

⇨ Crown Eyeglass plc
Stancliffe Street, Blackburn BB2 2QR
Phone: 0254 51535

Optical centres

Outlets
Number of outlets
Company owned outlets: 03
Franchised: 75
Pilot: No information supplied
1988 franchise target: No information supplied

Costs
Total: See comment below
Franchise fee: £9,000
Other charges: None
Royalties
No information supplied
Bank rating No information supplied
Territory No information supplied
Strings Tied to Crown for supply of products
Training Practical and management training provided
Cost: Nil – included in franchise fee
Training value: No information supplied

Culligans Water Softeners

Support No information supplied
Operating Manual No information supplied
Profit 'Some of our franchisees are making in excess of £700 per week before expenses'.
Risk Franchise takes opportunity from recent law change which means optician has to hand prescription to patient, giving patient freedom to choose glasses anywhere. But will people really go elsewhere? No one knows; that's the risk.
Management only No information supplied

Franchisor's formula for success
Crown Eyeglass franchisees provide the public with top quality spectacles on prescription for as little as £9.95 a pair.
A Crown Franchise includes promotion, training, a starter pack, and no stock headaches. In addition to replacing stock with each order every month we send a number of brand new designs, you then send back to us the same number of frames which you consider are your slowest sellers.

Good Franchise Guide comment: The brochure sent to prospective franchisees states: 'How much does it cost me? – The total cost of the franchise package is shown and explained in detail in the enclosed Crown Fact Sheet. There are no hidden extras.' That fact sheet says 'A Crown Franchise to enable you to open a Crown Optical Centre costs just £9,000 plus VAT'. Everything else is paid for by the franchisor. So doubtful were we that we phoned Crown for confirmation, which was forthcoming at once – everything but everything is included in the franchise fee.

Number of franchisee addresses provided by franchisor: 00

➪ Culligans Water Softeners
Blenheim Road, High Wycombe, Bucks HP12 3RS
Phone: 0494 36484

Water treatment company

No information on royalties, profits etc

Size and reach
Overseas connections: A division of Culligan International, USA 1000 franchises in N America. Franchises in 90 other countries as well.

Franchisor's formula for success
As part of the Culligan dealer/company team our dealers have the most accepted and best-known brand name in the industry behind them; are part of the most productive and reputable dealer organisation in the water conditioning business; are backed by the most diversified manufacturing and marketing organisation in the industry.

Good Franchise Guide comment: Would-be franchisees are sent a massive range of information on the product and parent company, which is very impressive, but precious little on the subject of the franchise, and its costs. From what we can see it looks to be more like a distributorship.

Number of franchisee addresses provided by franchisor: 00

➪ Dampco (UK) Ltd
21 Lythalls Lane, Coventry, CV6 6FN
Phone: 0203 687683

Treatment of rising damp, woodworm and dry rot

Outlets
Number of outlets
Company owned outlets: 03
Franchised: 04
Pilot: 00
1988 franchise target: 20
Current reach:

South	01	South west	00	South east	00
Midlands	06	East Anglia	00	North east	00
North west	00	Scotland	00	Wales	00
N Ireland	00	Rep Ireland	00	I of Man/CI	00

Costs
Total £10,500
Franchise fee: £10,500
Other charges: Nil
Min cash excluding bank: No information supplied
Min overdraft required: No information supplied
Normal bank advance: £7,000
Working capital first 2 months: £2,000
Associated banks: Nat West
Capital items required: All equipment supplied franchisor pays 20% deposit on vehicle
Associated leasing co: None

Royalties
　10.0% of turnover
　0.0% accounts service
　0.0% for advertising fund
Total 10.0% monthly sales
　No standing royalty independent of turnover

Bank rating Banks helpful
Territory Half a Yellow Pages area
Strings Strong ties but part of the operation not controlled
Training 2 to 3 weeks practical training
1 week management training
Cost: Nil – included in franchise fee
Training value: Adequate

Support Good
Operating Manual Good
Profit Worse than expected but surviving
Risk Every week there seems to be a new company starting up in this field

Management only 'Franchise would start as a one man operation and build up to about 8 men'

Size and reach
Original company launched: 1958 (first franchise 1987)
Overseas connections: None
UK connections: None
Viable for whole UK? Yes
Trade bodies BCDA, BWPA

Dampcure/30 Ltd

Franchisor's formula for success
The strength of the franchise lies in the fact that we are a family business run by working directors and shareholders. The franchisee is fully equipped by us, right down to the screws, scrap pads, fluids etc. Indeed we try hard to think of things they may need so that we can suppy them all included in the franchise fee.

Inside story from the franchisees
'I would encourage other franchisees to take up a franchise as long as they knew something about the work involved.'

Insider tips
'I have seen other people take up the sort of work that we do and have no idea about building work and therefore have to contract most of their out to others.' Don't bother unless you really can cope.

Moans and groans
None, save lower than expected profits.

Number of franchisee addresses provided by franchisor: 3

⇨ **Dampcure/30 Ltd**
(also known as Dampcure-Woodcure)
Darley House, Cow Lane, Garston, Watford, Herts WD2 6PH
Phone: 0923 223842; 663322; 241514

Guaranteed treatment of rising damp and timber (for woodworm and dry rot). Work comes from building societies, local authorities, architects, surveyors and specifiers dealing with the maintenance of property.

Outlets
Number of outlets
Company owned outlets: 01
Franchised: 40
Pilot: 00 Company started 1959
1988 franchise target: 100
Current reach:

South	08	South west	02	South east	14
Midlands	04	East Anglia	02	North east	03
North west	05	Scotland	02	Wales	02
N Ireland	00	Rep Ireland	00	I of Man/CI	00

Costs
Total £9,000
Franchise fee: £9,000
Other charges: Nil
Min cash excluding bank: According to applicant
Min overdraft required: £3,000
Normal bank advance: Variable
Working capital first 2 months: £3,000
Associated banks: All banks
Capital items required: Vehicle
Associated leasing co: None

Royalties
              15.0% of turnover
              0.0% accounts service
              0.0% for advertising fund
Total   15.0% monthly sales

No standing royalty independent of turnover

Bank rating No information supplied, but we doubt if there would be much of a problem
Territory 80,000 households per territory
Strings No information supplied

82

Damptechnik UK

Training	2 weeks practical training 2 weeks management training Cost: Nil – included in franchise fee Training value: No information supplied
Support	No information supplied
Operating Manual	No information supplied
Profit	No information supplied
Risk	A lot of competition about, but this is an established company
Management only	Reasonable return for owner with management ability
Size and reach	
Original company launched:	1959 (Dampcure-Woodcure Group)
Overseas connections:	None
UK connections:	Crimecure/30 Ltd
Viable for whole UK?	Yes
Trade bodies	British Chemical Damp Course Assn; British Wood Preserving Assn

Franchisor's formula for success
Part of the Dampcure-Woodcure/30 group which has been established since 1959. We issue maintenance contracts for all work carried out. Where a Crimecure/30 is also established in the same area, this is of great benefit for the Dampcure-Woodcure/30 branch in motivation, referrals etc. We now have one Crimecure/30 and Dampcure/30 franchisee sharing the same office, which we believe to be the first of its kind in the country.

Insider tips
This is part of the Cure/30 Group of Companies Ltd comprising Dampcure/30, Woodcure/30 and Crimecure/30. A listing under Cure/30 does appear in some reference books, although there is no franchise as such under that general title.

Good Franchise Guide comment: 15% seems rather high to us for a royalty; we would like to know what the franchisees think. But it certainly isn't the highest figure asked, and it may be justified.

Number of franchisee addresses provided by franchisor: 00

⇨ Damptechnik UK

Damptechnik House, George Street, Mandale Triangle, Thornaby, Cleveland TS17 6DE
Phone: 0642 606484
Prospective franchisees may use the free Link Line 0800 591 741

Damp proofing, replastering, tanking, timber treatments and cavity Tie-Bar replacement services

Outlets
Number of outlets	No information supplied

Costs
Total	£11,000
Franchise fee:	£4,000
Other charges:	Training and equipment – see below
Min cash excluding bank:	No information supplied
Min overdraft required:	No information supplied
Normal bank advance:	No information supplied
Working capital first 2 months:	No information supplied
Associated banks:	None
Capital items required:	Equipment, deposit on vehicle etc, £4,000
Associated leasing co:	None

Dash Ltd

Royalties

	7.5% of turnover
	5.0% of contract value guarantee fee
	0.0% for advertising fund
Total	12.5% monthly sales
	No standing royalty independent of turnover
Bank rating	No information supplied
Territory	No information supplied
Strings	No information supplied
Training	2 weeks practical and management training for two people
	Cost: £3,500 – not included in franchise fee
	Training value: No information supplied
Support	No information supplied
Operating Manual	No information supplied
Profit	Net profit in first year quoted as £16,210
Risk	Clearly thousands of houses need this treatment, and there is an ever-growing desire to avoid cowboys and work with established companies.
Management only	Could be run by manager but with limited profit

Size and reach

Original company launched:	1939
Overseas connections:	None
UK connections:	Fred Kidd & Sons (Engineers) Ltd
Viable for whole UK?	Yes
Trade bodies	None

Franchisor's formula for success
To succeed you must be adequately capitalised, hard working, able to deal with the public and keen to work in partnership with the franchisor, dedicated to developing the business in your area and prepared to accept that your interests must be long term. But in the event of your wishing to sell the franchise you may do so.

Good Franchise Guide comment: An ever-growing area of franchising, and there does seem to be an endless demand, but we do think franchisees deserve more information than this.

Number of franchisee addresses provided by franchisor: 00

⇨ Dash Ltd

PO Box, Rowdell Road, Northolt, Middx UB5 6BS
Phone: 01-845 7777

Dash are currently writing to all prospective franchisees stating that as a result of the figures for the first full year of franchising the company has decided (for the time at least) to stop further franchise openings. Future stand-alone shops are being confined to company-owned sites only.

⇨ Data Maid Ltd

47 First Avenue, Deeside Industrial Park, Clwyd CH5 2NU
Phone: 0244 823177

Computerised analysis system that specialises in tachograph analysis and returns to customers a low-cost detailed report of drivers' activities highlighting any infringements that have occurred

Outlets
Number of outlets
Company owned outlets: 02
Franchised: 45
Pilot: 01 started 1982
1988 franchise target: 200

Current reach: The franchisor has only supplied information on areas covered rather than the number of franchisees in each area.

South	00	South west	00	South east	00
Midlands	Yes	East Anglia	Yes	North east	Yes
North west	Yes	Scotland	00	Wales	00
N Ireland	00	Rep Ireland	00	I of Man/CI	00

Costs
Total   £10,450
Franchise fee: £10,450
Other charges: Nil
Min cash excluding bank: Nil
Min overdraft required: Nil
Normal bank advance: Nil
Working capital first 2 months: £150
Associated banks: None
Capital items required: None
Associated leasing co: None

Royalties
Total
0.0% of turnover
0.0% accounts service
0.0% for advertising fund
0.0% monthly sales

£1,250 annual licence renewal independent of turnover payable quarterly in advance
After two weeks a charge of £15 per week will be made to cover overheads for checking work, plus 25p per update made to ensure work returned is correct. Charges cease when works reaches an acceptable level.

Bank rating   No information supplied
Territory   Allocation of drivers' charts for analysis. Drivers' company usually local to franchisee.
Strings   Tied to one operator
Training   5 days practical training
                     No management training
                     Cost: £150 – included in franchise fee for one person
                     Training value: No information supplied
Support   No information supplied
Operating Manual No information supplied
Profit   'Average monthly profit £891'
Risk   No information supplied
Management only Depends on the number of drivers used

The Cream of Franchise Opportunities...

Join us and run your own business supplying the retail and catering trade with our extensive and diverse range of speciality food and dairy products.

The demand is there... and we want you there

WE OFFER
NATIONAL GROWTH :: PROFESSIONAL MARKETING
NATIONAL PRESTEL ADVERTISING :: ATTRACTIVE PRODUCT RANGE :: TRIED AND TESTED FORMAT
:: FULL COMPANY BACKUP

OUR SUCCESS IS YOUR SUCCESS AND YOUR SUCCESS IS OURS...

Who could ask for a better business marriage?
CALL US – WE OUGHT TO TALK

DAYTELLO FOODS LTD

Unit 4, Nuffield Close
Nuffield Road Industrial Estate
Cambridge CB4 1SS
Telephone: (0223) 315215

Dayvilles

Size and reach
Original company launched: 1986 (but absorbing concept and practical structure dating from 1981)
Overseas connections: None
UK connections: None except that it shares the same directors and management expertise as Photomaid Ltd
Viable for whole UK? Yes
Trade bodies: Applications pending

Franchisor's formula for success
In each lorry on the road throughout most of the EEC there is a tachograph recorder. The driver of the lorry must use a tachograph chart and this chart must be kept for one year so that the Department of Transport are able to inspect the records to check if any infringements have occurred. More and more transport operators are finding it an increasing burden to keep an accurate check on the drivers activities; the Data Maid system relieves the industry from this task by specialising in tachograph analysis.

Good Franchise Guide comment: In one sense this looks rather like an outworker scheme rather than a franchise, although that is not to say it is not a good way of making money. We are concerned that the franchisor's target of 200 franchises by the end of 1988 (ie 3 per week) may stretch the resources of the company given the need to check early work. The implication is that once the system is set up you really are on your own. The three directors and shareholders of Data Maid Ltd are the same three directors of the management buyout in 1986 of the Kis UK subsidiary.

Number of franchisee addresses provided by franchisor: 00

⇨ Dayvilles
78/92 Stamford Road, London N15 4PQ
Phone: 01-801 7331

Original American ice cream parlours

Costs
Total: £15,000
Franchise fee: No information supplied
Other charges: No information supplied
Min cash excluding bank: No information supplied
Min overdraft required: No information supplied
Normal bank advance: No information supplied
Working capital first 2 months: £2,650
Associated banks: None
Capital items required: Equipment – £5,000; shopfitting up to £10,000
Associated leasing co: None

Royalties
No information supplied
Bank rating No information supplied
Territory No information supplied
Strings Total tie to the franchisor's products
Training There is training on the day of opening
Support No information supplied
Operating Manual No information supplied
Profit 'Profit on return 55.8%'
Risk You are up against the established UK brands such as Lyons Maid
Management only Not likely to be much money available for a manager

Decorative Fine Arts Ltd

Size and reach
Original company launched: No information supplied
Overseas connections: American based company
UK connections: None
Viable for whole UK?   Yes
Trade bodies   None

Franchisor's formula for success
Dayvilles ice cream differs from the majority of other brands because we use fresh whole milk, fresh double cream and natural ingredients. Flavours are regularly changed, the variety of innovation offered by Dayvilles is unrivalled by any other manufacturer.

Good Franchise Guide comment: Page after page of mouth watering recipes for ice creams of every description, but hardly a word about costs. In effect you are paying for the right to sell one company's products.

Number of franchisee addresses provided by franchisor: 00

➪ Decorative Fine Arts Ltd

2 – 12 St Albans Road, Dartford, Kent DA1 1TF

This franchise has been listed in some reference books and magazines. Mail sent to this address is accepted, but we have been unable to obtain information either in response to general requests from would-be franchisees or specifically for this publication. In the light of this experience we suggest a certain amount of caution may be in order if the franchise does eventually reappear.

➪ Deep Pan Pizza Company

289 Oxford Street, London W1R 1LB
Phone: 01-491 3038

This franchise has been listed in some reference books and magazines.
The company has informed us that this is an error – it does not franchise any of its outlets.

➪ Descamps Ltd

197 Sloane Street, London SW1X 9QX

This franchise has been listed in some reference books and magazines.
The company is a supplier of bedspreads, duvet covers etc, and is not a franchise under any definition of the word.

➪ Dial a Char Ltd

77 London Road, East Grinstead, Sussex RH19 1EQ
Phone: 0342 28391

Domestic services, party help etc

Outlets
Number of outlets
Company owned outlets: 03
Franchised: About 15
Pilot: No information supplied
1988 franchise target: No information supplied

Dial a Char Ltd

Costs
Total	£12,500
Franchise fee:	£7,500
Other charges:	No information supplied
Min cash excluding bank:	£5,000
Min overdraft required:	No information supplied
Normal bank advance:	60%
Working capital first 2 months:	£5,000
Associated banks:	Barclays
Capital items required:	None
Associated leasing co:	None

Royalties
	5.0% of turnover
	0.0% accounts service
	3.0% for advertising fund
Total	8.0% monthly sales
	No standing royalty independent of turnover

Bank rating — No information supplied
Territory — No information supplied
Strings — Only Dial a Char products may be used – you are totally tied

Training — 4 weeks practical and management training
Cost: Nil – included in franchise fee
Training value: No information supplied

Support — Help is promised with staff selection, premises office procedure, marketing

Operating Manual — No information supplied

Profit — Little salary to spare for a manager in our estimation, but no information supplied by franchisor

Risk — Other firms are moving into this field fast

Management only — Could be run by manager but with limited profit

Size and reach
Original company launched:	No information supplied
Overseas connections:	None
UK connections:	None
Viable for whole UK?	Yes
Trade bodies	FTA

Franchisor's formula for success
Current services include cleaning, ironing, convalescent help, interior decorating, lawn mowing, heavy gardening, car valeting, shopping, home hairdressing, babysitting, party help, catering, window cleaning, pet care, caretaking of homes, granny sitting, and yacht cleaning.

Good Franchise Guide comment: Everyone tells us that the problem is with allocating and keeping staff. We would have welcomed the opportunity to talk with franchisees and ascertain their views.

Number of franchisee addresses provided by franchisor: 00

Dinol-Protectol Ltd,

⇨ Dinol-Protectol Ltd,
Conduit Place, 100 Ock Street, Abingdon, Oxon OX14 5DH
Phone: 0833 38090

Dinol-Protectol is listed in some publications as operating from Durham, although our would-be franchisee received his reply on headed paper showing the Abingdon address with the head office quoted as Montalbo Road, Barnard Castle, Co Durham. The Abingdon address and phone number are the same as for Tuff-Kote Dinol (qv), whose emblem appears on the Dinol-Protectol headed paper (although the two companies are often listed as separate entities).

Dinol-Protectol state that they do not operate 'on a formal franchise basis'. They are only interested in dealing with existing garages or bodyshops, and will only give details of their operation to individuals who have such an establishment in an area in which they do not already have an agent. We have been unable to discover any further information.

⇨ Direct Salon Services Ltd
Newport Way, Cannon Park, Middlesbrough, Cleveland TS1 5JW
Phone: 0642 217978

Suppliers of hair and beauty products to hairdressers and beauty salons via company and franchised van sales, and a cash and carry warehouse

Outlets
Number of outlets — No information supplied

Costs
Total	£20,000
Franchise fee:	£4,500
Other charges:	£6,000 stock included in £20,000
Min cash excluding bank:	£4,025
Min overdraft required:	Nil – cash business
Normal bank advance:	£12,075
Working capital first 2 months:	No information supplied
Associated banks:	Lloyds
Capital items required:	Included in £20,000: Ford Transit van
Associated leasing co:	None

Royalties
No royalties – franchisees get a commission on sales

Bank rating — No information supplied
Territory — No information supplied
Strings — Tied to the company's products

Training
2 weeks practical and management training
Cost: Nil – included in franchise fee
Training value: No information supplied

Support — No information supplied
Operating Manual — No information supplied
Profit — Net profit for first year quoted as £7,396
Risk — To work a van sales system you need to be a good salesmen. If you are not your risk factor is high
Management only — One-man-band operation

Size and reach
Original company launched:	1973
Overseas connections:	None
UK connections:	None
Viable for whole UK?	Yes
Trade bodies	None

Don Millers Hot Bread Kitchens Ltd

Franchisor's formula for success
Our experience in van sales is spread over 15 years and we have established a proven business package. Audited company single van sales show quarterly totals ranging from £16,910 and £26,964. The franchise fee includes £6,000 worth of stock.

Good Franchise Guide comment: Van sales operations are only as good as the franchisees – try to talk to some before getting committed to the hefty launch payments.

Number of franchisee addresses provided by franchisor: 00

⇨ Dirtsearchers
79 Lower Eastern Green Lane, Coventry CV5 7DT

This carpet and upholstery cleaning franchise has declined to supply us with information, and is not replying to letters from would-be franchisees. Our latest information is that the franchise still exists but is not seeking franchisees at present.

⇨ DISC Ltd
Chemical Road, West Wilts Trading Estate, Westbury, Wilts BA13 4JN

This franchise in industrial solvents and chemicals is no longer on offer, as, according to a spokesman for the company, 'two previous station operators defrauded the company'.

⇨ Diversey Ltd
Weston Favell Centre, Northampton NN3 4PD
Phone: 0604 405311

This franchise offers the supply of materials to garages. In their own literature they describe their regional representatives as holding a 'distributorship' rather than a franchise. The company has refrained from supplying the *Good Franchise Guide* with information. Potential franchisees have received a letter back stating that there are no more distributorships available 'in your area', which appears to preclude the possibility of anyone moving.

⇨ Don Millers Hot Bread Kitchens Ltd
166 Bute Street Mall, Arndale Centre, Luton LU1 2TL
Phone: 0582 422781

Retail chain of high street hot bread kitchens

Outlets
Number of outlets   No information supplied

Costs
Total   £34,500 to £65,000
Franchise fee: £10,000
Other charges: £3,000 to £6,000 professional fees
Min cash excluding bank: No information supplied
Min overdraft required: No information supplied
Normal bank advance: No information supplied
Working capital first 2 months: £4,000 (described as startup cost)
Associated banks: Nat West, Barclays, Royal Bank of Scotland
Capital items required: Major plant £17,500 to £45,000
                                Shopfitting £18,000 to £70,000
Associated leasing co: None

91

Doran Products

Royalties

	8.0% of turnover
	0.0% accounts service
	0.0% for advertising fund
Total	8.0% monthly sales
	No standing royalty independent of turnover

Bank rating	No information supplied
Territory	No information supplied
Strings	No information supplied
Training	No information supplied
Support	No information supplied
Operating Manual	No information supplied
Profit	Net profit quoted as £27,070 on annual sales of £156,000
Risk	Difficult to imagine bread going out of fashion
Management only	Reasonable return for owner with management ability

Size and reach

Original company launched:	No information supplied
Overseas connections:	None
UK connections:	A member of the Whitworths group
Viable for whole UK?	Yes
Trade bodies	None

Franchisor's formula for success

The company's rapid growth is one of the high street's biggest success stories ever . . . and is widely recognised by Britain's bread-loving families as the original and major influence in popularising the return of delicious fresh bread. The company's open-fronted shops and the aroma of freshly baked products are drawing in the customers and profits as the Don Millers success story goes from strength to strength.

Good Franchise Guide comment: This looks a very substantial franchise – it is a shame the franchisor would not tell us more.

Number of franchisee addresses provided by franchisor: 00

⇨ Doran Products

22 Tanners Hill, London SE8 4PJ

This franchise has been listed in some reference books and magazines. Mail sent to this address is accepted, but we have been unable to obtain information either in response to general requests from would-be franchisees or specifically for this publication. In the light of this experience we suggest a certain amount of caution may be in order if the franchise does eventually reappear.

⇨ Draincure/30 Ltd

Darley House, Cow Lane, Garston, Watford, Herts WD2 6PH
Phone: 0923 223842; 663322; 241514

This is part of the Cure/30 Group of Companies Ltd comprising Dampcure/30, Woodcure/30 and Crimecure/30. A listing under Draincure/30 does appear in some reference books. Although the franchisor has supplied information on Dampcure, Woodcure and Crimecure no information has been supplied under the name Draincure. (A similar situation has arisen under the name Electricure.)

Dyno-Electrics

⇨ Drainmasters (London) Ltd
443 Brighton Road, South Croydon, Surrey CR2 6EU
Phone: 01-668 6189

This franchise has recently been taken over by another firm, and franchises are no longer on offer.

⇨ Dutch Pancake Houses Ltd
34 James Street, London W1M 5HS

A franchise at this name and address has been listed in some reference books and magazines, although the address has been listed erroneously as St James Street elsewhere. Mail sent to this address is accepted, but we have been unable to obtain information either in response to general requests from would-be franchisees or specifically for this publication. In the light of this experience we suggest a certain amount of caution may be in order if the franchise does eventually reappear.

⇨ Dyno-Electrics
143 Maple Road, Surbiton, Surrey KT6 4BJ
Phone: 01-549 9711

Emergency repair and installation service to domestic and commercial properties.

Outlets
Number of outlets
Company owned outlets: 01
Franchised: 16
Pilot: 00
1988 franchise target: No information available
Current reach:
No analysis provided by franchisor

Costs
Total
Franchise fee: } Varies according to size
Other charges: Nil
Min cash excluding bank: From £1,250
Min overdraft required: From £500
Normal bank advance: 70%
Working capital first 2 months: From £500
Associated banks: Nat West, Royal Bank of Scotland, Midlands, Lloyds
Capital items required: Large new van
Associated leasing co: Usually work with one particular firm but name not supplied

Royalties

22.5% upwards royalty according to area
0.0% accounts service
0.0% for advertising fund
Total 22.5% upwards monthly sales
No standing royalty independent of turnover

Bank rating No information supplied
Territory Calculated by computer analysis using postcodes, franchisee base and market potential within proposed area.
Strings No information supplied

93

Dyno-Plumbing

Training	5 days practical training plus twice yearly appraisals 5 days management training Cost: Nil – included in franchise fee Training value: No information supplied
Support	No information supplied
Operating Manual	No information supplied
Profit	No information supplied
Risk	Low risk – the Dyno name is so well known
Management only	From one-man-band operation upwards depending on the size of area.

Size and reach

Original company launched:	1963
Overseas connections:	5 (2 joint ventures)
UK connections:	Associate companies include Dyno-Rod, Dyno-Plumbing and Dyno-Locks.
Viable for whole UK?	Yes
Trade bodies	BFA

Insider tips
A further franchise under the name 'Drips Plumbing' at the same address has been listed in some magazines although it is not mentioned by the parent company, and enquiries to the address have brought no response.

Good Franchise Guide comment: This is Dyno – home of Dyno-Rod, and that says a lot. The only trouble is that when our would-be franchisee wrote for details he got a Dyno-Rod pack.

Number of franchisee addresses provided by franchisor: 00

⇨ Dyno-Plumbing

143 Maple Road, Surbiton, Surrey KT6 4BJ
Phone: 01-549 9467

Dyno-Plumbing offers an emergency plumbing repair and installation service

Outlets
Number of outlets

Company owned outlets:	No information supplied
Franchised:	10
Pilot:	No information supplied
1988 franchise target:	No information supplied

Costs

Total	£1,250 each; but may vary according to territory size

No other information supplied

Royalties

Total	22.5% of turnover 0.0% accounts service 0.0% for advertising fund 22.5% monthly sales
	No standing royalty independent of turnover
Bank rating	With only £1,250 required a loan is unlikely to be required
Territory	Calculated by computer anaysis using postcodes, franchisee base and market potential within proposed
Strings	No information supplied

Dyno-Rod plc

Training	5 days practical training plus twice yearly appraisals
	5 days management training
	Cost: Nil – including in the franchise fee
	Training value: No information supplied
Support	No information supplied
Operating Manual	No information supplied
Profit	The company is using the Dyno name which should gain instant recognition from anyone who once suffered a blocked drain and now suffers a broken pipe
Risk	With low costs and the Dyno name – slight
Management only	From one-man-band operation upwards depending on the size of area

Size and reach

Original company launched:	1963
Overseas connections:	5 (2 joint ventures)
UK connections:	Parent: Dyno-Rod plc
Viable for whole UK?	Yes
Trade bodies	BFA

Franchisor's formula for success
Work is passed from the franchisor's HQ to franchisees. The Dyno name is used to increase public awareness.

Good Franchise Guide comment: For some reason we have found it hard to gain much information on this new development from the same team that gave the world Dyno-Rod. Given the Dyno-Rod success it seems unlikely that this franchise will fail.

Number of franchisee addresses provided by franchisor: 00

⇨ Dyno-Rod plc
143 Maple Road, Surbiton, Surrey KT6 4BJ
Phone: 01-549 9467

Market leader in drain, pipe and sewer cleaning and maintenance.

Outlets
Number of outlets

Company owned outlets:	03
Franchised:	94 excluding overseas
Pilot:	00
1988 franchise target:	102
Current reach:	No analysis provided by franchisor

Costs

Total	} Varies according to size
Franchise fee:	
Other charges:	Nil
Min cash excluding bank:	Varies
Min overdraft required:	From £500
Normal bank advance:	70%
Working capital first 2 months:	From £500
Associated banks:	Nat West, Royal Bank of Scotland, Lloyds, Midlands
Capital items required:	Large new van
Associated leasing co:	Usually work with one particular firm; details not supplied

Royalties

	22.5% upwards royalty according to area.
	0.0% accounts service
	0.0% for advertising fund
Total	22.5% upwards monthly sales
	No standing royalty independent of turnover

Electricure/30 Ltd

Bank rating	Helpful
Territory	Calculated by computer analysis using postcodes, franchisee base and market potential within proposed area
	Franchisees report: Just right
Strings	Some ties but lots of freedom too
Training	5 days practical training plus twice yearly appraisals
	5 days management training
	Cost: Nil – included in franchise fee
	Training value: Adequate
Support	Good
Operating Manual	Good
Profit	Higher than projected
Risk	This is clearly the market leader with highly visible presence promoting the name, but there are competitors.
Management only	From one-man-band operation upwards depending on area.

Size and reach

Original company launched:	1963
Overseas connections:	5 (2 joint ventures)
UK connections:	Associate companies include Dyno-Electrics, Dyno-Plumbing and Dyno-Locks.
Viable for whole UK?	Yes
Trade bodies	BFA

Franchisor's formula for success
Dyno-Rod has been the clear leader in drain, pipe and sewer cleaning and maintenance for 20 years, offering reliable, courteous service which is available day and night, 365 days a year throughout the UK and overseas.

Insider tips
A further franchise under the name 'Drips Plumbing' at the same address has been listed in some magazines although it is not mentioned by the parent company, and enquiries to the address have brought no response.

Inside story from the franchisees
A good franchise, but the franchisee must make the most of the Dyno-Rod name in order to maximise profit potential.

Moans and groans
'Pay special attention to any resale clauses. These can be restrictive and undervalued if the business is successful.'

Number of franchisee addresses provided by franchisor: 3

⇨ Electricure/30 Ltd

Darley House, Cow Lane, Garston, Watford, Herts WD2 6PH
Phone: 0923 223842; 663322; 241514

This is part of the Cure/30 Group of Companies Ltd comprising Dampcure/30, Woodcure/30 and Crimecure/30. A listing under Electricure/30 does appear in some reference books. Although the franchisor has supplied information on Dampcure, Woodcure and Crimecure no information has been supplied under the name Electricure. (A similar situation has arisen with Draincure, again at the same address.)

⇨ Electron Glaze
Unit 46 Meadow Mills Industrial Estate, Dixon Street, Kidderminster, Worcs DY10 1HH

A franchise at this name and address has been listed in some reference books and magazines. In fact Electron Glaze offer a photoglazing unit for glazing photographs onto plates, plaques, glass, wood, stainless steel and plastics. It represents what might be a worthwhile one-man-band operation, but it is not a franchise.

⇨ English Rose Franchises
Ideal Timber Products Ltd, Broadmeadow Industrial Estate, Dumbarton, Glasgow G82 2RG
Phone: 0389 61777

English Rose Kitchen Centres display and sell a well known brand name backed by marketing support

Outlets
Number of outlets
Company owned outlets: 05; one to be replaced by new franchised outlet
Franchised: 02
Pilot: 05 started 1983
1988 franchise target: 12
Current reach:

South	00	South west	00	South east	00
Midlands	00	East Anglia	00	North east	00
North west	00	Scotland	06	Wales	00
N Ireland	00	Rep Ireland	00	I of Man/CI	00

Costs
Total   £30,000 to £35,000
Franchise fee: £5,000
Other charges: Shopfitting, displays, legal fees
Min cash excluding bank: £30,000 to £35,000
Min overdraft required: £10,000
Normal bank advance: 70%
Working capital first 2 months: £10,000
Associated banks: Royal Bank of Scotland
Capital items required: Private car (not included in £30,000)
Associated leasing co: None

Royalties
Total
0.0% of turnover
0.0% accounts service
2.0% for advertising fund
2.0% monthly sales
No standing royalty independent of turnover

Bank rating   No information supplied
Territory   Varies depending on location; by post codes or map references
Strings   Ties are to one particular manufacturer
Training   1 day practical training
6 days management training
Cost: Nil – included in franchise fee
Training value: No information supplied

Entre Computer Centres Europe Ltd

Support	No information supplied
Operating Manual	No information supplied
Profit	No information supplied
Risk	Profit must eventually depend on the public's perception of this brand of furniture.
Management only	Reasonable return for owner with management ability. In year 2 or 3 should be profitable enough to support a manager in addition to owner.

Size and reach

Original company launched:	1955 as manufacturing base only
Overseas connections:	None
UK connections:	None
Viable for whole UK?	Yes for selected areas of high density population
Trade bodies	None

Franchisor's formula for success

English Rose centres and First Avenue are the retail trading names of Ideal Timber Products Ltd, a manufacturing company first established in Scotland in 1955 and now Scotland's largest kichen manufacturer. Among the parent company's many claims to fame is the fact that it is credited with introducing flat pack furniture to the UK and since then it has continued to build its reputation and turnover with innovative ideas and quality products using the latest technology and manufacturing processes. At one time the company was a subsidiary of the Woolworth/Comet group but in 1986 it was the subject of a management buy-out and a new board was formed. Its turnover for the current year is £11,500,000.

Good Franchise Guide comment: The company supplied the addresses of the first two franchisees – but neither was willing to spend time helping us – something very understandable in the early days of a franchise. This leaves us unable to validate the claims of the franchisor, but the openness of the franchisor in supplying addresses at this early stage says a lot for the company.

Number of franchisee addresses provided by franchisor: 02

⇨ Entre Computer Centres Europe Ltd

Entre House, 17 Bath Road, Slough, Berks

A franchise at this name and address has been listed in some reference books and magazines. Mail sent to this address is accepted, but we have been unable to obtain information either in response to general requests or specifically for this publication. Some information to hand suggests that this franchise ceased trading, although without the co-operation of the franchisor we are unable to confirm this. In the light of this experience we suggest a certain amount of caution may be in order.

⇨ ESC Ltd

Stirling House, Stirling Road, Chichester, West Sussex PO19 2EN

A franchise at this address has been listed in some reference books and magazines. Mail sent to this address is now being returned by the Post Office marked 'Gone Away'. Enquiries have revealed that no forwarding address has been left, although it is possible that the franchise may have been set up once more in another part of the country. In the light of this experience we suggest a certain amount of caution may be in order.

Euroclean

⇨ Estate Express
34 Drummond Road, Ilkeston, Derbyshire DE7 5HA

A franchise providing temporary advertising signs for estate agents, central heating contractors and the like existed at the above address in 1985, and appeared at that time to be expanding rapidly. Mail sent to this address is accepted, but we have been unable to obtain information either in response to general requests from would-be franchisees or specifically for this publication. In the light of this experience we suggest a certain amount of caution may be in order if the franchise does eventually reappear.

⇨ Euroclean
15 The Mall, Heathway, Dagenham, Essex RM10 8RE
Phone: 01-595 4234

New franchisees should apply to:
13 Stratford Office Village, 4 Romford Road, London E15 4BZ
Phone: 01 – 519 5873

Drycleaning franchise

Outlets
Number of outlets
Company owned outlets: No information supplied
Franchised: About 20
Pilot: No information supplied
1988 franchise target: No information supplied

Costs
Total £55,375
Franchise fee: £4,500
Other charges: Nil
Min cash excluding bank: £22,150
Min overdraft required: No information supplied
Normal bank advance: 60%
Working capital first 2 months: No information supplied
Associated banks: None
Capital items required: Process equipment (£3,875)
Shopfitting etc (£13,500)

Associated leasing co: None

Royalties
   No information supplied
Bank rating No information supplied
Territory No information supplied
Strings No information supplied

Training No information supplied

Support No information supplied
Operating Manual No information supplied
Profit 'Five figure profit by second year'
Risk Fairly high competition
Management only Little salary to spare for a manager

Size and reach
Original company launched: No information supplied
Overseas connections: None
UK connections: Black Arrow Group plc
Viable for whole UK? Yes
Trade bodies None

Eurodance Ltd

Franchisor's formula for success
'Brushing aside many of the old traditions and costly methods of running dry cleaning shops Euroclean has developed a business system that can be run by two people (a classical husband and wife franchise) and capable of second year earnings well into five figures' (from leaflet put out by The Franchise Shop).

Good Franchise Guide comment: It has proved very difficult to gain much information on this franchise; we can, of course, only comment on what we know, and wonder why the franchisor and his agents are so reluctant to tell us more.

Number of franchisee addresses provided by franchisor: 00

⇨ Eurodance Ltd

12-16 Byron Road, Wealdstone, Harrow, Middx

A franchise at this name and address has been listed in some reference books and magazines. Mail sent to this address is now being returned by the Post Office marked 'Gone Away'. Enquiries have revealed that no forwarding address has been left, although it is possible that the franchise may have been set up once more in another part of the country. In the light of this experience we suggest a certain amount of caution may be in order.

⇨ Everett, Masson & Furby Ltd (EM & F)

18 Nalsworth Road, Hitchin, Herts
Phone: 0462 32377

One of the largest country's largest business transfer agents

Outlets
Number of outlets
Company owned outlets: 02
Franchised: 22
Pilot: 01 (non UK; started 1987)
1988 franchise target: 28
Current reach:

South	06	South west	03	South east	08
Midlands	04	East Anglia	02	North east	00
North west	00	Scotland	00	Wales	01
N Ireland	00	Rep Ireland	00	I of Man/CI	00

Costs
Total   £25,000
Franchise fee: £15,000
Other charges: £10,000
Min cash excluding bank: £20,000
Min overdraft required: Not applicable
Normal bank advance: Variable
Working capital first 2 months: £5,000
Associated banks: Barclays
Capital items required: Computerisation included in £25,000
Associated leasing co: None

Royalties
                              10.0% of turnover
                              0.0% accounts service
                              0.0% for advertising fund
Total   10.0% monthly sales
                              No standing royalty independent of turnover

Exchange Travel

Bank rating	Banks helpful
Territory	Approx county boundaries
	Franchisees report: Just right in most cases
Strings	Some ties, but a lot of freedom
Training	30 days practical training
	10 days management training
	Cost: £4,000 – included in franchise fee
	Training value: Adequate
Support	Very good
Operating Manual	Some franchisees reported it was good, some said there was no manual!
Profit	As expected or better
Risk	Not a high risk area, as long as the economy expands
Management only	Reasonable return for owner with good management ability

Size and reach

Original company launched:	1963
Overseas connections:	1 pilot – Spain
UK connections:	None
Viable for whole UK?	Depends on result of pilot scheme
Trade bodies	Most franchisees are members of National Assn of Estate Agents

Franchisor's formula for success
Ideal franchise for person with middle management experience. No limit to potential earnings. Vacancies only exist for new franchisees in N England and Scotland.

Inside story from the franchisees
'An excellent business with forward looking management'

Insider tips
'Very good business for someone with the right background'

Moans and groans
'No manual, only guidelines'

Number of franchisee addresses provided by franchisor: 25

⇨ J Evershed & Son Ltd
Dolphin Road, Shoreham by Sea, West Sussex BN4 6QE

Evershed's have informed us that with the acquisition of the company by Booker/Circle K (UK) the franchise operation will not be continued.

⇨ Exchange Travel
Exchange House, Parker Road, Hastings, East Sussex TN34 3UB
Phone: 0424 443684

Large family owned travel and leisure group centring on a retail travel agency. In 1985 the firm sold 39 company owned branches (including 22 franchises) to another travel retailer allowing the branches to continue to use the Exchange Travel name. New franchises date from 1986 onwards.

Outlets
Number of outlets

Company owned outlets:	25
Franchised:	50
Pilot:	01 started 1984
1988 franchise target:	90

Exchange Travel

Current reach:

South	20	South west	06	South east	20
Midlands	08	East Anglia	03	North east	04
North west	08	Scotland	03	Wales	03
N Ireland	00	Rep Ireland	00	I of Man/CI	00

Costs

Total	£65,000 to £100,000
Franchise fee:	£7,500
Other charges:	No information supplied
Min cash excluding bank:	£30,000
Min overdraft required:	£35,000
Normal bank advance:	Normal gearing criteria apply
Working capital first 2 months:	No information supplied
Associated banks:	All major banks
Capital items required:	Shop fitting
Associated leasing co:	None

Royalties

	12.5% of turnover
	0.0% accounts service
	5.5% for advertising fund
Total	18.0% monthly sales
	No standing royalty independent of turnover

Bank rating	No problems getting finance
Territory	Population; catchment; travel spend and existing agents
	Franchisees report: Just right
Strings	Some ties, but not restrictive
Training	20 days practical training
	10 days management training
	Cost: Training included in franchise fee, but not accommodation at the training centre
	Training value: Generally considered adequate, but on-going training is considered expensive by some due to the travel and accommodation charges.
Support	Not considered particularly highly by franchisees
Operating Manual	Responses ranged from 'rubbish' to 'excellent'
	Since our survey a new manual has been produced
Profit	Most are meeting projections, but it can take up to two years to establish a place in the market
Risk	All travel agency work is highly competitive.
Management only	Reasonable return for owner with management ability

Size and reach

Original company launched:	1950s
Overseas connections:	None
UK connections:	Exchange Travel Holdings
Viable for whole UK?	Yes
Trade bodies	ABTA, IATA, BFA

Franchisor's formula for success

Exchange Travel is unique in having produced a franchise package which opens the door into the world of retail travel. Few vocations offer greater interest and variety, few are more difficult for the newcomer to enter. For those with communication skills, enthusiasm, high motivation and who like to be involved and don't mind hard work then travel agency work is right.

Inside story from the franchisees
Overall a very good response from franchisees who view the franchsior as 'honest', and the work as 'rewarding' and 'interesting'. Out of the franchisees that we contacted all gave promising reports save one who found the training, support, manual and back-up all poor, and reported a much lower than expected return on investment. Quite why or how one franchisee should have such bad experiences alongside others' good experience we don't fully understand.

Insider tips
Ensure you have sufficient capital. It is possible to cut back on the set-up costs.

Moans and groans
Initial projections can be too high, and with the high discounts that have to be given income can be lower than projected.

Number of franchisee addresses provided by franchisor: 15

⇨ Exide Batteries
Chequers Lane, Dagenham, Essex RM9 6PX
Phone: 01-592 4560

Mobile wholesale for Exide products, batteries, torches and lanterns

Outlets
Number of outlets
Company owned outlets:	01
Franchised:	20
Pilot:	No information supplied
1988 franchise target:	No information supplied

Costs
Total	No information supplied
Franchise fee:	£3,000
Other charges:	£3,000 stock
Min cash excluding bank:	No information supplied
Min overdraft required:	No information supplied
Normal bank advance:	66%
Working capital first 2 months:	No information supplied
Associated banks:	'All banks'
Capital items required:	Van
Associated leasing co:	None

Royalties
	0.0% of turnover
	0.0% accounts service
	1.33% for advertising fund
Total	1.33% monthly sales
	No standing royalty independent of turnover

Bank rating	No information supplied
Territory	No information supplied
Strings	Tied to Exide for products
Training	Training provided, but no information given
Support	No information supplied
Operating Manual	No information supplied
Profit	No information supplied
Risk	Depends how good a salesman you are
Management only	One-man-band operation

Express Dairy Ltd

Franchisor's formula for success
The Chloride Group is one of the largest manufacturers in the world of batteries for cars, commercial vehicles, motive power and standby power, best known by the brand name of Exide. In 1981 the company decided to expand its dry battery operation by making them available to selected franchisees to sell on to retail industrial and commercial customers.

Good Franchise Guide comment: It looks like a viable one-man-band operation selling a recognised product.

Number of franchisee addresses provided by franchisor: 00

➪ Express Dairy Ltd
Broadfield Road, Sheffield S8 0XP

This franchise comes from the famous milk delivery group, looking to develop their strong position in the dairy market.
Mail sent to this address is accepted, but we have been unable to obtain information either in response to general requests from would-be franchisees or specifically for this publication. It may be that the company is now only looking for franchisees in certain areas, but if this is the reason it would have been nice to let the would-be franchisees know.

➪ Express Hoses Ltd,
Darlaston Central Trading Estate, Wednesbury, West Midlands

This franchise is currently listed in some reference books and magazines. Mail sent to this address is accepted, but we have been unable to obtain information either in response to general requests from would-be franchisees or specifically for this publication. In the light of this experience we suggest a certain amount of caution may be in order if the franchise does eventually reappear.

➪ 4th Dimension Computer Systems Ltd
Ryknild House, Burnett Street, Sutton Coldfield B74 3EL

A franchise at this name and address has been listed in some reference books and magazines. Mail sent to this address is now being returned by the Post Office marked 'Gone Away'. Enquiries have revealed that no forwarding address has been left, although it is possible that the franchise may have been set up once more in another part of the country. In the light of this experience we suggest a certain amount of caution may be in order.

➪ Fastframe Franchises Ltd
28 Blandford Street, Sunderland SR1 3JH
Phone: 091-565 2233

All manner of framing undertaken including oil paintings, lithography, screen work, photographs, tapestries, water colours, certificates, stamps, picture cards, coins, medals etc

Outlets
Number of outlets
Company owned outlets: 03
Franchised: 51
Pilot: 02 started 1983
1988 franchise target: 85

Fastframe Franchises Ltd

Current reach:

South	08	South west	08	South east	04
Midlands	04	East Anglia	04	North east	12
North west	04	Scotland	08	Wales	01
N Ireland	01	Rep Ireland	00	I of Man/CI	00

Costs
Total	£34,000
Franchise fee:	£7,500
Other charges:	No information available
Min cash excluding bank:	£15,000
Min overdraft required:	£1,000 to £5,000
Normal bank advance:	66%
Working capital first 2 months:	Variable
Associated banks:	Lloyds, NatWest and Barclays
Capital items required:	Equipment package £6,500
Associated leasing co:	None

Royalties

Total
6.25% of turnover
6.25% marketing services fund
0.0% for advertising fund
12.5% monthly sales
No standing royalty independent of turnover

Bank rating Everyone very helpful. No problems with finance reported by anyone.

Territory Based on population; defined by post code
Franchisees report: 'Just right'

Strings Strong ties but parts of the operation are not strongly controlled, leaving much franchisee freedom.

Training 12 days minimum practical training
6 days minimum management training
Plus on-site ongoing support
Cost: £1,500 to £2,000 included in franchise fee
Training value: Responses vary from adequate to excellent

Support Very good
Operating Manual Excellent
Profit Most franchisees report better than expected results
Risk Some competition but mostly it is nowhere near as well organised as this franchise.

Management only Proven franchise with good return on investment

Size and reach
Original company launched:	1983
Overseas connections:	Los Angeles 3, Australia 1
UK connections:	Part of Unit Offset Group, Newcastle on Tyne
Viable for whole UK?	Yes
Trade bodies	BFA, Fine Arts Trade Guild

Franchisor's formula for success
Fastframe is the market leader offering expert picture framing instantly combining the traditional skills of quality framing with a bright, tastefully decorated retail environment. Over 100 different mouldings are held in stock and a simple efficient pricing system enables speedy handling of customer's requirements. Work is completed on the average frame in only 15 minutes.

A Fastframe franchise has the added advantage of being a cash business with little seasonal fluctuation or changes in fashion. It combines the benefits of a retail shop and manufacturing unit, creating an end product over which the franchisee has complete control.

Fatso's Pasta Joint

Inside story from the franchisees
Very good response from franchisees who, to a man (and woman) felt that the franchise was very worthwhile with support always available when asked for.
'Thoroughly recommended' was the average comment.

Insider tips
Prospective franchisee should have a sales and/or business background and should be highly self-motivated.
'Fantastic return on capital and as long as attitude is positive a great future is anticipated'

Moans and groans
Some franchisees found it hard to get the larger commercial work coming their way but beyond that there were no real problems.

Number of franchisee addresses provided by franchisor: 51

⇨ **Fatso's Pasta Joint**
3 Palace Gate Parade, Hampton Court, East Molesey, Surrey KT8 9BN

This franchise is listed in *Franchise Opportunities* directory as being a 'Restaurant where diners may eat as much pasta and sauces as they wish for £2.60.' It sounded just the place to take the editors' children, but sadly although mail sent to this address is accepted, we have been unable to obtain information either in response to general requests from would-be franchisees or specifically for this publication.
Taking Up a Franchise states that this is a subsidiary of Theme Holdings plc, requires a start up capital of £70,000 and has a franchise fee of £5,000. Royalties are quoted as 8 per cent per month, with the first franchise being launched in February 1987. However in the light of our own experience in trying to get any information we can offer no comment.

⇨ **Fersina International**
Cestrum House, Industry Road, Carlton Industrial Estate, Carlton, Barnsley, S Yorks S70 3NH
Phone: 0226 728310

Manufacture, installation and sale of uPVC doors and windows

Outlets
Number of outlets
Company owned outlets: 01
Franchised: 70
Pilot: 02 started 1984
1988 franchise target: 100
Current reach:

South	00	South west	*10	South east	*20
Midlands	05	East Anglia	03	North east	09
North west	12	Scotland	04	Wales	04
N Ireland	01	Rep Ireland	01	I of Man/CI	01

* Includes a number of franchises in the south of England

Costs
Total   £40,000
Franchise fee: £8,000
Other charges: No details supplied
Min cash excluding bank: £12,000
Min overdraft required: £28,000
Normal bank advance: 70%
Working capital first 2 months: No details supplied
Associated banks: '4 major banks'
Capital items required: Machinery and vehicles (part of £40,000)
Associated leasing co: None

Financial Consultants Ltd

Royalties	2.5% of turnover
	0.0% accounts service
	0.0% for advertising fund
Total	2.5% monthly sales
	No standing royalty independent of turnover
Bank rating	No problems reported with raising finance
Territory	250,000 population
	Franchisees report: Just right
Strings	Very strong ties for materials etc
Training	1 month initial practical training
	3 day initial management training
	Cost: Nil – included in franchise fee
	Training value: Adequate
Support	Very good
Operating Manual	Very good
Profit	As projected or better
Risk	Although Fersina appears to be the only franchise undertaking exactly this type of work, there are other non-franchised firms in this competitive field.
Management only	Proven franchise with good return on investment
Size and reach	
Original company launched:	1981
Overseas connections:	Companies in Italy, Canada, Spain, Germany, Norway, Singapore, Malaysia, Tunisia, Switzerland
UK connections:	None
Viable for whole UK?	Yes
Trade bodies	BFA

Franchisor's formula for success
Through the years Fersina have been building local networks of selected manufacturers all bearing the same name style, image and all displaying the same logo. This consistent corporate image identifies the small local company as part of the bigger international Fersina family, thus producing customer confidence.

Inside story from the franchisees
Franchisees very enthusiastic about this franchise and the franchisor. The only complaint relates to the industry itself, not this particular franchise.

Insider tips
Manpower Services Commission grant may be available for additional training.

Moans and groans
'Enter the window industry at your own risk. It is full of crooks who would rip off any unsuspecting franchisee. Be prepared to have 100% commitment to succeed. There is no easy way. You even have to dream about windows.'

Number of franchisee addresses provided by franchisor: 12

⇨ Financial Consultants Ltd
30 Silent Street, Ipswich, Suffolk IP1 1TG

This franchise has been listed in some reference books and magazines. When a would-be franchisee wrote to them, however, he was offered a loan of £100,000 at an APR of 12.01%. There appears to be no franchise.

⇨ Fire Technology Ltd
Townfield House, Townfield Street, Oldham, Lancs OL4 1HL
Phone: 061-627 0721

Handles the worldwide sales and marketing of PROTEX flameproofing products

Outlets
Number of outlets
Company owned outlets: 01
Franchised: 06
Pilot: 02 started 1986
1988 franchise target: 30
Current reach:

South	05	South west	02	South east	04
Midlands	02	East Anglia	01	North east	02
North west	02	Scotland	03	Wales	03
N Ireland	01	Rep Ireland	01	I of Man/CI	02

Current reach figures include franchises licensed but not yet operational.

Costs
Total	No information supplied
Franchise fee:	£12,500
Other charges:	Nil
Min cash excluding bank:	'Up to the franchisee'
Min overdraft required:	'Up to the franchisee'
Normal bank advance:	'Up to the franchisee'
Working capital first 2 months:	£2,000
Associated banks:	'Yes' – no details given
Capital items required:	A car or a van
Associated leasing co:	'Yes' – no details given

Royalties
Total
- 10.0% of turnover
- 0.0% accounts service
- 0.0% for advertising fund
- 10.0% monthly sales

No standing royalty independent of turnover

Bank rating   No information supplied
Territory   Post codes, except London
Strings   Total tie into one product

Training
- 3 days practical training
- 2 days management training
- Cost: Nil – included in franchise fee
- Training value: No information supplied

Support   No information supplied
Operating Manual   No information supplied
Profit   No figures supplied
Risk   With a total tie in to one product everything depends on the quality of that product. Franchisor does supply a lot of technical information to propsective franchisees
Management only   Reasonable return for owner with management ability

Size and reach
Original company launched: 1985
Overseas connections: Active in overseas market
UK connections: D H Heywood (Int) Ltd and Glomart Ltd
Viable for whole UK?   Yes
Trade bodies   'Negotiable with individual franchisees'

Fires and Things

Franchisor's formula for success
The PROTEX system is not a fire retardant but a process for rendering upholstery, soft furnishings, paper and wood flameproof. Materials treated with PROTEX will not burn. This unique product produces a result which exceeds the British Standards for non-flammability at present in force. The product is a proven success and has been applied to such varying items as rolls of fabric, curtains, textile, wallcoverings, upholstery, upholstered screens, paper screens, Christmas decorations and dried flowers.

Good Franchise Guide comment: Not having the technical background to validate the specifications which are central to this product, we would have welcomed the chance to examine the marketability of the product through the experiences of existing franchisees. New legislation and the current high level of concern makes this look an increasingly attractive area of operation.

Number of franchisee addresses provided by franchisor: 00

⇨ Fires and Things
4 Brighton Road, Horsham, West Sussex RH13 5BA
Phone: 0403 56227

Retail outlets for household fire products

Outlets
Number of outlets
Company owned outlets: 03
Franchised: About 6

Costs
Total   £25,000
Franchise fee: £4,000
Other charges: No information supplied
Min cash excluding bank: £8,500
Min overdraft required: No information supplied
Normal bank advance: 66%
Working capital first 2 months: No information supplied
Associated banks: None
Capital items required: None
Associated leasing co: None

Royalties
                                  1.0% of turnover
                                  0.0% accounts service
                                  0.0% for advertising fund
Total   1.0% monthly sales

                                  No standing royalty independent of turnover

Bank rating   No information supplied
Territory   No information supplied
Strings   No information supplied

Training   No information supplied

Support   No information supplied
Operating Manual   No information supplied
Profit   No information supplied
Risk   No information supplied
Management only   No information supplied

Size and reach
Original company launched: 1985
Overseas connections: None
UK connections: Apex Associated Group Holdings
Viable for whole UK?   Yes
Trade bodies   None

Fixit Tools Ltd

Good Franchise Guide comment: The company has responded neither to our requests for information nor to that from our test franchisee, and such information as we have been able to obtain has been gleaned from other sources.

Number of franchisee addresses provided by franchisor: 00

⇨ Fixit Tools Ltd

98 Braemar Avenue, South Croydon, Surrey CR2 0QB
Phone: 01-668 4567

Provide a fast and efficient local service to builders, electricians, heating engineers, plumbers and other users of tools and fixings. Stock is held on board a van for instant delivery.
Note that the company also trades as Fixit Mobile Fastening Centre

Outlets
Number of outlets
Company owned outlets: 01
Franchised: 02
Pilot: 01 started 1985
1988 franchise target: 05
Current reach:

South	00	South west	02	South east	01
Midlands	00	East Anglia	00	North east	00
North west	00	Scotland	00	Wales	00
N Ireland	00	Rep Ireland	00	I of Man/CI	00

Costs
Total £12,000
Franchise fee: No information provided
Other charges: £1,750
Min cash excluding bank: £5,000
Min overdraft required: £4,500
Normal bank advance: £9,000
Working capital first 2 months: £2,000
Associated banks: Nat West
Capital items required: Lease of fully fitted and liveried vehicle
Associated leasing co: No information provided

Royalties

  0.0% of turnover
  1.0% for advertising fund from year 2
  2.0% for advertising fund from year 3
Total 1% in year 2; 2% from year 3
  No standing royalty independent of turnover

Bank rating All establishments helpful with finance
Territory Population; eg 500,000 from base
  Franchisees report: Areas too big
Strings Very strong ties for materials
Training 2 weeks practical training
  No management training
  Cost: Nil – included in franchise fee
  Training value: 'Not enough'

Support Good
Operating Manual Poor
Profit Not as good as projected
Risk Similar to other operations
Management only One-man-band operation

Flash Trash

Size and reach
Original company launched: 1973
Overseas connections: None
UK connections: None
Viable for whole UK? Yes
Trade bodies None

Franchisor's formula for success
Fixit Tools Ltd was formed in January 1973 to supply the construction industry with a comprehensive range of fixings, fastening, hand tools and power tools. It fills a gap left by the larger companies in providing a fast and efficient local service to builders, electricians, heating engineers plumbers etc.

Inside story from the franchisees
Franchisees believe the concept is sound, but as the company is in its first year as a franchisor there may not always be enough experience to foresee the problems that franchisees encounter.

Number of franchisee addresses provided by franchisor: 02

⇨ **Flash Trash**
269 Regent Street, London W1R 7PA
Phone: 01-491 4215

'A striking image for a new concept in retailing.'

Outlets
Number of outlets
Company owned outlets: 02
Franchised: 03
Pilot: 02 – no date given
1988 franchise target: 52 locations listed, but no date given
Current reach:

South	00	South west	00	South east	03
Midlands	00	East Anglia	00	North east	00
North west	00	Scotland	00	Wales	00
N Ireland	00	Rep Ireland	00	I of Man/CI	00

Costs
Total £59,000
Franchise fee: £8,500
Other charges: £15,000 stock
Min cash excluding bank: £20,000
Min overdraft required: No information supplied
Normal bank advance: £39,000
Working capital first 2 months: £10,500 plus £7,000 to cover VAT
Associated banks: None
Capital items required: £25,000 shopfitting
Associated leasing co: None

Royalties
Total
0.0% of turnover
0.0% accounts service
3.0% for marketing fund
3.0% monthly sales

No standing royalty independent of turnover

Bank rating No information supplied
Territory No information supplied
Strings No information supplied

Training No information supplied

Foto-Inn

Support	No information supplied
Operating Manual	No information supplied
Profit	Year 1 net profit £24,000
Risk	High street style = high risk, but it looks good on paper
Management only	We would expect the manager to be working in the shop for the first few years |//

Size and reach
Original company launched:	No information supplied
Overseas connections:	None
UK connections:	'Major capital investor – CIN Industrial'
Viable for whole UK?	Throughout the south of England, large towns in the Midlands and major cities in the north. A full list of possible locations is provided by the franchisor.
Trade bodies	None

Franchisor's formula for success
Flash Trash sell accessories, bags and belts, co-ordinates, earrings, gloves, hosiery, jewellery, make-up etc etc.

Good Franchise Guide comment: Ten out of ten for style of information sent to franchisees. Franchisors sending out flimsy photocopied sheets should take a look at what can be done. Franchisees tempted by a couple of pages of duplicated generality should see what real style looks like. None of which means you will make a fortune, but it shows the franchisor is taking a bit of trouble.
Too early to have reports from franchisees, but our feelings are positive.

Number of franchisee addresses provided by franchisor: 00

➪ Foto-Inn

35 South Molton Street, London W1Y 1HA
Phone: 01-629 7911

60 minute photographic developing and printing

Outlets
Number of outlets
Company owned outlets:	01
Franchised:	By mid-July 1986 – 6; no subsequent information
Pilot:	01 started 1981
1988 franchise target:	No information supplied

Costs
Total	£39,675
Franchise fee:	£5,000
Other charges:	Mostly shopfitting (see below)
Min cash excluding bank:	£25,000
Min overdraft required:	No information supplied
Normal bank advance:	£25,000
Working capital first 2 months:	£10,000
Associated banks:	None
Capital items required:	£20,000 shopfitting, £5,500 equipment, deposit for lease
Associated leasing co:	None

Royalties
	7.0% of turnover
	0.0% accounts service
	2.0% for advertising fund
Total	9.0% monthly sales
	No standing royalty independent of turnover

Fotofast

Bank rating	No information supplied
Territory	No information supplied
Strings	No information supplied
Training	No information supplied
	No information supplied
	Cost: Nil – included in franchise fee
	Training value: No information supplied
Support	No information supplied
Operating Manual	No information supplied
Profit	Net profit for year one quoted as £15,200
Risk	Quick developing is a growing area, which may mean an increased risk.
Management only	Could be run by manager but with limited profit

Size and reach

Original company launched:	1981
Overseas connections:	None
UK connections:	None
Viable for whole UK?	Yes
Trade bodies	None

Franchisor's formula for success

Mini-labs, the main tool of our business, are basically compact photo-finishing machines using the latest in computer technology. So confident are we about our expertise, product and service that we have a policy to acquire good sites, set them up and run them prior to their being franchised. This means that you can either purchase a 'fast start' franchise almost immediately, or start a new outlet in your chosen location, which will take about 3 months.

Good Franchise Guide comment: A rapidly developing area which may eventually see a shake out in the industry.

Number of franchisee addresses provided by franchisor: 00

➪ Fotofast

4th Floor, Carolyn House, 22/26 Dingwall Road, Croydon CR0 9XF

Phone: None of the literature received for prospective franchisees carries the company's phone number. The London number quoted in other reference material gave the unobtainable tone when we tried.

Processing of photographs

Outlets

Number of outlets	No information supplied

Costs

Total	£23,000
Franchise fee:	£5,000
Other charges:	£18,000
Min cash excluding bank:	£15,000
Min overdraft required:	No information supplied
Normal bank advance:	£8,000 (possibly including overdraft)
Working capital first 2 months:	£3,000
Associated banks:	None
Capital items required:	Shopfitting £10,000
Associated leasing co:	None

Royalties

	*7.5% of turnover
	0.0% accounts service
	0.0% for advertising fund
Total	*7.5% monthly sales

Frame Express

	*Figure dervied from examples and may be only approximate
	No standing royalty independent of turnover
Bank rating	No information supplied
Territory	No information supplied
Strings	No information supplied
Training	No information supplied
Support	No information supplied
Operating Manual	No information supplied
Profit	£30,000 gross profit quoted on turnover of £75,000
Risk	An increasingly competitive field
Management only	No information supplied

Size and reach

Original company launched:	No information supplied
Overseas connections:	None
UK connections:	None
Viable for whole UK?	Yes
Trade bodies	None

Franchisor's formula for success

Fotofast is a successful proven commercial enterprise involved in the retailing of photo-processing services and related consumer products to business and professional customers, and the general public. The operational base is in Greater London, and the aim is to expand within the capital and beyond through franchises to interested people who we believe will respond to and enhance our ten-year success story.

Good Franchise Guide comment: The information that we have comes in the form of a package sent to a prospective franchisee making general enquiries. Within the franchise contract provided is the statement that 'The usual length of agreement is for a period of three years whereupon as a successful member of Fotofast you will be invited to continue your association with us. The agreement may be terminated by us at any time with 24 hours notice. This would in practice generally longer (sic) and is necessary to protect our interest and reputation.' We find that disconcerting to say the very least. Odd about the phone number too.

Number of franchisee addresses provided by franchisor: 00

⇨ **Frame Express**

1 Queens Road, London SW19 8NG
Phone: 01-879 3366

Picture framing

IMPORTANT: See *Good Franchise Guide* comment below

Outlets
Number of outlets

Company owned outlets:	No information supplied
Franchised:	25 – possibly more, mostly in London
Pilot:	No information supplied
1988 franchise target:	No information supplied

Frame Express

Costs
Total	£30,000
Franchise fee:	£6,500
Other charges:	£500 training
Min cash excluding bank:	£10,000
Min overdraft required:	£6,000
Normal bank advance:	£14,000
Working capital first 2 months:	£4,500
Associated banks:	None
Capital items required:	Shop equipment £5,500, shopfitting £8,000
Associated leasing co:	None

Royalties

10.0% of turnover
0.0% accounts service
0.0% for advertising fund

Total 10.0% monthly sales

No standing royalty independent of turnover

Bank rating	No information supplied
Territory	No information supplied
Strings	No information supplied
Training	No information supplied on length of training
	Cost: £500 – included in franchise fee
	Training value: No information supplied
Support	No information supplied
Operating Manual	No information supplied
Profit	First year net profit quoted as £17,340
Risk	A very large number of firms are presenting picture framing with its bright and breezy image
Management only	Could be run by manager but with limited profit

Size and reach
Original company launched:	No information supplied
Overseas connections:	None
UK connections:	None
Viable for whole UK?	Yes
Trade bodies	None

Franchisor's formula for success

Frame Express is changing the face of the picture framing market. The shops are bright, modern and attractive, situated in prominent trading positions. The shop interior has been carefully designed to convey a modern business image with a traditional air while maintaining a corporate identity.

Good Franchise Guide comment: Despite repeated attempts we have found it singularly difficult to obtain up-to-date information from this franchisor, and we have been forced to use figures and data above which may be up to two years out of date. We urge caution when using the information provided. It is an area of growing competition.

Number of franchisee addresses provided by franchisor: 00

The Frame Factory Franchise Ltd

⇨ The Frame Factory Franchise Ltd
67 Vivian Avenue, London NW4 3XE
Phone: 01-202 2499

Framing service plus provision of originally designed posters, prints etc

Outlets
Number of outlets
Company owned outlets: 03
Franchised: 06
Pilot: 01 started 1982
1988 franchise target: 16
Current reach:

South	00	South west	00	South east	08
Midlands	00	East Anglia	01	North east	00
North west	00	Scotland	00	Wales	00
N Ireland	00	Rep Ireland	00	I of Man/CI	00

Costs
Total: £28,000
Franchise fee: £7,500
Other charges: £20,500
Min cash excluding bank: £7,000 to £10,000
Min overdraft required: £5,000
Normal bank advance: 75%
Working capital first 2 months: £5,000
Associated banks: Barclays
Capital items required: 'We operate a leasing deal'
Associated leasing co: Anglo

Royalties

Total:
8.0% of turnover
0.0% accounts service
0.0% for advertising fund
8.0% monthly sales

No standing royalty independent of turnover

Bank rating No information supplied
Territory Population – approx 200,000 to 300,000
Strings Franchisor stresses that they like each shop to reflect the personality of the franchisee

Training 11 days practical and management training
Cost: Nil – included in franchise fee
Training value: No information supplied

Support No information supplied
Operating Manual No information supplied
Profit Net profit quoted as £16,420 in first year
Risk There is a growing number of framing franchises – the risk relates to how many firms the market can take.
Management only Could be run by manager but with limited profit

Size and reach
Original company launched: 1979
Overseas connections: French and Irish links in progress
UK connections: None
Viable for whole UK? Yes
Trade bodies None

Franchise Development Services Ltd

Franchisor's formula for success
We believe that the strength of this particular franchise is that it allows individual freedom of the franchisee to work within the franchise format. By visiting any one of our locations a potential franchisee will soon see the individual mark of each current franchisee stamped on that shop. We are currently looking throughout the UK for more individual franchisees to share our financial success.

Good Franchise Guide comment: Framing shops can be successful, but can the market really take several franchises plus all the local stores? Everyone now runs the risk of having a rival franchise open up just along the street; even if they are not as good they will still take away some of your business.

Number of franchisee addresses provided by franchisor: 00

⇨ Frameorama
The Bridge, Forty Foot, Ramsey, Cambs PE17 1XN

Leaflets produced by Frameorama describe the company as 'a nationwide network offering you a professional, individual framing service for those treasured photographs, favourite picture or even that piece of needlework laying in drawer.' (sic)

The company has not responded to any enquiries regarding its operation.

⇨ Franchise Development Services Ltd
Castle House, Castle Meadow, Norwich NR2 1PJ
Phone: 0603 620301

International licensing, UK franchisor development, services to prospective franchisors, publications, services to franchisees, promotions and seminars and ancillary services

Outlets
Number of outlets
Company owned outlets: 01
Franchised: 02
Pilot: 01 started 1985
1988 franchise target: 07 UK, 21 overseas
Current reach:

South	01	South west	00	South east	00
Midlands	00	East Anglia	01	North east	00
North west	00	Scotland	00	Wales	00
N Ireland	00	Rep Ireland	00	I of Man/CI	00

Costs
Total: £25,000 to £100,000
Franchise fee: Details available on request
Other charges: Nil
Min cash excluding bank: 50%
Min overdraft required: Not applicable
Normal bank advance: 70%
Working capital first 2 months: £5,000
Associated banks: Lloyds, Barclays
Capital items required: Prestige office accommodation
Associated leasing co: None

Royalties
'Information available on application'
Total percentage of monthly sales: 'Confidential'

Bank rating No information supplied
Territory UK trading regions
Strings No information supplied

Free-Room (UK) Ltd

Training	6 months practical training
	3 months management training
	Cost: £7,500 – included in franchise fee
	Training value: No information supplied
Management only	Reasonable return for owner with management ability
Size and reach	
Original company launched:	1981
Overseas connections:	Canada, Holland, Singapore, Hong Kong, Trinidad
UK connections:	None
Viable for whole UK?	Yes
Trade bodies	CBI, FTA

Franchisor's formula for success

While franchising accounts for only 7.5% of all retail sales in this country it represents over 40% in France and the USA. As franchising continues to expand in all areas of retailing, sales and distribution, so too does the sales potential of the franchisee who has the financial capability and business skills. Many companies around the world have entered the franchise field and the majority have prospered, especially those based on sound operating and franchising principles. The use of competent consultants is essential to the successful development of any franchise investment.

Good Franchise Guide comment: We have not been able to obtain enough material for us properly to evaluate this franchise. However, we feel that the projected target of 7 outlets in the UK may possibly be optimistic considering that by the end of 1987 there was still only the one pilot, started in 1985. We also wonder if there are enough franchisable operations left for consultants to aid, but we could be wrong. We are also hopelessly biased on the subject of consultants (see our comments in the introduction).

Number of franchisee addresses provided by franchisor: 00

⇨ Free-Room (UK) Ltd

30 Church Road, Lymm, Cheshire WA13 0QQ
Phone: 0925 757171

Sale of promotional packages

Outlets
Number of outlets
Company owned outlets: No information supplied
Franchised: 07
Pilot: No information supplied
1988 franchise target: No information supplied
Current reach:

South	00	South west	02	South east	00
Midlands	02	East Anglia	00	North east	00
North west	01	Scotland	01	Wales	01
N Ireland	00	Rep Ireland	00	I of Man/CI	00

Costs
Total	£5,860
Franchise fee:	£7,100
Other charges:	No information supplied
Min cash excluding bank:	No information supplied
Min overdraft required:	No information supplied
Normal bank advance:	No information supplied
Working capital first 2 months:	No information supplied
Associated banks:	None
Capital items required:	Vehicle
Associated leasing co:	None

Royalties

No mention of a royalty is made in the brochure

Freezavan Ltd

Bank rating	No information supplied
Territory	No information supplied
Strings	You are selling one idea, and so are totally tied to that idea.
Training	10 days practical and management training Cost: Nil – included in franchise fee Training value: No information supplied
Support	No information supplied
Operating Manual	No information supplied
Profit	Net profit in example provided by franchisor quoted as £20,895
Risk	It looks like a novel idea – but there is no way of knowing if it will continue to work
Management only	Could be run by manager but with limited profit

Size and reach

Original company launched:	No information supplied
Overseas connections:	None
UK connections:	None
Viable for whole UK?	No information supplied
Trade bodies	None

Franchisor's formula for success
Your clients give vouchers to their customers as a bonus or free gift with specific order values. Alternatively they are used as part of employee incentive schemes. The holder of Free Room vouchers can stay at a superb hotel without paying for the room providing they agree to take breakfast and dinner in the hotel at the regular prices. We never sell the product direct to members of the general public.

Good Franchise Guide comment: We find the presentation made by the franchisor rather confusing and we end up unsure of exactly what the franchisee does, and how the franchisor makes his money. It is as if the writer of the brochure assumes you know what it is all about before you start reading.

Number of franchisee addresses provided by franchisor: 00

⇨ Freezavan Ltd

Fleet Estate Office, Fleet, Spalding, Lincs PE12 8LR
Phone: 0406 22727

Door to door frozen food delivery service

Outlets
Number of outlets
Company owned outlets: 00
Franchised: 25
Pilot: 00
1988 franchise target: 40
Current reach:

South	00	South west	00	South east	*25
Midlands	00	East Anglia	25	North east	00
North west	00	Scotland	00	Wales	00
N Ireland	00	Rep Ireland	00	I of Man/CI	00

*The East Anglia and South east totals combined make 25

Freezavan Ltd

Costs
Total	
Franchise fee:	£7,000
Other charges:	£4,500
Min cash excluding bank:	£2,500
Min overdraft required:	£3,000
Normal bank advance:	£4,000
Working capital first 2 months:	£5,000
Associated banks:	£3,000
Capital items required:	Nat West
Associated leasing co:	None
	Transfleet

Royalties

Total
7.5% of turnover
8.0% additional royalty
0.0% for advertising fund
15.5% monthly sales

No standing royalty independent of turnover

Bank rating Financial institutions helpful
Territory No information available from franchisor
One franchisee reported area was too large
Strings Strong ties for the product
Training 1 week initial practical and management training

Cost: Nil – included in franchise fee
Training value: Adequate

Support Good
Operating Manual One complaint – it was badly written
Profit As projected
Risk Little competition; not high risk
Management only One-man-band operation

Size and reach
Original company launched: 1983
Overseas connections: None
UK connections: Wholly owned subsidiary of Frozen Quality Ltd (Froqual)
Viable for whole UK? Yes
Trade bodies BFA Associate

Franchisor's formula for success
The benefits of a Freezavan franchise can be summarised as
1. Startup costs are fixed and predetermined
2. Continual business management advice and financial advice available
3. Sound sales and marketing help
4. Excellent promotional and advertising support
5. Priviledged access to banking facilities subject to status
6. With hard work a potential to earn in excess of £16,000 pa

Insider tips
Have faith in the product and sell it; there is a good market for the goods.

Moans and groans
Startup costs are expensive in a new territory.

Number of franchisee addresses provided by franchisor: 10

FuelBoss Ltd

⇨ Fudge Kitchen (UK) Ltd

Coniscliffe House, Darlington DL3 7EX
Phone: 0325 488688

Fudge Kitchen, a retail confectionery franchise specialising in fudge, toffee, ice cream etc, have informed us that they have not been offering new franchises for some months, and there are 'no plans to start again in the foreseeable future'.

⇨ FuelBoss Ltd

The Courtyard, Corby Castle, Great Corby, Carlisle, Cumbria
Phone: 0228 61416

Heating system control unit

Outlets
Number of outlets
Company owned outlets:	No information supplied
Franchised:	About 25
Pilot:	No information supplied
1988 franchise target:	No information supplied

Costs
Total	£3,000 approx
Franchise fee:	No information supplied
Other charges:	No information supplied
Min cash excluding bank:	No information supplied
Min overdraft required:	No information supplied
Normal bank advance:	No information supplied
Working capital first 2 months:	No information supplied
Associated banks:	None
Capital items required:	None
Associated leasing co:	None

Royalties — No information supplied
Bank rating — No information supplied
Territory — Although this appears to be more of a distributorship than a franchise the brochure offers an 'exclusive area'
Strings — Total tie in to one product
Training — 1 day practical and management training
Cost: Nil – included in franchise fee
Training value: No information supplied

Support — 24 hour hotline offers technical advice
Operating Manual — No information supplied
Profit — No information supplied
Risk — Totally depends on the product
Management only — One-man-band operation

Size and reach
Original company launched:	No information supplied
Overseas connections:	None
UK connections:	None
Viable for whole UK?	Yes
Trade bodies	None

Franchisor's formula for success
By using a microchip FuelBoss Control Systems eliminate unnecessary fuel waste in heating systems, giving the user much greater control and a more comfortable living and working environment. Results show that a typical fuel saving achieved is a staggering 35%.

Good Franchise Guide comment: Possibly a good product but precious little information.

Number of franchisee addresses provided by franchisor: 00

G and T Video Services

⇨ G and T Video Services

35 Balena Close, Creekmore Industrial Estate, Poole, Dorset BH17 7EB
Phone: 0202 610851

Selling videos to retail outlets

Outlets
Number of outlets
Company owned outlets: 01
Franchised: No information supplied
Pilot: 01 started 1984
1988 franchise target: 60

Costs
Total £36,660
Franchise fee: £5,000
Other charges: £2,000 stock control system
Min cash excluding bank: £16,000 to £20,000
Min overdraft required: No information supplied
Normal bank advance: £16,000 to £20,000
Working capital first 2 months: No information supplied
Associated banks: None
Capital items required: Vehicle (3 months lease £960)
Associated leasing co: None

Royalties

Total
7.0% of turnover
0.0% accounts service
3.0% for advertising fund
10.0% monthly sales

Note: these percentages are derived from example figures provided by the franchisor, who does not quote the exact percentage in the literature. We have to admit that we can't quite see how the quoted figures are derived in percentage terms – our percentages are therefore approximate.

Bank rating	No information supplied
Territory	No information supplied
Strings	Tied to franchisor for selection of videos
Training	'2 weeks initial comprehensive training'.
Support	No information supplied
Operating Manual	No information supplied
Profit	Illustrations provided by franchisor suggest net profit of £30,000 to £40,000 once 42 accounts are achieved.
Risk	Video remains high risk because of the saturation of the market experienced in the mid-80s.
Management only	To us it looks like a one-man-band operation but the sample figures provided suggest that it is might offer a reasonable return for owner with management ability

Size and reach
Original company launched: 1984
Overseas connections: None
UK connections: None
Viable for whole UK? Yes
Trade bodies None

Franchisor's formula for success
Each franchisee services a network of independent retail outlets who realise that by offering a choice of video films they are able to boost their weekly takings. To many retailers, the video film boom has increased shop traffic by over 25% with a corresponding increase in sales of additional lines.

Good Franchise Guide comment: We still think it is high risk – talk to other franchisees before proceeding.

Garden Building Centres Ltd

Number of franchisee addresses provided by franchisor: 00

➪ Garage Door Company
Unit 5, Russell Road Industrial Estate, Edinburgh EH11 2NN

A franchise at this address was available recently. Mail sent to this address is accepted, but we have been unable to obtain information either in response to general requests from would-be franchisees or specifically for this publication. In the light of this experience we suggest a certain amount of caution may be in order if the franchise does eventually reappear.

➪ Garden Building Centres Ltd
Coppice Gate, Lye Head, Bewdley, Worcs DY12 2UX
Phone: 0299 266361

The selling of garden buildings from sites leased on a concession basis within garden centres. The concession runs for the same term as the franchise agreement.

Outlets
Number of outlets
Company owned outlets: 03
Franchised: 14
Pilot: 02 started 1986
1988 franchise target: 30 to 36
Current reach:

South	01	South west	00	South east	01
Midlands	12	East Anglia	01	North east	00
North west	00	Scotland	00	Wales	02
N Ireland	00	Rep Ireland	00	I of Man/CI	00

Costs
Total: £25,000
Franchise fee: £5,000
Other charges: No information supplied
Min cash excluding bank: £10,000
Min overdraft required: £15,000
Normal bank advance: Depends on status
Working capital first 2 months: No information supplied
Associated banks: Midland, Barclays, Nat West, Lloyds, Royal Bank of Scotland
Capital items required: Display models and vehicles
Associated leasing co: Franchise Finance

Royalties
Total:
6.0% of turnover
2.5% accounts service
0.0% for advertising fund
8.5% monthly sales

No standing royalty independent of turnover

Bank rating No problems with finance
Territory Radius of site
Franchisees report: Just right
Strings Some ties but lots of freedom
Training 5 days + practical training
3 days + management training
Cost: Nil – included in franchise fee
Training value: Not enough training

George Strachan & Co Ltd (Strachan Studio)

Support	Good
Operating Manual	Good
Profit	On target or better
Risk	Competition from other garden centres
Management only	Could be run by manager but with limited profit

Size and reach

Original company launched:	1985
Overseas connections:	None
UK connections:	Wholly owned subsidiary of D V Pound Garden Buildings Ltd
Viable for whole UK?	Yes
Trade bodies	BFA Register, Conservatory Assn

Franchisor's formula for success

The way many people spend their spare time has led to a multi-billion pound market – the leisure market. The lists of leisure and leisure related activities are endless and home and garden activities account for the biggest sector. The ever increasing range of gardening tools, equipment, furniture, barbecues and add-on products makes this one of the major growth areas on the retail scene.

Inside story from the franchisees

Lots of support from the franchisor in most areas other than 'a total lack of marketing input' reported by one franchisee.

Insider tips

A good franchise but 'look closely at setting up costs of site'

Moans and groans

Training programme not properly structured.

Number of franchisee addresses provided by franchisor: 17

⇨ George Strachan & Co Ltd (Strachan Studio)

Cross Green Way, Leeds LS9 0RS
Phone: 0532 495694

Strachan Studio outlets retail craftsman made quality fitted bedroom furniture. Strachan Studios are acknowledged within the industry as one of the leading and most successful manufacturers and retailers of fitted bedroom furniture.

Outlets
Number of outlets

Company owned outlets:	32
Franchised:	04
Pilot:	00
1988 franchise target:	40

Current reach:

South	06	South west	07	South east	03
Midlands	03	East Anglia	02	North east	04
North west	06	Scotland	02	Wales	01
N Ireland	02	Rep Ireland	02	I of Man/CI	01

Costs

Total	£65,000
Franchise fee:	£5,000
Other charges:	£30,000
Min cash excluding bank:	No information supplied
Min overdraft required:	£5,000
Normal bank advance:	66%
Working capital first 2 months:	£2,000
Associated banks:	Nat West
Capital items required:	Furniture displays
Associated leasing co:	None

Gestetner Ltd

Royalties	0.0% of turnover
	0.0% accounts service
	0.0% for advertising fund
Total	0.0% monthly sales
	Standing royalty independent of turnover on specific non-Strachan items
Bank rating	No information supplied
Territory	Post codes allied to population census
Strings	You are tied to one manufacturer
Training	7 days practical training
	7 days management training
	Cost: £2,500 not included in franchise fee
	Training value: No information supplied
Support	No information supplied
Operating Manual	No information supplied
Profit	Year 1 profit projected as £27,500
Risk	You are tied to the success of one manufacturer although franchisees do sell non-Strachan products
Management only	Could be run by manager but with limited profit in smaller outlets but for larger outlets this could be viewed as offering a chance for a manager to make a good return on investment

Size and reach

Original company launched:	1957
Overseas connections:	None
UK connections:	Strachan Studio Ltd
Viable for whole UK?	Yes
Trade bodies	BFA membership applied for

Franchisor's formula for success
We have a philosophy about furniture that began in 1850 when James Strachan plied his trade as a master wood carver. It was the beginning of generations of fine furniture makers; the Strachans insisted on the highest standards of craftsmanship, investing all the care and expertise available to create collectors' furniture of ultimate quality.

Good Franchise Guide comment: We would have welcomed access to the franchisees in order to validate the first year profit claim.

Number of franchisee addresses provided by franchisor: 00

⇨ Gestetner Ltd
(operating as Copygirl)
210 Euston Road, London NW1

A franchise at this name and address was available in recent years and a few dozen franchises were reported to have been issued, with an eventual target being reported as over 100. Subsequent reports suggest that the franchise has now been withdrawn. Mail sent to this address is accepted, but we have been unable to obtain information either in response to general requests from would-be franchisees or specifically for this publication.

Giltsharp Ltd

⇨ Giltsharp Ltd
Steeple House, Percy Street, Coventry CV1 3BY

A franchise at this address was available recently. Mail sent to this address is accepted, but we have been unable to obtain information either in response to general requests from would-be franchisees or specifically for this publication. In the light of this experience we suggest a certain amount of caution may be in order if the franchise does eventually reappear.

⇨ GKD
Lanrick House, Lanrick Road, London E14 0JF

A franchise at this name and address has been referred to in some publications relating to fitted bedrooms. GKD inform us that they are no longer considering franchising but instead are developing new business through GKD showrooms.

⇨ Global Cleaning Contracts
8 to 10 High Street, Sutton, Surrey SM1 1HN
Phone: 01-643 0146

Office cleaning franchise in which salesmen obtain office cleaning contracts and sell them to contractors who do the cleaning as independent businessmen in their own right

Outlets
Number of outlets
Company owned outlets: 02
Franchised: 24
Pilot: 01 started 1975
1988 franchise target: 30
Current reach:
Area breakdown not supplied

Costs
Total £100,000 minimum
Franchise fee: £8,000
Other charges: Nil
Min cash excluding bank: £40,000
Min overdraft required: Nil
Normal bank advance: 66%
Working capital first 2 months: Nil
Associated banks: All banks
Capital items required: 3 vehicles, 1 computer
Associated leasing co: Universal Consolidated Leasing Ltd

Royalties
7.0% of turnover approx
0.0% accounts service
3.0% for advertising fund approx
Total 10.0% monthly sales
No standing royalty independent of turnover

Bank rating Very helpful
Territory No information supplied by franchisor
Franchisees found territory 'just right'
Strings Some ties but lots of freedom.
Training No practical training
10 days management training
Cost: £1,500 – included in franchise fee
Training value: Adequate

The Gold Vault Ltd

Support	Very good
Operating Manual	Very good
Profit	Most stated their profit was 'as expected' but some were doing 'very very well'
Risk	Not high risk for return
Management only	Proven franchise with good return on investment

Size and reach

Original company launched:	1975
Overseas connections:	None
UK connections:	Subsidiary of the Global Group Ltd (See listing under The Maids)
Viable for whole UK?	'Details on application'
Trade bodies	BFA

Franchisor's formula for success
Service industry with repeat revenue; no shop premises; no Saturdays

Inside story from the franchisees
Very positive response which heaped praise on this franchise. 'This is one of the best franchises if not the best on offer.'

Insider tips
Very hard work and must have the right aptitude; but the rewards are high.

Moans and groans
The manual is very long (but this appears to be unavoidable).

Number of franchisee addresses provided by franchisor: 6

⇨ Gold Car Ltd

Unit 1 Cliffe Industrial Estate, Lewes, Sussex

A franchise at this address has been listed in some publications. The franchisor has now left this address and we have been unable to find any further trace.. In the light of this we suggest a certain amount of caution may be in order if the franchise does reappear.

⇨ The Gold Vault Ltd

in association with PMR Dental Ltd
Pen-y-Bryn House, 26 Sketty Park Road, Sketty, Swansea SA2 9AS
Phone: 0792 207194

Purchasers of precious metals and suppliers of dental products

Outlets

Number of outlets	No information supplied

Costs

Total	No information supplied
Franchise fee:	No information supplied
Other charges:	£2,000

Information supplied to prospective franchisees includes several references to a licence fee, but seemingly no reference to the amount of the fee.

Royalties	No royalties – franchisees receive varying rates of commission on their sales and purchases.
Bank rating	No information supplied
Territory	Geography, population, market potential
Strings	No information supplied

Goldprint Ltd

Training	4 weeks management and practical training Cost: Nil – included in franchise fee Training value: No information supplied
Support	No information supplied
Operating Manual	No information supplied
Profit	Net taxable income shown as £13,475 for year one.
Risk	Difficult to estimate
Management only	One-man-band operation
Size and reach	
Original company launched:	No information supplied
Overseas connections:	None
UK connections:	The link between PMR and The Gold Vault remains (to us at least) unclear
Viable for whole UK?	Yes – we all use dentists
Trade bodies	None

Franchisor's formula for success
The franchise will be at the outset a one man business operating a large exclusive territory promoting and selling dental products direct to the dental surgery and to dental technicians, also purchasing secondary previous metals from the same outlets.

Good Franchise Guide comment: This franchisor did not reply to our letters requesting information. Potential franchisees writing to The Gold Vault receive a four page newspaper from PMR Dental describing an employment agency franchise opportunity. This has nothing to do with employment agencies in the conventional sense but is in fact the Gold Vault, quoting the address as 9 – 10 Walter Road, Swansea SA1 5NF.
Despite the mass of words used – probably more than used by any other franchisor to describe the opportunity, we remain uncertain as to what most of the document means. It is, to say the least, written in a singularly idiosyncratic style in which headlines often have little to do with the text that follows. Perhaps those in the trade will be able to make more sense of it all. PMR, we should add, have been around for some time and have a solid base within the dental market.

Number of franchisee addresses provided by franchisor: 00

⇨ **Goldprint Ltd**
93 Newton Road, Newbury, Berks RG14 7DD
Phone: 0635 35567

Sale of foil printing machines.

Outlets
This company sells a printing machine – there is no territory assigned, and no restriction as to outlets

Costs
Total (cost of machine)	£1,495
Franchise fee:	Nil
No other information supplied	

Royalties
No royalties

Bank rating	Ask for a business development loan
Territory	No territory; your neighbour could buy one the day after you.
Strings	None – you buy the machine
Training	'No previous printing experience is required. The machine is purchased with a package of accessories which allows you to start printing immediately.'

128

Graffiti Management

Support	'Full backup on machine; technical advice; refresher and advanced course in the use of the machine; courses in marketing and sales promotion; monthly newsletter on ideas and opportunities...'
Operating Manual	No information supplied
Profit	Company quotes 5 hours a week as generating £100 profit
Risk	Like we say, anyone can do it
Management only	One-man-band operation

Size and reach

Original company launched:	No information supplied
Overseas connections:	None declared
UK connections:	None
Viable for whole UK?	Yes
Trade bodies	None

Franchisor's formula for success
Demand for foil printed products is huge. One of the biggest markets is promotional items – key rings, diaries and the like. Many foil printers make large profits from bookmatches alone. Exclusive business cards is a wide open repeat business.

Good Franchise Guide comment: Obviously not a franchise, although this company does turn up in some franchise lists. But it is a way of starting a business without too much investment, and without having to pay franchise fees.

Number of franchisee addresses provided by franchisor: 00

➪ Goldstrike Products

142 Cromwell Road, South Kensington, London SW7 4EF

A franchise at this name and address has been listed in some reference books and magazines. Mail sent to this address is accepted, but we have been unable to obtain information either in response to general requests from would-be franchisees or specifically for this publication. In the light of this experience we suggest a certain amount of caution may be in order if the franchise does eventually reappear.

➪ Graffiti Management

5 The Hamiltons, Shaldon, Devon
Phone: No number quoted on headed paper, but enquiries have led us to 0626 872488

Removal of graffiti

Outlets
Number of outlets

Company owned outlets:	01
Franchised:	No information supplied
Pilot:	No information supplied
1988 franchise target:	'Plan to complete licensee recruitment in 1988'
Current reach:	No information supplied

129

The Great Adventure Game

Costs
Total	£13,500
Franchise fee:	£3,000 (rural) to £4,750 (urban)
Other charges:	Materials, tools, insurance
Min cash excluding bank:	No information supplied
Min overdraft required:	£5,000
Normal bank advance:	No information supplied
Working capital first 2 months:	No information supplied
Associated banks:	None
Capital items required:	Vehicle (£3,000)
Associated leasing co:	None

Royalties

'A small royalty is payable'
No further information supplied

Bank rating — No information supplied
Territory — No information supplied
Strings — Complete tie to franchisor for materials
Training — No information supplied
Cost: £250 – not included in franchise fee
Training value: No information supplied

Support — No information supplied
Operating Manual — No information supplied
Profit — Gross margins quoted as 50% + on contracting work 27% to 30% on product sales.
Risk — Vandalism is endemic, and from photographs provided to us the materials appear to work brilliantly
Management only — Insufficient information for us to reach a conclusion

Size and reach
Original company launched:	1984
Overseas connections:	None
UK connections:	None
Viable for whole UK?	Yes (there's vandalism everywhere)
Trade bodies	None

Franchisor's formula for success
Licensees are expected to be sales orientated and demonstrate significant enthusiasm. Some experience of building fabric is necessary. Due to the continuing interest we are generating, it has been decided to provide the first national seminar on vandalism and graffiti, and promote this as part of a national campaign called Vandal Action 1988. This is being supported by a large police force, two substantial public transport organisations and several local authorities.

Good Franchise Guide comment: Rightly or wrongly we always feel concern when a franchisor fails to tell potential franchisees what the royalty is in the initial documents. Against this, the idea of the national campaign looks like a good bit of PR; let's hope it gets the coverage.

Number of franchisee addresses provided by franchisor: 00

⇨ **The Great Adventure Game**
Bergen Mews, 158a Blythe Road, London W14 0HL
Phone: 01-940 7644

'Capture the flag' styled outdoor activity. Franchises are available to people willing to lease at least 25 markers (pistols).

The Great Adventure Game

Outlets
Number of outlets
Company owned outlets: 01
Franchised: 04
Pilot: 01 started 1987
1988 franchise target: No information supplied
Current reach:

South	02	South west	00	South east	03
Midlands	00	East Anglia	00	North east	00
North west	00	Scotland	00	Wales	00
N Ireland	00	Rep Ireland	00	I of Man/CI	00

Costs
Total: £12,006.25
Franchise fee: £7,000
Other charges: No information supplied
Min cash excluding bank: No information supplied
Min overdraft required: No information supplied
Normal bank advance: No information supplied
Working capital first 2 months: No information supplied
Associated banks: None
Capital items required: £4,000* (25 marker pistols)
£1,006.25 visors and accessory packs
Associated leasing co: None
*First year lease

Royalties
No royalties, save yearly lease on pistols (see above)

Bank rating No information supplied

Territory No information supplied

Strings The main tie is to the lease on the pistols. If your venture fails you could be tied to that lease which is costing good money for no return.

Training None mentioned in literature

Support Limited to initial promotional material and demonstration kit

Operating Manual Not mentioned in literature

Profit Players pay £25 per game each. Income also from pellets

Risk Could be a fad; could be badly affected by weather (although one picture shows men in battle fatigues playing the game in snow).

Management only Could be run by manager but with limited profit

Size and reach
Original company launched: No information supplied
Overseas connections: 66% of the board are Canadian. Links with Canada, USA and New Zealand
UK connections: None
Viable for whole UK? Yes – subject to availability of sites
Trade bodies: None

Franchisor's formula for success

Each player is equipped with a marking pistol. Opponents who are shot are eliminated from the game; players shoot one another with water soluble dye pellets propelled from a specially designed semi-automatic marker pistol. We provide the franchisee with a marker that will shoot pellets as quickly as your customer can pull the trigger. During a 5 to 6 hour day your customers will normally use 80 to 100 pellets each. Pellets are retailed at 12.5p each.

Greenbank Finance Ltd

Good Franchise Guide comment: A major restriction is presumably finding the right sites and finding mid-week players during the rainy season, although there are signs that some companies are looking at this type of game as a way of putting their junior managers through their paces. (It sounds like fun but we're glad our company doesn't go to such lengths.)

Number of franchisee addresses provided by franchisor: 00

➪ Greenbank Finance Ltd

34 Victoria Road, Fulwood, Preston, Lancs PR2 4NE

A franchise at this name and address has been listed in some reference books and magazines. The franchise (which has a registered office at 3/5 Mill Lane, Blackburn) has declined to supply *The Good Franchise Guide* with any information. Letters from individuals interested in the franchise are responded to with a standard three line letter which states 'would you be good enough to contact this office by telephone'. No information or background material of any kind is supplied, despite requests.

➪ Group 4 Securities

Farncombe House, Broadway, Worcs
Phone: 0684 295250

A franchise exists as this address. Unfortunately the franchisor has declined to supply information either to ourselves or a would-be franchisee. When the would-be franchisee telephoned she was told that the firm was no longer expanding and there was therefore no point in them replying to requests for information.

➪ Guarantee System UK Ltd

74 Roding road, London Industrial Park, London E6

Carpet dyeing, cleaning, restoration etc

A franchise at this name and address has been listed in some reference books and magazines. Mail sent to this address is now being returned by the Post Office marked 'Gone Away' and the phone number quoted is now used by a different firm. Enquiries have revealed that no forwarding address has been left, although it is possible that the franchise may have been set up once more in another part of the country. In the light of this experience we suggest a certain amount of caution may be in order.

➪ Gun-Point Ltd

Thavies Inn House, 3–4 Holborn Circus, London EC1N 2PL
Phone: 01-353 6167

Specialist repointing system using mechanical method

Outlets
Number of outlets
Company owned outlets: 03
Franchised: 20
Pilot: 01 started 1984
1988 franchise target: 28
Current reach:

South	06	South west	04	South east	05
Midlands	04	East Anglia	01	North east	00
North west	01	Scotland	00	Wales	02
N Ireland	00	Rep Ireland	00	I of Man/CI	00

Gun-Point Ltd

Costs
Total	£14,500
Franchise fee:	£6,000
Other charges:	£8,500
Min cash excluding bank:	£6,000
Min overdraft required:	£5,000
Normal bank advance:	70% total cost
Working capital first 2 months:	£5,000
Associated banks:	None
Capital items required:	Transit vehicle
Associated leasing co:	No information supplied

Royalties

7.0% of turnover
0.0% accounts service
2.5% for advertising fund
Total 9.5% monthly sales

£94 per month standing royalty independent of turnover for rental of patented mortar pump

Bank rating Helpful
Territory Population of 350,000 defined in postcode areas
Strings Some ties but lots of freedom
Training 15 days practical training
5 days management training
Cost: Nil – included in franchise fee
Training value: Adequate

Support Good
Operating Manual Good
Profit As projected
Risk Not a high risk area
Management only Reasonable return for owner with management ability when operating more than one team

Size and reach
Original company launched:	1983
Overseas connections:	None
UK connections:	Subsidiary of commodity brokers
Viable for whole UK?	Yes
Trade bodies	BFA Register

Franchisor's formula for success
With our six million homes more than 50 years old, the market for repointing in the UK is enormous and enduring. The unique Gun-Point equipment has been designed to do the job of repointing efficiently to a high standard, but ultimately it is only as good as the person using it. The major problem in this franchise is in getting the labour to do the work. Those franchisees who can control and discipline labour do well.

Inside story from the franchisees
A sound franchise with good support when required. No major problems in getting work, which can be transferred in from neighbouring franchise areas when one operator is overloaded and another has spare time.

Insider tips
Franchisees must be prepared to work manually at first to gain experience to enable them to manage staff successfully later.

Moans and groans
Low profit in early stages. You must like outdoor work.

Number of franchisee addresses provided by franchisor: 01

Handy Sam Ltd

➪ Handy Sam Ltd

172 Baker Street, Enfield, Middx
Phone: 01-367 7768

A franchise exists at this address. Unfortunately the franchisor has declined to supply information either to ourselves or a would-be franchisee. When the would-be franchisee telephoned she was told that the firm would send some information through the post but so far it has not arrived.

➪ Hayden Timber Ltd

Angel Drove, Ely, Cambs CB7 4DT
Phone: 0353 5764

This franchise has been advertising in some newspapers. The company has informed us that at this stage in its development the company is only covering a very small area of the country, and future plans remain modest.

Hayden Timber manufacture custom designed timber buildings – chalets, sheds, saunas etc. The franchised outlets – The Shed Shops – exist in East Anglia and are moving west into Northants. Lloyds Bank are quoted as being associated with Hayden Timber. 12 franchises exist at present.

➪ Herbal World

North Eastern Chambers, Station Square, Harrogate HG1 1SY
Phone: 0423 525865

Sale of natural products for body care products and ancillary items

Outlets
Number of outlets — No information supplied

Costs
Total — £35,000
Franchise fee: — £5,000
Other charges: — None
Min cash excluding bank: — £17,500
Min overdraft required: — No information supplied
Normal bank advance: — 50%
Working capital first 2 months: — No information supplied
Associated banks: — None
Capital items required: — £14,500 shopfitting
Associated leasing co: — None

Royalties

Total —
5.0% of turnover
0.0% accounts service
0.0% for advertising fund
5.0% monthly sales

No standing royalty independent of turnover

Bank rating — No information supplied
Territory — No information supplied
Strings — Tied to franchisor for all products
Training — A full training course is given mostly 'in the classroom' at the company head office.
Cost: Nil – included in franchise fee
Training value: No information supplied

Highway Windscreens UK Ltd

Support	No information supplied
Operating Manual	No information supplied
Profit	Gross profit quoted as £34,650 on medium sized operation with turnover of £140,000
Risk	A growing market – moderate risk from intensive competiton.
Management only	Reasonable return for owner with management ability
Size and reach	
Original company launched:	No information supplied
Overseas connections:	None
UK connections:	Owned by Herbal World Natural Body Care
Viable for whole UK?	Yes
Trade bodies	None

Franchisor's formula for success

The publicity given to the natural way of living in recent years has created a demand for naturally based products in many areas of our lives. The growth in the market for health foods and vegetarian products reflects the public interest in a healthy body from within. It is logical therefore that the interest should also focus on the body's external appearance and well being, using natural products researched and manufactured without animals being involved in the process at any stage of development.

Good Franchise Guide comment: Competition will grow – if you want to go into this type of market make sure you choose the strongest possible franchise. Others may fall by the wayside.

Number of franchisee addresses provided by franchisor: 00

➪ Highway Windscreens UK Ltd

Arodene House, 41-55 Perth Road, Gants Hill, Ilford, Essex IG2 6BX
Phone: 0296 433113

Windscreen replacement service operating from mobile outlets

Outlets	
Number of outlets	
Company owned outlets:	06
Franchised:	15
Pilot:	02 started 1980
1988 franchise target:	35
Current reach:	
	No information supplied
Costs	
Total	£18,000
Franchise fee:	£7,000
Other charges:	£11,000*
Highway make a £6,000 interest free loan over 2 years for purchase of stock	
Min cash excluding bank:	£6,000
Min overdraft required:	£5,000
Normal bank advance:	50% +
Working capital first 2 months:	£5,000
Associated banks:	'Not particularly'
Capital items required:	Two vans and one Amstrad microcomputer
Associated leasing co:	Lombard
Royalties	
	12.5% of turnover
	0.0% accounts service
	0.0% for advertising fund
Total	12.5% monthly sales
	No standing royalty independent of turnover

Hire Technicians Group Ltd

Bank rating	No information supplied
Territory	Yellow Pages area
Strings	No information supplied
Training	3 weeks practical training
	1 week management training
	Cost: Nil – included in franchise fee
	Training value: No information supplied
Support	No information supplied
Operating Manual	No information supplied
Profit	No information supplied
Risk	Highly competitive area with many rival businesses seeking a place in the market.
Management only	'Proven franchise with good return on investment'

Size and reach

Original company launched:	1973
Overseas connections:	None
UK connections:	None
Viable for whole UK?	Yes and overseas
Trade bodies	None

Franchisor's formula for success
Since its inception Highway has developed a company-owned fleet of mobile workshops, now numbering more than 35 vehicles, covering an area based mainly in London and the south east. In 1979 the first area franchisees were appointed, including the highly successful partnership of Philip Milburn and Tim Harbur who have now developed their operation into a multi-vehicle half-million-pound business.

Good Franchise Guide comment: From the information provided this appears to be a well researched franchise which is growing at an acceptable pace. We would have welcomed the chance to talk to franchisees to see if this opinion is borne out.

Number of franchisee addresses provided by franchisor: 00

➪ Hire Technicians Group Ltd
Chalk Hill House, Chalk Hill, Watford, Herts WD1 4BH

This franchise has been listed in some reference books and magazines. Mail sent to this address is accepted, but we have been unable to obtain information either in response to general requests from would-be franchisees or specifically for this publication. In the light of this experience we suggest a certain amount of caution may be in order if the franchise does eventually reappear.

➪ Holiday Inn International Hotels
Windmill House, 80/82 Windmill Road, Brentford, Middx TW8 0QH
Phone: 01-568 8800

International hotels

Outlets
Number of outlets

Company owned outlets:	02 (UK only)
Franchised:	14 (UK only)
Pilot:	01 started 1970s
1988 franchise target:	20 UK only

Current reach:

South	01	South west	02	South east	06
Midlands	03	East Anglia	00	North east	01
North west	00	Scotland	02	Wales	01
N Ireland	00	Rep Ireland	00	I of Man/CI	00

Home Choose Carpets

Costs
Total	£1.5 million
Franchise fee:	No information supplied
Other charges:	No information supplied
Min cash excluding bank:	£500,000
Min overdraft required:	£1,000,000
Normal bank advance:	No information supplied
Working capital first 2 months:	£100,000
Associated banks:	All major banks
Capital items required:	No information supplied
Associated leasing co:	None

Royalties
	3.0% of turnover
	1.0% marketing service
	1.0% for advertising fund
Total	5.0% monthly sales
	Standing royalty independent of turnover for Holidex Terminal Fee Reservation (no information on cost)

Bank rating	No information supplied
Territory	Company strategy and development plans
Strings	No information supplied
Training	No information supplied
Management only	Proven franchise with good return on investment

Size and reach
Original company launched:	1952
Overseas connections:	1700 hotels (approx) worldwide
UK connections:	Subsidiary of parent company: Holiday Corporation Memphis, Tennessee, USA
Viable for whole UK?	Yes and Europe, Middle East, Africa
Trade bodies	BFA

Good Franchise Guide comment: Only limited information was provided by the franchisor. However, given the fact that this is a worldwide chain of the highest repute, and given that the minimum cost of buying a franchise is £1.5 million, any comments we could make would be superfluous.

Number of franchisee addresses provided by franchisor: 00

⇨ Holland and Barrett

Healthways House, 45 Station Approach, West Byfleet, Surrey KT14 6NE

Holland and Barrett, the health food chain, inform us that they are no longer expanding their franchise network. No further information has been supplied.

⇨ Home Choose Carpets

Jublilee House, Jubilee Court, Dersingham, King's Lynn, Norfolk PE31 6HH
Phone: 0485 43021

Mobile carpet showroom

Outlets
Number of outlets
Company owned outlets:	01
Franchised:	00
Pilot:	No information supplied
1988 franchise target:	No information supplied

Home Tune Ltd

Costs
Total	£7,523
Franchise fee:	£6,600
Other charges:	£923 deposit on van
Min cash excluding bank:	No information supplied
Min overdraft required:	No information supplied
Normal bank advance:	No information supplied
Working capital first 2 months:	No information supplied
Associated banks:	None
Capital items required:	Van ('A mobile showroom')
Associated leasing co:	None

Royalties

10.0% of turnover
0.0% accounts service
0.0% for advertising fund

Total   10.0% monthly sales

No standing royalty independent of turnover

Bank rating   No information supplied
Territory   No information supplied
Strings   No information supplied

Training   10 days practical and management training
Cost: Nil – included in franchise fee
Training value: No information supplied

Support   No information supplied
Operating Manual   No information supplied
Profit   Projected net profit £27,277
Risk   No information supplied
Management only   Little salary to spare for a manager

Size and reach
Original company launched:	1978
Overseas connections:	None
UK connections:	A member of the Derek Sellers Group
Viable for whole UK?	Yes
Trade bodies	None

Franchisor's formula for success
A large operating area, low overheads (business is normally operated from home), no increase in licence fee for second area, no initial stock purchase required.

Good Franchise Guide comment: Derek Sellers Home Choose Carpets Ltd is entitled to print the royal crest on its paper as providing carpets 'By Appointment to Her Majesty Queen Elizabeth II'. Although the company refrained from giving *us* information, the details it sends out to would-be franchisees does include a full list of franchisees already operating – one up to them.

Number of franchisee addresses provided by franchisor: 00

⇨ Home Tune Ltd
77 Mount Ephraim, Tunbridge Wells, Kent TN4 8BS
Phone: 0892 510532

We had this franchise listed at Effingham in Surrey, and although mail is still accepted at that address it appears that the company is in fact at the address and phone number given above. We have not been able to obtain more information thus far.

House of Something Different Group Ltd

⇨ Hot Wheels
1145 Christchurch Road, Bournemouth, Dorset
Phone: 0202 425744

This franchise clearly exists, but they have failed to reply to our questionnaire, and to the written enquiries of our would-be franchisees. When, in desperation, one would-be franchisee telephoned he was told that no information could be given on the phone, but if he would care to write information would be sent . . .

⇨ The House of Regency
5 Kingsway Buildings, Bridgend Industrial Estate, Bridgend, Mid-Glamorgan CF31 3SN

This franchise has been listed in some reference books and magazines. Mail sent to this address is accepted, but we have been unable to obtain information either in response to general requests from would-be franchisees or specifically for this publication. In the light of this experience we suggest a certain amount of caution may be in order if the franchise does eventually reappear.

⇨ House of Skinner (UK) Ltd
Rutherford Square, Bruceford Industrial Park, Livingston, West Lothian EH54 9BU
Phone: 0506 412112

This franchise clearly exists, but they have failed to reply to our questionnaire, and to the written enquiries of our would-be franchisees. When, in desperation, one would-be franchisee telephoned she was told that no information could be given there and then, nor was anything sent through the post. If she would like to phone back later the person who dealt with franchising might be in and would be able to help. . . She did, he wasn't, and she gave up spending money on phone calls.

⇨ House of Something Different Group Ltd
Suite 17, Teme Street, Tenbury Wells, Worcs WR5 8AA
Phone: 0584 811515

Manufacturers and retailers of fireplaces

Outlets
Number of outlets
Company owned outlets: No information supplied
Franchised/company owned: 12; 6 more opening shortly
1988 franchise target: No information supplied
Current reach:

South	00	South west	00	South east	09
Midlands	00	East Anglia	00	North east	00
North west	01	Scotland	02	Wales	00
N Ireland	00	Rep Ireland	00	I of Man/CI	00

House of Wetherby

Costs
Total	£54,268
Franchise fee:	£6,000
Other charges:	£1,800 training
Min cash excluding bank:	No information supplied
Min overdraft required:	No information supplied
Normal bank advance:	70%
Working capital first 2 months:	None
Associated banks:	Most major high street banks
Capital items required:	Van (£1,250 van lease deposit included above)
	Shopfitting (£22,500 included above)
Associated leasing co:	None

Royalties
	5.0% of turnover
	0.0% accounts service
	0.0% for advertising fund
Total	5.0% monthly sales
	No standing royalty independent of turnover

Bank rating	No information supplied
Territory	By negotiation
Strings	Tied totally to the franchisor's products
Training	No information supplied
	Cost: £1,800 not included in franchise fee
	Training value: No information supplied
Support	No information supplied
Operating Manual	No information supplied
Profit	First year gross profit estimated at £120,416
	Nett profit at £33,887
Risk	Mainly that you are selling a style-related product
Management only	Certainly possible

Size and reach
Original company launched:	1978
Overseas connections:	None
UK connections:	None
Viable for whole UK?	Yes
Trade bodies	None

Franchisor's formula for success
House of Something Different has established a reputation over ten years as one of the UK's leading manufacturers and retailers of a superior range of modern and traditional fireplaces, dog grates and frets, gas coal fires, fireside accessories, electric fires, regency mouldings and tudor beams. Franchisees take over fully fitted showrooms under ten year licence agreements.

Good Franchise Guide comment: All franchises which involve opening shops to sell a set product from one manufacturer contain an inherent risk, and we would have welcomed the opportunity to speak to franchisees to establish how closely they got to the impressive first year profit projection.

Number of franchisee addresses provided by franchisor: 00

➪ House of Wetherby

101 – 105 Balby Road, Doncaster DN4 0RE
Phone: 0302 64216

Property renovations

Profit, royalties etc
The following statement is made by the company:

H Plan Manufacturing Co Ltd

Dealer/Company Working Split
On each order to cover cost of sales/marketing and overheads (which includes your salary) 45%
On each order cost of material 15%
The remaining 40% is handled as follows:
Contracting 20%
Company administration charge 5%
Gross (in this case Net) profit 15%

The net profit will be split equally as follows:
Dealer 7.5%
Company 7.5%

Size and reach
Original company launched:	No information supplied
Overseas connections:	No information supplied
UK connections:	No information supplied
Viable for whole UK?	Yes
Trade bodies	Wethertex carries the Agrement Certificate

Franchisor's formula for success
The market leaders in external renovation are offering for the first time an opportunity for you to run your own business while minimising the risk (a failure rate of almost 90%) of starting a small business from the beginning.
The Wethertex heavy duty system is the number 1 system for the transformation of exterior walls. More than 3000 tonnes has already been successfully applied in the UK alone.

Good Franchise Guide comment: We have faithfully reproduced the franchisor's report on dealer/company split, because in all honesty we can't quite make out what it all means.

Number of franchisee addresses provided by franchisor: 00

⇨ H Plan Manufacturing Co Ltd
Dallow Road, Luton, Beds LU1 1SP
Phone: 0582 424222

Furniture manufacture and retailer

Outlets
Number of outlets
Company owned outlets:	No information supplied
Franchised:	No information supplied
Pilot:	No information supplied
1988 franchise target:	No information supplied

Costs
Total	£50,000
Franchise fee:	£3,000
Other charges:	£15,000 lease premium (inc in above)
Min cash excluding bank:	£12,000
Min overdraft required:	No information supplied
Normal bank advance:	70% advance available from franchisor
Working capital first 2 months:	No information supplied
Associated banks:	Nat West, Barclays
Capital items required:	Fixtures and fittings £30,000
Associated leasing co:	None

Royalties
No percentage royalty, 40% sales commision

£20 per week standing charge independent of turnover for the option administration package
£670 per month advertising levy
£500 per year promotional material charge

HPR

Bank rating	No information supplied
Territory	No information supplied
Strings	Total tie to one manufacturer
Training	No information supplied
Support	No information supplied
Operating Manual	No information supplied
Profit	Typical showroom quoted as generating net profit of £61,621
Risk	Established franchisor – limited risk
Management only	No information supplied

Franchisor's formula for success
H Plan Fitted Bedroom Furniture is manufactured using only the highest quality raw materials and fittings. The furniture is of a modular construction which is manufactured to the customer's order from the extensive range of units offered.

Good Franchise Guide comment: Established franchise, but with a lot of set payments unrelated to turnover. We'd like to know what the franchisees think of it.

Number of franchisee addresses provided by franchisor: 00

⇨ HPR

c/o KR Harford, Unit B5, Bumpers Farm Industrial Estate, Chippenham, Wiltshire SN14 6LH

A franchise at this address has been listed in some reference books and magazines. The franchise related to the repair of plastic car bumpers, dash boards, grilles etc. This franchise has now been abandoned and HPR is now the main distributor of plastic welding and retexturing equipment.

Under the new distributorship arrangements HPR offer a half day training course free with each kit purchased. The basic kit starts at £295, and the ex-franchisor makes the following statement:

> 'To replace a car bumper could cost anything from £30 to £300, so think of the potential market just waiting to be tapped from offering a quick and efficient repair service. We already know that the market exists, but don't take our word for it, go out for yourself and do your own market research . . .'

⇨ Hughes, David and Partners

c/o The Franchise Shop Ltd, 26 High Stret, Merstham, Surrey RH1 3EA

Business transfer agent

Outlets	No information supplied
Costs	
Total	£8,000
Franchise fee:	No information supplied
Other charges:	No information supplied
Min cash excluding bank:	£10,000
Min overdraft required:	No information supplied
Normal bank advance:	50%
Working capital first 2 months:	£12,000
Associated banks:	None
Capital items required:	No information supplied
Associated leasing co:	None
Royalties	No information supplied
Training	8 weeks practical and management training
	Cost: Nil – included in franchise fee
	Training value: No information supplied

Support	No information supplied
Operating Manual	No information supplied
Profit	£20,000 profit is projeted in first 18 months
Risk	Becoming a very competitive area indeed with numerous franchises appearing.
Management only	One-man-band operation

Size and reach

Original company launched:	No information supplied
Overseas connections:	None disclosed
UK connections:	None
Viable for whole UK?	Yes
Trade bodies	None

Franchisor's formula for success
Income is derived from the commission earned on the sale of each business.

Good Franchise Guide comment: Little information available, and no response to our requests from the agent. With such competition about we suggest extreme caution.

Number of franchisee addresses provided by franchisor: 00

⇨ Hyde-Barker Travel
Market Street, Mansfield, Notts NG18 1SR
Phone: 0623 31121

Travel shops

Outlets
Number of outlets

Company owned outlets:	01
Franchised:	07
Pilot:	No information supplied
1988 franchise target:	No information supplied

Costs

Total	£12,500
Franchise fee:	£2,500
Other charges:	Nil
Min cash excluding bank:	No information supplied (Total start up capital £35,000)
Min overdraft required:	No information supplied
Normal bank advance:	No information supplied
Working capital first 2 months:	£2,000 (GFG estimate from published figures)
Associated banks:	None
Capital items required:	£10,000 shopfitting (included in £12,500 above)
Associated leasing co:	None

Royalties

	10.0% of turnover
	0.0% accounts service
	0.0% for advertising fund
Total	10.0% monthly sales
	Royalty has a minimum of £3,600 pa irrespective of turnover

Bank rating	No information supplied
Territory	No information supplied
Strings	Very strong ties. Income comes from a 9.5% commission on turnover. 10% of the turnover (not 10% of the commission) has to be paid back as a royalty.
Training	No information at all supplied on training

Hydrosoft Ltd

Support	No information supplied
Operating Manual	No information supplied
Profit	Assuming a small branch and franchisee acting as manager with no staff, net profits *after deduction of salary* start at £1,000 in year 2 and reach £9,000 by year 4. But if another member of staff is needed then maximum drawings would appear to be £9,000. Not very exciting.
Risk	Travel is very high risk, but if you really want to get into the business franchising is probably the only way.
Management only	One-man-band operation (see 'profit' above)

Size and reach

Original company launched:	1948
Overseas connections:	None
UK connections:	None
Viable for whole UK?	Yes
Trade bodies	IATA appointed

Franchisor's formula for success

By judicious buying in bulk from the major operators Hyde-Barker Travel can make special offers to its clients on selected departures. The company has a thriving '55 + club' which caters for the ever-growing needs of the over-55 years age group, a discerning well-to-do and ever more travelled section of the public with more and more spare time on its hands. The company also packages its own most successful programme of 2 – 8 day minibreaks in the UK.

Good Franchise Guide comment: Our information comes from the brochure provided to franchisees, and our reading of the profit potential makes this seem a very modest proposition. Equally we can't see why the franchisor gives the franchisee a 9.5% commission on sales, and then takes 10% of the turnover back again. There might be explanations, and we might have misunderstood their figures, but without comment from the franchisor we are left with our suppositions.

Number of franchisee addresses provided by franchisor: 00

⇨ Hydrosoft Ltd

Unit 1a North Orbital Trading Estate, St Albans, Herts AL1 1XB

This franchise has been listed in some reference books and magazines. Mail sent to this address is accepted, but we have been unable to obtain information either in response to general requests from would-be franchisees or specifically for this publication. In the light of this experience we suggest a certain amount of caution may be in order if the franchise does eventually reappear.

⇨ Ideal Showers

64 Heming Road, Washford Industrial Estate, Redditch, Worcs B98 0EA

This franchise has been listed in some reference books and magazines. Mail sent to this address is accepted, but we have been unable to obtain information either in response to general requests from would-be franchisees or specifically for this publication. In the light of this experience we suggest a certain amount of caution may be in order if the franchise does eventually reappear.

Independent Gas Heating

⇨ Identicar

(also known as Midas Identicar)
Shenley Hall, Rectory Lane, Shenley, Radlett, Herts WD7 9AN
Phone: 09276 4747

Security system for vehicles

A franchise at this address has been listed in some reference books and magazines. The company has informed us that it has moved away from a franchised operation. No further information has been supplied.

⇨ In Business Systems Ltd

Church Street, Seaford, Sussex BN25 1HD
Phone: 0323 897469
'Business automation with a personal touch'

This franchisor did not return a questionnaire to us, but did supply information to would-be franchisees. The following statement is taken from the document supplied: 'Thousands of companies are ready to use microcomputers in many parts of their business – such as stock control, maintenance, word processing, typesetting, accounting, records, to name just a few – the problem is there are, surprisingly, not enough people able to understand particular business applications and provide them with a suitable microcomputer based solution. In Business Systems has addressed that particular problem by recognising that the solution lies not in trying to find scarce computer experienced people and training them in specific business application (sic), but to find people with deep experience in particular areas of business, commerce, engineering and the professions and train them in microcomputing.'

Some financial information is also given:

Year one turnover: £50,000 plus
Total expenditure including salary of approx £10,000 around £50,000, indicating a break-even in the first year.
Negative cash flow for year one will peak at around £13,000, including the payment of the franchise fee of £8,000.

Good Franchise Guide comment: In our view the franchisor uses a lot of words, but doesn't actually say too much. It would be good to have a clear statement of what the franchisee actually does on a day-to-day basis, along with a lot more financial information.

⇨ Independent Gas Heating

21 Market Street, Abergele, Clwyd LL22 7AG

This franchise has been listed in some reference books and magazines. Mail sent to this address is accepted, but we have been unable to obtain information either in response to general requests from would-be franchisees or specifically for this publication. In the light of this experience we suggest a certain amount of caution may be in order if the franchise does eventually reappear.

Infopoint Ltd

⇨ Infopoint Ltd
4 – 5 Hanborough Business Park, Long Hanborough, Oxon OX7 2LH
Phone: 0993 881991

Infopoint is a vending machine that dispenses non-deteriorating glossy plastic cards containing information on the local environment at 50p each

Outlets
Number of outlets
Company owned outlets: 06 units
Franchised: 03 units (one franchisee)
Pilot: 03 units started 1986
1988 franchise target: 200 units (12 franchisees)
Current reach:

South	01	South west	00	South east	00		
Midlands	05	East Anglia	00	North east	03		
North west	00	Scotland	00	Wales	00		
N Ireland	00	Rep Ireland	00	I of Man/CI	00		

Costs
Total   £4,000 approx
Franchise fee: £3,000
Other charges: £280 cardstock, £800 artwork
Min cash excluding bank: No information available
Min overdraft required: No information available
Normal bank advance: 60%
Working capital first 2 months: No information available
Associated banks: Nat West
Capital items required: None, but car is advisable
Associated leasing co: None

Royalties
No royalties: the franchisee is responsible for research and production of artwork to an agreed format. The franchisee contracts to buy 1000 cards per month for a period of one year for each Infopoint unit at a cost of 28p per card. From then on 750 cards need to be ordered per month at 28p with additional supplies at 25p each.

Bank rating	No information supplied
Territory	On city/town basis
Strings	No information supplied
Training	Approx 3 days practical and management training
	Cost: Nil – included in franchise fee (except hotel) Training value: No information supplied
Support	No information supplied
Operating Manual	No information supplied
Profit	No information supplied
Risk	Nothing directly comparable, but if a site fails to produce sufficient sales to pay for the cards the franchisee is committed to buying, then a substantial sum will be lost in a business which then has no re-sale value.
Management only	Reasonable return for owner with management ability

Size and reach
Original company launched: 1986
Overseas connections: None
UK connections: None
Viable for whole UK?   Yes
Trade bodies   BFA Developing member

Franchisor's formula for success
Good rewards for very little workload once it has been established.

The Institute of Tukido

Good Franchise Guide comment: The franchisor supplied us with the name and address of the one franchisee currently operating, but he declined to answer our questions. This is a franchise which could be a dream – set up the information point, prepare the cards and watch the money roll in, but we wonder if there might not be major variations from site to site. We are also worried about maintaining the level of card sales at outdoor sites during the winter months, and at any sites during December. If these concerns are valid (and at present these are merely our suppositions) then the flat fee payments incurred in purchasing a set number of cards might be inappropriate.

Number of franchisee addresses provided by franchisor: 01

⇨ Instagram
Thornfield, Withins, Bolton, Lancs BL2 5DZ

This franchise has been listed in some reference books and magazines. Mail sent to this address is accepted, but we have been unable to obtain information either in response to general requests from would-be franchisees or specifically for this publication. In the light of this experience we suggest a certain amount of caution may be in order if the franchise does eventually reappear.

⇨ Institute of Psychology and Para-Psychology Ltd
56 Lime Grove, Chaddesden, Derbys DE5 1BY

A franchise at this address has been listed in some reference books and magazines. Mail sent to this address is now being returned by the Post Office marked 'Gone Away'. Enquiries have revealed that a director of the company can be reached on 0332 673943 although when we telephoned we were unable to obtain a reply on this number. In the light of this experience we suggest a certain amount of caution may be in order.

Good Franchise Guide comment: Perhaps contact may be made on a higher level.

⇨ The Institute of Tukido
2 Conifer Place, Lenzie, Glasgow G66 4EJ

Information available from Saffery Champness Consultancy Services, Fairfax House, Fulwood Place, Gray's Inn, London WC1V 6UB
Phone: 01-405 2828

We were unable to obtain a reply to our questionnaire from the Institute. Our would-be franchisee received a most curious reply from Saffery Champness, who act as consultants to this firm and Specpoint (qv). The consultants offered to supply information, but first asked the applicant for more information – in particular where the applicant first heard of the Institute, why was he asking about more than one franchise, if he was acting as a spy for another consultancy, and why he was not on the phone. (This last was in fact untrue – he was on the phone but had refrained from putting his number on the letter.)
At this point the editors became involved and declared their interest. The consultant replied in full, explaining his problems with another larger franchise consultancy, and thereafter everyone was happy. Saffery Champness passed our questionnaire on to the Institute but we have not had a reply from them, and thus still lack any information on the franchise.

Insurance Management Services

➪ Insurance Management Services
4 Longstaff Way, Hartford, Huntingdon, Cambs PE18 7XT

This franchise failed to reply to our questionnaires, but did write back to our would-be franchisees. The letter explained that no royalty was required but that 'A one time fee of £1,500 secures an operating manual and assistance with agency applications . . . We have in the past produced three issues of an information booklet which has been out of date the moment it was printed. We have therefore ceased bothering with this and simply invite any enquirers to contact us on 0480 63969 . . .'

The letter does not explain exactly what the franchise is or does. There is a link with Coversure, at the same address.

➪ Intacab Ltd
Service House, West Mayne, Basildon, Essex SS15 6RW
Phone: 0268 415891

Intacab supply would-be franchisees for their taxi franchise with two booklets. The franchise prospectus gives no hard facts, (we learn for example that one of the directors had a grammar school education). The Action File does give details but starts with the statement that 'This Action File is the property of Intacab Ltd the contents of which constitute a confidential disclosure made by Intacab Ltd to prospective franchisees solely for their use in the evaluation of the franchise system . . .'

➪ Interface Network
Bilton Road, Kingsland Industrial Park, Basingstoke, Hants

A franchise at this address offering a computer service has been listed in some reference books and magazines. Mail sent to this address is now being returned by the Post Office marked 'Gone Away' and the phone line has been disconnected by BT. Enquiries have revealed that no forwarding address has been left, although it is possible that the franchise may have been set up once more in another part of the country. In the light of this experience we suggest a certain amount of caution may be in order.

➪ Interlink Express Parcels Ltd
Brunswick Court, Brunswick Square, Bristol BS2 8PE
Phone: 0272 426900

Parcel transport and delivery service

All franchises in the company have been taken up and the franchisor has informed us that they are rarely available on the open market. No further information has been supplied.

➪ International Promotions
20 South End, Croydon, Surrey CR0 1DN

A franchise at this name and address has been listed in some reference books and magazines. Mail sent to this address is now being returned by the Post Office marked 'Gone Away'. Enquiries have revealed that no forwarding address has been left, although it is possible that the franchise may have been set up once more in another part of the country. In the light of this experience we suggest a certain amount of caution may be in order.

Intoto Ltd
Wakefield Road, Gildersome, Leeds LS27 0QW
Phone: 0532 524131

Intoto is the trading name of a chain of independently owned quality kitchen centres acting either as solus stores or stores-within-stores and offering design, installation, tiles, accessories and furniture. Kitchens are manufactured by Wellmann and electrical appliances by Philips.

Outlets
Number of outlets
Company owned outlets: 01
Franchised: 33
Pilot: 01 started 1980
1988 franchise target: 50
Current reach:

South	02	South west	03	South east	07
Midlands	04	East Anglia	02	North east	05
North west	03	Scotland	08	Wales	00
N Ireland	00	Rep Ireland	00	I of Man/CI	00

Costs
Total: £35,000 to £40,000
Franchise fee: £5,000
Other charges: £30,000 to £35,000
Min cash excluding bank: £10,000 to £15,000
Min overdraft required: £10,000 to £15,000
Normal bank advance: Usually £30,000 to £40,000 depending on status
Working capital first 2 months: £5,000 to £10,000
Associated banks: Barclays, Nat West
Capital items required: All included in set-up cost
Associated leasing co: None

Royalties
Total:
0.0% of turnover
0.0% accounts service
0.0% for advertising fund
0.0% monthly sales
£250 per month standing royalty independent of turnover

Bank rating No problems with finance

Territory Approx 200,000 population
Franchisees report: Just right

Strings Strong ties to franchisor

Training 2 months practical training and management training plus on going 3 days per month
Cost: Nil – included in franchise fee
Training value: Adequate

Support Good

Operating Manual Good but not up to date

Profit An exceptionlly varied response from franchisees ranging from 'we are doing very very well indeed' to 'close to bankruptcy'

Risk Highly competitive area. Responses suggest that the input and ability of the franchisee, combined with local conditions, can have a fundamental effect on the ability of the franchisee to make money.

Management only Reasonable return for owner with management ability

Isodan (UK) Ltd

Size and reach
Original company launched: 1980
Overseas connections: Holding company is German
UK connections: None
Viable for whole UK? Yes
Trade bodies: BEA

Franchisor's formula for success
Intoto stores retail quality rigid kitchens, providing to the customer a complete service from design through to installation of kitchens and built-in appliances, with furniture manufactured by probably the most progressive kitchen manufacturer in Germany.

Inside story from the franchisees
The response indicate that some people are doing very well and feel it is a good franchise. Even those not doing very well do not blame the franchisor and feel it is the local market causing problems.

Insider tips
Undertake as much market research for your territory as possible.

Moans and groans
The manual: basically good but badly out of date.

Number of franchisee addresses provided by franchisor: 33

⇨ Isodan (UK) Ltd

55b Colebrook Road, Royal Tunbridge Wells, Kent TN4 9DP
Phone: 0892 44822

Wall insulation system

Outlets
Number of outlets
Company owned outlets: 00
Franchised: Over 60
Pilot: No information supplied
1988 franchise target: No information supplied

Costs
Total: £7,500
Franchise fee: £3,500
Other charges: No information supplied
Min cash excluding bank: Nil
Min overdraft required: No information supplied
Normal bank advance: 100%
Working capital first 2 months: No information supplied
Associated banks: None
Capital items required: Vehicle and tools (operating machine provided)
Associated leasing co: None

Royalties
Total:
0.0% of turnover
0.0% accounts service
0.0% for advertising fund
0.0% monthly sales

No standing royalty independent of turnover

Bank rating No information supplied
Territory No information supplied
Strings Tied to Isodan system

Kall-Kwik Printing (UK) Ltd

Training	No information supplied
Support	No information supplied
Operating Manual	No information supplied
Profit	No information supplied
Risk	An exclusive system, so risk should be minimised
Management only	No information supplied

Size and reach

Original company launched:	1973
Overseas connections:	None
UK connections:	None
Viable for whole UK?	Yes
Trade bodies	None

Franchisor's formula for success
No information supplied

Good Franchise Guide comment: As with all exclusive systems they can be a great success if the materials and machinery really work at a price people will pay. There are no royalties and so we presume that the franchisor simply gives a discount on the sales achieved by each franchisee.

Number of franchisee addresses provided by franchisor: 00

⇨ Janus Introduction Bureaux

8 Gaskell Avenue, Knutsford, Cheshire
Phone: 0565 52516

Introduction bureau

Janus have informed us that they have set up two franchisees, but both have subsequently closed following poor results. The franchisor has now ceased promoting the franchise for the time being pending a revision of the operation in order to ensure that further difficulties are not encountered. They do indicate that they are willing to discuss further franchising with any interested parties.

⇨ Kall-Kwik Printing (UK) Ltd

Kall-Kwik House, 106 Pembroke Road, Ruislip, Middx HA4 8NW
Phone: 0895 632700

Print, copy and design service

Outlets
Number of outlets

Company owned outlets:	01
Franchised:	130
Pilot:	02 started 1974/5
1988 franchise target:	160

Current reach:

South	11	South west	09	South east	71
Midlands	10	East Anglia	04	North east	06
North west	09	Scotland	07	Wales	02
N Ireland	00	Rep Ireland	00	I of Man/CI	01

Kall-Kwik Printing (UK) Ltd

Costs
Total	£80,000 including working capital
Franchise fee:	£12,000
Other charges:	£23,850 equipment, £16,000 shopfitting £4,000 stock/marketing
Min cash excluding bank:	up to £30,000
Min overdraft required:	up to £10,000
Normal bank advance:	66% (around £60,000)
Working capital first 2 months:	£9,670
Associated banks:	5 major joint stock banks
Capital items required:	Equipment (£24,000) shopfitting (£16,000)
Associated leasing co:	None

Royalties

Total
6.0% of turnover
0.0% accounts service
4.0% for advertising fund
10.0% monthly sales

No standing royalty independent of turnover

Bank rating — No information supplied
Territory — No information supplied
Strings — No information supplied

Training
12 days practical training
25 days management training
Cost: £3,000 – included in franchise fee
Training value: No information supplied

Support — No information supplied
Operating Manual — No information supplied
Profit — 'Once established the level of pre-tax profitability achievable should run at 20–25% of sales turnover.'
Risk — High level of competition, but apparently an ever growing demand.
Management only — Proven franchise with good return on investment

Size and reach
Original company launched:	1978 (USA 1971)
Overseas connections:	Over 1100 outlets in USA, Canada, Australia, S Africa, Israel
UK connections:	None
Viable for whole UK?	All commercial areas
Trade bodies	None

Franchisor's formula for success
Quick printing has advantages of the traditional printing industry in that it offers accessibility through its high street shops; speed through the use of the latest technology; and that vital element no machine will ever replace, personal service.

Inside story from the franchisees
Kall Kwik was virtually the only franchise to supply a leaflet containing commentaries from franchisees, with the franchisees identified by name and address, which we think says a lot for their willingness to stand up and be counted. On the other hand, they refused to send us a list of franchisees. Naturally we do not suspect there is anything wrong with the selection chosen by Kall-Kwik, but it would have been nice for us to be able to undertake our own research.

Insider tips
All letters supplied by franchisor as testimonials speak of the great success they have had. No special tips, no moans and groans.

Number of franchisee addresses provided by franchisor: 00

⇨ Keith Hall Hairdressing

2 Oxford Street, Long Eaton, Nottingham NG10 1JR

A franchise at this name and address has been listed in some reference books and magazines. Mail sent to this address is now being returned by the Post Office marked 'Gone Away'. Enquiries have revealed that no forwarding address has been left, although it is possible that the franchise may have been set up once more in another part of the country. In the light of this experience we suggest a certain amount of caution may be in order.

⇨ Kemmytex

129 Windham Road, Bournemouth, Dorset BH1 4RJ
Phone: 0202 304875

Manufacturers and suppliers of chemical render for external walls of buildings

Outlets
Number of outlets
Company owned outlets:	No information supplied
Franchised:	14
Pilot:	No information supplied
1988 franchise target:	No information supplied

Costs
Total	£15,000

Note: Franchisor states 'We ask for a minimum investment of £15,000 for which we set you up totally in your own business.' No further information supplied.

Franchise fee:	No information supplied
Other charges:	No information supplied
Min cash excluding bank:	Presumably zero – see below
Min overdraft required:	No information supplied
Normal bank advance:	'100% of the investment can be raised via the Building Society'
Working capital first 2 months:	No information supplied
Associated banks:	None
Capital items required:	None
Associated leasing co:	None

Royalties
No information supplied

Bank rating	No information supplied
Territory	No information supplied
Strings	Total tie to one product
Training	2 weeks practical and management training
	Cost: Nil – included in franchise fee
	Training value: No information supplied
Support	No information supplied
Operating Manual	No information supplied
Profit	All current franchisees reported to be netting over £1,000 per week
Risk	All depends on the viability of the product
Management only	One-man-band operation

Size and reach
Original company launched:	1980
Overseas connections:	None
UK connections:	None
Viable for whole UK?	Yes
Trade bodies	None

Kentucky Fried Chicken

Franchisor's formula for success
Kemmytex is a totally maintenance free coating and is backed with a full 15 year unconditional guarantee, but this said we know that if the product is applied correctly it will protect the building for over 30 years.

Good Franchise Guide comment: Only take this up if you are sure that the product is as good as it is claimed to be. We are dubious about any business which is set up on a 100% loan. And why via a building society? If the suggestion is that money can be raised as a mortgage against your house, then beware – you may not qualify for tax relief, and if your business folds you could lose the roof over your head.

Number of franchisee addresses provided by franchisor: 00

⇨ Kentucky Fried Chicken
Wicat House, 403 London Road, Camberley, Surrey GU15 3HL
Phone: 0276 686151

This franchise has informed us that it is not currently seeking new franchisees. According to the authoritative *Taking up a Franchise* the franchisor has, in recent years, been closing franchised outlets. It is reported that as the franchise changes to a restaurant type chain more outlets will close. The franchisor has formed a joint venture with Trusthouse Forte to operate the chain and meanwhile ex-franchisees are continuing to trade but under new names. A pressure group exists to protect the interests of the remaining franchisees.

⇨ Kimberleys
Unit 3, Stafford Park, Hornchurch, Essex RM11 2SJ
Phone: 040 24 76078

This company has informed us that it is no longer offering franchises.

⇨ Kis Services
Kis House, South Bank Business Centre, Unit A, Nine Elms Lane, London SW8 5BA
Phone: 01-627 4000

Rapid development of photographs

This franchise has been listed in some reference books and magazines. However, material sent to would-be franchisees states: 'Kis respects the freedom of its customers to own a Kis Photo system, you are not forced to comply with a long series of obligations . . . to pay for the name . . . to report your sales . . . to pay sales percentages and on and on and on. 'To the contrary with Kis Photo equipment KIS supplies an extensive package of publicity and advertising materials perfectly adapted to help start-up and maintain an "Instant Service" operation.'

Good Franchise Guide comment: Not a franchise.

The Knight Guard Ltd

➪ Kitchen Design and Advice
Unit A4, North Orbital Trading Estate, Napsbury Lane, St Albans, Herts
Phone: 0727 37227

This franchise clearly exists, but they have failed to reply to our questionnaire, and to the written enquiries of our would-be franchisees. When, in desperation, one would-be franchisee telephoned she was told that no information could be given there and then as the person she needed to speak to was not there, nor was anything sent through the post. If she would like to phone back later the person who dealt with franchising might be in and would be able to help . . . She did try later, but was unable to make further progress.

➪ Kitchen Gear Ltd
65 Deansgate, Manchester M3 2BW
Phone: 061-834 5348

Kitchen Gear do not operate as a franchise, despite what has been said in various journals and magazines. In effect the company commissioned a study of franchising, and is still evaluating the results – it is unlikely that there will be a decision before 1989.

➪ The Knight Guard Ltd
14 – 16 Tonbridge Road, Maidstone, Kent ME16 8RP
Phone: 0622 686363

Security service with uniformed and plain clothes guards

Outlets
Number of outlets
Company owned outlets: No information supplied
Franchised: No information supplied
Pilot: No information supplied
1988 franchise target: No information supplied

Costs
Total No information supplied
Franchise fee: £9,750
No other information provided on costs

Royalties
Up to £250,000 gross income 10.0%
£250,000 to £500,000 gross income 7.5%
£500,000 and above gross income 5.0%

Bank rating No information supplied
Territory No information supplied
Strings No information supplied

Training 4 day practical and management training
Cost: Nil – included in franchise fee
Training value: No information supplied

Support No information supplied
Operating Manual No information supplied
Profit Profit yield quoted at £7,737 per year at lowest level

Risk Possibly more physical than financial
Management only No information supplied

155

Knobs & Knockers Franchising Ltd

Size and reach
Original company launched: No information supplied
Overseas connections: None
UK connections: None
Viable for whole UK?   Yes
Trade bodies   None

Franchisor's formula for success
There is no doubt that the need and therefore the market for manpower security is expanding. The incidence of crime and wanton vandalism is increasing at an alarming rate. Our excellent police force – which is without doubt overworked, undermanned and underfunded – cannot be expected to cope with the current tide.

Good Franchise Guide comment: Hard to judge on the information supplied

Number of franchisee addresses provided by franchisor: 00

⇨ **Knobs & Knockers Franchising Ltd**
36–40 York Way, London N1 9AB
Phone: 01-278 8925

Leading retailers in the field of elegant and distinctive internal and external door furniture

Outlets
Number of outlets
Company owned outlets: 65
Franchised: 05
Pilot: 01 started 1986
1988 franchise target: 80
Current reach:

South	10	South west	08	South east	25
Midlands	06	East Anglia	02	North east	05
North west	05	Scotland	02	Wales	00
N Ireland	00	Rep Ireland	00	I of Man/CI	00

Costs
Total   No information supplied
Franchise fee: £7,000
Other charges: No information supplied
Min cash excluding bank: £20,000
Min overdraft required: £55,000 to £60,000
Normal bank advance: 70%
Working capital first 2 months: No infomation supplied
Associated banks: None
Capital items required: Shopfitting
Associated leasing co: None

Royalties
                             7.5% of turnover
                             0.0% accounts service
                             0.0% for advertising fund
Total   7.5% monthly sales

                             No standing royalty independent of turnover

Bank rating   No information supplied
Territory   Non-territorial; town/city agreed
Strings   Strong ties for products
Training   10 days practical training
                              3 days management training
                              Cost: Nil – included in franchise fee
                              Training value: No information supplied

KVC Franchise UK

Support	No information supplied
Operating Manual	No information supplied
Profit	First year projected profit shown as £4,224
Risk	Limited – the large number of company owned outlets shows how well the package has been prepared
Management only	Owner-operator essential to develop business in early stages

Size and reach

Original company launched:	1969
Overseas connections:	None
UK connections:	None
Viable for whole UK?	Yes
Trade bodies	BFA

Franchisor's formula for success
The success of Knobs & Knockers is due to our experience in the selection and display of merchandise together with proven attractive pricing. This has made Knobs & Knockers the leading retail group specialising in internal and external door furniture in brass, black iron and porcelain together with co-ordinating brass light switches, dimmers and sockets.

Good Franchise Guide comment: None of the outlets we contacted was willing to discuss matters with us.

Number of franchisee addresses provided by franchisor: 18 (plus large number of instore shops) but no indication of which were the 5 franchised outlets.

⇨ KVC Franchise UK
Lakeside House, Triangle, Ripponden, West Yorks HX6 3LZ
Phone: No phone number quoted on literature

Car valeting

Outlets

Number of outlets	No information supplied

Costs

Total	£15,000

Note the £15,000 is described as including everything needed for the job. No further information supplied.

Associated banks:	Lloyds
Capital items required:	No information supplied
Associated leasing co:	'Access to all major sources of finance'

Royalties

No information supplied

Bank rating	No information supplied
Territory	No information supplied
Strings	No information supplied
Training	4 weeks practical and management training Cost: Nil – included in franchise fee Training value: No information supplied
Support	No information supplied
Operating Manual	No information supplied
Profit	Gross profit quoted at under £4,000
Risk	Ever increasing number of competitors, from well organised franchises like AutoSheen to local non-franchised companies
Management only	One-man-band operation

Kwik Silver Print

Size and reach
Original company launched:	1968
Overseas connections:	None
UK connections:	Owned by Kleenacar Valeting Co Ltd
Viable for whole UK?	Yes
Trade bodies	None

Franchisor's formula for success
Expensive office and cleaning bays with the costs they incur are not required as 90% of the work is carried out on-site at your contract's own premises. With paper work being kept to a minimum the administration can be controlled from your own home. No expensive additional vehicle is required as the equipment selected by KVC can be transported in the average family car.

Good Franchise Guide comment: application brochure is well detailed in some aspects (eg training) and poor on others (such as finance). The phone number quoted in some reference books (0422 834179) has been disconnected. Directory Enquiries do not have this firm listed under KVC.

Number of franchisee addresses provided by franchisor: 00

⇨ **Kwik Silver Print**
263 Commercial Road, Portsmouth, Hants PO1 4BP
Phone: 0705 730205

Print mini-lab franchise

Outlets
Number of outlets	No information supplied
1988 franchise target:	Leaflet supplied to franchisees lists 64 towns and states a further 200 will be available from August 1988

Costs
Franchise fee:	£10,000

No other financial information supplied

Royalties
	7.5% of turnover
	0.0% accounts service
	0.0% for advertising fund
Total	7.5% monthly sales

Profit	On 70 films a day net profit is quoted at £37,809
Risk	More competition appears almost daily.
Management only	No information supplied

Size and reach
Original company launched:	No information supplied
Overseas connections:	None
UK connections:	Part of Windsor Estates group owned by Cavels Ltd
Viable for whole UK?	Yes
Trade bodies	None

Good Franchise Guide comment: The licence includes the right to use the Kodak Express Quality Control service and much will depend on the nature of the relationship with Kodak. Otherwise what we find is a glossy brochure containing a lot about franchising in general and virtually nothing about this franchise in particular.

Number of franchisee addresses provided by franchisor: 00

Kwik Strip (UK) Ltd

Units 1/2 The 306 Estate, 242 Broomhill Road, Brislington, Bristol BS4 5RA
Phone: 0272 772470 or 716537

Suppliers of a process that strips paint, varnish and polyurethanes from wood and metal

Outlets
Number of outlets
Company owned outlets: 01
Franchised: 17
Pilot: 01 started 1982
1988 franchise target: 24
Current reach:

South	01	South west	04	South east	07		
Midlands	04	East Anglia	00	North east	00		
North west	00	Scotland	01	Wales	01		
N Ireland	00	Rep Ireland	00	I of Man/CI	00		

Costs
Total: £8,500
Franchise fee: £3,000
Other charges: £5,500
Min cash excluding bank: £6,000
Min overdraft required: £2,000
Normal bank advance: 66%
Working capital first 2 months: £4,000
Associated banks: All major banks
Capital items required: Lease of vehicle (quarter's rent up front)
Associated leasing co: None

Royalties

5.0% of turnover
0.0% accounts service
0.0% for advertising fund
Total 5.0% monthly sales

No standing royalty independent of turnover

Bank rating Very helpful. 'Practically threw the stuff at me'
Territory Based on population density; franchisee view: 'About right'
Strings Strong ties for chemicals etc
Training 3 days practical training
2 days management training
Cost: Nil – included in franchise fee
Training value: Adequate

Support Poor
Operating Manual Poor
Profit Lower than projected in most cases
Risk Could be risky if fashion for stripped pine fades
Management only Could be run by manager but with limited profit

Size and reach
Original company launched: 1982
Overseas connections: None
UK connections: None
Viable for whole UK? Yes
Trade bodies None

Franchisor's formula for success
Main advantages are that no knowledge of woods or furniture restoration is rquired, and no credit is given to customers.

La Mama Ltd

Inside story from the franchisees
Good response to our questionnaire. General feeling is that it is a good franchise, but support is a bit weak and profits less than hoped for.

Insider tips
It helps to be practically minded. Franchisees must ensure that they really do have enough capital to get through the first year. Over-estimate your financial needs.

Moans and groans
Not enough practical training.

Number of franchisee addresses provided by franchisor: 18

⇨ La Mama Ltd

70 – 78 York Way, Kings Cross, London N1 9AG

Maternity clothes shops

In November 1985 the Young's Franchise Group which included La Mama went into receivership. Total group debts approach £4 million. The group was then bought by Mr C Spencer who pulled out of La Mama leaving the franchisees on their own. Our latest information is that under a quarter of the La Mama franchisees survive. The original franchisor was a senior member of the BFA. Loans for most franchisees came from National Westminster Bank.

⇨ Lady K Salon Services Ltd

Manor Farmhouse, Charity Lane, Carlton Scroop, Grantham, Lincs NG32 2AT
Phone: 0400 50012

Mobile hair salon supplies

Outlets
Number of outlets	No information supplied

Costs
Total	£7,500
Franchise fee:	£3,500
Other charges:	£3,000 stock
Min cash excluding bank:	No information supplied
Min overdraft required:	No information supplied
Normal bank advance:	No information supplied
Working capital first 2 months:	No information supplied
Associated banks:	None
Capital items required:	Van
Associated leasing co:	None

Royalties
No royalties

Bank rating	No information supplied
Territory	No information supplied
Strings	Tied to franchisor for stock selection
Training	No information supplied
Support	No information supplied
Operating Manual	No information supplied
Profit	'Your potential earnings £12,000 to £20,000'
Risk	Very dependent on products
Management only	One-man-band operation

Late Late Supershop

Size and reach
Original company launched: 1985
Overseas connections: None
UK connections: Owned by Hairdressing Franchises Ltd
Viable for whole UK? Yes
Trade bodies None

Franchisor's formula for success
A new concept in the direct to consumer business involving supplies to hairdressing salons from a fully fitted walk in van, with our own distinctive livery on all sides.

Insider tips
This franchise also advertises as Hairdressing Franchises Ltd.

Good Franchise Guide comment: Some difficulty in finding this franchise, as two other addresses are listed in other reference books: Unit 5, Belton Lane, Grantham, Lincs, and Lancaster House, Ancaster, Grantham, Lincs. What we wonder is why the franchisor doesn't bother to have his mail forwarded each time he moves.

Number of franchisee addresses provided by franchisor: 00

➪ Lamacrest Ltd
Crown Works, Cold Bath Road, Harrogate, North Yorks HG2 0NR

This franchise has been listed in some reference books and magazines. Mail sent to this address is accepted, but we have been unable to obtain information either in response to general requests from would-be franchisees or specifically for this publication. In the light of this experience we suggest a certain amount of caution may be in order if the franchise does eventually reappear.

➪ Late Late Supershop
CWS Ltd, New Century House, PO Box 53, Manchester M60 4ES
Phone: 061-834 1212 ext 5417

Retail stores selling highest quality branded and Co-op brand goods at competitive prices, open extended hours

Outlets
Number of outlets
Company owned outlets: 02
Franchised: 10
Pilot: 02 started 1984 and 1986
1988 franchise target: No information available
Current reach:

South	00	South west	00	South east	06
Midlands	00	East Anglia	00	North east	00
North west	04	Scotland	02	Wales	00
N Ireland	00	Rep Ireland	00	I of Man/CI	00

Costs
Total: £75,000 approx
Franchise fee: £8,000
Other charges: No details supplied
Min cash excluding bank: 30%
Min overdraft required: No details supplied
Normal bank advance: 70%
Working capital first 2 months: £2,000
Associated banks: Co-operative Bank
Capital items required: Fixtures and fittings
Associated leasing co: None

Learning Point

Royalties
	1.5% of turnover
	0.0% accounts service
	0.5% for advertising fund
Total	2.0% monthly sales
	No standing royalty independent of turnover

Bank rating	There should be no problem since the Co-op has its own bank which lends to franchisees
Territory	No information supplied
Strings	Tied to CWS but you do have the option to include additional sales through wines, papers, car accesories, video club, DIY etc
Training	16 days practical training
	4 days management training
	Cost: Nil – included in franchise fee
	Training value: No information supplied
Support	No information supplied
Operating Manual	No information supplied
Profit	High potential
Risk	Small – the Co-ops are hardly likely to go bust
Management only	No information supplied

Size and reach
Original company launched:	1984
Overseas connections:	None
UK connections:	Subsidiary of Co-operative Wholesale Society Ltd
Viable for whole UK?	South east, north west and Scotland
Trade bodies	BFA

Franchisor's formula for success

Today's shoppers are usually in a hurry and often don't get time to shop properly – or when they do, they forget things. The Late Late Supershop is open from early morning until late at night – 8am till at least 8pm, six or seven days a week, 52 weeks a year. Shoppers will soon learn they can reply on their local Supershop – in fact will come to depend on it.

Good Franchise Guide comment: Although this franchise did not send us a list of franchisees they did (unlike so many other franchisors) have the courtesy to phone and explain their decision. It is difficult to imagine the Co-op not getting its franchise act right, especially when it owns the bank that lends the money.

Number of franchisee addresses provided by franchisor: 00

➪ Learning Point

8 Castillian Terrace, Northants NN1 1LD
Phone: 0604 37311

Learning Point did not respond to our questionnaires, but did write back to our would-be franchisee stating that 'at this present time we are no longer seeking applicants'. No reason or explanation was given.

➪ Lomax Designs Ltd

Previously listed at: 44 St John Street London EC1M 4DT

Vehicle security marking system

M & B Marquees Ltd

A franchise at this address has been listed in some reference books and magazines. Enquiries have revealed that the company is now trading from 59 Charlotte Road, London EC2A 3QT, phone 01-739 6486. The company is not a franchise, although it does sell the vehicle security equipment described in some magazines as part of the franchise.

⇨ London Stone
Southampton House, 192 – 206 York Road, London SW11 3SA

This franchise has been listed in some reference books and magazines. Mail sent to this address is accepted, but we have been unable to obtain information either in response to general requests from would-be franchisees or specifically for this publication. In the light of this experience we suggest a certain amount of caution may be in order if the franchise does eventually reappear.

⇨ Lyons Maid Ltd
Bridge Park, Oldfield Lane North, Greenford, Middx UB6 0BA
Phone: 01-575 2004

Lyons Maid offer three franchise packages: Mister Softee (soft ice cream), Lyons Maid (scooped ice cream) and Tonibell (soft ice cream).
There are no fees or royalties.

Would-be franchisees are given the following information in response to their enquiries:

A franchise gives the franchisee the full use of the trade marks of the appropriate trading company on mobile sales vehicles within an agreed permitted territory. It also gives him preferential trading terms, together with a support package. In return the franchisee agrees to sell only that company's products from the sales vehicle . . .
The financial requirement for setting up in business is largely dependent upon the number of sales vehicles envisaged. It is possible to obtain a good second-hand scooping van for as little as £3,000 but a soft serve van would be double that figure. Essential back-up equipment such as storage cabinets for ice cream would cost about £500 for a small operation.
Profitability can vary between 50% and 80% on return of capital dependent upon the type of franchise.

No other information has been supplied.

Good Franchise Guide comment: Beware! They sent the local rep round, and that on the basis of a two line letter of enquiry.

⇨ M & B Marquees Ltd
Unit 16 Swinborne Court, Burnt Mills Industrial Estate, Basildon, Essex SS13 1QA
Phone: 0268 728361

Hire of free standing marquees without ropes or stakes, plus matting, floors, stages, platforms, tables, chairs, patio and garden furniture. Also the provider of catering, photographic, music and other services.

Outlets
Number of outlets
Company owned outlets: 01
Franchised: 13
Pilot: 00
1988 franchise target: 15 to 18

163

M & B Marquees Ltd

Current reach:

South	01	South west	03	South east	03
Midlands	03	East Anglia	02	North east	00
North west	01	Scotland	00	Wales	00
N Ireland	00	Rep Ireland	00	I of Man/CI	00

Costs
Total	£20,000
Franchise fee:	£16,900
Other charges:	No information supplied
Min cash excluding bank:	£8,000 to £10,000
Min overdraft required:	No information supplied
Normal bank advance:	66%
Working capital first 2 months:	£1,000
Associated banks:	Barclays
Capital items required:	None
Associated leasing co:	None

Royalties

Total:
9.0% of turnover
0.0% accounts service
1.0% for advertising fund after 1st year
10.0% monthly sales from 2nd year

No standing royalty independent of turnover

Bank rating No information supplied

Territory Approx 30 miles radius – more if population is low

Strings Strong ties for product

Training
1 week practical training
1 week management training
Cost: £1,200 – included in franchise fee
Training value: No information supplied

Support No information supplied

Operating Manual No information supplied

Profit 'Complete financial projections, which tend to disclose many of our operational secrets, will only be presented in detail . . . at a meeting, however as a guide during your first full year in business you should expect to achieve a turnover in the region of £35,000 from marquee hire alone, producing a net profit in excess of £13,000.'

Risk Some competition, but not a massive amount

Management only Reasonable return for owner with management ability

Size and reach
Original company launched:	1977
Overseas connections:	None
UK connections:	None
Viable for whole UK?	Yes
Trade bodies	Applied to BFA

Franchisor's formula for success
Probably the most important aspect of the marquees is that they can be erected on soft or hard surfaces. Lawn or concrete, wooden flooring or tarmac, it makes no difference as the rigid frame structure is designed to allow the marquee to be free standing. They are made from easily cleaned and maintained material to BSI standards with little or no stock depreciation.

Good Franchise Guide comment: This sounds a good franchise – but we notice that M & B shares with Modular Marquees (qv) an excessive desire for secrecy. Could it be, we wonder, that they are trying to hide information from each other?

Number of franchisee addresses provided by franchisor: 00

⇨ Magic Windshields (UK)

13 Beehive Lane, Gants Hill, Ilford, Essex IG1 3RG
Phone: 01-518 6430

Windscreen repairs

Outlets
Number of outlets
Company owned outlets: 02
Franchised: 06
Pilot: 01 started 1984
1988 franchise target: 20
Current reach:

South	02	South west	00	South east	03
Midlands	01	East Anglia	00	North east	00
North west	00	Scotland	00	Wales	00
N Ireland	01	Rep Ireland	01	I of Man/CI	00

Costs
Total: No information supplied
Franchise fee: £5,000
Other charges: None
Min cash excluding bank: No information supplied
Min overdraft required: No information supplied
Normal bank advance: No information supplied
Working capital first 2 months: £500
Associated banks: None
Capital items required: Car or van
Associated leasing co: Yes – but no details given

Royalties

Total:
0.0% of turnover
0.0% accounts service
0.0% for advertising fund
0.0% monthly sales

No standing royalty independent of turnover

Advertising royalties may be added later.

Bank rating: No information supplied
Territory: Appropriate Yellow Pages area
Strings: No information supplied

Training: 30 hours practical training
10 hours management training
Cost: Nil – included in franchise fee
Training value: No information supplied

Support: No information supplied
Operating Manual: No information supplied
Profit: We calculate £21,000 net profit in year one (derived from figures supplied)

Risk: Modest
Management only: Reasonable return for owner with management ability

Size and reach
Original company launched: 1984
Overseas connections: Magic Windshield USA
UK connections: None
Viable for whole UK? Yes
Trade bodies: None

Magna-Dry

Franchisor's formula for success
When a laminated windshield is struck by a stone at high velocity, because of the plastic/glass construction a small stress fracture occurs. This causes either a chip, star break, or ugly bullet hole type of damage. In fact, a small fragment of glass has been removed. If left unattended due to vibration, change of temperature, or change of pressure, the damage will inevitably spread and crack. Now due to a revolutionary new system which has been developed and successfully employed for more than 10 years in the USA the damage can be repaired, using a secret formula liquid glass, which has the same refractive index as glass.

Number of franchisee addresses provided by franchisor: 00

⇨ Magna-Dry

Euston House, 81 – 103 Euston Street, London NW1 2EW

This franchise has been listed in some reference books and magazines. Mail sent to this address is accepted, but we have been unable to obtain information either in response to general requests from would-be franchisees or specifically for this publication. In the light of this experience we suggest a certain amount of caution may be in order if the franchise does eventually reappear.

⇨ The Maids Ltd

8 – 10 High Street, Sutton, Surrey SM1 1HN
Phone: 01-643 0138

Home cleaning service provided by uniformed teams of cleaners either on a scheduled or one-off basis

Outlets
Number of outlets
Company owned outlets: 02
Franchised: 12
Pilot: 01 started 1983
1988 franchise target: 30
Current reach:

South	01	South west	01	South east	06
Midlands	02	East Anglia	02	North east	00
North west	00	Scotland	02	Wales	00
N Ireland	00	Rep Ireland	00	I of Man/CI	00

Costs
Total   £35,000
Franchise fee: £8,000
Other charges: No information supplied
Min cash excluding bank: £15,000
Min overdraft required: Nil
Normal bank advance: 66%
Working capital first 2 months: Nil
Associated banks: Bank of Scotland, Lloyds, Barclays
                                  Nat West, Midland
Capital items required: None
Associated leasing co: Universal Consolidated Leasing

Royalties
(figures are   7.0% of turnover
approximate)   0.0% accounts service
                                  3.0% for advertising fund
Total   10.0% monthly sales

                                  No standing royalty independent of turnover

166

Management Selection Services

Bank rating	Banks helpful
Territory	Combination of population and radius from base. Franchisees' report: 'Just right'
Strings	Lots of ties, but lots of freedom.
Training	5 days + practical training
	5 days + management training
	Cost: £1,500 – included in franchise fee
	Training value: Adequate
Support	Good
Operating Manual	Good
Profit	As projected
Risk	Increased due to number of rival firms in market
Management only	Reasonable return for owner with management ability

Size and reach

Original company launched:	1983
Overseas connections:	None
UK connections:	Subsidiary of The Global Group Ltd
	Universal Consolidated Leasing is part of The Global Group as is Global Franchise Services (see listing under that name)
Viable for whole UK?	Yes
Trade bodies	None

Franchisor's formula for success
Low investment service industry with tremendous customer demand. Recurring revenue without shop premises and no Saturday working.

Inside story from the franchisees
Good response from franchisees, all of whom think the franchise is sound and has improved lately.

Insider tips
Staff are the main problem; they are not as easy to recruit as you might think. Get the right staff and you will make money with hard work.

Moans and groans
More practical training would be useful; on-going training is not as good as the initial training.

Number of franchisee addresses provided by franchisor: 10

⇨ Mainly Marines

6 Trojan Way, Croydon, Surrey CR0 4XL
Phone: 01-681 8421

We have been unable to obtain information from this franchise. Our would-be franchisee telephoned and confirmed that this was a company that deal with aquaria in the retail market. More information was promised, but as yet it has not arrived.

⇨ Management Selection Services

34 Victoria Road, Fulwood, Preston PR2 4NE

This franchise has been listed in some reference books and magazines. Mail sent to this address is accepted, but we have been unable to obtain information either in response to general requests from would-be franchisees or specifically for this publication. In the light of this experience we suggest a certain amount of caution may be in order if the franchise does eventually reappear.

Manns & Norwich Brewery Co Ltd

⇨ Manns & Norwich Brewery Co Ltd

Lodge Way, Harlestone Road, Northampton NN5 7UU
Phone: 0604 52452

Regional company of Watney Mann and Truman Brewers, part of the Brewing Division of Grand Metropolitan, which has 5000 tenanted public houses throughout England and Wales ranging from small village pubs to busy town centre outlets.

Outlets
Number of outlets
Company owned and
franchised: 1,300
Pilot: 00
1988 franchise target: 1,300
Current reach:

South	00	South west	00	South east	00
Midlands	600	East Anglia	700	North east	00
North west	00	Scotland	00	Wales	00
N Ireland	00	Rep Ireland	00	I of Man/CI	00

Costs
Total   £12,000 to £40,000
Franchise fee: Nil
Other charges: Nil
Min cash excluding bank: £12,000
Min overdraft required: See working capital
Normal bank advance: No information
Working capital first 2 months: £2,000
Associated banks: Nat West
Capital items required: Fixtures, fittings and stock
Associated leasing co: None

Royalties
Total   9.0% of turnover
                                            0.0% accounts service
                                            0.0% for advertising fund
                                            9.0% monthly sales

No standing royalty independent of turnover

Bank rating   Should be no problem with this famous public house chain.
Territory   Existing location of public houses
Strings   Total tie for main product – the beer

Training   5½ days practical and management training
                   Cost: £400 per couple – included in purchase fee
                   Training value: No information supplied

Support   No information supplied
Operating Manual No information supplied
Profit   No information supplied
Risk   Unless you lose your licence (for trading contrary to the licensing laws) a pub is a good way of making a reasonable living.

Management only   Variable depending on size. Manns is primarily seeking owner operators.

Size and reach
Original company launched: 1844
Overseas connections: None
UK connections: Regional company within Grand Metropolitan
Viable for whole UK?   Midlands and East Anglia only
Trade bodies   Brewers Society, British Institute of Innkeepers

Marketing Methods Ltd

Franchisor's formula for success
Low start up costs (from £12,000), with the capital invested being retained in business as an asset (including fixtures and fittings) which can be recovered on sale of business. There are substantial profit margins, comprehensive support package and the opportunity for career progression to larger outlets.

Good Franchise Guide comment: This brewery has a wide range of brands in its portfolio – Carlsberg, Fosters, Holstein, Websters Bitter, Ruddles, Ben Truman plus various regional drinks, which offers a good base for anyone with imagination to turn an unexciting pub into a highly profitable venture. But it must be very hard work, and none of us reckon we could stand it!

Number of franchisee addresses provided by franchisor: 00

⇨ Marketing Methods Ltd
(trading as Telsell)
1 Buxton Road West, Disley, Stockport, Cheshire SK12 2AF
Phone: 0663 65882
Telephone sales, recruitment and training

Telsell is a trade name, used for the Telephone Marketing Division of Marketing Methods. Operated on a local area network basis, Marketing Methods is a national company listed by the DTI and the Industrial Development Board for Northern Ireland as suppliers of marketing services. Other services include advertising and promotional goods, direct mail services, marketing consultancy services, sales promotion, advertising and design services. The Telsell section is involved in lead generation and appointment making, account servicing, market research, coupon response, direct mail screening and follow up, rallying calls and telephone sales.

Outlets
Number of outlets
Company owned outlets: 01
Franchised: 09
Pilot: 01 started 1984
1988 franchise target: 20
Current reach:

South	01	South west	00	South east	05
Midlands	00	East Anglia	00	North east	01
North west	02	Scotland	00	Wales	00
N Ireland	01	Rep Ireland	00	I of Man/CI	00

Costs
Total	£13,700
Franchise fee:	£6,000
Other charges:	£7,700
Min cash excluding bank:	£6,000
Min overdraft required:	£6,000
Normal bank advance:	£7,700
Working capital first 2 months:	£6,000
Associated banks:	None
Capital items required:	One car
Associated leasing co:	None

Royalties
Total
5.0% to 10% of turnover
0.0% accounts service
1.5% for advertising fund
6.5% to 11.5% monthly sales
No standing royalty independent of turnover

169

Massor UK Ltd

Bank rating	Helpful
Territory	A combination of counties, post codes and population of business in the area
	Franchisees report: 'Just right'
Strings	Lots of ties, but lots of freedom too
Training	Min 10 days practical training
	Min 5 days management training
	Cost: £1,900 – included in franchise fee
	Training value: Excellent
Support	Excellent
Operating Manual	Good
Profit	As expected or better
Risk	Only one competitor thus far, but this is an obvious market for expansion
Management only	Proven franchise with good return on investment

Size and reach

Original company launched:	1976
Overseas connections:	None
UK connections:	45% owned by Great Yew Investments, 52 The Drive, Sevenoaks, Kent
Viable for whole UK?	Yes
Trade bodies	None

Franchisor's formula for success
Our approach is unique in that we operate on the basis of a network of offices each run by a franchisee, linked to one another to create a shared national resource. Structured in this way we are able to serve the direct marketing needs of companies large and small through the UK.

Inside story from the franchisees
Everyone is very enthusiastic about this franchisor

Insider tips
Franchisees must have a sales or marketing background to succeed.

Moans and groans
'No real complaints'
'As yet not any area which one could fault'

Number of franchisee addresses provided by franchisor: 10

⇨ **Massor UK Ltd**

Adelphi House, Bollington, Macclesfield, Cheshire

This franchise has been listed in some reference books and magazines. Mail sent to this address is accepted, but we have been unable to obtain information either in response to general requests from would-be franchisees or specifically for this publication. In the light of this experience we suggest a certain amount of caution may be in order if the franchise does eventually reappear.

⇨ **Mast Midlands**

15 Guy's Cliffe Road, Leamington Spa CV32 5BG
Phone: 0926 24067

We originally had this franchise listed at a different address in Leamington Spa, and after mail had been returned we found their new location through Directory Enquiries. However neither we nor our would-be franchisee received any information even after we mailed them at their right address.

Master Thatchers Ltd

Rose Tree Farm, 29 Nine Mile Ride, Finchampstead, Wokingham, Berks RG11 4QD
Phone: 0734 732361

Thatching and re-thatching service

Outlets
Number of outlets
Company owned outlets: 01
Franchised: 18
Pilot: 04 started 1983
1988 franchise target: 21
Current reach:

South	03	South west	03	South east	03
Midlands	04	East Anglia	04	North east	00
North west	01	Scotland	00	Wales	00
N Ireland	00	Rep Ireland	00	I of Man/CI	00

Costs
Total £12,000
Franchise fee: £8,400
Other charges: £3,600 deposit
Min cash excluding bank: £12,000
Min overdraft required: Nil
Normal bank advance: £10,000
Working capital first 2 months: £2,000
Associated banks: Lloyds
Capital items required: Pick up truck required by end of six months' training
Associated leasing co: None

Royalties
Total
- 10.0% of turnover
- 0.0% accounts service
- 0.0% for advertising fund
- 10.0% monthly sales

No standing royalty independent of turnover

Bank rating No problems raising finance
Territory Normally based on circle of 15 mile radius. Franchisees find the territory satisfactory
Strings Strong ties but part of operation not controlled
Training 6 months practical and management training
Cost: £3,000 – included in franchise fee
Training value: Good
Note the franchisee is paid £600 per month by the franchisor during training.
Support Very good
Operating Manual 'None as such'
Profit Most franchisees are exceeding projections
Risk Limited risk unless the market suddenly changes – a very specialist area
Management only Little salary to spare for a manager

Size and reach
Original company launched: 1974
Overseas connections: None
UK connections: Subsidiary of Thatching Advisory Service
Viable for whole UK? Southern areas only
Trade bodies: BFA, Guild of Master Craftsmen

MBC Distributorships

Franchisor's formula for success
The company not only has a considerable reputation for roof thatching but also for servicing many other facets of the thatch industry including specialised thatched property insurance, sales of various products and material related to thatching, and the highly successful Thatch Owners Protection Scheme and associated Thatched Property Estate Agency.

Inside story from the franchisees
Very positive response. All franchisees we contacted felt this to be an excellent franchise with very good training.

Insider tips
Must like outside work and be prepared to work alone at first.

Moans and groans
As there is no operating manual more guidance on the book-keeping side would help.

Number of franchisee addresses provided by franchisor: 17

⇨ MBC Distributorships

Miniprints Ltd, Knowle Green, Longridge, Preston PR3 2YN

Although listed as a franchise in some publications this is in fact a distributorship, although to make matters more confusing the literature quotes Wimpy, Dyno-Rod, Prontaprint as distributorships of a similar nature. The company produce miniprints as photographic business cards, plus library photographs, individually designed brochures and photographic labels.

Good Franchise Guide comment: We think that some of this is playing with words, but this could be a nice little additional earner for anyone interested in cameras. More information required.

⇨ McDonald's

11 – 59 High Road, East Finchley, London N2 8AW

The initial McDonald's operation has been run by the company itself and not as a franchise. The company has asked that we do not list further details in *The Good Franchise Guide*.

⇨ Med-Ped SA

Plaza Med-Ped, Palma Nova, Majorca, Spain
Phone: (34-71) 68-16-32

Med-Ped operates moped and scooter hire outlets located in the most popular Spanish tourist resorts. All franchisees are currently British

Outlets
Number of outlets
Company owned outlets: 04
Franchised: 10
Pilot: 00
1988 franchise target: 20
Current reach:
                            All outlets are in Spanish tourist resorts

Metro Express

Costs
Total — No information supplied
Initial franchise fee: £7,500
Other charges: No information supplied
Min cash excluding bank: £35,000
Min overdraft required: No information supplied
Normal bank advance: No information supplied
Working capital first 2 months: £3,000
Associated banks: None
Capital items required: Fleet of mopeds
Associated leasing co: None

Royalties
6.0% of turnover
0.0% accounts service
0.0% for advertising fund
Total — 6.0% monthly sales

No standing royalty independent of turnover

Bank rating — No information supplied
Territory — Based on number of hotel beds in each resort
Strings — No information supplied
Training
2 weeks practical training
2 weeks management training
Cost: Nil – included in franchise fee
Training value: No information supplied

Support — No information supplied
Operating Manual — No information supplied
Profit — No information supplied
Risk — Operators will be subject to local laws – a subject on which we are not qualified to give an opinion.
Management only — Reasonable return for owner with management ability

Size and reach
Original company launched: 1976
Overseas connections: Wholly owned by Mediterranean Mopeds SA
UK connections: Spanish company
Viable for whole UK? Spanish resorts only
Trade bodies: None

Good Franchise Guide comment: An interesting idea which could be everyone's dream of easy summer money. But we'd like to know just how much franchisees are making at it.

Number of franchisee addresses provided by franchisor: 00

⇨ Metro Express
22 John Street, London EC1

Transport and delivery service

There is no doubt that this is a flourishing franchise. We have simply been unable to obtain any information from them.

Metro Rod Franchising Ltd

⇨ **Metro Rod Franchising Ltd**
Metro House, Churchill Way, Macclesfield, Cheshire SK11 6AY
Phone: 0625 34444

Drain cleaning service

Outlets
Number of outlets
Company owned outlets: 01
Franchised: 41
Pilot: 01 started 1983
1988 franchise target: 48
Note reach figures that follow are percentages, not actual franchises
Current reach:

South	10	South west	05	South east	20
Midlands	20	East Anglia	15	North east	00
North west	15	Scotland	05	Wales	10
N Ireland	00	Rep Ireland	00	I of Man/CI	00

Costs
Total	£30,000
Franchise fee:	£8,000
Other charges:	Balance for capital equipment
Min cash excluding bank:	£10,000
Min overdraft required:	£5,000
Normal bank advance:	£20,000
Working capital first 2 months:	£1,000
Associated banks:	Lloyds, Barclays, Midland
Capital items required:	Van
Associated leasing co:	Various and own

Royalties
	'No royalties – management fees are charged'
	23.0% of turnover (average)
	0.0% accounts service
	0.0% for advertising fund
Total	23.0% monthly sales
	No standing royalty independent of turnover

Bank rating	No information supplied
Territory	Yellow Pages areas
Strings	No information supplied
Training	1 month practical training
	Continuous management training
	Cost: Nil – included in franchise fee
	Training value: No information supplied
Support	No information supplied
Operating Manual	No information supplied
Profit	No information supplied
Risk	Presumably fighting Dyno-Rod
Management only	Reasonable return for owner with management ability

Size and reach
Original company launched:	1982
Overseas connections:	None
UK connections:	None
Viable for whole UK?	Yes
Trade bodies	Institute of Public Health and Hygiene, High Pressure Water Jetting Assn

Franchisor's formula for success
No information supplied

Good Franchise Guide comment: We were in fact given a lot more information by this franchisor but it came in a pack marked 'This ACTION FILE is delivered subject to the express condition that its contents will not be reproduced in whole or in part, and that its contents will not be revealed to any person not an authorised employee . . .' etc. It's a shame because that document contains a lot of good stuff. We suggest would-be franchisees try to get it; it would seem that anyone who wants to can obtain the file simply by writing and asking.

Number of franchisee addresses provided by franchisor: 00

⇨ MGN Consultants Ltd
Orchard Cottage, Rectory Lane, North Runcton, King's Lynn, Norfolk PE33 0QS
Phone: 0553 841621

Conveyancing services

Outlets
Number of outlets
Company owned outlets:	01
Franchised:	17
Pilot:	01 started 1984
1988 franchise target:	29

No regional breakdown provided

Costs
Total	No information supplied
Franchise fee:	£8,750*
Other charges:	See training, below
Min cash excluding bank:	No information supplied
Min overdraft required:	No information supplied
Normal bank advance:	No information supplied
Working capital first 2 months:	No information supplied
Associated banks:	None
Capital items required:	No information supplied
Associated leasing co:	None

*Includes computer and software. Remove £1,500 where franchisees supply own computer.

Royalties
Total	0.0% of turnover 0.0% accounts service 0.0% for advertising fund 0.0% monthly sales
	£35 per transaction standing royalty independent of turnover
Bank rating	No information supplied
Territory	No information supplied
Strings	No information supplied
Training	150 hours practical and management training Cost: £8,750 – not included in franchise fee Training value: No information supplied
Support	No information supplied
Operating Manual	No information supplied
Profit	Gross profit per year based on 2 clients per week £23,920
Risk	Could be risky if solicitors start fighting back by reducing their fees
Management only	Conveyancer is the manager

Micrex Microfilm Express Ltd

Size and reach
Original company launched: No information supplied
Overseas connections: None
UK connections: None
Viable for whole UK?   England and Wales only
Trade bodies   None

Franchisor's formula for success
There have been considerable changes in conveyancing legislation. The purpose of these changes was to introduce licensed conveyancers who have to be employed in a solicitor's or licensed conveyancer's office for a minimum of 2 years before qualifying. There are now 3 categories of conveyancers, first solicitors, secondly licensed conveyancers, and thirdly conveyancing agents.
Our proven training course is singularly for this third group of conveyancers. Linked to a document drafting service with full legal, marketing and administration co-ordination and back-up, you will be able to build up your own successful and highly profitable business.

Good Franchise Guide comment: Could be worthwhile – but depends on what the opposition gets up to.

Number of franchisee addresses provided by franchisor: 00

⇨ Micrex Microfilm Express Ltd
Microfilm House, Thrupp Lane, Radley, Oxon OX14 3NG
Phone: 0235 22275

Microfilm service centre

Outlets
Number of outlets
Company owned outlets: 01
Franchised: New franchise
Pilot: 01 started 1974
1988 franchise target: 07
Current reach:

South	01	South west	00	South east	00
Midlands	00	East Anglia	00	North east	00
North west	00	Scotland	00	Wales	00
N Ireland	00	Rep Ireland	00	I of Man/CI	00

Costs
Total   £40,000
Franchise fee: Nil
Other charges: 'Flexible'
Min cash excluding bank: 'Flexible'
Min overdraft required: 'Flexible'
Normal bank advance: 50% to 66%
Working capital first 2 months: £5,000
Associated banks: 'All main banks'
Capital items required: Vehicle and technical equipment
Associated leasing co: None

Royalties
  10.0% of turnover
  0.0% accounts service
  2.5% for advertising fund
Total   12.5% monthly sales

  No standing royalty independent of turnover

Bank rating   No information supplied
Territory   Yellow Pages area
Strings   No information supplied

Microlec

Training	2 weeks practical training
	1 week management training
	Cost: £2,000 included in franchise fee
	Training value: No information supplied
Support	No information supplied
Operating Manual	No information supplied
Profit	No information supplied
Risk	Very specialist field – ensure you know something about it.
Management only	Reasonable return for owner with management ability

Size and reach

Original company launched:	1987
Overseas connections:	To be explored in 1988
UK connections:	None
Viable for whole UK?	Yes
Trade bodies	NAMB

Franchisor's formula for success

The Microfilm Express franchise is the first attempt in the world to form a franchise from the concept of a microfilm service centre. It has attracted great attention from the relatively few people who saw it at its first public exposure at NEC Birmingham this year [1987]. It boasts a dignified life style as a consultant to a sales company dealing almost exclusively with other businesses, local authorities, hospitals, government, architects etc, and offers a high return on investment from a very small customer base who are likely to be offering repeat orders for many years. These customers are easily located by direct mail campaigns with follow-up appointments. Husband and wife teams are ideal and high street premises are most definitely *not* required. Arrangements have been agreed with a major bank subsidiary to factor invoices so lowering the working capital cost.

Good Franchise Guide comment: An interesting new venture – possibly one to watch. But beware: factoring can be an expensive way of funding a business. Go as far as possible on your overdraft.

Number of franchisee addresses provided by franchisor: 00

⇨ **Micro Management (ECS) Ltd**

Latchetts, Chacewater, Truro, Cornwall

This franchise has been listed in some reference books and magazines. Mail sent to this address is accepted, but we have been unable to obtain information either in response to general requests from would-be franchisees or specifically for this publication. In the light of this experience we suggest a certain amount of caution may be in order if the franchise does eventually reappear.

⇨ **Microlec**

1a United Downs Industrial Park, St Day, Redruth TR16 5HY
Phone: See *Good Franchise Guide* comment

Heating control system

Outlets

Number of outlets	
Company owned outlets:	01
Franchised:	00
Pilot:	No information supplied
1988 franchise target:	No information supplied

Microlec

Costs
Total	No information supplied
Franchise fee:	£15,000
Other charges:	No information supplied
Min cash excluding bank:	No information supplied
Min overdraft required:	No information supplied
Normal bank advance:	No information supplied
Working capital first 2 months:	No information supplied but franchisor suggests 6 months working capital is required
Associated banks:	None
Capital items required:	No information supplied
Associated leasing co:	None

Royalties

Nil – franchisor acts as wholesaler

Bank rating — No information supplied
Territory — No information supplied
Strings — Tied to one product

Training — 4 day practical and management training
Cost: Nil – included in franchise fee
Training value: No information supplied

Support — No information supplied
Operating Manual — No information supplied
Profit — Gross profit quoted at £7,350 per month
Risk — Totally related to the viability of the product and skill of your salesman

Management only — Little salary to spare for a manager

Size and reach
Original company launched:	No information supplied
Overseas connections:	None
UK connections:	Controlled by Micro Management (ECS) Ltd
Viable for whole UK?	Yes
Trade bodies	None

Franchisor's formula for success
Microlec is a sophisticated but simple to operate heating system controlled by a computer and monitored by a very accurate sensor which offers up to five temperature changes in each 24 hour period. Franchisees need no experience in the central heating or electrical field. Franchisees do require an installation engineer and a direct salesman, both trained by the franchisor.

Good Franchise Guide comment: Microlec reply to would-be franchisees by supplying the information given above, and stating that prior to making a formal presentation 'it is our policy to ask for more information to enable us to accurately assess your potential as a future Microlec franchisee'. A questionnaire is enclosed. Noticeably Microlec didn't respond to *our* questionnaire.
The letter sent to our would-be franchisee contained no phone number, but the parent company does operate from 0872 560958.

Number of franchisee addresses provided by franchisor: 00

➪ Midas (Great Britain) Ltd
107 Mortlake High Street, London SW14 8HH
Phone: 01-878 7803

Car exhaust and brake specialists

Outlets
Number of outlets	
Company owned outlets:	30 (approx)
Franchised:	10 (approx)
Pilot:	No information supplied
1988 franchise target:	No information supplied

Costs
Total	£80,000
Franchise fee:	£10,000
Other charges:	£35,000 'Assets'
	£25,000 stock
Min cash excluding bank:	£25,000
Min overdraft required:	No information supplied
Normal bank advance:	30%
Working capital first 2 months:	No information supplied
Associated banks:	None
Capital items required:	Shop equipment £3,500
Associated leasing co:	None

Royalties
	6.0% of turnover
	0.0% accounts service
	0.0% for advertising fund
Total	6.0% monthly sales
	No standing royalty independent of turnover

Bank rating	No information supplied
Territory	No information supplied
Strings	No information supplied
Training	Training exists but no information has been supplied
	Cost: Nil – included in franchise fee
	Training value: No information supplied
Support	No information supplied
Operating Manual	No information supplied
Profit	Brochure quotes a gross operating profit for year 1 as £24,265
Risk	Competitive area
Management only	Could be run by manager but with limited profit

Size and reach
Original company launched:	1967
Overseas connections:	Started in USA in 1955
UK connections:	Subsidiary of I C Industries
Viable for whole UK?	Yes
Trade bodies	BFA

Franchisor's formula for success
Running your own independent exhaust and brake centre you'd be right out on a limb. As a Midas franchisee you'll be part of the world's largest specialist exhaust and brake organisation – selling an established 'household name' service – and backed by in-depth management resources and unrivalled know-how.

Good Franchise Guide comment: Although Midas did not reply to our questionnaire, would-be franchisees are sent a list of existing operating addresses – which contrasts strongly with those firms which mark such information 'strictly secret'.

Midland Magazines Ltd

Number of franchisee addresses provided by franchisor: 00 (Addresses supplied to franchisees do not distinguish between franchisees and franchisor operated outlets.)

⇨ Midland Magazines Ltd
25-35 Hobmoor Road, Small Heath, Birmingham B10 9AY

This franchise has been listed in some reference books and magazines. The company is operating as a conventional wholesaler of books and magazines, and we have seen no signs of franchising. We have been unable to obtain information either in response to general requests from would-be franchisees or specifically for this publication. In the light of this experience we suggest that the most likely explanation is that this is not a franchise.

⇨ Midland Waterlife Franchising Ltd
154 High Street, Bromsgrove, Worcs B61 8AR
Phone: 0527 70676

Aquatic centre and water gardening business run from garden centres and high street locations

Outlets
Number of outlets
Company owned outlets: 04
Franchised: 03
Pilot: 00
1988 franchise target: 14
Current reach:

South	00	South west	00	South east	01
Midlands	06	East Anglia	00	North east	00
North west	00	Scotland	00	Wales	00
N Ireland	00	Rep Ireland	00	I of Man/CI	00

Costs
Total   £35,000
Franchise fee: £3,000
Other charges: No information supplied
Min cash excluding bank: £35,000
Min overdraft required: No information supplied
Normal bank advance: 66%
Working capital first 2 months: £1,000
Associated banks: Nat West
Capital items required: Fixtures and fittings
Associated leasing co: Lombard

Royalties

Total
0.0% of turnover
0.0% accounts service
2.0% for advertising fund
2.0% monthly sales

No standing royalty independent of turnover

Bank rating   Banks very helpful
Territory   Normally radius from franchise base
                    Franchisees report: Just right
Strings   Strong ties for the product
Training   20 days management and practical training
                    Cost: Nil – included in franchise fee
                    Training value: Not enough training given

Millie's Cookies (UK) Ltd

Support	Good
Operating Manual	Very good
Profit	Reasonable – return as expected
Risk	Not a high risk area, but beware the growth of competition
Management only	Could be run by manager – profit depends on location
Size and reach	
Original company launched:	Information not supplied
Overseas connections:	None
UK connections:	None
Viable for whole UK?	Most areas
Trade bodies	None

Franchisor's formula for success
All garden centres and high street locations are thoroughly investigated and it is only after Midland Waterlife are completely satisfied that the site is a viable proposition that it will be offered as exclusive territory to a potential franchisee.

Inside story from the franchisees
Considered a very good business, with good potential

Insider tips
'Make sure the wholesaler can supply all your needs and requirements'

Moans and groans
Wholesaler does 'not supply basic needs fast enough'

Number of franchisee addresses provided by franchisor: 3

⇨ Millie's Cookies (UK) Ltd

24a Perivale Industrial Park, Horsenden Lane South, Greenford, Middx UB6 7RJ
Phone: 01-997 9793

Fresh baked chocoloate chip cookie

Outlets	
Number of outlets	
Company owned outlets:	No information supplied
Franchised:	No information supplied
Pilot:	No information supplied
1988 franchise target:	No information supplied
Costs	
Total	Variable from £17,500 for a mobile cart unit to £45,000 for shop
Franchise fee:	£7,500
Other charges:	No information supplied
Min cash excluding bank:	No information supplied
Min overdraft required:	No information supplied
Normal bank advance:	65%
Working capital first 2 months:	No information supplied
Associated banks:	Barclays
Capital items required:	shop equipment package £30,000
Associated leasing co:	None
Royalties	
	8.0% of turnover
	0.0% accounts service
	2.0% for advertising fund
Total	10.0% monthly sales
	No standing royalty independent of turnover
Bank rating	No information supplied
Territory	No information supplied
Strings	Strong – all ingredients provided by franchisor

Mister Donut UK

Training	Practical and management training given but no details of length provided.
	Cost: Nil – included in franchise fee
	Training value: No information supplied
Support	No information supplied
Operating Manual	No information supplied
Profit	Net profit quoted as £17,400 on £100,000 turnover
Risk	Depends on whether the high street will really take such a specialised food outlet
Management only	Could be run by manager but with limited profit

Size and reach

Original company launched:	No information supplied
Overseas connections:	We presume so, but no information supplied
UK connections:	None
Viable for whole UK?	Yes
Trade bodies	None

Franchisor's formula for success

Imagine when people see fresh, sof'n' chewy chunky chocolate chip cookies being baked on your premises; when they smell that scrumptious warm aroma, they'll queue up and come back for more. However, one fresh idea isn't enough. We've also introduced real fruit milk shakes, plus our fresh baked super cones...

Good Franchise Guide comment: Talk to existing franchisees before you do anything – everything depends on the long term viability of the cookie market.

Number of franchisee addresses provided by franchisor: 00

⇨ Mister Donut UK

353 North End Road, London SW6
(Previously at Gloucester Road, London SW7)
Phone: 01-386 9133

Suppliers of doughnuts, coffee, sandwiches etc

Outlets
Number of outlets

Company owned outlets:	01 in UK
Franchised:	704 in 14 countries
Pilot:	01 started 1987
1988 franchise target:	07

Current reach:

South	00	South west	00	South east	01
Midlands	00	East Anglia	00	North east	00
North west	00	Scotland	00	Wales	00
N Ireland	00	Rep Ireland	00	I of Man/CI	00

Costs

Total	£60,000
Franchise fee:	£5,000
Other charges:	No information supplied
Min cash excluding bank:	No information supplied
Min overdraft required:	No information supplied
Normal bank advance:	70%
Working capital first 2 months:	£5,000 to £7,000
Associated banks:	Midland
Capital items required:	'Equipment'
Associated leasing co:	None

Mixamate Concrete (Mixamate Holdings Ltd)

Royalties	5.0% of turnover
	0.0% accounts service
	0.0% for advertising fund
Total	5.0% monthly sales
	No standing royalty independent of turnover
Bank rating	No information supplied
Territory	To be negotiated
Strings	No information supplied
Training	30 hours practical training
	30 days management training
	Cost: Nil – included in franchise fee
	Training value: No information supplied
Management only	See *Good Franchise Guide* comment
Size and reach	
Original company launched:	1955 – USA
Overseas connections:	Outlets throughout the world
UK connections:	Affiliate of International Multifoods
Viable for whole UK?	Yes
Trade bodies	None

Good Franchise Guide comment: This is a well established American franchise whose newness to the UK market, combined with a seeming reluctance to supply information (not just to us!) makes them difficult to evaluate. If the American experience can be transferred to the UK market then this should be an attractive proposition. If you have any doubts wait and see what happens.

Number of franchisee addresses provided by franchisor: 00

⇨ Mister Softee

This franchise has been listed in some reference books and magazines. It is, however, a part of the Lyons Maid (qv) operation.

⇨ Mixamate Concrete (Mixamate Holdings Ltd)

Bourne Way, Hayes, Kent BR2 7EY
Phone: 01-462 8011

Flexible concrete delivery service, with the concrete mixed on site to the customer's actual requirement (not to rough estimates)

Outlets
Number of outlets
Company owned outlets: 03
Franchised: 13
Pilot: 03 started 1976
1988 franchise target: 24 plus
Current reach:

South	06	South west	02	South east	04
Midlands	02	East Anglia	00	North east	01
North west	00	Scotland	00	Wales	00
N Ireland	01	Rep Ireland	00	I of Man/CI	00

183

Mixamate Concrete (Mixamate Holdings Ltd)

Costs

Total	£15,000
Franchise fee:	£3,000
Other charges:	£9,000 for vehicle; £3,000 for plant
Min cash excluding bank:	£5,000
Min overdraft required:	£1,000
Normal bank advance:	70%
Working capital first 2 months:	£2,000
Associated banks:	All five major banks
Capital items required:	Fork lift £1,500, shovel £1,500
Associated leasing co:	LMS Ltd

Royalties

	6.0% of turnover
	0.0% accounts service
	0.0% for advertising fund
Total	6.0% monthly sales
	No standing royalty independent of turnover

Bank rating — Good

Territory — 18 mile radius
Franchisees report: Just right

Strings — Strong ties – eg you must get your vehicle from them

Training
7 to 10 days practical training
2 to 3 days management training
Cost: Included in franchise fee except hotel and meals
Training value: Adequate

Support — Very good
Operating Manual — Good
Profit — As anticipated or better
Risk — Not a high risk area
Management only — Variable opportunities from one-man-band operation upwards

Size and reach

Original company launched:	1976
Overseas connections:	None
UK connections:	Mixamate Ltd runs 3 company owned operations
Viable for whole UK?	Yes
Trade bodies	None

Franchisor's formula for success
With Mixamate the customer neither has to mix the concrete himself nor take a bulk delivery of ready mixed concrete. When the Mixamate vehicle arrives on site the driver starts to mix the concrete ready for the customer to lay. So the customer gets only the amount of freshly made concrete that he needs for the job – no more no less, unlike traditional ready-mixed concrete where the customer either under-orders because of poor estimating or over-orders because he wants to make sure he is not left short. With Mixamate this is not a concern.

Inside story from the franchisees
Considered to be a good franchise; no complaints save that it is hard work.

Insider tips
It's a specialist area. You must know the trade and be fit.

Moans and groans
'Physically very demanding but I would encourage others.'

Number of franchisee addresses provided by franchisor: 17

Mobiletuning Ltd

7a Nelson Road, London SE10 9JB
Phone: 01-853 1520

Tuning of motor vehicle engines at client's homes with electronic equipment

Outlets
Number of outlets
Company owned outlets: 01
Franchised: 60
Pilot: 02 started 1973
1988 franchise target: 72
Current reach:

South	06	South west	06	South east	22
Midlands	07	East Anglia	05	North east	05
North west	05	Scotland	02	Wales	03
N Ireland	00	Rep Ireland	00	I of Man/CI	00

Costs
Total: No information supplied
Franchise fee: £3,000
Other charges: £7,500 to £12,000
Min cash excluding bank: 50%
Min overdraft required: No information supplied
Normal bank advance: 50%
Working capital first 2 months: £500
Associated banks: None
Capital items required: Van, diagnostic equipment
Associated leasing co: None

Royalties

Total
- 10.0% of turnover
- 0.0% accounts service
- 0.0% for advertising fund
- 10.0% monthly sales

No standing royalty independent of turnover

Bank rating Finance houses reported as being more helpful than banks. No problems raising money at all reported.

Territory Territories contain minimum of 250,000 population. Of the 16 franchisees who replied 15 said the territory was just right, 1 said it was too big.

Strings Some ties, but lots of freedom

Training 9 days practical training
1 day management training
Cost: £400 – *not* included in franchise fee
Training value: Rated as excellent by virtually everyone

Support Excellent
Operating Manual Excellent
Profit Good
Risk Lots of competition as in most motor trade operations
Management only One-man-band operation

Size and reach
Original company launched: 1976
Overseas connections: None
UK connections: None
Viable for whole UK? Yes
Trade bodies: BFA

Modular Marquees Ltd

Franchisor's formula for success
The first year profit on capital employed should be 70%. The start up costs of £13,800 can be reduced to £9,200 if the franchisee elects to start with used equipment, and it is also possible to start on a part-time basis while still in employment elsewhere. There is on offer a nil deposit financial package.

Inside story from the franchisees
Out of all the franchises where we have contacted franchisees this one had the most positive response from those in the field. Everyone rated it a well-run franchise; the training is particularly rated very highly.

Insider tips
This is not a get rich quick business but a good living can be had for those willing to work.

Moans and groans
Absolutely none.

Number of franchisee addresses provided by franchisor: 60

⇨ Modular Marquees Ltd
The Yard, High Green, Catterick Village, Richmond, N Yorks
Phone: 0748 811511

Hire of marquees

Outlets
Number of outlets
Company owned outlets:	01				
Franchised:	06				
Pilot:	01 started 1978				
1988 franchise target:	08				
Current reach:					
South	00	South west	01	South east	01
Midlands	00	East Anglia	01	North east	01
North west	01	Scotland	01	Wales	01
N Ireland	00	Rep Ireland	00	I of Man/CI	00

Costs
Total	£22,000
Franchise fee:	£3,000
Other charges:	No information supplied
Min cash excluding bank:	No information supplied
Min overdraft required:	No information supplied
Normal bank advance:	No information supplied
Working capital first 2 months:	No information supplied
Associated banks:	None
Capital items required:	None
Associated leasing co:	None

Royalties
Total	5.0% of turnover 0.0% accounts service 0.0% for advertising fund 5.0% monthly sales
	No standing royalty independent of turnover

Bank rating	No information supplied
Territory	No information supplied
Strings	No information supplied
Training	No information supplied on training Cost: Nil – included in franchise fee Training value: No information supplied

Molly Maid

Support	No information supplied
Operating Manual	No information supplied
Profit	No information supplied
Risk	One other franchise, plus local competition
Management only	One-man-band operation

Size and reach

Original company launched:	No information supplied
Overseas connections:	None
UK connections:	None
Viable for whole UK?	Yes
Trade bodies	Made Up Textiles Assn

Good Franchise Guide comment: The company has declined to supply any form of brochure or a list of franchisees. It did return our questionnaire but declined to answer any questions put. Would-be franchisees receive a short letter inviting a phone call, but no detailed information. It should be noted that M and B Marquees (qv) also suffer from a surfeit of secrecy.

Number of franchisee addresses provided by franchisor: 00

⇨ **Molly Maid**
10 – 12 Henry Road, Slough, Berks SL1 2QL
Phone: 0753 35343

House cleaning

Outlets

Number of outlets	
Company owned outlets:	No information supplied
Franchised:	23 UK
Pilot:	No information supplied
1988 franchise target:	No information supplied

Costs

Total	£6,000
Franchise fee:	£5,500
Other charges:	Nil
Min cash excluding bank:	No information supplied
Min overdraft required:	No information supplied
Normal bank advance:	No information supplied
Working capital first 2 months:	£500
Associated banks:	None
Capital items required:	None
Associated leasing co:	None

Royalties

	8.0% of turnover
	0.0% accounts service
	2.0% for advertising fund
Total	10.0% monthly sales
	No standing royalty independent of turnover

Bank rating	No information supplied
Territory	25,000 to 35,000 households
Strings	Franchisor supplies materials

Morley's

Training	5 day practical and management training
Support	No information supplied
Operating Manual	No information supplied
Profit	£10,260 net profit projected
Risk	High – strong competition from other franchises plus a growing feeling among local companies that you don't need a franchise to do this sort of thing.
Management only	One-man-band operation operating from home

Size and reach

Original company launched:	1978 Canada; 150 franchises Canada, 200 USA
Overseas connections:	None
UK connections:	Controlled by Agostpolar Ltd UK
Viable for whole UK?	Yes
Trade bodies	None

Franchisor's formula for success
'On a weekly or bi-weekly basis a team of two Molly Maids arrive at the customer's home and with drill-team precision, thoroughly clean the home in a relatively short period of time. The household is systemised, methods are standardised and management practices are uniform.'

Good Franchise Guide comment: Reports reaching us suggest that the biggest problem of all with these house cleaning franchises is getting and holding on to reliable staff. Our strong suggestion is that no one should take on such an operation without first talking to other franchisees.

Number of franchisee addresses provided by franchisor: 00

➪ Morley's

162 Clapham High Street, London SW4 7UG
Phone: 01-622 4821

Fast food restaurants

Outlets
Number of outlets

Company owned outlets:	00
Franchised:	05
Pilot:	No information supplied
1988 franchise target:	No information supplied

Costs

Total	£60,000
Franchise fee:	£8,000
Other charges:	£20,000 equipment
Min cash excluding bank:	No information supplied
Min overdraft required:	No information supplied
Normal bank advance:	No information supplied
Working capital first 2 months:	No information supplied
Associated banks:	None
Capital items required:	Shopfitting £20,000
Associated leasing co:	None

Royalties

	4.0% of turnover
	0.0% accounts service
	3.0% for advertising fund
Total	7.0% monthly sales
	No standing royalty independent of turnover

Bank rating	No information supplied
Territory	No information supplied
Strings	No information supplied

Training	Practical and management training provided Cost: £2,000 – included in franchise fee Training value: No information supplied
Support	No information supplied
Operating Manual	No information supplied
Profit	Projected return on investment 69.3%
Risk	We are not really sure if the high street can take any more fast food chains
Management only	Could be run by manager but with limited profit

Size and reach

Original company launched:	No information supplied
Overseas connections:	None
UK connections:	Currie Motors Group
Viable for whole UK?	Yes
Trade bodies	None

Franchisor's formula for success
Morleys are an expanding fast food chain offering a wide range of quality fast foods.

Good Franchise Guide comment: See risk

Number of franchisee addresses provided by franchisor: 00

⇨ Motabitz (Franchising) Ltd

18 Church Green East, Redditch, Worcs B98 8BP
Phone: 0527 584878

Van delivery system supplying 2000 items ranging from light bulbs to drills, hoses to fuses servicing all types of business

Outlets
Number of outlets

Company owned outlets:	14
Franchised:	04
Pilot:	04 started 1985
1988 franchise target:	32
Current reach by area:	No information supplied

Costs

Total	£15,000
Franchise fee:	£4,000
Other charges:	£1,000 training, and launch £3,000 stock
Min cash excluding bank:	No information supplied
Min overdraft required:	No information supplied
Normal bank advance:	No information supplied
Working capital first 2 months:	'A small amount'
Associated banks:	'Yes' – but no information supplied
Capital items required:	Vehicle – deposit £3,000
Associated leasing co:	None

Royalties

No information supplied

Bank rating	No information supplied
Territory	Radius from franchisee's base
Strings	Strong ties – van must be the one selected by franchisor; products as selected
Training	1 week practical training Continuous management training Cost: £1,000 – see fees above Training value: No information supplied

Motoplas Ltd

Size and reach
Original company launched: 1978
Overseas connections: None
UK connections: None
Viable for whole UK?   Yes
Trade bodies   None

Franchisor's formula for success
Only first class products sold ranging from light bulbs to drills, from hoses to fuses, yet at very competitive prices. A very strong management structure especially set up to advise and assist franchisees. A sales director, a general manager and a training manager make up this team.

Good Franchise Guide comment: A crowded area; the risk factor here could be high. We are a little unsure about the ability of what is essentially a one-man franchise operation selling maintenance products from a van to make a profit of £23,000 by year two – but we have only a limited amount of material supplied to us by the franchisor and his agent, The Franchise Shop, Surrey.

Number of franchisee addresses provided by franchisor: 00

⇨ **Motoplas Ltd**
1 Carn Industrial Estate, Portadown, N Ireland BT63 5RH
Phone: 0762 333193

Motoplas have perfected a process which repairs broken, cracked or scuffed plastic leaving it as new

Outlets
Number of outlets
Company owned outlets: 01
Franchised: 08
Pilot: 01 started 1984
1988 franchise target: 12
Current reach:

South	00	South west	00	South east	00
Midlands	04	East Anglia	01	North east	01
North west	00	Scotland	00	Wales	01
N Ireland	02	Rep Ireland	00	I of Man/CI	00

Costs
Total   £15,000
Franchise fee: £6,000
Other charges: No information supplied
Min cash excluding bank: £6,000
Min overdraft required: £9,000
Normal bank advance: £10,000 to £15,000
Working capital first 2 months: £3,500
Associated banks: Nat West and Barclays
Capital items required   PME £2,000; Build £4,000
Associated leasing co: Lombard

Royalties
                                   0.0% of turnover
                                   0.0% accounts service
                                   0.0% for advertising fund
Total   0.0% monthly sales

                                   No standing royalty independent of turnover

Bank rating   No information supplied
Territory   Population and industrial density
Strings   No information supplied

Mr Boilerserviceman

Training	28 days practical training
	2 days management training
	Cost: Nil – included in franchise fee
	Training value: No information supplied
Support	No information supplied
Operating Manual	No information supplied
Profit	No information supplied
Risk	The franchise is advertised as a 'completely new concept in the world of plastics.' The risk therefore is that the new concept may either not catch on, or fail.
Management only	Reasonable return for owner with management ability

Size and reach

Original company launched:	1984
Overseas connections:	None
UK connections:	Motoplas Services Ltd
Viable for whole UK?	Yes
Trade bodies	None

Franchisor's formula for success

Motoplas represents the most revolutionary and growth orientatied of any automotive franchise to date. The use of plastics in most industrial situations is on the increase, yet when a car bumper is damaged the solution to date has been to replace with a new one. Motoplas now provides a much cheaper alternative. This not only applies to paint finished plastic but also the the impregnated and dark grey textured finished bumpers.

Good Franchise Guide comment: As no franchise royalties are required it appears that the franchisor must make money from the supply of materials.
None of the 8 franchisees we contacted was willing to give us information on their progress with the franchise.

Number of franchisee addresses provided by franchisor: 8

⇨ Mr Big (UK) Ltd

15 Bellacre Gardens, Letchworth, Herts SG6 2BY

This franchise has been listed in some reference books and magazines. Mail sent to this address is accepted, but we have been unable to obtain information either in response to general requests from would-be franchisees or specifically for this publication. In the light of this experience we suggest a certain amount of caution may be in order if the franchise does eventually reappear.

⇨ Mr Boilerserviceman

148 Highfield Road, Hall Green, Birmingham B28 0HT

A franchise at this address is listed in some reference books and on some consultancy leaflets. Mail sent to this address is now being returned by the Post Office marked 'Gone Away' and the phone number given has been withdrawn by BT. Enquiries have revealed that no forwarding address has been left and there is no trace of a company of this name in the Birmingham area, although it is possible that the franchise may have been set up once more in another part of the country. A leaflet circulated by The Franchise Shop stated that the minimum cash requirement was £4,750 with a total cost of £9,500. The franchise is described as 'A superb maintenance and repair service in an expanding domestic service industry . . . A really first class business – well promoted too.' We have been unable to obtain further information from The Franchise Shop in response to our enquiries concerning this franchise. In the light of this experience we suggest a certain amount of caution may be in order.

Mr Clutch Franchising Ltd

⇨ Mr Clutch Franchising Ltd
20 Lower Coombe Street, Croydon, Surrey CR0 1AA
Phone: 01-686 9330

Replacement of car clutches

Outlets
Number of outlets
Company owned outlets:	03
Franchised:	No information supplied
Pilot:	No information supplied
1988 franchise target:	No information supplied

Costs
Total	£25,000
Franchise fee:	£3,500
Other charges:	£4,000 initial stock
Min cash excluding bank:	£12,500
Min overdraft required:	No information supplied
Normal bank advance:	60%
Working capital first 2 months:	No information supplied
Associated banks:	None
Capital items required:	Second hand van £1,000
	Renovations £4,500
	Equipment £12,000
Associated leasing co:	None

Royalties
	10.0% of turnover
	5.0% marketing contribution
	0.0% for advertising fund
Total	15.0% monthly sales.
	No standing royalty independent of turnover

Bank rating	No information supplied
Territory	No information supplied
Strings	Few, as far as we can judge
Training	No detailed information – described as 'comprehensive'
Support	No information supplied
Operating Manual	No information supplied
Profit	'Profit expectation after including a salary for the franchisee but before bank interest charges' in worked examples year 1 profits range from £3,544 to £22,825
Risk	Cars do need replacement clutches (at least one of ours does) which seems to indicate its a reasonable concept with low risk.
Management only	One-man-band operation

Size and reach
Original company launched:	No information supplied
Overseas connections:	None
UK connections:	None
Viable for whole UK?	Yes
Trade bodies	None

Franchisor's formula for success
There are 20.7 million cars on the road in the UK and given that almost all of them will need a replacement clutch at some time or other a company that can provide a fast, efficient and economical service to the motorist is clearly going to be a winner.
By specialising only in clutch replacements, the company has developed its own exclusive system whih ensures a speedy turn-around resulting in an incredibly successful and profitable business.

Mr Fish on Wheels

Good Franchise Guide comment: High level of royalty – we would like to know if existing franchisees feel that is good value for money. A basic, non-gloss brochure given to would-be operators, that actually gives the relevant facts and figures – at least you know they are not wasting your money on useful flashy handouts.

Number of franchisee addresses provided by franchisor: 00

⇨ Mr Cod Ltd

6 – 7 High Street, Woking, Surrey
Phone: 048 62 5493

This franchise clearly exists, but they have failed to reply to our questionnaire, and to the written enquiries of our would-be franchisees. When, in desperation, one would-be franchisee telephoned she was told that the number rung (that given above) was in fact the fish shop. A further number was given as the 'office' but when our franchisee phoned that she was told that it was in fact the local pub. At this point she (and we) gave up.

⇨ Mr Fish on Wheels

c/o The Franchise Shop Ltd, Mertsham, Surrey RH1 3EA
Phone: 073 74 4211

Fresh fish delivery to homes

Outlets
Number of outlets	
Company owned outlets:	No information supplied
Franchised:	03
Pilot:	No information supplied
1988 franchise target:	No information supplied

Costs
Total	£40,000
Franchise fee:	No information supplied
Other charges:	No information supplied
Min cash excluding bank:	£20,000
Min overdraft required:	No information supplied
Normal bank advance:	50%
Working capital first 2 months:	No information supplied
Associated banks:	None
Capital items required:	None
Associated leasing co:	None

Royalties   No information supplied
Bank rating   No information supplied
Territory   No information supplied
Strings   Presumably strong ties for supply of fish
Training   No information supplied
Support   No information supplied
Operating Manual   No information supplied
Profit   Up to £30,000 profit suggested in brochure
Risk   All delivery services have a built in risk; you are up against local rivals, who may well have well established rounds and strong customer loyalties
Management only   Reasonable return for owner with management ability

193

Mr Lift Ltd

Size and reach
Original company launched: 1983
Overseas connections: None
UK connections: None
Viable for whole UK?   Yes
Trade bodies   None

Franchisor's formula for success
From your own distribution centre you operate a fleet of superbly equipped vehicles to bring back those much sought-after virtues of personal service and quality/freshness. The switch to fresh food, so much the mood of the 80s, means that direct deliveries are welcomed by households, hotels and restaurants.

Good Franchise Guide comment: No information supplied by consultant

Number of franchisee addresses provided by franchisor: 00

⇨ **Mr Lift Ltd**
Gloucester Road, Almondsbury, Bristol BS12 4HY
Phone: 0454 618181

Sale, hire and service of used fork-lift trucks, plus importing of reconditioned trucks from Japan with the emphasis on service when the customer needs it

Outlets
Number of outlets
Company owned outlets: 01
Franchised: 04
Pilot: 01 started 1984
1988 franchise target: 10
Current reach:

South	00	South west	01	South east	03
Midlands	00	East Anglia	00	North east	00
North west	00	Scotland	01	Wales	00
N Ireland	00	Rep Ireland	00	I of Man/CI	00

Costs
Total   £82,500
Franchise fee: £7,500
Other charges: No information supplied
Min cash excluding bank: £82,500
Min overdraft required: £30,000
Normal bank advance: £55,000
Working capital first 2 months: £15,000
Associated banks: None
Capital items required: Stock £25,000, vehicles £15,000, premises £10,000
Associated leasing co: None

Royalties
Total   5.0% of turnover
                                   0.0% accounts service
                                   2.5% for advertising fund
                                   7.5% monthly sales
                                   No standing royalty independent of turnover

Bank rating   No information supplied
Territory   Postcodes within population of given area
Strings   Strong ties for product
Training   15 days practical training
                     15 days management training
                     Cost: £5,000 – included in franchise fee
                     Training value: No information supplied

Support	No information supplied
Operating Manual	No information supplied
Profit	First year projection is 'breakeven or better'
Risk	Difficult to say
Management only	Reasonable return for owner with management ability

Size and reach

Original company launched:	1983
Overseas connections:	None
UK connections:	Tony Day Handling plc – related company
Viable for whole UK?	Yes
Trade bodies	BFA Register, Fork Lift Truck Organisation

Franchisor's formula for success

Mr Lift Service means service when the customer needs it. By being prepared to pay a service call to a customer at any time, day or night, Mr Lift cemented working relationships with customers and started them thinking the Mr Lift way.

Good Franchise Guide comment: At least this franchisor has the honesty to admit that the first year ends at a break-even point. It would have been good to talk to franchisees to see just how well they did. This clearly is a specialist area and those entering will undoubtedly know more about reconditioned fork-lift trucks than we do.

Number of franchisee addresses provided by franchisor: 00

⇨ Mr Slade Dry Cleaning

Maritime Chambers, Howard Street, North Shields, Tyne and Wear NE30 1AR
Phone: 091-296 0707

Dry cleaning shops

Mr Slade has informed us that it is no longer franchising shops, having disposed of the franchise network to Sketchley plc in 1987. It is however possible that Mr Slade will be launching a new format drycleaning franchise during the latter part of 1988.

⇨ Mr Slot

PO Box 196, Corsham, Wilts SN13 9HY
Phone: 0249 716441

Mr Slot has been a 'most successful "down-market" TV rental company for some years'. They have however been contracting of late, and are not offering any franchises or dealerships. The explanation for the problems besetting the firm relates to the highly competitive stance taken by the majors and the credit facilities available to everyone which makes it easy to buy a set.
This is probably the most honest reply we have seen from a franchisor whose franchise isn't working. It augurs well for the firm should they ever move back into franchising.

⇨ MTR Training Centre

Unit B5, Bumpers Farm Trading Estate, Chippenham, Wilts

This franchise has been listed in some reference books and magazines. Mail sent to this address is accepted, but we have been unable to obtain information either in response to general requests from would-be franchisees or specifically for this publication. In the light of this experience we suggest a certain amount of caution may be in order if the franchise does eventually reappear.

National Security

⇨ **National Security**
Denbigh House, Denbigh Road, Bletchley, Milton Keynes MK1 1YP
Phone: 0908 270007
Suppliers of National Security Alarm System requiring no redecorating

Outlets
Number of outlets
Company owned outlets: 02
Franchised: 40
Pilot: 02 started 1986
1988 franchise target: 70
Current reach:

South	05	South west	02	South east	06
Midlands	12	East Anglia	00	North east	08
North west	04	Scotland	02	Wales	00
N Ireland	01	Rep Ireland	00	I of Man/CI	00

Costs
Total: No information supplied
Franchise fee: £2,500
Other charges: Nil
Min cash excluding bank: £1,500
Min overdraft required: Nil
Normal bank advance: 50%
Working capital first 2 months: No information supplied
Associated banks: 500
Capital items required: None
Associated leasing co: None

Royalties
  10.0% of turnover
  0.0% accounts service
  0.0% for advertising fund
Total 10.0% monthly sales

£50 per month standing royalty independent of turnover

Bank rating No information supplied
Territory Population approx 150,000
Strings No information supplied
Training 28 hours practical training
14 hours management training
Cost: Nil – included in franchise fee
Training value: No information supplied

Management only Reasonable return for owner with management ability

Size and reach
Original company launched: 1986
Overseas connections: None
UK connections: None
Viable for whole UK? Yes
Trade bodies IAAI

Franchisor's formula for success
The phenomenal growth of the home security market over the last 10 years is largely the result of an increased awareness among ordinary people that they may become victims of burglaries, and their feeling of a need to do something about it.

Good Franchise Guide comment: Home security systems is a major growth area and as such it may be one from which excellent profits can be derived. Our only concern in relation to this line of business is the speed with which new low-price technology imported from the Far East is making old systems obsolete. While we have no information to suggest that this franchise may have problems some franchises may tie franchisees to increasingly old fashioned technology.

National Vacuum Cleaner Services

Number of franchisee addresses provided by franchisor: 00

⇨ National Slimming Centres
3 Trinity House, 161 Old Christchurch Road, Bournemouth, Dorset DH1 1JU
Phone: 0202 25233

Slimming combined with private medicine

Outlets
Number of outlets
Company owned outlets: No information supplied
Franchised: 11
Pilot: No information supplied
1988 franchise target: 32

Support   No information supplied
Operating Manual   No information supplied
Profit   £50,000 plus year 2 net profit
Risk   No information supplied
Management only   No information supplied

Franchisor's formula for success
All NSC centres employ fully qualified doctors who are also trained in the NSC slimming methods. Each patient has a private consultation with a doctor who will advise on diet and lifestyle. The patient will then be supplied with medication, NSC diets and menus tailored to suit his or her own specific needs.

Good Franchise Guide comment: Our would-be franchisee received a brochure with no indications of costs, and was invited to fill in an application form.

Number of franchisee addresses provided by franchisor: 00

⇨ National Vacuum Cleaner Services
Richmond House, 1 Richmond Street, Herne Bay, Kent CT6 5LU
Phone: 0227 374656

Servicing and repairs of domestic, commercial and industrial vacuum cleaners

Outlets
Number of outlets
Company owned outlets: 00
Franchised: 65
Pilot: 00
1988 franchise target: 90
Current reach:

South	19	South west	04	South east	11
Midlands	12	East Anglia	06	North east	03
North west	02	Scotland	04	Wales	03
N Ireland	01	Rep Ireland	00	I of Man/CI	00

Costs
Total   £3,890
Franchise fee: Nil
Other charges: Nil
Min cash excluding bank: £3,890
Min overdraft required: No information supplied

197

National Vacuum Cleaner Services

Normal bank advance:	Variable
Working capital first 2 months:	Varies according to personal circumstances
Associated banks:	None
Capital items required:	Workshop, vehicle, telephone
Associated leasing co:	None
Royalties	No royalties are paid
Bank rating	Virtually everyone found money available at once with the institutions very helpful.
Territory	2 to 15 miles from base; population; newspapers; Yellow Pages areas
Strings	Strong ties in some areas
Training	100 hours and ongoing practical training 10 hours management training Cost: £2,500 – included in franchise fee Training value: Excellent (one franchisee just said 'Adequate')
Support	Good
Operating Manual	Some franchisees said 'good', others reported there was no manual at all!
Profit	Good
Risk	Not a particularly high risk area
Management only	'All our members succeed if selected'

Size and reach

Original company launched:	1983
Overseas connections:	None
UK connections:	None
Viable for whole UK?	Yes
Trade bodies	M Inst D, M Inst M

Franchisor's formula for success

We are a very caring organisation and members are loyal to the cause. We are confident FDS Norwich would support our claim. The package is an excellent one and we serve an honourable profession.

Inside story from the franchisees

Very positive response. A good franchise with good initial and good ongoing training. As far as we can see the company claim of 100% success for selected franchisees is correct. 'A lot depends on how much the individual puts into his area.'

Insider tips

Hard work, but very rewarding. Even previously unemployed make a go of this franchise. The lack of royalty is attractive, we presume the franchisor is profiting from wholesaling items to franchisees.
One franchisee got an Enterprise Allowance – worth looking into.

Moans and groans

None, save the lack of a manual according to some franchisees, and the fact that it did not cover everything, according to others (but even this didn't seem to hinder those taking up the franchise).

Number of franchisee addresses provided by franchisor: 04

Natural Beauty Products Ltd

⇨ Nationwide Investigations
Nationwide House, 86 Southwark Bridge Road, London SE1 0EX
Phone: 01-248 0211

We have been unable to obtain information from this franchise. Our would-be franchisee telephoned and confirmed that this was a company offered franchises in the private investigation field. More information was promised, but as yet it has not arrived.

⇨ Natural Beauty Products Ltd
Western Avenue, Bridgend Industrial Estate, Mid Glamorgan CF31 3RT
Phone: 0656 766566

Natural Beauty Products manufactures full ranges of skin care, hair care, bath and body care, toiletries, perfumes, colognes, contouring treatments, decorative cosmetics, essential oils and aromatherapy oils. The Body Reform Shops are specialised retail outlets. A master licensee undertakes to develop a territory, normally through opening one or more Body Reform Shops and recruiting sub-franchisees to open Body Reform Shops throughout the rest of the territory.

Outlets
Number of outlets
Company owned outlets: 08
Franchised: 35
Pilot: 01 started 1986
1988 franchise target: 100
Current reach:

South	01	South west	01	South east	02		
Midlands	02	East Anglia	01	North east	03		
North west	03	Scotland	03	Wales	02		
N Ireland	02	Rep Ireland	08	I of Man/CI	00		

Costs
Total: £35,000 to £50,000
Franchise fee: £6,000
Other charges: Stock and site conversion
Min cash excluding bank: £12,000
Min overdraft required: £24,000
Normal bank advance: 66%
Working capital first 2 months: £1,000
Associated banks: Nat West
Capital items required: Site conversion
Associated leasing co: None

Royalties
10% of turnover
0.0% accounts service
0.0% for advertising fund
Total: 10.0% monthly sales

No standing royalty independent of turnover

Bank rating: Banks helpful; money raised first time round
Territory: 100,000 to 250,000 population or city centre
Franchisees report: either 'Just right' or 'Not wide enough'
Strings: Strong ties for materials, but some freedom elsewhere
Training: 5 days, plus 5 days on site practical training
5 days management training
Cost: Nil – included in franchise fee
Training value: Adequate

Natural Life Health Foods

Support	Very good
Operating Manual	Very good
Profit	Variable reports from 'better' to 'worse' than anticipated
Risk	An area of growing competition
Management only	Master franchise with 3 shops: reasonable return for owner with management ability
	Where franchisee is a shop manager: one-woman-band operation

Size and reach

Original company launched:	1985
Overseas connections:	7 overseas master franchisees
	Factory being constructed in Peking, China
UK connections:	Reform Cosmetics and Body Reform Centres
Viable for whole UK?	Yes – low density areas supported through direct sales
Trade bodies	None

Franchisor's formula for success

The franchisor is the manufacturer of the widest range of natural products in the UK for serious skin care as well as simple herbal cosmetics. A wide company base of operations (predominantly export) supports the franchise operation which is the smaller and newest part of the overall company. Business format turnkey operations offered. Products are not tested on animals.

Inside story from the franchisees

'It depends on how much you are prepared to put into it yourself'

Insider tips

Watch out for time taken on supply and delivery of goods

Moans and groans

'Training made us more aware of the products but much more time should have been spent on training.'

Although the manual was considered to be very good the complaint was raised that it was 'Too long – impossible to take it all in'.

Number of franchisee addresses provided by franchisor: 09

⇨ **Natural Life Health Foods**

15 Queen Street, Salisbury, Wilts SP1 1EY
Phone: 0584 811515

Health food shops plus coffee shops and restaurants

Outlets
Number of outlets

Company owned outlets:	01
Franchised:	04
Pilot:	No information supplied
1988 franchise target:	No information supplied

Costs

Total	£56,000
Franchise fee:	£7,500
Other charges:	£15,000 stock
Min cash excluding bank:	£17,000
Min overdraft required:	No information supplied
Normal bank advance:	70%
Working capital first 2 months:	£5,000
Associated banks:	None
Capital items required:	Shopfitting – £25,000
Associated leasing co:	None

Nectar Cosmetics

Royalties

	4.5% of turnover
	0.0% accounts service
	2.0% maximum for advertising fund
Total	6.5% maximum monthly sales
	No standing royalty independent of turnover

Bank rating	No information supplied
Territory	No information supplied
Strings	No information supplied
Training	Training takes place but no information supplied
Support	No information supplied
Operating Manual	No information supplied
Profit	No information supplied
Risk	There are a lot of health food shops around
Management only	Little salary to spare for a manager

Size and reach

Original company launched:	1985
Overseas connections:	None
UK connections:	None
Viable for whole UK?	Yes
Trade bodies	None

Franchisor's formula for success
Our products appeal to a growing market of discriminating customers who believe that good health is an asset worth preserving. The product range includes wholemeal bread, honey, vitamin food supplements, takeaway foods, dried fruit, nuts etc.

Good Franchise Guide comment: Limited hard information in the franchisor's presentation to franchisees. We were unable to get an answer on the phone number quoted above. The company is not listed via Directory Enquiries.

Number of franchisee addresses provided by franchisor: 00

➪ Nectar Cosmetics

Carrickfergus Industrial Estate, Carrickfergus, County Antrim BT38 8PW
Phone: 09603 69133

Beauty shops selling natural cosmetics with an 'olde worlde' image

Outlets
Number of outlets

Company owned outlets:		01			
Franchised:		26			
Pilot:		01 started 1984			
1988 franchise target:		55 to 60			
Current reach:					
South	02	South west	00	South east	04
Midlands	01	East Anglia	00	North east	01
North west	00	Scotland	02	Wales	00
N Ireland	06	Rep Ireland	03	I of Man/CI	00

Also 7 outlets in Sweden

Nectar Cosmetics

Costs
Total	£55,000 – £60,000
Franchise fee:	£7,500
Other charges:	No information supplied
Min cash excluding bank:	No information supplied
Min overdraft required:	£5,000
Normal bank advance:	66%
Working capital first 2 months:	£5,000
Associated banks:	Nat West
Capital items required:	None
Associated leasing co:	None

Royalties
	0.0% of turnover
	1.5% PR fund
	0.0% for advertising fund
Total	1.5% monthly sales
	No standing royalty independent of turnover

Bank rating	Institutions helpful, but it was necessary to shop around
Territory	Radius and population Franchisees report: Just right
Strings	Strong ties in some areas, but other parts not strongly controlled
Training	3 days practical and management training before opening and 3 days after opening. Cost: Nil – included in franchise fee Training value: 'Not enough'
Support	Opinions vary
Operating Manual	Opinions vary
Profit	Both our respondents were in their first year of trading – one doing better than expected, one doing worse.
Risk	There are similar operations around, but the market is growing.
Management only	Reasonable return for owner with management ability

Size and reach
Original company launched:	1981
Overseas connections:	7 shops Sweden, 1 shop Malaysia
UK connections:	None
Viable for whole UK?	Yes
Trade bodies	None

Franchisor's formula for success
After many years researching and developing our Natural Collection we believe we have one of the most exciting franchises in the UK. Clearly there has been a dramatic change in the way in which we care for ourselves. The way you look makes a clear statement to others of the type of person you are. Natural cosmetics are not a fad, so this is an opportunity to share in the success of a phenomenal growth market. Our attractive olde worlde image has a very strong visual effect in which customers just pop in to browse and eventually buy.

Inside story from the franchisees
This is a new franchise, the franchisor gave us 11 addresses, all of whom we wrote to. One letter came back marked 'not known, gone away', and two answered our questions, but each gave a very different picture. The problem is that matters can change radically in a short time with new businesses, and our respondents may soon be changing their views. We suggest would-be franchisees contact the existing outlets to see the latest position.

Insider tips
'Tell the franchisor – they listen to improvements I suggest'.

Moans and groans
More advertising needed to bring public awareness up.

Number of franchisee addresses provided by franchisor: 11

ᐅ New Moves
Previously at: 15 South Street, Exeter EX1 1DZ

This estate agency, mortgage and insurance franchise appears to have ceased trading in late 1987 or early 1988.

ᐅ Newlook Bath Services
Business and Technology Centre, Bessemer Drive, Stevenage, Herts
Phone: 0438 310008

A franchise at this name and address has been listed in some reference books and magazines. Mail sent to this address is accepted, but we have been unable to obtain information either in response to general requests from would-be franchisees or specifically for this publication. The telephone also works, but when we have tried it is connected to an answering machine. Requests for information left on the machine have not resulted in any subsequent action.

ᐅ Northern Dairies Ltd
Triumph Road, Lenton, Nottingham NG7 2GH
Phone: 0602 789344

Milk delivery service

Outlets
Number of outlets	
Company owned outlets:	No information supplied
Franchised:	No information supplied
Pilot:	No information supplied
1988 franchise target:	No information supplied

Costs
Total	No information supplied
Franchise fee:	£3,450
Other charges:	£3,000 returnable bond
Min cash excluding bank:	No information supplied
Min overdraft required:	No information supplied
Normal bank advance:	No information supplied
Working capital first 2 months:	Nil
Associated banks:	None
Capital items required:	Vehicle lease £20 pw
Associated leasing co:	None

Royalties
	0.0% of turnover
	0.0% accounts service
	0.0% for advertising fund
Total	0.0% monthly sales
	£1,690 pa depot charge independent of turnover

Bank rating	No information supplied
Territory	No information supplied
Strings	Totally tied to Dale Farm produce
Training	Training given, but no information supplied

Novus Windscreen Repair

Support	No information supplied
Operating Manual	No information supplied
Profit	'Earnings before tax, NI, accountants' fees, £13,506' Based on 450 customers and 80 gallons of milk a day
Risk	Very low
Management only	One-man-band operation

Size and reach
Original company launched:	No information supplied
Overseas connections:	None
UK connections:	None
Viable for whole UK?	From Northampton to Middlesborough plus North Wales
Trade bodies	None

Franchisor's formula for success
Following successful completion of training you will become a Dale Farm franchisee operating an existing business selling and promoting our impressive range of Dale Farm products and services to our customers.

Good Franchise Guide comment: Beware of penalty payments for under-achieving daily rate.

Number of franchisee addresses provided by franchisor: 00

➪ Novus Windscreen Repair

3rd floor, Pensnett House, The Pensnett Estate, Kingswinford, West Midlands DY6 7PP
Phone: 0384 291509

Windscreen repair

Outlets
Number of outlets
Company owned outlets:	01
Franchised:	20
Pilot:	02 started 1986
1988 franchise target:	40+

Current reach:
South	05	South west	01	South east	02		
Midlands	04	East Anglia	00	North east	02		
North west	02	Scotland	01	Wales	01		
N Ireland	01	Rep Ireland	02	I of Man/CI	00		

Costs
Total	£3,950
Franchise fee:	No information supplied
Other charges:	No information supplied
Min cash excluding bank:	No information supplied
Min overdraft required:	No information supplied
Normal bank advance:	No information supplied
Working capital first 2 months:	£1,000
Associated banks:	Not currently
Capital items required:	None
Associated leasing co:	None

Royalties
Total	8.0% of turnover planned
	0.0% accounts service
	2.0% for advertising fund planned
	10.0% monthly sales
	No standing royalty independent of turnover

Nulon Products Ltd

Bank rating	No information supplied
Territory	Based on vehicle population
Strings	No information supplied
Training	3 days practical and management training
	Cost: Nil – included in franchise fee
	Training value: No information supplied
Support	No information supplied
Operating Manual	No information supplied
Profit	See franchisor's statement below
Risk	Looks low risk at this stage but the number of rivals is growing
Management only	Anything from one-man-band operation upwards depending on number of outlets

Size and reach

Original company launched:	1986
Overseas connections:	Novus Inc, established 1972; turnover about $35,000,000
UK connections:	None
Viable for whole UK?	Yes
Trade bodies	IFA

Franchisor's formula for success
The franchise has the advantage of a totally unexploited market which is growing at approximately 25% per annum. The initial investment is moderate and the ongoing commitment is low. The return on investment is exceptional with some operators recovering their capital in two or three months. Overheads are extremely low. There is an 85 – 90% gross margin which offers the opportunity to achieve a profitable operation at a relatively low turnover. The franchise has proved successful in both affluent and deprived parts of the UK. There have been no failures to date.

Good Franchise Guide comment: Sounds very promising. We await comments from franchisees next time round. But do watch out for rivals suddenly appearing on the scene.

Number of franchisee addresses provided by franchisor: 00

⇨ Nulon Products Ltd

Unit 3D, Summerhouse Works, Summerhouse Lane, Harefield, Middx UB9 6UH
Phone: 089 582 5244

Oil additive

Size and reach

Original company launched:	1985
Overseas connections:	Australian made product
UK connections:	None
Viable for whole UK?	Yes – but mostly in the south
Trade bodies	None

Franchisor's formula for success
Nulon is a unique metal treatment that once added to the normal oil of an engine or any driven machine will bond itself permanently on to the metal by way of friction.

Good Franchise Guide comment: A distributorship, with the distributor being expected to buy a product range in before opening for business.

Number of franchisee addresses provided by franchisor: 00

Nurse-Call

⇨ Nurse-Call
69 Westgate Street, Ipswich IP1 3DZ
Phone: 0473 210843

Nursing services

Outlets
Number of outlets					
Company owned outlets:	03				
Franchised:	No information supplied				
Pilot:	01 No information on date started				
1988 franchise target:	06				
Current reach:					
South	00	South west	00	South east	01
Midlands	00	East Anglia	02	North east	00
North west	00	Scotland	00	Wales	00
N Ireland	00	Rep Ireland	00	I of Man/CI	00

Costs
Total	No information supplied
Franchise fee:	£5,000
Other charges:	£6,700
Min cash excluding bank:	£4,000
Min overdraft required:	£8,000
Normal bank advance:	66%
Working capital first 2 months:	No information supplied
Associated banks:	Lloyds
Capital items required:	Computer and office equipment
Associated leasing co:	None

Royalties
	7.5% of turnover
	0.0% accounts service
	0.0% for advertising fund
Total	7.5% monthly sales
	No standing royalty independent of turnover

Bank rating	No information supplied
Territory	Number of private and NHS hospital beds
Strings	No information supplied
Training	10 days practical training
	6 days management training
	Cost: £750 – included in franchise fee
	Training value: No information supplied
Support	No information supplied
Operating Manual	No information supplied
Profit	Net profit year 1 £11,000
Risk	An area of growing demand
Management only	Reasonable return for owner with management ability

Size and reach
Original company launched:	1962
Overseas connections:	None
UK connections:	None
Viable for whole UK?	Yes
Trade bodies	FRES; Reg by Dept of Employment

Franchisor's formula for success
Nursing agencies cover one of the fastest growing areas of the recruitment and employment industry. The operation is computer based. The job of interviewing, selecting and placing nurses must be carried out by a Registered Nurse although the franchisee need not be a Registered Nurse.

Oasis Trading

Good Franchise Guide comment: Recent franchise in a growth area from an established company; should be a viable proposition. It would have been helpful to know more from the franchisees' point of view.

Number of franchisee addresses provided by franchisor: 00

⇨ **Oasis Trading**
7/8 Cave Street, Oxford, OX4 1BA
Phone: 0865 723561

Importers of ladies clothing, jewellery, fashion accessories, gifts, basketware, rugs, dhurries and living items

Outlets
Number of outlets
Company owned outlets: 11
Franchised: 18
Pilot: 01 started 1981/2
1988 franchise target: 35
Current reach:

South	15	South west	04	South east	00
Midlands	04	East Anglia	02	North east	01
North west	00	Scotland	03	Wales	00
N Ireland	00	Rep Ireland	00	I of Man/CI	00

Costs
Total   £55,000 to £65,000
Franchise fee: £10,000
Other charges: Nil
Min cash excluding bank: £20,000
Min overdraft required: No information supplied
Normal bank advance: 66%
Working capital first 2 months: £15,000
Associated banks: All major clearing banks
Capital items required: No information supplied
Associated leasing co: None

Royalties

Total
0.0% of turnover
0.0% accounts service
2.0% for advertising fund
2.0% monthly sales

10.0% of rental cost of lease for shop standing royalty independent of turnover

Bank rating   Very helpful
Territory   Each location is dependent on the size of town
                     Franchisees report: Felt to be just about right
Strings   Very strong ties for products
Training   14 days practical training
                     14 days management training
                     Cost: Nil – included in franchise fee
                     Training value: 'Not enough'

Support   Very good
Operating Manual Good
Profit   Much lower than expected
Risk   High street fashion is one of the riskiest areas there is.
Management only Reasonable return for owner with management ability.

O'Corrain Heraldry

Size and reach

Original company launched:	1975
Overseas connections:	Export to USA, Ireland and Europe
UK connections:	None
Viable for whole UK?	Yes
Trade bodies	BFA

Franchisor's formula for success
One of the few franchises available in ladies fashion and accessories. We design, source and manufacture our products. The image we seek to achieve is of a co-ordinated look for women who want to buy their clothing from a shop offering unusual designs at sensible prices.

Inside story from the franchisees
Out of the 15 franchisees we contacted three were willing to answer our questions. All were very negative, but all acknowledged that changes are taking place, and all expected things to get better.

Insider tips
Check up that changes have taken place in 1988.

Moans and groans
Training not sufficient, products not good enough, delivery too late.

Good Franchise Guide comment: When things are going wrong people complain, when they are going well they just get on with the job. What we may have here is a case of three franchisees having a hard time who have felt the need to complain, while the rest are doing all right. The moral must be to get in touch with as many franchisees as possible before making any decision.

Number of franchisee addresses provided by franchisor: 15

➪ O'Corrain Heraldry

c/o Alphacrest Ltd, Charterland House, 2251 Coventry Road, Sheldon, Birmingham

This franchise has been listed in some reference books and magazines. We have been unable to obtain information either in response to general requests from would-be franchisees or specifically for this publication. In the light of this experience we suggest that a cautious approach may be best if this franchise does reappear.

➪ Olivers UK Ltd

Eagle Court, Harpur Street, Bedford MK40 1JZ
Phone: 0234 32818

Coffee shops and bakeries

Outlets

Number of outlets	
Company owned outlets:	11
Franchised:	17 plus three bakeries
Pilot:	No information supplied
1988 franchise target:	No information supplied

Current reach:

South	02	South west	01	South east	06
Midlands	01	East Anglia	02	North east	03
North west	02	Scotland	12	Wales	02
N Ireland	00	Rep Ireland	00	I of Man/CI	00

Opportunity Exchange

Costs

Total	£250,000
Franchise fee:	£10,000
Other charges:	£32,000 professional fees
Min cash excluding bank:	£90,000
Min overdraft required:	No information supplied
Normal bank advance:	No information supplied
Working capital first 2 months:	No information supplied
Associated banks:	Nat West
Capital items required:	Shopfitting £120,000
	Heating, equipment etc £80,000
Associated leasing co:	None

Royalties

	8.0% of turnover
	0.0% accounts service
	0.0% for advertising fund
Total	8.0% monthly sales
	No standing royalty independent of turnover

Bank rating	No information supplied
Territory	No information supplied
Strings	Although the material we have doesn't specifically say so we presume all food is bought from Olivers
Training	Up to 3 months practical and management training (depending on previous experience)
	Cost: No information supplied
	Training value: No information supplied
Support	No information supplied
Operating Manual	No information supplied
Profit	Year 1 net profit shown as £51,000
Risk	Looks well established; limited risk
Management only	Could be run by manager but with limited profit

Size and reach

Original company launched:	No information supplied
Overseas connections:	No information supplied
UK connections:	No information supplied
Viable for whole UK?	Yes
Trade bodies	BFA

Franchisor's formula for success

Our reputation for wholesome fresh food and good service in a pleasant eating environment makes us ideally suited for today's high street, where shopping for pleasure is the order of the day.

Good Franchise Guide comment: No information from the franchisor supplied to us, but this is an established franchise and with £250,000 set up costs we presume you are not going to take this on without finding out more.

Number of franchisee addresses provided by franchisor: 00

➪ **Opportunity Exchange**

Previously at: Snow House, 103 Southwark Street, London SE1 0JF

A business services franchise at this name and address has been listed in some reference books and magazines. Mail sent to this address is now being returned by the Post Office marked 'Gone Away'. Enquiries have revealed that no forwarding address has been left and there is no telephone number listed for the firm in London, although it is possible that the franchise may have been set up once more in another part of the country. In the light of this experience we suggest a certain amount of caution may be in order.

Original Art Shops Ltd

⇨ Original Art Shops Ltd
12 Southchurch Road, Southend-on-Sea, Essex SS1 2NE
Phone: 0702 460391

Retail art outlets

Outlets
Number of outlets	
Company owned outlets:	5 (approx)
Franchised:	25 (approx)
Pilot:	No information supplied
1988 franchise target:	No information supplied

Costs
Total	£30,000
Franchise fee:	£2,500
Other charges:	No information supplied
Min cash excluding bank:	£12,000
Min overdraft required:	£30,000
Normal bank advance:	No information supplied
Working capital first 2 months:	No information supplied
Associated banks:	Barclays, Lloyds
Capital items required:	None
Associated leasing co:	None

Royalties: 10% of turnover (no information on advertising proportion)

Bank rating	No information supplied
Territory	No information supplied
Strings	No information supplied
Training	Described as comprehensive
Support	No information supplied
Operating Manual	No information supplied
Profit	Net profit in example provided by franchisor shown as £18,819
Risk	No information supplied
Management only	Little salary to spare for a manager

Size and reach
Original company launched:	1981
Overseas connections:	None
UK connections:	None
Viable for whole UK?	Yes
Trade bodies	BFA Register

Franchisor's formula for success
Original Art Shops Ltd was formed in 1981 in order to bridge the gap which so obviously exists in the market by providing a wide range of realistically priced paintings and pictures ranging from original oils to reproduction lithographs, complemented by a framing service that perfectly finishes the picture.

Good Franchise Guide comment: Glossy brochure weak on hard facts about royalties etc. But if finances are OK could be fun for someone desperate to be in the art world.

Number of franchisee addresses provided by franchisor: 00

➪ The Original Kitchen Company Ltd
131 Penwith Road, London SW18 4PZ
Phone: 01-870 6179

Retailers of hand painted kitchen furniture, made to customer order selling for £2,000 to £15,000 with an associated kitchen design service and an open ended guarantee. (See note under 'Inside Story' below.)

Outlets
Number of outlets
Company owned outlets: 04
Franchised: 03
Pilot: 04 started 1981
1988 franchise target: 12
Current reach:

South	03	South west	01	South east	03
Midlands	00	East Anglia	00	North east	00
North west	00	Scotland	00	Wales	00
N Ireland	00	Rep Ireland	00	I of Man/CI	00

Costs
Total   No information supplied
Franchise fee: £3,000
Other charges: £77,000 maximum
Min cash excluding bank: £30,800
Min overdraft required: £20,000
Normal bank advance: 70%
Working capital first 2 months: £14,000
Associated banks: Barclays
Capital items required: Shopfitting mainly
Associated leasing co: None

Royalties
                    10.0% of turnover
                    0.0% accounts service
                    0.0% for advertising fund
Total   10.0% monthly sales
                    No standing royalty independent of turnover

Bank rating   No information supplied
Territory   Radius from base
Strings   Tied to one manufacturer

Training   14 days practical training
                   14 days management training
                   Cost: £4,000 – included in franchise fee
                   Training value: No information supplied

Support   No information supplied
Operating Manual   No information supplied
Profit   No information supplied – no figures in brochure
Risk   Much competition, but as long as houses remain an investment for the middle classes the should be no falling off in demand

Management only   Reasonable return for owner with management ability

Size and reach
Original company launched: 1980
Overseas connections: None
UK connections: None
Viable for whole UK?   Mainly in the south
Trade bodies   None

Panarama Sunroofs Ltd

Franchisor's formula for success
Our furniture is made to customer order – not stacked in a warehouse – so individual requirements can, and will be catered for. The hand painting gives free rein to the imagination, and the company aims to offer a quality of service now sadly lacking elsewhere.

Inside story from the franchisees
The company is in the early stages of establishing a complete franchise network and it is not yet entirely clear if it will eventually do so. For this reason the company has not supplied details of franchisees.

Good Franchise Guide comment: A franchise just starting to feel its way; the franchisor's caution does him credit at a time when so many others appear to be rushing in at full speed without thinking of the dangers.

Number of franchisee addresses provided by franchisor: 00

➪ Panarama Sunroofs Ltd

25/26 Kernan Drive, Bishops Meadow Industrial Estate, Loughborough, Leics LE11 0JF
Phone: 0509 233033

Sunroofs for cars

Although listed as a franchise in some publications this appears to us to be a straight dealership, judging by the material supplied to our would-be franchisee. No royalties or other fees were mentioned – our franchisee was merely asked to fill out an application form for an account.

Training   Optional training course available to management training
                        Cost: Nil – included in franchise fee
                        Training value: No further information on training supplied

Size and reach
Original company launched: 1976
Overseas connections: None
UK connections: Part of TKD Industries
Viable for whole UK?   Yes
Trade bodies: None

Franchisor's formula for success
Panarama Sunroofs are produced at our factory where only the best materials are used incorporating the latest manufacturing technology. Quality is always a priority and our sunroofs are fully guaranteed.

Number of franchisee addresses provided by franchisor: 00

➪ The Pancake Place

30 New Road, Milnathort, Kinross KY13 7XT
Phone: 0577 63969

Pancake restaurants

Outlets
Number of outlets
Company owned outlets: 01
Franchised: 20
Pilot: No information supplied
1988 franchise target: No information supplied

The Pancake Place

Costs
Total	£87,000 to £98,000
Franchise fee:	£5,000
Other charges:	Kitchen equipment (£20,000 included in total above)
Min cash excluding bank:	No information supplied
Min overdraft required:	No information supplied
Normal bank advance:	No information supplied
Working capital first 2 months:	No information supplied
Associated banks:	None
Capital items required:	Shopfitting £55,000, tables etc £12,000, kitchen equipment above
Associated leasing co:	None

Royalties

5.0% of turnover
0.0% accounts service
3.0% for advertising and research fund
Total — 8.0% monthly sales

No standing royalty independent of turnover

Bank rating — No information supplied
Territory — No information supplied
Strings — No information supplied
Training — 4 weeks practical and management training
Cost: Nil – included in franchise fee
Training value: No information supplied

Support — No information supplied
Operating Manual — No information supplied
Profit — Net profit quoted at 20%
Risk — Always a risk basing a restaurant around one product – either from fashions changing, or from a rival setting up next door.

Management only — Could be run by manager but with limited profit

Size and reach
Original company launched:	No information supplied
Overseas connections:	None
UK connections:	None
Viable for whole UK?	Yes
Trade bodies	No information supplied

Franchisor's formula for success
The Pancake Place is a unique restaurant concept. Menus consist almost entirely of pancakes crammed with savoury fillings or smothered in sweet toppings all of which are prepared in a variety of portion sizes to cater for differing appetites. Such is the success of our operation that Pancake Places may be found throughout the country – each maintaining our readily identifiable corporate image.

Good Franchise Guide comment: Would-be franchisees currently receive a standard letter stating 'Recent market research has indicated that some changes to our present concept in terms of decor and menu should open up previously untapped sectors of the market for us and we hope also produce a higher spend per head (sic). For the time being we are not actively seeking new sites for franchisees in view of these developments . . .' At least they are honest enough to suggest the concept needs modifying, although just how much they need to improve spend per head, we don't know. Our advice: wait and see.

Number of franchisee addresses provided by franchisor: 00

Paper Place

⇨ Paper Place

c/o The Franchise Shop Ltd, 26 High Street, Merstham, Surrey RH1 3EA
Phone: 073 74 4211

Retail outlets for address books to writing paper

Outlets
Number of outlets
Company owned outlets:	No information supplied
Franchised:	No information supplied
Pilot:	No information supplied
1988 franchise target:	No information supplied

Costs
Total	£27,000
Franchise fee:	No information supplied
Other charges:	No information supplied
Min cash excluding bank:	£13,000
Min overdraft required:	No information supplied
Normal bank advance:	50%
Working capital first 2 months:	No information supplied
Associated banks:	None
Capital items required:	None
Associated leasing co:	None

Royalties
No information supplied

Bank rating No information supplied
Territory No information supplied
Strings No information supplied

Training No information supplied
Support No information supplied
Operating Manual No information supplied
Profit 'Earnings of the order of £20,000 to £30,000 per annum'
Risk High – an attempt to take on the greeting card shop on the one hand and WH Smith on the other.

Management only Could be run by manager but with limited profit

Size and reach
Original company launched:	No information supplied
Overseas connections:	None
UK connections:	None
Viable for whole UK?	Yes
Trade bodies	None

Franchisor's formula for success Paper Place stock address books, bags, boxes, bulldog clips, carriers, cases, drawing pins, files, gift tags, gift wrap, greetings cards, invitations, mobiles, napkins, notelets, notepads, paper clips, paper cups, paper decorations, paper plates, portfolios, postcards, posters, ribbon, stickers, tissue paper, writing paper.

Good Franchise Guide comment: Inadequate information to make any real judgement. No reply from the consultant to our questions. There is a move to more specialist shops these days, but that does not mean they will all make a fortune.

Number of franchisee addresses provided by franchisor: 00

Party Rentals

⇨ Paramount Syndications
34 Ivor Place, London NW1 6EA
Phone: 01-724 0848

Card retailers

Outlets
Number of outlets	
Company owned outlets:	01
Franchised:	00
Pilot:	No information supplied
1988 franchise target:	No information supplied

Costs
Total £10,000
No other information supplied

Profit	£350 per annum per location forecast
Risk	No information supplied
Management only	One-man-band operation

Size and reach
Original company launched:	No information supplied
Overseas connections:	None
UK connections:	None
Viable for whole UK?	Yes
Trade bodies	None

Franchisor's formula for success
We have developed a unique new way of selling greeting cards on a shop in shop basis. In just six months the success of our unique marketing system can be seen in 3000 retail outlets throughout the UK. In most department stores the greeting card department is usually contracted out to an outside operator. Sunny Message cards are sold as normal except that our merchandising unit only takes up one square foot of floor space.

Good Franchise Guide comment: Another neat idea, but no real information in brochure

Number of franchisee addresses provided by franchisor: 00

⇨ Party Rentals
16 North Road, Whittlesford, Cambridge CB2 4NZ
Phone: 0223 833100

Catering equipment rental

Outlets
Number of outlets	
Company owned outlets:	01
Franchised:	00
Pilot:	No information supplied
1988 franchise target:	No information supplied

Costs
Total	£28,000
Franchise fee:	£5,500
Other charges:	£12,700 stock
Min cash excluding bank:	£13,000
Min overdraft required:	£5,000
Normal bank advance:	£18,000
Working capital first 2 months:	No information supplied
Associated banks:	None
Capital items required:	£3,800 'Equipment'
Associated leasing co:	None

No other information provided on royalties etc

215

Pass & Co Ltd

Size and reach
Original company launched: No information supplied
Overseas connections: None
UK connections: Division of Cambridge Catering Equipment Hire
Viable for whole UK?   Yes
Trade bodies   None

Franchisor's formula for success
Become a Party Rentals franchise and you will be able to draw upon the experience and expertise we have accumulated in over 30 years of working in this trade. You will feel confident in knowing that as well as marquees and accessories, silverware, table linen, serving dishes and glassware, we have available over 6000 place settings in three qualities of china and cutlery.

Good Franchise Guide comment: Good basic finance information supplied by franchisor for franchisees, but we could only see a note which says there is a management charge – no indication of how much – or any profit projections. On the other hand there is more here than supplied by the other companies in the marquee hire business.

Number of franchisee addresses provided by franchisor: 00

⇨ Pass & Co Ltd
Passco House, 635 High Road, Leytonstone, London E11 4RD
Phone: 01-539 1105

Timber preservation

Outlets
Number of outlets
Company owned outlets: 01
Franchised: 11
Pilot: No information supplied
1988 franchise target: No information supplied

Costs
Total   £11,500
Franchise fee: No information supplied
Other charges: No information supplied
Min cash excluding bank: £5,000
Min overdraft required: No information supplied
Normal bank advance: 60%
Working capital first 2 months: No information supplied
Associated banks: None
Capital items required: Van
Associated leasing co: None

Royalties
                             Sales letter quotes 10% but gives no information on division between advertising account and other uses of the royalty.

Bank rating   No information supplied
Territory   No information supplied
Strings   Tied to the franchisor for materials
Training   Training is given but no details provided
Support   No information supplied
Operating Manual   No information supplied
Profit   Net profit £12,500 quoted
Risk   Not a high risk area
Management only   One-man-band operation

Size and reach
Original company launched: Company 'over 25 years old'
Overseas connections: None
UK connections: None
Viable for whole UK? Yes, except Ireland
Trade bodies British Wood Preserving Assn, BFA

Franchisor's formula for success
Pass & Co are specialists in timber preservation and damp eradication. Our services have been available for over two decades and we are extremely well known in the industry and with potential customers.

Good Franchise Guide comment: Constant demand for this service, but we lack information. Over 40 territories are said to remain available.

Number of franchisee addresses provided by franchisor: 00

⇨ Pava Products
15 Banks Lane, Bexleyheath, Kent DA6 6BH
Phone 01-301 0333

We have been unable to obtain information from this franchise. Our would-be franchisee telephoned and confirmed that this was a company offered franchises. More information was promised, but as yet it has not arrived. Note however that this franchise is still listed under an old Tunbridge Wells address in some reference books.

⇨ PDC Copyprint (Franchise) Ltd
1 Church Lane, East Grinstead, West Sussex RH19 3AZ
Phone: 0342 315321

All-British fast print and copy shops

Outlets
Number of outlets
Company owned outlets: 01
Franchised: 18
Pilot: 01 started 1975
1988 franchise target: 26
Current reach:

South	04	South west	01	South east	06
Midlands	02	East Anglia	00	North east	00
North west	02	Scotland	04	Wales	00
N Ireland	00	Rep Ireland	00	I of Man/CI	00

Costs
Total £62,000
Franchise fee: £9,500
Other charges:
Min cash excluding bank: £21,000
Min overdraft required: ⎫
Normal bank advance: ⎬ £41,000
Working capital first 2 months: ⎭
Associated banks: Nat West
Capital items required: Printing equipment and photocopier
Associated leasing co: None

Royalties
 6.0% of turnover
 0.0% accounts service
 4.0% for advertising fund reducing to 2%
Total 10.0% monthly sales reducing to 8%

Peak Insulation Ltd

	No standing royalty independent of turnover
Bank rating	Most franchisees found banks 'not too helpful'
Territory	Sufficient to open 2 to 3 shops
	Franchisees report: Just right
Strings	Lots of ties but some freedom too.
Training	5 days practical training
	15 days management training
	Cost: Nil – included in franchise fee
	Training value: 'Not enough'
Support	Good
Operating Manual	Not too good
Profit	As projected or 'just under'
Risk	A lot of similar franchises around in this very competitive market.
Management only	Reasonable return for owner with management ability

Size and reach

Original company launched:	1982
Overseas connections:	'Scandinavia' – no further information given
UK connections:	None
Viable for whole UK?	Yes
Trade bodies	BFA, British Assn of Print and Copyshops

Franchisor's formula for success
1. Intake restricted to 6 pa to give maximum support in vital first year.
2. Reducing royalty scheme.
3. Bigger territories – room for expansion
4. Holiday relief scheme available.

Inside story from the franchisees
'Franchise is cheaper than other franchises to start with but you get what you pay for.'

Insider tips
'One of the most comprehensive and clear guides to a franchise that we have received.'

Moans and groans
None save that in one or two cases profit was slightly lower than expected.

Number of franchisee addresses provided by franchisor: 17

⇨ **Peak Insulation Ltd**
60 Buxton Road, Hazel Grove, Stockport SK7 6AE
Phone: 061-456 9498

Suppliers and installers of Peak Rock-wool cavity insulation fibre

Outlets
Number of outlets

Company owned outlets:	00
Franchised:	06
Pilot:	00
1988 franchise target:	30

Current reach:

South	01	South west	00	South east	00
Midlands	01	East Anglia	00	North east	01
North west	02	Scotland	00	Wales	00
N Ireland	01	Rep Ireland	00	I of Man/CI	00

Peak Insulation Ltd

Costs
Total	Nil
Franchise fee:	Nil
Other charges:	Cost of machine
Min cash excluding bank:	£10,000
Min overdraft required:	No information supplied
Normal bank advance:	No information supplied
Working capital first 2 months:	No information supplied
Associated banks:	Nat West
Capital items required:	35cwt Luton bodied van; £6,500
Associated leasing co:	None

Royalties

Total
- 0.0% of turnover
- 0.0% accounts service
- 0.0% for advertising fund
- 0.0% monthly sales

No standing royalty independent of turnover

Bank rating	No information supplied
Territory	Radius from base
Strings	No information supplied
Training	4 days practical training
	4 hours management training
	Cost: No charge made
	Training value: No information supplied
Support	No information supplied
Operating Manual	No information supplied
Profit	No information supplied
Risk	Moderate risk industry; image affected by 'cowboys'
Management only	Could be run by manager but with limited profit

Size and reach
Original company launched:	1966
Overseas connections:	None
UK connections:	None
Viable for whole UK?	Yes
Trade bodies	Approved by British Board of Agrement

Franchisor's formula for success
With Peak Rock-wool you have complete peace of mind. On every Peak approved installation your customer will receive a guarantee, backed by Peak and Pilkington Insulation, one of Britain's leading companies. The product is guaranteed by Pilkington Insulation for a period of 50 years. The installer can recover the investment in his/her business in one year by installing just one job per day. The customer can recover the cost of their installation in reducing heating bills within 3 – 4 years.

Good Franchise Guide comment: The company make their profit by selling the machines and materials to the franchisee. No royalties are paid. Sadly we were unable to obtain a list of franchisees to ascertain how well this non-royalty system works.

Number of franchisee addresses provided by franchisor: 00

Perfect Pizza

⇨ Perfect Pizza

65 Staines Road, Hounslow, Middx TW3 3HW
Phone: 01-577 1711

Pizza take-away and delivery service

Outlets
Number of outlets
Company owned outlets: 03
Franchised: 77
Pilot: 00
1988 franchise target: 140
Current reach:

South	61	South west	04	South east	05
Midlands	08	East Anglia	01	North east	01
North west	00	Scotland	00	Wales	00
N Ireland	00	Rep Ireland	00	I of Man/CI	00

Costs
Total	approx: £70,000
Franchise fee:	£4,000
Other charges:	No information supplied
Min cash excluding bank:	£25,000
Min overdraft required:	No information supplied
Normal bank advance:	66%
Working capital first 2 months:	No information supplied
Associated banks:	All major high street banks
Capital items required:	Ovens, about £8,000
Associated leasing co:	None

Royalties

Total
5.0% of turnover
0.0% accounts service
3.0% for advertising fund
8.0% monthly sales

No standing royalty independent of turnover

Bank rating No information supplied
Territory No information supplied
Strings No information supplied

Training
7 days practical training
No management training
Cost: Nil – included in franchise fee
Training value: No information supplied

Support No information supplied
Operating Manual No information supplied
Profit No information supplied
Risk Pizza is a highly competitive area, but the association of Wimpy and United Biscuits would appear to reduce the risk dramatically

Management only Proven franchise with good return on investment

Size and reach
Original company launched:	1978
Overseas connections:	None
UK connections:	Parent company: United Biscuits
Viable for whole UK?	Just south of England
Trade bodies	Pizza and Pasta Assn, BFA

Phone-In UK Ltd

Franchisor's formula for success
Perfect Pizza enjoys the franchising expertise of Wimpy, and the deep product understanding of Pizzaland, both of which are United Biscuits companies. In addition Perfect Pizza is a member of the British Franchise Association. Thus the interests of both franchisor and Perfect Pizza franchisees are represented and protected at every level.

Good Franchise Guide comment: This franchisor was very forthcoming and among other things supplied us with the phone numbers of various franchisees (although not the addresses). It was *The Good Franchise Guide* that decided against phoning rather than writing – we ask a lot of franchisees in providing us with information, and to interrupt their work with a prolonged phone call seemed to be asking too much.

Number of franchisee addresses provided by franchisor: 52

ᗧ **Phildar (UK) Ltd**
4 Gambrel Road, Northampton NN5 5NF
Phone: 0604 583111

This franchise informs us that the company is fully committed for the foreseeable future, in terms of franchising, but is now offering alternative trading options as follows:

1. Semi-specialist account, whereby 'you may stock Phildar yarn alongside other products – ie haberdashery, fabrics etc, but excluding competitors' yarns. This account is operated on an annual contract basis and offers a 10.5% discount off invoice for all goods (excluding items of furniture).'

2. Multi-brand account whereby 'you may stock the Phildar range alongside any competitors' products. There are no contractual obligations but we do offer a quantity bonus on your purchases.'

What we don't understand is that if anyone can open these accounts and so sell the products, what is special about the franchise?

ᗧ **Phone-In UK Ltd**
Thomas Watson House, Northumberland Street, Darlington, Co Durham DL3 7HJ
Phone: 0325 483859

Telephone shops with good visual image supplying domestic and business users

Outlets
Number of outlets
Company owned outlets: 03
Franchised: 04
Pilot: 03 started 1985 and 1986
1988 franchise target: 20
Current reach:

South	00	South west	00	South east	00
Midlands	00	East Anglia	00	North east	06
North west	01	Scotland	00	Wales	00
N Ireland	00	Rep Ireland	00	I of Man/CI	00

Costs
Total   £22,000
Franchise fee: £3,000
Other charges: £9,750 franchise package
Min cash excluding bank: £12,000
Min overdraft required: £3,000
Normal bank advance: £7,090
Working capital first 2 months: £3,000
Associated banks: 'Close association with two major banks'
Capital items required: Vehicle (HP), shopfittings, demonstration units
Associated leasing co: Yes – no details given

Phone-In UK Ltd

Royalties

	3.0% of turnover
	3.0% accounts service
	0.0% for advertising fund
Total	6.0% monthly sales
	No standing royalty independent of turnover

Bank rating — Banks helpful – no problem
Territory — Minimum population 80,000. Decided on population and household types relating to census data.
Franchisees report: Just right
Strings — Lots of ties but lots of freedom too
Training — 2 weeks practical training
1 week management training
Cost: £500 – included in franchise fee
Training value: Good
Support — Very good
Operating Manual — Very good
Profit — No information supplied
Risk — Growing sector, but competition is growing apace
Management only — Reasonable return for owner with management ability

Size and reach

Original company launched:	1985
Overseas connections:	None
UK connections:	None
Viable for whole UK?	Yes
Trade bodies	Founder member of Telecommunications Industry Assn

Franchisor's formula for success
The independent telecommunications market is one of the fastest growing sectors of the British economy. Since the privatisation of British Telecom and the liberalisation of the industry, more and more people are choosing to buy their own equipment rather than continue to rent. A conservative estimate of the current retail sales value of the telephone market in the UK is £100 million per annum.

Inside story from the franchisees
Manual covers everything from starting the shop right through. 'It's our bible.'
'I firmly believe in Phone-In. Everyone is very approachable for even the simplest query and we are all kept well informed of new developments. Although small at the moment, the company has, and deserves, good prospects in the future.'

Insider tips
One franchisee got an Enterprise Allowance – worth looking into.
'Must be aware of the time, effort and commitment required and be prepared for the worst before it gets better.'

Moans and groans
None, except for the fact that it is hard work.

Number of franchisee addresses provided by franchisor: 04

Photomaid Ltd

⇨ Photomaid Ltd
47 First Avenue, Deeside Industrial Park, Deeside, Clwyd, CH5 2NU
Phone: 0244 823177

One hour photo developing and printing

Outlets
Number of outlets
Company owned outlets: 300 +
Franchised: 00
Pilot: 04 started 1987
1988 franchise target: 40
Current reach:

South	00	South west	00	South east	00
Midlands	00	East Anglia	00	North east	00
North west	00	Scotland	00	Wales	00
N Ireland	00	Rep Ireland	00	I of Man/CI	00

Costs
Total: £28,000
Franchise fee: £4,500
Other charges: No information supplied
Min cash excluding bank: £6,000
Min overdraft required: £2,000
Normal bank advance: No information supplied
Working capital first 2 months: £2,000
Associated banks: None
Capital items required: Photographic minilab
Associated leasing co: Yes – no details supplied

Royalties
In the quoted example of a series of typical years the licence fee is shown as decreasing as the turnover increases.

£4,500 standing royalty independent of turnover

Bank rating No franchisees as yet to supply information
Territory Based on 20,000 population
Strings No information supplied

Training
4 days practical training
1 day management training
Cost: Nil – included in franchise fee
Training value: No franchisees as yet to supply views

Support No franchisees as yet to supply views
Operating Manual No franchisees as yet to supply views
Profit Operating profit in first year quoted at £19,990
Risk No information supplied
Management only Could be run by manager but with limited profit

Size and reach
Original company launched: 1987
Overseas connections: None
UK connections: Captoch Ltd has supplied and fitted out 300 plus similar units within last three years; owner-operated.

Viable for whole UK? Yes
Trade bodies None

Franchisor's formula for success
Apart from the growth of the overall market, one hour photo processing is the fastest growing sector and almost doubles its market share each year. Kodak predict that by 1990 one hour shops will account for 25% of the market and will eventually attain 40%.

Photomarkets (UK) Ltd

Good Franchise Guide comment: A brand new franchise for which we have limited information. However, it has the virtue of a wide franchisor owned base and four separate pilots. The company also offer the Data Maid franchise (qv). Could be one to watch although there are a number of other franchises recently launched in this field, and some high street stores offering in-house services.

Number of franchisee addresses provided by franchisor: 00

➪ Photomarkets (UK) Ltd
Previously at Unit 9, Raynham Road Industrial Estate, Bishop's Stortford, Herts

A franchise at this name and address has been listed in some reference books and magazines. Mail sent to this address is now being returned by the Post Office marked 'Gone Away' and the telephone number quoted has been reissued to Abbey Life. Enquiries have revealed that no forwarding address has been left, and Telecom have no listing for this company within Bishop's Stortford, although it is possible that the franchise may have been set up once more in another part of the country. In the light of this experience we suggest a certain amount of caution may be in order.

➪ Pickwicks of England
Unit 5 Cross Fields Industrial Estate, Lichfield, Staffs WS13 6RJ
Phone: 0543 258454

Unique mobile catering from hand built Victorian kitchen equipment

Outlets
Number of outlets — No information supplied – see comment below

Costs
Total — Up to: £20,000
Franchise fee: — Nil
Other charges: — Nil – customers simply purchase the equipment

Working capital first 2 months: £300

Royalties
No royalties payable

Bank rating — Depends on applicant
Territory — No restrictions
Strings — None – the company sells the machine and you are on your own.

Training — Half day practical training
No management training
Cost: None
Training value: No information supplied

Support — None
Operating Manual — Instruction book only
Profit — Depends on operator
Risk — Anyone can buy a machine, so you could find yourself in direct competition.
Management only — Varies depending on how many sites the owner has

Size and reach
Original company launched: 1979
Overseas connections: Distributors in Europe
UK connections: None
Viable for whole UK? Yes
Trade bodies None

Franchisor's formula for success
Pickwicks is synonymous with unique mobile catering and is renowned for being the company that started an industry. The inherent beauty of the classic machines is supported by quality engineering. These hardworking commercial units will earn their keep for years to come.

Insider tips
Pickwicks is not a franchise in the normal sense of the word in that the company merely sell its food vending machines with their traditional design. The link with franchising comes from the fact that the food machines are unique in appearance and commonly found at shows and the like, thus leading to a corporate identity in the public mind. A typical item, the King George Victorian counter oven with warming oven, costs £896.00.

Number of franchisee addresses provided by franchisor: 00

⇨ PIP Printing (Franprint Ltd)
Black Arrow House, 2 Chandos Road, London NW10 6NF
Phone: 01-965 0700

Franprint is the master licence holder of the American fast printing and copying retailer PIP Instant Printing

Outlets
Number of outlets
Company owned outlets:	03
Franchised:	55
Pilot:	07 started 1965 in USA
1988 franchise target:	100
Current reach:	
	No regional information supplied

Costs
Total	£73,000 including working capital
Franchise fee:	£8,500
Other charges:	Nil
Min cash excluding bank:	£23,000
Min overdraft required:	£18,000
Normal bank advance:	Up to 70%
Working capital first 2 months:	£25,000 (specified as opening working capital)
Associated banks:	All major banks
Capital items required:	Printing press and plate making camera; equipment package £23,000; shopfitting £15,000
Associated leasing co:	None

Royalties
	7.5% of turnover
	0.0% accounts service
	2.5% for advertising fund
Total	10.0% monthly sales
	No standing royalty independent of turnover

Bank rating	No information supplied
Territory	Location of franchise within a defined marketing area
Strings	Strong ties for materials
Training	4 weeks practical and management training Cost: Nil – included in franchise fee Training value: No information supplied

Pizza Hut

Support	No information supplied
Operating Manual	No information supplied
Profit	'You can expect to lose money in your first year'
Risk	Highly competitive area in which only those firms with polished presentations will survive.
Management only	Little salary to spare for a manager in first shop but better management prospects with several shops

Size and reach

Original company launched:	1964; in 1985 the UK Master Franchise was purchased by FranPrint Ltd trading as PIP UK
Overseas connections:	1200 + stores overseas
UK connections:	Wholly owned subsidiary of Franchise Investors Ltd – city backed firm devoted to franchising
Viable for whole UK?	Yes
Trade bodies	BFA, BAPC

Franchisor's formula for success

Quick printing has proved one of the most successful and profitable types of franchise and has become over the last 20 years an industry in its own right. Pip Printing is the leader in the field.

Good Franchise Guide comment: It took a while to get a PIP brochure, and when it came we found it opened with the statement that 'you won't ever be sold by PIP – hard, soft or negative'. And that makes a change from all the franchisors who do try and sell hard with the phone calls and visits, often without presenting essential finance information first. An excellent brochure which bodes well for the company, even though we didn't get to talk to franchisees.

Number of franchisee addresses provided by franchisor: 00

⇨ Pizza Hut

Eurafme House, 2 Woodgrange Avenue, Kenton, Middx HA3 0XD
Phone: 01-959 3677

Pizza Hut, part of Pepsico Food Service International, are reported not to have any franchises on offer at present. Our would-be franchisee received a letter asking which country he was interested in – when he replied England, no further communication was received.
Obviously Pizza Hut is a major operator, backed by Pepsico.

⇨ PizzaExpress

29 Wardour Street, Soho, London W1V 3HB
Phone: 01-437 7215

Pizza shops using a unique recipe

Outlets
Number of outlets
Company owned outlets: 12
Franchised: 29
Pilot: 07 started 1965
1988 franchise target: 60
Current reach:

South	02	South west	01	South east	36
Midlands	00	East Anglia	01	North east	00
North west	00	Scotland	00	Wales	00
N Ireland	00	Rep Ireland	00	I of Man/CI	01

PizzaExpress

Costs
Total	£150,000
Franchise fee:	£12,500
Other charges:	No information supplied
Min cash excluding bank:	No information supplied
Min overdraft required:	No information supplied
Normal bank advance:	No information supplied
Working capital first 2 months:	£5,000
Associated banks:	None
Capital items required:	Oven, marble top tables, other furniture, light fittings
Associated leasing co:	None

Royalties

Total
4.0% of turnover
0.0% accounts service
0.5% for advertising fund (not yet levied)
4.0% monthly sales currently

No standing royalty independent of turnover

Bank rating Very helpful
Territory No territories are allocated
Strings Lots of ties but lots of freedom too

Training 30 days practical training
20 days management training
Cost: Nil – included in franchise fee
Training value: Excellent

Support Excellent
Operating Manual Very good
Profit Better than expected
Risk Very high competition both from other franchises and individual operators
Management only Proven franchise with good return on investment

Size and reach
Original company launched:	1965
Overseas connections:	None
UK connections:	None
Viable for whole UK?	Yes
Trade bodies	BFA, Franchise Association

Franchisor's formula for success
The PizzaExpress concept is right, it offers food that's quick and inexpensive – yet delicious, satisfying and appealing to all ages and socio-economic groups. And it does so in an atmosphere that's stylish, stimulating and fun.

Inside story from the franchisees
Very positive comments, summed up by one franchisee who said, without prompting, 'PizzaExpress is an excellent company'. After such a statement there seems little to be added.

Insider tips
None given – everything appears to be as stated by the franchisor.

Moans and groans
None

Good Franchise Guide comment: The fact that this fast food operator has been going since 1965 says a lot – it is becoming a very very competitive field.

Number of franchisee addresses provided by franchisor: 17

PJs Drive In Ltd

⇨ PJs Drive In Ltd
282a High Street, Bangor, Gwynedd
Phone: No phone number quoted on any literature

Drive-in restaurant

Outlets
Number of outlets
Company owned outlets: 01
Franchised: 00
Pilot: No information supplied
1988 franchise target: No information supplied

Costs
Total £35,500
Franchise fee: £3,500
Other charges: £4,000 Business package
Min cash excluding bank: No information supplied
Min overdraft required: No information supplied
Normal bank advance: No information supplied
Working capital first 2 months: No information supplied
Associated banks: None
Capital items required: None
Associated leasing co: None

Royalties
7.5% of turnover
0.0% accounts service
0.0% for advertising fund
Total 7.5% monthly sales

No standing royalty independent of turnover

Bank rating No information supplied
Territory No information supplied
Strings No information supplied
Training 'Intensive' – no indication of how long it lasts is given in the brochure
Support No information supplied
Operating Manual No information supplied
Profit First year net profit quoted as £14,965
Risk Drive-ins are springing up elsewhere – we have a major one within a couple of miles of our editorial offices. If they do take off expect all the majors to be active within 18 months.
Management only Could be run by manager but with limited profit

Size and reach
Original company launched: No information supplied
Overseas connections: None
UK connections: None
Viable for whole UK? Yes
Trade bodies None

Franchisor's formula for success
'PJs Drive In is the first American style drive in takeaway fast food operation in Britain ... PJs Drive In is a unique concept in the British fast food market that not only brings together all that's best in the most successful American drive in takeaway operations but also gives you all the professional help you need – literally from the ground up.'

Good Franchise Guide comment: This could work well – especially as the pilot is running in Bangor – not known as the centre of progressive restauranting. It really is a shame that the franchisor would not tell us more.

Number of franchisee addresses provided by franchisor: 00

➪ Plastercure/30 Ltd

Darley House, Cow Lane, Garston, Watford, Herts WD2 6PH
Phone: 0923 223842; 663322; 241514

This is part of the Cure/30 Group of Companies Ltd comprising Dampcure/30, Woodcure/30 and Crimecure/30. A listing under Plastercure/30 does appear in some reference books. Although the franchisor has supplied information on Dampcure, Woodcure and Crimecure no information has been supplied under the name Plastercure. (A similar situation has arisen under the name Electricure, Draincure and Plumbingcure.)

➪ Plumbingcure/30 Ltd

Darley House, Cow Lane, Garston, Watford, Herts WD2 6PH
Phone: 0923 223842; 663322; 241514

This is part of the Cure/30 Group of Companies Ltd comprising Dampcure/30, Woodcure/30 and Crimecure/30. A listing under Plumbingcure/30 does appear in some reference books. Although the franchisor has supplied information on Dampcure, Woodcure and Crimecure no information has been supplied under the name Plumbingcure. (A similar situation has arisen under the name Electricure, Draincure and Plastercure.)

➪ Polymer Protection Ltd

Stone Lodge, Inkbarrow, Worcester WR7 4JJ

This 'property revitalisation' franchise has been listed in some reference books and magazines. Mail sent to this address is accepted, but we have been unable to obtain information either in response to general requests from would-be franchisees or specifically for this publication. In the light of this experience we suggest a certain amount of caution may be in order if the franchise does eventually reappear.

➪ Ponderosa Inc

PO Box 578, Dayton, Ohio 45401-0578, USA
Phone: (513) 454-2400

Note: A Ponderosa office for the UK is quoted in one magazine, but all information sent to our would-be franchisee came from the American address and made no reference to any UK address at all. Our correspondence to the UK address went unanswered.

Steak houses

Outlets
Number of outlets
Company owned outlets:	03 UK
Franchised:	01 UK
Pilot:	No information supplied
1988 franchise target:	No information supplied

Costs
Total	$1,055,000
Franchise fee:	$ 25,000
Other charges:	Nil
Min cash excluding bank:	$125,000
Min overdraft required:	No information supplied
Normal bank advance:	No information supplied
Working capital first 2 months:	$ 40,000
Associated banks:	None
Capital items required:	Equipment $250,000; building $380,000; real estate $250,000; site development $110,000
Associated leasing co:	None

Poppies UK Ltd

Note: applicants for franchises must have a verifiable net worth of $500,000 excluding personal residence

Royalties

	4.0% of turnover
	0.0% accounts service
	4.0% max for advertising fund
Total	8.0% max monthly sales
	No standing royalty independent of turnover
Bank rating	No information supplied
Territory	No information supplied
Strings	No information supplied
Training	No information supplied
Support	No information supplied
Operating Manual	No information supplied
Profit	Ought to be good with that much investment
Risk	The question is will the British take to the product
Management only	Proven franchise outside UK with good return on investment

Size and reach
Original company launched: 1965 (Indiana)
Overseas connections: American parent company with 700 franchises in USA, Canada, Puerto Rico, Virgin Islands, Europe and Far East
UK connections: None
Viable for whole UK? No information supplied
Trade bodies They must be members of some!

Franchisor's formula for success
Ponderosa steakhouses enjoy a broad economic and demographic customer base by offering outstanding value through quality food, with generous portions at reasonable prices. Ongoing market research allows the company to pinpoint changes necessary to maintain our leadership position in the family steakhouse market.

Good Franchise Guide comment: Do people worth half a million dollars (excluding the house) really want to open a steak house? Perhaps they do, and perhaps the very American styled approach will catch on here, but you have to be convinced to put up that much money.

Number of franchisee addresses provided by franchisor: 00

⇨ Poppies UK Ltd

31 Houndgate, Darlington, Co Durham DL1 5RH
Phone: 0325 488699

Cleaning service to domestic and commercial properties including spring cleans, emergency cleaning, mother's help, cleaning before and after removals, gardening etc

Outlets
Number of outlets
Company owned outlets: 01
Franchised: 70
Pilot: 01 started 1980
1988 franchise target: 120
Current reach:
  No breakdown provided for England
  Scotland   02   Wales   01
  N Ireland   01   Rep Ireland   00   I of Man/CI   00

Poppies UK Ltd

Costs
Total	£12,860
Franchise fee:	£4,000
Other charges:	No information supplied
Min cash excluding bank:	£4,000
Min overdraft required:	£2,000 to £3,000
Normal bank advance:	70% of initial cost plus working capital
Working capital first 2 months:	Varies
Associated banks:	None; finance available from all main banks
Capital items required:	Liveried vehicle included in franchise package
Associated leasing co:	Forward Trust

Royalties

Total
- 0.0% of turnover
- 0.0% accounts service
- 0.0% for advertising fund
- 0.0% monthly sales
- £2,000 pa standing royalty independent of turnover

Bank rating — No information supplied

Territory — Areas individually researched based on minimum number of potential customer households

Strings — No information supplied

Training
8 days practical training
5 days management training
Cost: Nil – included in franchise fee
Training value: No information supplied

Support — No information supplied
Operating Manual — No information supplied
Profit — No information supplied
Risk — A growing area of demand, but with several franchises plus local firms moving in. It will take a little time before the inevitable shake out occurs.

Management only — Reasonable return for owner with management ability

Size and reach
Original company launched:	1980
Overseas connections:	None
UK connections:	None
Viable for whole UK?	Yes
Trade bodies	Full member BFA

Franchisor's formula for success
Poppies' success is based on providing a specialist service to the domestic market and treating commercial customers in a caring and personal way. From providing regular weekly cleaning to private households Poppies has grown to offer a wide range of related services.

Inside story from the franchisees
Five addresses were supplied to us, but none of the franchisees was willing to answer our questions.

Number of franchisee addresses provided by franchisor: 5

Poppy's Body Centre Ltd

⇨ Poppy's Body Centre Ltd
87 Skipton Road, Harrogate HG1 4LF
Phone: 0423 500206

Retail of natural body products

Outlets
Number of outlets
Company owned outlets:	No information supplied
Franchised:	No information supplied
Pilot:	No information supplied
1988 franchise target:	No information supplied

Costs
Total	£45,000
Franchise fee:	£3,000
Other charges:	Lease premium
Min cash excluding bank:	£25,000
Min overdraft required:	No information supplied
Normal bank advance:	No information supplied
Working capital first 2 months:	No information supplied
Associated banks:	None
Capital items required:	None
Associated leasing co:	None

Royalties
	No information supplied
Support	No information supplied
Operating Manual	No information supplied
Profit	Pre-tax profit quoted at £15,750 from year one
Risk	Products all provided by Poppy's (beware you only get 21 days credit)
Management only	Could be run by manager but with limited profit

Franchisor's formula for success
Poppy's trades from prime retail high street sites of around 1000 square feet taking advantage of one of the most significant market trends of recent years, a major and continuous escalation in demand for products which are pure and natural.

Good Franchise Guide comment: Limited information available from this franchise moving into an area already dominated by one successful franchisor. The question is, how much demand is there for this type of outlet? Only the franchisees can tell us the answer.

Number of franchisee addresses provided by franchisor: 00

⇨ Portico Canopies
Abbotsfield Road, St Helens, Lancs WA9 4HU
Phone: 0744 821321

Supply of canopies for shops etc

Outlets
Number of outlets
Company owned outlets:	01
Franchised:	00
Pilot:	No information supplied
1988 franchise target:	No information supplied

Costs etc
'The usual start-up fees have been waived in order to quickly establish a network of dedicated franchisees who will be able to concentrate on building a successful business without the burden of a costly start-up. Portico derives its income solely from supplying canopies to the franchisees.'

Potholes Ltd

Franchisor's formula for success
'Canopies are recognised as a low cost high impact method of promoting an image. Their visual appeal can advertise a business, or enhance a house. Conventional canopies are constructed from plastic film stretched over a metal frame. Portico canopies are constructed as one piece integral moulding from fibreglass. They cannot rip, tear or sag. They have a tensile strength relative to steel and inherent durability of image which outshines plastic.'

Good Franchise Guide comment: The style of the presentation is that of a franchise – a word used throughout the brochure. The firm gets a listing in the normally discerning *Franchise Opportunities Directory*, and yet there is nothing we can see here to distinguish this operation from a standard distributorship run without a pilot.

Number of franchisee addresses provided by franchisor: 00

⇨ **Posh Wash**
460 Carr Place, Walton Summit, Bamber Bridge, Preston, Lancs PR5 8AU
Phone: 0772 314641

We have been unable to obtain information from this franchise despite letters both from ourselves and our would-be franchisee. Our would-be franchisee telephoned and confirmed that this was a company which offered franchises. More information was promised, but as yet it has not arrived.

⇨ **Postal Centres International Ltd**
Also known as the Taylor Harrison Group
Previously at Goodyear House, 52 – 56 Osnaburgh Street, London NW1 3ND

This franchise offered vending and advertising display centres for establishment in public places. The company went into liquidation in 1986 and was the subject of a major enquiry on Radio 4 in 1987. According to the BBC report the company claimed that it had negotiated a deal with the Post Office that it would gain a discount on postage stamps sold through its machines. This was untrue. It also claimed to have sold large numbers of advertisements for display on the machines and would pay franchisees a set commission on these sales – in fact none was sold and the advertisements appearing on demonstration models were given away – no commission was paid. It was further reported on the BBC that one day before the company went into liquidation it took a further £15,000 from a franchisee who, like most other franchisees, lost everything. The company was able to boast a supporting package from several high street banks.
Despite its record and liquidation the franchise continues to be listed in some reference books and magazines. Mail sent to this address is now being returned by the Post Office marked 'Gone Away'. Enquiries have revealed that previous directors of the company are now setting up a new franchise connected with video. In the light of this experience we suggest a certain amount of caution may be in order with any franchise involving the Taylor Harrison Group or anyone connected with it.

⇨ **Potholes Ltd**
Prospect Road, Alresford, Hants
Phone: 096 273 3025/3289

Repair and maintenance of concrete and asphalt for industry, farms and businesses.

Outlets
Number of outlets
Company owned outlets: 01
Franchised: 07
Pilot: 02 started 1983 and 1985
1988 franchise target: 23

Potholes Ltd

Current reach:

South	03	South west	01	South east	00
Midlands	01	East Anglia	00	North east	01
North west	01	Scotland	01	Wales	00
N Ireland	00	Rep Ireland	00	I of Man/CI	00

Costs
Total	£12,000 plus working capital
Franchise fee:	£7,500
Other charges:	Nil
Min cash excluding bank:	Varies – about £15,000
Min overdraft required:	Varies – about £100,000
Normal bank advance:	No fixed arrangement but banks have advanced £12,000 +
Working capital first 2 months:	£3,000
Associated banks:	None
Capital items required:	Used 35cwt transit (£2,500 to £4,000)
Associated leasing co:	None

Royalties
	6.0% of turnover
	0.5% public and employee liability
	0.0% for advertising fund
Total	6.5% monthly sales
	No standing royalty independent of turnover

Bank rating — No information supplied

Territory — 'This is our biggest problem; normally a county or two London boroughs.' Various other solutions have been tried

Strings — No information supplied

Training — 2 days initial practical training and site training as needed where an experienced man assists with any work the Franchisee needs help on
1 day management training plus unlimited follow-up
Cost: £3,000 approx – included in franchise fee
Training value: No information supplied

Management only — From a one-man-band operation up depending on the size of franchise taken on.

Size and reach
Original company launched:	1973
Overseas connections:	Middle East, Far East (no details supplied)
UK connections:	None
Viable for whole UK?	Yes
Trade bodies	None

Franchisor's formula for success
No special skills are needed; start-up as a one-man-band is practical and in many ways best; start-up as a sizeable operation is feasible for the right person with sufficient capital; quick movement into profit; suitable for both sexes.
'We are currently accepting one in three who, after three meetings, wish to join us. We never contact people, but leave it to them to contact us, thus ensuring that nobody feels under any pressure. Out of every 12 meetings we expect one to proceed to a second meeting and try, as nicely as possible, to suggest to the majority of the other 11 that our business is not for them.'

Good Franchise Guide comment: It is particularly sad that we were unable to contact franchisees of these operations. The franchisor was more than willing to supply a wide range of details about the company, and we were most impressed by their policy of selecting such a tiny percentage of applicants. It would be most helpful to know just how these carefully selected franchisees view their chosen occupation.

Number of franchisee addresses provided by franchisor: 00

⇨ PPG Industries (UK) Ltd

PO Box 359, Rotton Park Street, Ladywood, Birmingham B16 0AD
Phone: 021-455 9866

This franchise distributes paint etc to car repair and respray requirements to garages via Spraystores. Our would-be franchisee received a note stating that 'the development of our franchised outlets and independent distributors is such that it is unlikely that we shall consider further Spraystores in the near future'.

⇨ Practical Used Car Rental Ltd

137 – 145 High Street, Bordesley, Birmingham B12 0JU
Phone: 021-772 8599

Car and van hire integrating with services already provided by firms already in the motor trade

Outlets
Number of outlets
Company owned outlets: 01
Franchised: 60
Pilot: 01 started 1985
1988 franchise target: 75
Current reach:

South	05	South west	06	South east	09
Midlands	13	East Anglia	06	North east	12
North west	03	Scotland	04	Wales	02
N Ireland	00	Rep Ireland	00	I of Man/CI	00

Costs
Total	£4,000 plus vehicles (see note below)
Franchise fee:	£4,000
Other charges:	Nil
Min cash excluding bank:	No information supplied
Min overdraft required:	No information supplied
Normal bank advance:	No information supplied
Working capital first 2 months:	No information supplied
Associated banks:	All clearing banks
Capital items required:	Vehicles
Associated leasing co:	Several – no names supplied

Note: because the franchise only applies to firms already operating as a garage, car recovery service or car dealer operating from existing premises the only finance normally required will be that for the cars themselves.

Royalties
Total	6.0% of turnover
	0.0% accounts service
	*4.0% for advertising fund
	*10.0% monthly sales
	*Advertising fund is called upon only as required – 2% in November 87
	No standing royalty independent of turnover
Bank rating	Banks very helpful – although because of low set-up costs some franchisees needed no financial aid.
Territory	Population
	Franchisees report: Just right
Strings	Some ties but not many

235

PRB Self Drive Hire

Training	2 days practical training
	3 days management training
	Cost: £480 – included in franchise fee
	Training value: Excellent
Support	Very good
Operating Manual	Very good
Profit	As projected or better
Risk	Competition only comes from the limited number of other used car rental firms, and there are not many. A low risk for firms with existing suitable premises.
Management only	Proven franchise with good return on investment

Size and reach

Original company launched:	1985
Overseas connections:	None
UK connections:	None
Viable for whole UK?	Yes
Trade bodies	BFA

Franchisor's formula for success

Hire is at about half the cost of other companies in the vehicle hire business, and operates as a secondary sales facility to boost repair and maintenance business, petrol sales etc.

Inside story from the franchisees

Well organised franchise with very good manual and support. A very enthusiastic reponse from franchisees.

Insider tips

Virtually impossible to undertake without the right premises, but if you have space and an existing facility the costs of setting it up are very small.

Moans and groans

Franchisees had no complaints at all

Good Franchise Guide comment: research was undertaken before current TV campaign started – which should boost sales even more. This franchisor said to us 'I'll let you have a list of our franchisees, you can ask them what they think' before we even asked. What a difference from the attitude of so many others.

Number of franchisee addresses provided by franchisor: 44

⇨ PRB Self Drive Hire

Unit 8, Cape Road Industrial Estate, Warwick CV34 4JW
Phone: 0926 499867

Car hire

Outlets
Number of outlets

Company owned outlets:	03 (approx)
Franchised:	15 (approx)
Pilot:	No information supplied
1988 franchise target:	No information supplied

Premier Videos

Costs
Total	£12,000
Franchise fee:	£7,500
Other charges:	Nil
Min cash excluding bank:	£6,000
Min overdraft required:	No information supplied
Normal bank advance:	50%
Working capital first 2 months:	No information supplied
Associated banks:	None
Capital items required:	None
Associated leasing co:	None

Royalties

Total
7.0% of turnover
0.0% accounts service
0.0% for advertising fund
7.0% monthly sales

No standing royalty independent of turnover

Bank rating	No information supplied
Territory	No information supplied
Strings	No information supplied
Training	No information supplied
Support	No information supplied
Operating Manual	No information supplied
Profit	No information supplied
Risk	Highly competitive area; you are up against some very large estabished companies
Management only	Could be run by manager but with limited profit

Size and reach
Original company launched:	1984
Overseas connections:	None
UK connections:	None
Viable for whole UK?	Yes
Trade bodies	None

Franchisor's formula for success
Taking up a Franchise describes the business as 'Nationwide vehicle hire depots using vehicles up to 12 months old, at a most competitive rate.'

Good Franchise Guide comment: Very limited information available, but from what we have found out it would appear that this franchise is taking on Hertz, Avis and the like. Our view is that the companies using older cars (such as Practical Used Car Rental and Wreck a Rent) are more likely to reap the rewards.

Number of franchisee addresses provided by franchisor: 00

⇨ **Premier Videos**
See Video Film Franchise

Primetime Video Centre Ltd

⇨ Primetime Video Centre Ltd
408 Manchester Road, Heaton Chapel, Stockport, Cheshire SK4 5BY
Phone: 061-432 0276

Outlets offer a wide choice of quality videos on hire

Outlets
Number of outlets
Company owned outlets:		15				
Franchised:		00				
Pilot:		01 started 1985				
1988 franchise target:		25 company, 15 franchised				

Current reach:
South	00	South west	00	South east	00
Midlands	00	East Anglia	00	North east	00
North west	15	Scotland	00	Wales	00
N Ireland	00	Rep Ireland	00	I of Man/CI	00

The company informs us that it has almost completed the signing on in the region of 25 franchised outlets.

Costs
Total	£50,000 to £60,000
Franchise fee:	£4,950
Other charges:	No information supplied
Min cash excluding bank:	£30,000 including working capital
Min overdraft required:	No information supplied
Normal bank advance:	70%
Working capital first 2 months:	£5,000
Associated banks:	Lloyds, Barclays, Royal Bank of Scotland, Nat West
Capital items required:	Stock, approx £21,000
Associated leasing co:	None

Royalties
	10.0% of turnover
	0.0% accounts service
	Advertising fund may be collected at the discretion of the franchisor
Total	10.0% monthly sales
	£750 pa standing royalty independent of turnover

Bank rating	No information supplied
Territory	Population based
Strings	No information supplied
Training	2 weeks practical and management training
	Cost: Nil – included in franchise fee
	Training value: No information supplied
Support	No information supplied
Operating Manual	No information supplied
Profit	£28,000 first year net profit predicted.
Risk	Many video companies have fallen by the wayside; franchisees will need to be convinced that this franchise has the approach just right.
Management only	Reasonable return for owner with management ability

Size and reach
Original company launched:	1981
Overseas connections:	None
UK connections:	None
Viable for whole UK?	Yes
Trade bodies	Video Trade Association

Prodata

Franchisor's formula for success
We operate on the simple philosophy of bringing a wide choice of quality material before the viewing audience in clean, professional outlets, but in unusually courteous and pleasant surroundings.

Good Franchise Guide comment: A limited amount of information from the franchisor makes this a hard franchise to judge, especially as video rental has proved to be a disaster-prone area thus far. It is interesting to note the growing number of franchises in this field while the number of non-franchised operations declines.

Number of franchisee addresses provided by franchisor: 00

➪ Prodata
6 Llys Dedwydd, Ebberston Road West, Rhos on Sea, Colwyn Bay, Clwyd LL28 4BG
Phone: No phone number is quoted on the computerised documentation sent. (No headed paper is used in writing to prospective franchisees.)
Directory Enquiries have no listing under Prodata for the Colwyn Bay area.

Bookkeeping service

Outlets
Number of outlets
Company owned outlets:	01
Franchised:	00
Pilot:	No information supplied
1988 franchise target:	No information supplied

Costs
Total	No information supplied
Franchise fee:	£3,000
Other charges:	No information supplied
Min cash excluding bank:	No information supplied
Min overdraft required:	No information supplied
Normal bank advance:	No information supplied
Working capital first 2 months:	No information supplied
Associated banks:	None
Capital items required:	Computer supplied by Prodata
Associated leasing co:	None

Royalties
Prodata charges franchisee for accountancy work as done at head office.

Bank rating	No information supplied
Territory	No information supplied
Strings	Computer comes from Prodata
Training	'Comprehensive'
Support	No information supplied
Operating Manual	No information supplied
Profit	£8,000 earnings projected for first year
Risk	There are rivals in the field, but it must be an attractive proposition to many small firms
Management only	One-man-band operation

Size and reach
Original company launched:	No information supplied; letter to franchisees not written on headed paper, and no information given on the company registration (as required under the Companies Act)
Overseas connections:	None
UK connections:	Owned by Burotech Ltd
Viable for whole UK?	Yes
Trade bodies	None

Professional Appearance Services (PAS) Ltd

Franchisor's formula for success
Prodata is a professional bookkeeping service for medium and small companies covering such businesses as ironmongers, plumbers, newsagents etc. Franchisees should have experience of bookkeeping or business administration. The work is carried out on the client's own premises.

Good Franchise Guide comment: Everything sent to our would-be franchisee is run off by a dot matrix printer – not one piece of typesetting in sight, save the cover. The effect is not pleasing, although it does allow offprints of typical work runs to be included. The lack of a phone number is disconcerting – at least Directory Enquiries should have heard of them.

Number of franchisee addresses provided by franchisor: 00

⇨ Professional Appearance Services (PAS) Ltd
1 Queen Square, Bath BA1 2HE
Phone: 0225 312756

Commercial contract cleaning, auto-valeting and carpet and upholstery cleaning

Outlets
Number of outlets
Company owned outlets: 00
Franchised: 12
Pilot: 02 started 1983 and 1987
1988 franchise target: 28
Current reach:

South	00	South west	01	South east	00
Midlands	05	East Anglia	02	North east	01
North west	00	Scotland	02	Wales	00
N Ireland	01	Rep Ireland	00	I of Man/CI	00

Costs
Total   £11,940
Franchise fee: £3,900
Other charges: £8,040
Min cash excluding bank: £5,500
Min overdraft required: £9,000
Normal bank advance: 70%
Working capital first 2 months: £2,500
Associated banks: Lloyds
Capital items required: Vehicle (leased); steam cleaner
Associated leasing co: Yes – no details supplied

Royalties
                                 8.0% of turnover
                                 0.0% accounts service
                                 0.0% for advertising fund
Total   8.0% monthly sales

No standing royalty independent of turnover

Bank rating Should be no problem with special Lloyds package available
Territory   Population, its type and the number of car dealers
Strings   No information supplied
Training   5 days practical training
                 4 days management training
                 Cost: £1,350 – included in franchise fee
                 Training value: No information supplied

The Progressive Conveyancing Company

Support	No information supplied
Operating Manual	No information supplied
Profit	No information supplied
Risk	Becoming increasingly competitive
Management only	Reasonable return for owner with management ability

Size and reach

Original company launched:	1980
Overseas connections:	None
UK connections:	None
Viable for whole UK?	Yes
Trade bodies	BFA Register

Franchisor's formula for success

The gross annual turnover in the car valeting and contract cleaning industry is greater than the defence budget. The markets are neither seasonal nor here today gone tomorrow. The service industry is the fastest growing industry in the UK and more stable than manufacturing or retail.

Good Franchise Guide comment: None of the three franchises whose addresses we were given was willing to answer our questionnaire.

Number of franchisee addresses provided by franchisor: 03

⇨ The Progressive Conveyancing Company

12 Church Road, Hove, Sussex BN3 2FL
Phone: 0273 720284

Conveyancing

Outlets
Number of outlets

Company owned outlets:	01
Franchised:	08
Pilot:	No information supplied
1988 franchise target:	No information supplied

Costs

Total	No information supplied
Franchise fee:	£10,000
Other charges:	No information supplied
Min cash excluding bank:	No information supplied
Min overdraft required:	No information supplied
Normal bank advance:	No information supplied
Working capital first 2 months:	No information supplied
Associated banks:	None
Capital items required:	None
Associated leasing co:	None

Royalties

No information supplied

Bank rating	No information supplied
Territory	No information supplied
Strings	Not likely to be too many
Training	2 week practical and management training
	Cost: Nil – included in franchise fee
	Training value: No information supplied

Prontaprint plc

Support	No information supplied
Operating Manual	No information supplied
Profit	First year profit projected as £9,700
Risk	People are turning away from solicitors at present, but watch out if solicitors dramatically cut their fees in order to claw back clients.
Management only	One-man-band operation

Size and reach

Original company launched:	No information supplied
Overseas connections:	None
UK connections:	None
Viable for whole UK?	Yes
Trade bodies	None

Franchisor's formula for success

'To carry out conveyancing of residential, commercial and industrial property in much the same way as is done by the best solicitors but with some special distinctions, particularly the greater emphasis on service provided for clients who quickly became aware that they were receiving a standard of care and attention often rare and unusual today.

Good Franchise Guide comment: Looks like a sensible operation. Although not many figures are given in the brochure those that are are well and clearly presented. But find out how much the royalty is before you proceed.

Number of franchisee addresses provided by franchisor: 00

⇨ Prontaprint plc

Coniscliffe House, Coniscliffe Road, Darlington DL3 7EX
Phone: 0325 483333

Europe's largest print and copy shop chain with outlets worldwide used mostly by small to medium sized businesses in the service sector

Outlets
Number of outlets

Company owned outlets:		01			
Franchised:		291			
Pilot:		01 started 1971			
1988 franchise target:		320			
Current reach:					
South	66	South west	20	South east	60
Midlands	41	East Anglia	09	North east	38
North west	34	Scotland	16	Wales	07
N Ireland	03	Rep Ireland	16	I of Man/CI	01

Note: N Ireland, Rep Ireland and Channel Isles are classed as 'International' outlets by Prontaprint.

Costs

Total	£60,000 to £65,000
Franchise fee:	£5,000
Other charges:	£9,000 (franchise package fee)
Min cash excluding bank:	£25,000
Min overdraft required:	Nil
Normal bank advance:	Up to 66% total cost
Working capital first 2 months:	Varies
Associated banks:	All major clearing banks
Capital items required:	Printing equipment and shopfitting
Associated leasing co:	None

Prontaprint plc

Royalties	5.0% of turnover
	5.0% marketing services fund contribution
	0.0% for advertising fund
Total	10.0% monthly sales
	No standing royalty independent of turnover
Bank rating	Banks found to be helpful
Territory	Usually post codes
	Franchisees report: 'Just right'
Strings	Ties, but lots of freedom too
Training	10 working days practical training
	10 working days management training
	Cost: Nil – included in franchise fee
	Training value: Adequate
Support	Very good
Operating Manual	Excellent
Profit	As projected or better
Risk	Very competitive market with several experienced well presented franchises aiming for the same businesses.
Management only	Proven franchise with good return on investment
Size and reach	
Original company launched:	1971
Overseas connections:	Prontaprint International; outlets in Europe, Africa, Australia, Scandinavia, Middle East
UK connections:	Wholly owned subsidiaries of Prontaprint Holdings Ltd, a Jersey company
Viable for whole UK?	Yes
Trade bodies	BFA

Franchisor's formula for success
The rapid success that Prontaprint has enjoyed in becoming Europe's largest print and copy shop chain, stems not only from its sound and innovative marketing but also from the rigorous application of proven financial principles. The shops are planned to operate efficiently with relatively low overheads to provide a healthy return on capital invested provided the well proven guidelines are followed with the necessary commitment and hard work from the franchisee.

Inside story from the franchisees
Very good franchise organisation with excellent manual and good support.

Insider tips
'The only people to have failed ignored the advice given by the franchisor and other franchisees.'

Moans and groans
Better deals on products are available than those delivered by the franchisor – often a complaint where a franchisee is tied to a franchisor for materials and supplies, but otherwise no complaints.

Number of franchisee addresses provided by franchisor: 6

Pronuptia de Paris Bridalwear

⇨ Pronuptia de Paris Bridalwear
70 – 78 York Way, London N1 9AG
Phone: 01-278 0343

Retail bridalwear

Outlets
Number of outlets
Company owned outlets: 18
Franchised: 50
Pilot: 00
1988 franchise target: 73
Current reach:

South	10	South west	05	South east	03
Midlands	*24	East Anglia	04	North east	02
North west	10	Scotland	06	Wales	02
N Ireland	01	Rep Ireland	01	I of Man/CI	00

*Midland figure includes Midlands and North (excluding North east and North west)

Costs
Total   £50,000 to £120,000
Franchise fee: £12,000 to £17,000
Other charges: Nil
Min cash excluding bank: £30,000 to £60,000
Min overdraft required: £20,000 to £60,000
Normal bank advance: 66%
Working capital first 2 months: £10,000
Associated banks: None
Capital items required: Shopfitting £25,000 to £50,000
Associated leasing co: None

Royalties
                                  10.0% of turnover
                                  0.0% accounts service
                                  0.0% for advertising fund
Total   10.0% monthly sales

                                  No standing royalty independent of turnover

Bank rating   No information supplied
Territory   Either a county or conurbation using post code areas
Strings   No information supplied
Training   24 days practical and management training in a
                      company shop
                      Cost: Nil – included in franchise fee
                      Training value: No information supplied

Support   No information supplied
Operating Manual No information supplied
Profit   No information supplied
Risk   See comment below
Management only   Reasonable return for owner with management ability

Size and reach
Original company launched: Pronuptia in 1977, Young's in 1948
Overseas connections: Pronuptia is a French company formed 1958
UK connections: Master franchise agreement with Pronuptia de Paris SA
Viable for whole UK?   Yes
Trade bodies   BFA

Prospectglen Ltd

Franchisor's formula for success
It is common for Young's Formal Wear and Pronuptia to operate together from the same store under a joint franchise.
As a Pronuptia franchisee you will be a vital part of our very successful retailing operation, personally enjoying all the status naturally given to an international company helping young brides look beautiful on their wedding day. With a high mark-up on each item, Pronuptia merchandise offers you an unusually attractive gross profit margin. And people will always pay top prices for exclusive quality products.

Good Franchise Guide comment: Young's franchise group went into receivership in 1985, and was bought shortly after. The new owners disposed of La Mama (qv) and have continued with Young's Franchise (qv) and Pronuptia. It is most likely that the new owners have resolved the problems that beset the previous regime, but nevertheless we would have welcomed the chance to talk with franchisees to gauge their feelings following this turbulent past.

Number of franchisee addresses provided by franchisor: 00

⇨ Prospectglen Ltd
99 High Street, Orpington, Kent BR6 0LG
Phone: 0689 36933

Specialists in office refreshment services

Outlets
Number of outlets	No information supplied

Costs
Total	£7,500
Franchise fee:	No information supplied
Other charges:	No information supplied
Min cash excluding bank:	No information supplied
Min overdraft required:	No information supplied
Normal bank advance:	No information supplied
Working capital first 2 months:	No information supplied
Associated banks:	None
Capital items required:	Car telephone
Associated leasing co:	No information supplied

Royalties
No information supplied

Bank rating	No information supplied
Territory	No information supplied
Strings	No information supplied
Training	'Comprehensive' – no further details
Support	No information supplied
Operating Manual	No information supplied
Profit	No information supplied
Risk	High – there appears to be no end of firms offering coffee machines for offices, and most of them keep calling on us.
Management only	One-man-band operation

Size and reach
Original company launched:	No information supplied
Overseas connections:	None declared
UK connections:	None
Viable for whole UK?	No information supplied
Trade bodies	None

Protoplas

Franchisor's formula for success
The company manufactures its own equipment and packages its own exclusive range of high quality and competitively priced ingredients, only available through its distributors. The range is suitable for most types of vending machines.
Customers include TSB, Midland Bank, Lloyds Bank, Barclays Bank, Burtons, Halfords, Top Shop etc.

Good Franchise Guide comment: As can be seen above, precious little information is given out – such information as we have comes from the leaflets sent with a preliminary application form. How can anyone make even a preliminary application on such a basis?

Number of franchisee addresses provided by franchisor: 00

⇨ Protoplas
1 Carn Industrial Estate, Portadown, N Ireland

A franchise at this name and address has been listed in some reference books. In fact the address and phone number given is that of Motoplas (qv). Motoplas make no mention of Protoplas in their promotional literature.

⇨ PSJ Business Consultants
Allied Dunbar House, 3 Church Street, Bishop's Stortford, Herts CM23 2LY

This franchise has been listed in some reference books and magazines. Mail sent to this address is accepted, but we have been unable to obtain information either in response to general requests from would-be franchisees or specifically for this publication. In the light of this experience we suggest a certain amount of caution may be in order if the franchise does eventually reappear.

⇨ Quest Estates International
11 Saint Mary's Place, Newcastle upon Tyne NE1 7PG
Phone: 091-232 1052
(Also at 15 Saint Thomas Street, Lymington, Hants)

Business transfer agency

Outlets
Number of outlets
Company owned outlets: No information supplied
Franchised: No information supplied
Pilot: No information supplied
1988 franchise target: No information supplied

Costs
Total No information supplied
Franchise fee: £7,500
No other inforamtion supplied

Royalties
Total
10.0% of turnover
0.0% accounts service
0.0% for advertising fund
10.0% monthly sales

No standing royalty independent of turnover

Bank rating No information supplied
Territory Yellow Pages area
Strings No information supplied

Quikframe

Training	No information supplied
Support	No information supplied
Operating Manual	No information supplied
Profit	First year net loss projected as £4,750
Risk	Very competitive area, and getting more so all the time
Management only	Brochure mentions 'husband and wife' team operating from home

Size and reach

Original company launched:	No information supplied
Overseas connections:	None
UK connections:	None
Viable for whole UK?	Yes
Trade bodies	None

Franchisor's formula for success
Three registers are operated: Inn Quest, Business Quest and Leisure Quest Estates. 'Our aim is to be the most effective and efficient agency of its kind no matter if it be in the traditional business of selling and transferring resort and country hotels, inns, restaurants, and guest houses through Inn Quest or quality businesses such as rest homes, wholesale operations, garage service stations, investment properties, service industries, engineering manufacturing services, superior retail business etc, through Business Quest, or overseas properties through Leisure Quest Estates.'

Good Franchise Guide comment: It is rare to find a franchise that actually has the nerve to suggest there may be a net loss in year 1, although undoubtedly many will make a loss, whatever the projections say. One up to this franchisor for honesty. Unfortunately the brochures could have gone on to say a lot more about the set-up costs, but didn't. Just how practical is it to get planning permission to run what is after all an estate agency, from home?

Number of franchisee addresses provided by franchisor: 00

⇨ Quikframe

c/o The Franchise Shop Ltd, 26 High Street, Merstham, Surrey RH1 3EA
Phone: 07374 4211

Instant picture framing

Outlets

Number of outlets	
Company owned outlets:	No information supplied
Franchised:	No information supplied
Pilot:	No information supplied
1988 franchise target:	No information supplied

Costs

Total	£22,000
Franchise fee:	No information supplied
Other charges:	No information supplied
Min cash excluding bank:	£10,000
Min overdraft required:	No information supplied
Normal bank advance:	50%
Working capital first 2 months:	No information supplied
Associated banks:	None
Capital items required:	None
Associated leasing co:	None

Rainbow Insurances

Royalties

	6.25% of turnover
	0.0% accounts service
	6.25% for marketing fund
Total	12.50% monthly sales
	No standing royalty independent of turnover

Bank rating	No information supplied
Territory	No information supplied
Strings	No information supplied
Training	No information supplied
Support	No information supplied
Operating Manual	No information supplied
Profit	No information supplied
Risk	Very high – a lot of competition
Management only	Could be run by manager but with limited profit

Size and reach

Original company launched:	No information supplied
Overseas connections:	None
UK connections:	None
Viable for whole UK?	Yes
Trade bodies	None

Franchisor's formula for success

We assess your area, help you find a shop, organise all the setting-up, equip it throughout, set up all the business systems, train you to do a really good job confidently, and launch you on the start of a really successful business future.

Good Franchise Guide comment: Inadequate information to make any real judgement. No reply from the consultant to our questions. There are many other franchises in this field – and many of those supplied more information than this one.

Number of franchisee addresses provided by franchisor: 00

➪ Rainbow Insurances

c/o The Franchise Shop Ltd, 25 High Street, Merstham, Surrey RH1 3EA
Phone: 07374 4211

This 'local building society and insurance agency franchise' has been advertised by The Franchise Shop. The brochure states that 'the local franchise agency services the saving, investing and insurance needs of the local community – in those areas where building societies are not represented – to provide a full deposit and withdrawal facility and to offer a complete range of general insurances . . .'
Capital required is about £10,000 depending on premises, with profits in excess of £12,000 in year 1. No other information has been provided.

➪ Red Baron

c/o The Franchise Shop Ltd, 26 High Street, Merstham, Surrey RH1 3EA
Phone: 07374 4211

Event catering company

Outlets

Number of outlets	25
Company owned outlets:	No information supplied
Franchised:	No information supplied
Pilot:	No information supplied
1988 franchise target:	No information supplied

Costs

Total	£6,300
Franchise fee:	No information supplied
Other charges:	No information supplied
Min cash excluding bank:	£3,150
Min overdraft required:	No information supplied
Normal bank advance:	50%
Working capital first 2 months:	No information supplied
Associated banks:	No information supplied
Capital items required:	No information supplied
Associated leasing co:	None

Royalties

No information supplied on royalties

Profit

'Company owned units have regularly taken £1,000 per day at weekends during the season with margins in excess of 50% – and there are opportunities to build up trade on other days of the week.'

Risk — Competitive area but expanding rapidly
Management only — 'Cash business ideal for husband and wife'

Size and reach

Original company launched:	No information supplied
Overseas connections:	No information supplied
UK connections:	None
Viable for whole UK?	Yes
Trade bodies	No information supplied

Franchisor's formula for success

Event catering in superb Bavarian chalets and a range of traditional and original German sausages.

Good Franchise Guide comment: The details on this franchise are available only through The Franchise Shop who have declined to supply further information.

Number of franchisee addresses provided by franchisor: 00

⇨ Regional Business Services Ltd

Regional House, Troy Road, Horsforth, Leeds LS18 5AZ
Phone: 0532 589225

Accountancy and bookkeeping service for small enterprises

Outlets

Number of outlets	
Company owned outlets:	01
Franchised:	00
Pilot:	No information supplied
1988 franchise target:	No information supplied

Costs and royalties etc

No information supplied

Training

4 weeks practical and management training
Cost: No information supplied
Training value: No information supplied

Support — No information supplied
Operating Manual — No information supplied
Profit — First year net profit quoted as £4,000
Risk — Only accountants can join in – they must know the risks better than we do.
Management only — Business centres on the accountant as owner-manager

Reliant Security System

Size and reach
Original company launched: 1971
Overseas connections: None
UK connections: None
Viable for whole UK? Yes
Trade bodies We imagine there must be, but none mentioned.

Franchisor's formula for success
The RBS Associate Scheme is a unique opportunity to establish your own accountancy practice within 3 years; exploiting the vast potential involved in servicing the small and medium sized business sectors.

Good Franchise Guide comment: Surprisingly little financial information given to our would-be franchisees, and being an accountant that was what she wanted. For the accountant who wants to be his own boss but can't see how, this type of franchise is possibly the answer.

Number of franchisee addresses provided by franchisor: 00

➪ Reliant Security System
Previously at: River Park, Berkhamsted, Herts HP4 1HL

A franchise at this name and address has been listed in some reference books and magazines. Mail sent to this address is now being returned by the Post Office marked 'Gone Away'. Enquiries have revealed that no forwarding address has been left, although it is possible that the franchise may have been set up once more in another part of the country.

In the light of this experience we suggest a certain amount of caution may be in order.

➪ Renubath Services Ltd
The Old House, Calmsden, Nr Cirencester, Glos GL7 5ET
Phone: 0285 66624

Renubath, who supply a bath repair service, have not responded to our requests for information. Our would-be franchisee gained a reply, but was told that there were no vacancies in his area. No further information was given, nor was any suggestion made that it might be possible to look at any other area in which there was not already a franchisee.

➪ Response Communications
177 Westward Road, Ebley, Stroud, Glos
Phone: 04536 71620

Suppliers of telecommunication equipment

Outlets
Number of outlets
Company owned outlets: 02
Franchised: 03
Pilot: 00
1988 franchise target: 20
Current reach:

South	00	South west	01	South east	01
Midlands	01	East Anglia	00	North east	00
North west	01	Scotland	00	Wales	01
N Ireland	00	Rep Ireland	00	I of Man/CI	00

Restor Antique Restoration Ltd

Costs
Total	£9,000
Franchise fee:	£2,000
Other charges:	Equipment and stock
Min cash excluding bank:	£5,000
Min overdraft required:	£5,000
Normal bank advance:	£5,000
Working capital first 2 months:	£2,000
Associated banks:	None
Capital items required:	None – vehicle ownership assumed
Associated leasing co:	Yes – no details provided

Royalties
	2.5% of turnover
	0.0% accounts service
	2.5% for advertising fund
Total	5.0% monthly sales
	No standing royalty independent of turnover

Bank rating	No information supplied
Territory	Based on population
Strings	No information supplied
Training	2 days practical training
	1 day management training
	Cost: Nil – included in franchise fee
	Training value: No information supplied
Support	No information supplied
Operating Manual	No information supplied
Profit	No information supplied
Risk	An area of increasing competition; many have already gone under
Management only	Reasonable return for owner with management ability

Size and reach
Original company launched:	1982
Overseas connections:	None
UK connections:	Western Communication Service, Guardine Telecommunications Ltd
Viable for whole UK?	Yes
Trade bodies	None

Franchisor's formula for success
No information supplied

Good Franchise Guide comment: Repeated requests for a brochure failed to bring one, so it is hard to get an overall picture, although the franchisor did answer our specific questions.

Number of franchisee addresses provided by franchisor: 00

⇨ Restor Antique Restoration Ltd
12 Macaulay House, Woodlead Road, London N16 0TR
Phone: 01-249 9483

Restor Antiques have informed us that they are no longer franchising.

Revolution Oil

⇨ Revolution Oil

Revolution House, Chesterway, Northwich, Cheshire CW9 5EZ
Phone: 0606 47961

Revolution manufacture engine and transmission oil additives, fuel additives, lubricating oils, car care products, industrial and hydraulic oils for vehicles, plant and machinery, selling to car accessory retailers, garage services, coach operators etc.

Outlets
Number of outlets
Company owned outlets:	00				
Franchised:	17				
Pilot:	01 started 1985				
1988 franchise target:	35 to 46				

Current reach:
South	02	South west	01	South east	03		
Midlands	02	East Anglia	02	North east	02		
North west	02	Scotland	01	Wales	02		
N Ireland	00	Rep Ireland	00	I of Man/CI	00		

Costs
Total	£5,500
Franchise fee:	£1,500
Other charges:	£4,000
Min cash excluding bank:	No information supplied
Min overdraft required:	No information supplied
Normal bank advance:	No information supplied
Working capital first 2 months:	£2,000
Associated banks:	Details of the franchise held by all major banks
Capital items required:	Delivery van, initial stock
Associated leasing co:	None

Royalties
No royalty payments required

Bank rating — No information supplied
Territory — Counties
Strings — No information supplied

Training
4 days practical training
1 day management training
Cost: Nil – included in franchise fee
Training value: No information supplied

Support — No information supplied
Operating Manual — No information supplied
Profit — No information supplied
Risk — No information supplied
Management only — Reasonable return for owner with management ability

Size and reach
Original company launched:	1978
Overseas connections:	None
UK connections:	None
Viable for whole UK?	Yes
Trade bodies	None

Franchisor's formula for success
We are a long established manufacturer of oil and related products with a very experienced management team, producing a comprehensive range of products for use through industry. Revolution is one of the fastest growing independent oil companies in the UK and the only oil company in the UK to date to be able to offer in-house printing and packaging facilities in all sizes of containers for own labelling.

Good Franchise Guide comment: A distributorship more than a franchise, but none the worse for that.

Number of franchisee addresses provided by franchisor: 00

➪ Riviera Plant Interiors Ltd
c/o The Franchise Shop Ltd, 25 High Street, Merstham, Surrey RH1 3EA
Phone: 07374 4211

This 'interior design and landscaping agency' has been advertised by The Franchise Shop. The brochure states that business is gained from hotels, restaurants, fast food establishments, etc, etc. The franchisee 'can earn as much as £15,000 in his first year', from a capital requirement of £10,000. No further information is available.

➪ Rotary Space Creators (North) Ltd
Whitestake, Preston, Lancs

This franchise has been listed in some reference books and magazines. The firm sells a style of shelving via agents who are trained by the company. Agents who do not subsequently fulfil the company's targets are then invoiced for the 'training etc'.

➪ RSH Consultants Ltd
Previously at 3 Jubilee Buildings, Sutton in Ashfield, Notts

A restaurant franchise at this name and address has been listed in some reference books and magazines. Mail sent to this address is now being returned by the Post Office marked 'Gone Away'. Enquiries have revealed that no forwarding address has been left, and no telephone listing can be found in the area, although it is possible that the franchise may have been set up once more in another part of the country. In the light of this experience we suggest a certain amount of caution may be in order.

➪ Ryman Ltd
59 Markham Street, London SW3 3NR
Phone: 01-351 5671

Office equipment and stationery retail chain

Outlets
Number of outlets
Company owned outlets: 50 (approx)
Franchised: 05 (approx)
Pilot: No information supplied
1988 franchise target: No information supplied

Costs
Total £90,000
Franchise fee: £6,500
Other charges: No information supplied
Min cash excluding bank: £27,000
Min overdraft required: No information supplied
Normal bank advance: 60%
Working capital first 2 months: No information supplied
Associated banks: None
Capital items required: None
Associated leasing co: None

Safeclean International

Royalties

	10.0% of turnover
	0.0% accounts service
	0.0% for advertising fund
Total	10.0% monthly sales
	No standing royalty independent of turnover

Bank rating   No information supplied
Territory   No information supplied
Strings   No information supplied

Training   No information supplied
Support   No information supplied
Operating Manual   No information supplied
Profit   No information supplied
Risk   Well known name which augers well, but lack of information makes a firm view difficult to formulate
Management only   No information supplied

Size and reach
Original company launched: 1985
Overseas connections: None
UK connections: None
Viable for whole UK?   Yes
Trade bodies   None

Franchisor's formula for success
No information supplied

Good Franchise Guide comment: Neither the editors nor our would-be franchisees got any reply to their requests for information. Not a good sign; what can explain this total lack of communication? We know it is a well respected large firm, but still . . .

Number of franchisee addresses provided by franchisor: 00

⇨ Safeclean International

Delmae House, Home Farm, Ardington, Wantage, Oxon OX12 8PN
Phone: 0235 833022

Cleaning of domestic furnishings in customer's home, using company's own equipment.

Outlets
Number of outlets
Company owned outlets: 00
Franchised: 70
Pilot: 02 started 1969
1988 franchise target: 85
Current reach:

South	10	South west	06	South east	17
Midlands	09	East Anglia	05	North east	01
North west	09	Scotland	03	Wales	03
N Ireland	01	Rep Ireland	05	I of Man/CI	00

Costs
Total   £9,750
Franchise fee: £3,000
Other charges: Nil
Min cash excluding bank: £2,850
Min overdraft required: £1,000
Normal bank advance: 66%
Working capital first months: 'Six months' living expenses'
Associated banks: Nat West, Lloyds
Capital items required: Car
Associated leasing co: None

Satinstyle Ltd

Royalties	
	0.0% of turnover
	0.0% accounts service
	0.0% for advertising fund
Total	0.0% monthly sales
	Max £1,800 pa standing royalty independent of turnover
Bank rating	Some found banks very helpful – others less so, but overall there was no problem
Territory	Post codes based on Acorn analysis of housing
	Franchisees report: 'Just right'
Strings	Strong ties in some areas but lots of freedom too
Training	4 days practical training
	4 days management training
	Cost: Nil – included in franchise fee
	Training value: Excellent
Support	Excellent
Operating Manual	Very good
Profit	'Worse than expected but surviving' was the main response
Risk	The guarantee given with the service should help reduce risk
Management only	One-man-band operation

Size and reach

Original company launched:	1969
Overseas connections:	Ireland 5, Belgium 1
UK connections:	None
Viable for whole UK?	Yes
Trade bodies	BFA

Franchisor's formula for success
A Safeclean business provides all the services necessary to help owners of fine furnishing to maintain the appearance of their homes and value of their possessions. In addition to cleaning you can provide a wide range of treatments to protect fabrics against soiling, stains, fire and static electricity.

Inside story from the franchisees
'Franchisor appears to be very honest and is also very helpful.'
Regular training throughout the year most helpful.

Insider tips
'The only reason I am doing worse than expected is due to my lack of effort!'
'Potential franchisees should be given a full list of franchisees to contact and see franchise in operation to see exactly what is involved before commiting oneself.'

Moans and groans
Index on the manual was very poor; also outdated in some places.

Number of franchisee addresses provided by franchisor: 55

⇨ Satinstyle Ltd
124b Kings Road, London SW3

A franchise at this address has been listed in some reference books and magazines. Mail sent to this address is accepted, but we have been unable to obtain information either in response to general requests from would-be franchisees or specifically for this publication. In the light of this experience we suggest a certain amount of caution may be in order if the franchise does eventually reappear.

Scan (Franchising) Ltd

⇨ Scan (Franchising) Ltd
50 East Over, Bridgwater, Somerset TA6 5AR
Phone: 0278 421744

Scan have informed us that as of February 1988 they are no longer franchising.

⇨ Securicor Carphones
24 Barton Street, Bath, Avon

A franchise at this name and address retailing car phones has been listed in some reference books and magazines. Mail sent to this address is now being returned by the Post Office marked 'Gone Away'. Enquiries have revealed that no forwarding address has been left, and Telecom have no listing for such a firm although it is possible that the franchise may have been set up once more in another part of the country. In the light of this experience we suggest a certain amount of caution may be in order.

⇨ Seekers (Thornganby) Ltd
200 Haverstock Hill, London NW3 2AG
Phone: 01-202 7882

Nationwide estate agency which sells houses on a fixed fee rather than a commission basis

Outlets

Number of outlets	
Company owned outlets:	00
Franchised:	58
Pilot:	02, no starting date given
1988 franchise target:	75 to 80
Current reach:	No area breakdown supplied. The company states: 'The majority of units are in the south with the majority on the peripherals of London and the Home Counties, several in the West Country and stretching up north to Walsall and Birmingham.'

Costs

Total	£30,000
Franchise fee:	£10,000
Other charges:	No other charges
Min cash excluding bank:	'Although we understand that Barclays, Nat West etc will fund up to 70%, this company considers that to be too highly geared for this type of business. 50% has to be available from incoming licensee.'
Min overdraft required:	No information supplied
Normal bank advance:	70%
Working capital first 2 months:	'Working capital aimed within £30,000 projections'
Associated banks:	None. 'We have been offered, but do not feel that this is necessary or appropriate'
Capital items required:	None
Associated leasing co:	None

Royalties

	10.0% of turnover
	0.0% accounts service
	5.0% for advertising fund
Total	15.0% monthly sales
	No standing royalty independent of turnover

Serviceman Franchise plc

Bank rating	No information supplied
Territory	Post codes or radius from franchisee's base
	Franchisees report: 'Just right'
Strings	Some ties but not too many
Training	6 days practical and management training absolute minimum for all staff. Other regular training courses and updated training notes.
	Cost: Nil – included in franchise fee
	Training value: 'Excellent' (but see comments below)
Support	Excellent (but see comments below)
Operating Manual	Very good (but see comments below)
Profit	Better than projected (but see comments below)
Risk	Lots of competition
Management only	Depends on area and manager

Size and reach

Original company launched:	1979
Overseas connections:	None
UK connections:	None
Viable for whole UK?	Yes – and Europe thereafter
Trade bodies	Application for BFA pending

Franchisor's formula for success
Comparatively low set-up costs, relatively immediate cashflow and potentially high return on investment. In respect of the franchise itself all licensees have access to a very considerable training and back-up facilities to enable them to maximise on every aspect of their business.

Inside story from the franchisees
A list of franchisees was supplied by Seekers following our request for information. However, we were then informed by two franchisees that the company had instructed all its franchisees not to deal with us despite a previous assurance from the franchisor that franchisees would be encouraged to co-operate. Further enquiries have not been answered by the firm.
Two franchisees did respond. One sent in a glowing report, which has been used as the basis for our assessment of training, support, the manual and profit. The other franchisee, who refused to divulge a name for fear of recriminations gave a totally negative report on the company. Our request for this franchisee to send in a written account of problems brought no response.

Insider tips
Hard work and the right attitude are essential.

Moans and groans
Manual is good as a starting point but too detailed to be used by staff.

Number of franchisee addresses provided by franchisor: 58 addresses, but franchisees subsequently told not to co-operate with us.

⇨ Serviceman Franchise plc

2nd Floor, Northgate House, High Pavement, Basildon, Essex SS14 1EA
Phone: 0268 293355

Car servicing

Outlets
Number of outlets

Company owned outlets:	03
Franchised:	09 (approx)
Pilot:	No information supplied
1988 franchise target:	No information for 1988, but 200 will complete the UK network

257

ServiceMaster Ltd

Costs
Total	£53,664
Franchise fee:	£18,135
Other charges:	£6,256 stationery, manuals etc
	£13,557 advance rental
	£10,000 stock
Min cash excluding bank:	No information supplied
Min overdraft required:	No information supplied
Normal bank advance:	70%
Working capital first 2 months:	No information supplied
Associated banks:	None
Capital items required:	No information supplied
Associated leasing co:	None

Royalties
	7.5% of turnover
	0.0% accounts service
	2.0% for advertising fund
Total	9.5% monthly sales
	No standing royalty independent of turnover

Bank rating	No information supplied
Territory	No information supplied
Strings	No information supplied
Training	8 weeks practical and management training
	Cost: £3,135 – included in franchise fee
	Training value: No information supplied
Support	No information supplied
Operating Manual	No information supplied
Profit	Year one projected as break-even on £100,000 turnover
Risk	Low – the location looks ideal
Management only	Reasonable return for owner with management ability

Size and reach
Original company launched:	1985
Overseas connections:	None
UK connections:	None
Viable for whole UK?	Yes
Trade bodies	None

Franchisor's formula for success
Serviceman franchise is a partnership with British Rail. Serviceman Service Centres are set up within selected station car parks throughout the UK. Each 8 bay Serviceman Centre is equipped with the most modern facilities which exceed MOT requirements.

Good Franchise Guide comment: What a tremendous idea! But is it really viable to set up a car servicing centre for over £50,000 and expect it to work from scratch? Remember many people always take their cars back to the same garage on a 'better the devil you know' basis. We look forward to hearing from franchisees in due course.

Number of franchisee addresses provided by franchisor: 00

⇨ ServiceMaster Ltd

50 Commercial Square, Freemans Common, Leicester LE2 7SR
Phone: 0533 548620

Worldwide cleaning franchise offering carpet cleaning, upholstery cleaning, curtain cleaning, carpet retufting, fire and flood restoration, smoke odour removal, soil proofing, sanitising, static proofing, stain removal, flame retardant treatment and moth treatment. Two franchises are on offer, Franchise A cleaning commercial premises daily, Franchise B cleaning domestic and commercial carpets and upholstery.

ServiceMaster Ltd

Outlets
Number of outlets
Company owned outlets: 00
Franchised: 195
Pilot: 00
1988 franchise target: 230
Current reach:

South	35	South west	15	South east	30
Midlands	35	East Anglia	10	North east	25
North west	25	Scotland	11	Wales	05
N Ireland	03	Rep Ireland	00	I of Man/CI	00

Costs
These refer to Franchise A and B (see above). Where only one rate is quoted it is the same for both franchises.

Total (A) £10,000 (B) £9,000
Franchise fee: (A) £5,000 (B) £4,000
Other charges: £5,000 starting pack
Min cash excluding bank: £3,000
Min overdraft required: No information supplied
Normal bank advance: 66%
Working capital first 2 months: Varies
Associated banks: Nat West, Royal Bank of Scotland
Capital items required: Vehicle in corporate colours
Other items included in starting pack

Associated leasing co: None

Royalties
(A) 10.0% of turnover
(B) 7.0% sliding scale down to 4%
0.0% accounts service
Sliding scale from £30 to £100 per month advertising fund

No standing royalty independent of turnover

Bank rating Very helpful
Territory (A) Population, (B) Radius from base
Franchisees report: Mostly satisfied, but a few wanted either a larger or smaller area

Strings Some ties but not very many

Training 4 weeks home study (part-time) 2 weeks practical training plus 1 week residential course.
Cost: Nil – included in franchise fee
Training value: Adequate

Support Opinion varied from 'not too good' to 'very good'
Operating Manual Very good
Profit Some were doing better than expected but a slightly larger percentage were doing worse than expected
Risk A lot of competition (which may explain some of the variance in replies)

Management only Reasonable return for owner with management ability

Size and reach
Original company launched: 1959
Overseas connections: 3500 franchisees world wide
UK connections: Subsidiary of the ServiceMaster Company Ltd Partnership, Downers Grove, Illinois, USA

Viable for whole UK? Yes
Trade bodies BFA, Carpet Cleaners' Association

Franchisor's formula for success
No information supplied

Servotomic Ltd

Inside story from the franchisees
Franchisees were very keen to talk to us, and most were very positive, but some were worried that the franchisor is pushing too hard for growth.

Insider tips
'Ensure that the franchisor's future intentions are clearly defined.'

Moans and groans
'New American management is going for expansion at the cost of existing franchisees to get total market penetration.'

Number of franchisee addresses provided by franchisor: 195

⇨ Servotomic Ltd

Jessamy Road, Weybridge, Surrey KT13 8LB

A franchise at this address has been listed in some reference books and magazines. Mail sent to this address is accepted, but we have been unable to obtain information either in response to general requests from would-be franchisees or specifically for this publication. In the light of this experience we suggest a certain amount of caution may be in order if the franchise does eventually reappear.

⇨ The Shooting Box

Upper Park Farm, Beckley, Oxford OX3 9TA
Phone: 086735 233

The Shooting Box offer a franchise, but have declined to supply any information to *The Good Franchise Guide* in relation to it. Our would-be franchisee received a letter stating that the company could not offer him a franchise as there was already another nearby. What we wonder is if the franchisor has ever considered the concept of people moving house in order to start a business.

⇨ Signtalk Ltd

266a Church Street, Blackpool, Lancs FY1 3PZ
Phone: 0253 295893

At the time of our enquiries the company had run out of its franchise prospectus and was unable to supply any information. We understand, however, that the company is involved in supplying items such as key fobs and licence holders. Start-up capital required is reported to be £5,000.

⇨ Silver Shield Windscreens Ltd

Wheler Rd, Whitley, Coventry CV3 4LA
Phone: 0203 307755

Silver Shield offer 24 hour mobile windscreen replacement service. All would-be franchisees who approach them receive a letter stating that 'we are fully subscribed at the moment, and therefore there are no areas available for sale'.

The company is a BFA member, with around 70 franchises in operation. The total cost of buying the franchise is around £20,000, with the franchise fee set at around £7,000 and the royalty set at 10%. Any franchise that sells all its areas is worth considering if any do become available.

⇨ Singer Consumer Products

Grafton Way, West Ham Industrial Estate, Basingstoke, Hants RG22 6HZ
Phone: 0256 56291

Retailers of sewing and knitting products

Outlets
Number of outlets	Over 160
Company owned outlets:	No information supplied
Franchised:	No information supplied
Pilot:	No information supplied
1988 franchise target:	No information supplied

Costs
Total	£9,200 (including machines)
Franchise fee:	£750
Other charges:	£250 towards fascia cost
Min cash excluding bank:	No information supplied
Min overdraft required:	No information supplied
Normal bank advance:	No information supplied
Working capital first 2 months:	No information supplied
Associated banks:	None
Capital items required:	£6,000 for machines
Associated leasing co:	None

Note: the £9,200 includes £8,200 for stock which is paid for over 3 months

Royalties
No royalties payable

Bank rating — No information supplied
Territory — No information supplied
Strings — Franchisees can also sell stock related items such as yarns, fabrics etc from leading suppliers.

Training
No information supplied
No information supplied
Cost: Nil – included in franchise fee
Training value: No information supplied

Support — No information supplied
Operating Manual — No information supplied
Profit — No information supplied
Risk — Well known brand, with the option to sell other products
Management only — Depends on size of shop, but should be possible

Size and reach
Original company launched:	No information supplied
Overseas connections:	No information supplied
UK connections:	SDL Ltd trading as Singer
Viable for whole UK?	Yes
Trade bodies	No information supplied

Good Franchise Guide comment: A brand name that is well known throughout the country; we would have welcomed more information from the company.

Number of franchisee addresses provided by franchisor: 00

Sketchley Franchises Ltd

⇨ Sketchley Franchises Ltd
PO Box 7, Rugby Road, Hinckley, Leics LE10 2NE
Phone: 0455 38133

Dry cleaning services, dyeing, repairs, alternation, made to measure curtains, flame retardation

Outlets
Number of outlets
Company owned outlets:	500 (approx)
Franchised:	10 (approx)
Pilot:	No information supplied
1988 franchise target:	No information supplied

Note: number of outlets derived from published material which may now be slightly inaccurate.

Costs
Total	£69,000
Franchise fee:	£4,000
Other charges:	£3,000 stock
Min cash excluding bank:	£25,000
Min overdraft / bank advance:	£52,000
Working capital first 2 months:	£5,000
Associated banks:	None
Capital items required:	Basic equipment £44,000
	Shopfitting £18,000
Associated leasing co:	None

Royalties
	10.0% of turnover
	0.0% accounts service
	0.0% for advertising fund
Total	10.0% monthly sales
	No standing royalty independent of turnover

Bank rating	Financial package available from franchisor
Territory	No information supplied
Strings	Site selection and rent negotiation organised by franchisor. Franchisor also has own shopfitting company, and supplies all equipment.
Training	Training is 'extremely thorough'
	Cost: No information supplied
	Training value: No information supplied
Support	Regular contact maintained
Operating Manual	No information supplied
Profit	Net Profit of £17,020 projected for year 1
Risk	Everyone needs dry cleaning, and Sketchley is obviously a leading name
Management only	Reasonable return for owner with management ability

Size and reach
Original company launched:	1885
Overseas connections:	Operations in USA and Europe
UK connections:	Sketchley plc with assets of over £5 million
Viable for whole UK?	Yes
Trade bodies	BFA

Franchisor's formula for success
We have 100 years' experience in the industry for franchisees to draw on. We operate company dry cleaning branches in nearly 500 locations and are still expanding. Allied to this we have a very large industrial divsion in the UK, USA and Germany supplying workwear, hospital, hotel and restaurant lines services. We are also expanding rapidly in the commercial office and store cleaning fields.

Skirmish Ltd

Good Franchise Guide comment: We would have welcomed details from franchisees of how well they are coping with such a well known firm that already has so many branches of its own.

Number of franchisee addresses provided by franchisor: 00

⇨ Skirmish Ltd

The Warehouse, Sandy Lane, Oxted, Surrey RH8 9LU
Phone: 0883 723422

A mock war is fought between sides played in 15 to 40 acres of woodland, each team attempting to capture the opponent's flag. Players are armed with a pistol that fires gelatine capsules filled with a water-based paint. The capsule breaks on impact and marks a struck player who is eliminated.

Outlets
Number of outlets
Company owned outlets: 03
Franchised: 23
Pilot: 00
1988 franchise target: 30 to 35
Current reach:

South	08	South west	02	South east	02
Midlands	05	East Anglia	01	North east	02
North west	02	Scotland	03	Wales	00
N Ireland	00	Rep Ireland	01	I of Man/CI	00

Costs
Total   £15,000
Franchise fee: £15,000
Other charges: Nil
Min cash excluding bank: 50%
Min overdraft required: No information supplied
Normal bank advance: Varies on status
Working capital first 2 months: £2,000
Associated banks: None
Capital items required: None
Associated leasing co: None

Royalties
Total
    0.0% of turnover
    0.0% accounts service
    0.0% for advertising fund
    0.0% monthly sales
    Yearly fees: £1,500 national advertising fund
    £600 development fund

Bank rating   No information supplied
Territory   Predetermined on population density and affluence
Strings   None apart from the game equipment

Training   1.5 days practical training
    1.5 days management training
    Cost: Nil – included in franchise fee
    Training value: Our respondent said 'no training'

Support   'Not too good'
Operating Manual   'Poor'
Profit   As projected
Risk   There are similar franchises operating; there are no royalties, but you pay a lot of money up front.

Management only   Reasonable return for owner with management ability

Slim Gym

Size and reach
Original company launched: 1984
Overseas connections: None until December 1988
UK connections: None
Viable for whole UK?   Yes
Trade bodies   None

Franchisor's formula for success
As in any entertainment or recreational business, the organisers must have people skills, and enthusiasm for the activity. It is also helpful to have some marketing experience. As the games are normally only played at weekends, it can be run as a part-time business. Alternatively, at a holiday location it could be run daily for a limited season.

Inside story from the franchisees
'We do not consider ourselves a franchise – more a licensee'

Insider tips
'Get professional advice all the way down the line'

Moans and groans
Gaming equipment considered expensive

Number of franchisee addresses provided by franchisor: 19

➪ Slim Gym

Bingswood Industrial Estate, Whaley Bridge, Stockport, Cheshire SK12 7LY
Phone: 06633 4545

Slim Gym runs a series of health clubs. At present the company is refraining from answering letters sent by would-be franchisees requesting information on the franchise. In answer to our telephone enquiries we were assured that the company was a franchise, but the spokeswoman answering the phone (who seem bemused that we should ask such a question) was unwilling to divulge any further information.

➪ Small Business Advisory Centres

1213 Stratford Road, Hall Green, Birmingham B28 9AD
Phone: 021-778 5105

'Somewhere to which the person already in business or the person thinking of starting a business can go for advice and assistance.'

Outlets
Number of outlets   12
Company owned outlets: No information supplied
Franchised: No information supplied
Pilot: No information supplied
1988 franchise target: No information supplied

Costs
Total   £10,000
Franchise fee: £5,000
Other charges: Nil
Min cash excluding bank: No information supplied
Min overdraft required: No information supplied
Normal bank advance: 50%
Working capital first 2 months: £3,000
Associated banks: None
Capital items required: Office fittings
Associated leasing co: None

Snap On Tools Ltd

Royalties
	12.5% of turnover
	0.0% accounts service
	0.0% for advertising fund
Total	12.5% monthly sales
	No standing royalty independent of turnover

Bank rating	No information supplied
Territory	No information supplied
Strings	Franchisees pass all financial work on to the head office, and give 'free' advice on general matters to clients.
Training	4 week training followed by further training on site
	Cost: Nil – included in franchise fee
	Training value: No information supplied
Support	No information supplied
Operating Manual	No information supplied
Profit	No information supplied
Risk	The number of small businesses is growing, which augurs well.
Management only	This is a purely management job.

Size and reach
Original company launched:	1983
Overseas connections:	None
UK connections:	Originally known as T Thompstone and Co
Viable for whole UK?	Yes
Trade bodies	None

Franchisor's formula for success
Every small business or self-employed person needs an accountant. This need is supplied by the Centre together with the associated services of bookkeeping, VAT, PAYE etc if needed. All clients can provide as a minimum their accounting fees each year, thus creating a business with a reliable repeating income. All accounting and other services are provided by Head Office. 'There is no comparable operation.'

Good Franchise Guide comment: The company should not be confused with the government agency of the same name; and we are worried about possible confusion that might result from the use of a name widely promoted by a government department. The concept of offering a free advisory service but picking up the resultant accountancy work is fascinating, and we would have welcomed the chance to talk with existing franchisees.

Number of franchisee addresses provided by franchisor: 00

⇨ Snap On Tools Ltd

Palmer House, 150–154 Cross Street, Sale, Cheshire M33 1AQ
Phone: 061-969 0126

Retailers to motor mechanics, commercial vehicle dealers, haulage contractors, plant hire companies, marinas, airports, agricultural dealers etc

Outlets
Number of outlets	over 350 dealers

Snappy Snaps

Costs
Total	No information supplied – fee covers purchase of initial stock
Franchise fee:	Nil
Other charges:	Nil
Min cash excluding bank:	No information supplied
Min overdraft required:	No information supplied
Normal bank advance:	No information supplied
Working capital first 2 months:	No information supplied
Associated banks:	None
Capital items required:	Tool display van
Associated leasing co:	None

Royalties
No royalty – dealers get a commission on each sale.

Bank rating No information supplied
Territory Depends on which part of the country you are in.
Strings You can only sell Snap On tools

Training A few weeks support from a field manager is given
Each field manager looks after 8 to 10 dealers and gives on-going assistance.
Cost: No information supplied
Training value: No information supplied

Support Above the field managers are 7 branches each supporting up to 80 dealers, and holding tool warehouses.
Operating Manual No information supplied
Profit No information supplied
Risk Much competition, but this is a well known name
Management only More of a one-man operation

Size and reach
Original company launched:	1920
Overseas connections:	None
UK connections:	None
Viable for whole UK?	Yes
Trade bodies	None

Franchisor's formula for success
As a Snap On dealer you will be in business for yourself. All aspects of the business will be handled by you. Operating a Snap On dealership requires dedication, hard work, planning, bookkeeping, efficient inventory management and the development of personal relations with your customers. However, at the end of the week, when your sales goals have been achieved or exceeded, the personal satisfaction and profits are yours.

Good Franchise Guide comment: As the franchisor comments show this is not a franchise in the normal sense, but a dealership, although Snap On is listed in many publications as a franchise.

Number of franchisee addresses provided by franchisor: 00

➪ Snappy Snaps
52 Notting Hill Gate, London W11 3HT
Phone: 01-727 6680

One-hour photo labs

Outlets
Number of outlets
Company owned outlets:	03
Franchised:	06
Pilot:	01 started 1983
1988 franchise target:	No information supplied

Costs
Total	£92,125
Franchise fee:	£8,000
Other charges:	Nil
Min cash excluding bank:	£20,000
Min overdraft required:	£12,125
Normal bank advance:	£2,000
Working capital first 2 months:	£12,000
Associated banks:	None
Capital items required:	Equipment package £50,000
	Shopfitting £12.500
Associated leasing co:	None

Royalties
	6.0% of turnover
	0.0% accounts service
	0.0% for advertising fund
Total	6.0% monthly sales
	No standing royalty independent of turnover

Bank rating	No information supplied
Territory	No information supplied
Strings	No information supplied
Training	No information supplied
Support	No information supplied
Operating Manual	No information supplied
Profit	Projected figures suggest you need a turnover of £100,000 plus to make any profit at all
Risk	Several rival franchises building up currently
Management only	Could be run by manager but with limited profit

Size and reach
Original company launched:	No information supplied, but recent
Overseas connections:	None
UK connections:	None
Viable for whole UK?	Yes
Trade bodies	None

Franchisor's formula for success
The Snappy Snaps Lab is a bright modern high street shop purpose designed to offer a service concept which is relatively new to the UK. The labs project a high tech, futuristic image, making available to the consumer the latest technological advances in the photofinishing field today.

Good Franchise Guide comment: The two franchisors are both ex-franchisees of Kall-Kwik, which should add an extra dimension of understanding. They didn't fill in our questionnaire, but the information sent to franchisees is helpful and fairly comprehensive.

Number of franchisee addresses provided by franchisor: 00

⇨ Snappy Tomato Pizza
1 Lyons Way, Greenford, Middx UB6 0BN
Phone: 01-578 5785

Take away and home delivery fast food service

Outlets
Number of outlets	400 outlets in 59 countries
Company owned outlets:	01
Franchised:	00
Pilot:	00
1988 franchise target:	00

The Sock Shop

Costs
Total	£28,000
Franchise fee:	£5,000 (about to rise to £6,900)
Other charges:	£23,000
Min cash excluding bank:	No information supplied
Min overdraft required:	No information supplied
Normal bank advance:	66%
Working capital first 2 months:	No information supplied
Associated banks:	None
Capital items required:	Shopfitting – £15,000 to £20,000 in addition to costs above
Associated leasing co:	None

Royalties
	5.0% of turnover
	0.0% accounts service
	0.0% for advertising fund
Total	5.0% monthly sales
	No standing royalty independent of turnover

Bank rating	Normally no problem where security is available
Territory	No information supplied
Strings	No information supplied
Training	3 to 4 weeks practical and management training Cost: Nil – included in franchise fee Training value: No information supplied
Support	Support includes a till linked to a modem which transmits data on all sales to company HQ to analyse sales, costs and offer remedial action where needed
Operating Manual	No information supplied
Profit	No information supplied
Risk	Great competition, and fashions can change
Management only	Manager is involved in building the pizzas

Size and reach
Original company launched:	1970
Overseas connections:	Controlled by Slush Puppie Corp who bought it in 1985 from Snappy Tomato Pizza
UK connections:	Controlling UK company: Able Foods Ltd
Viable for whole UK?	Yes
Trade bodies	None

Franchisor's formula for success
Pizza is the fastest growing product in the fast food and disciplined menus market both in England and America. In America, the home of fast food, pizza outsells hamburgers by miles, and what America did yesterday the rest of the world will do today.

Good Franchise Guide comment: Just how far England will follow America in terms of eating pizzas remains to be seen; but this is a proven American product and service which might translate to the UK. But beware of the competition, of which there is an enormous amount.

Number of franchisee addresses provided by franchisor: 00

⇨ The Sock Shop

2c Nine Elms Industrial Estate, Kirtling Street, London SW8 5BP
Phone: 01-627 8080

The Sock Shop at the above address has been listed in some reference books and magazines as a franchise. However Richard Ross, the managing director, informs us that the company does not franchise or wholesale.

Sovereign Services

⇨ Southern Health Food Stores

c/o The Franchise Shop Ltd, 26 High Street, Merstham, Surrey RH1 3EA
Phone: 07374 4211

Health food retailing chain

Outlets
Number of outlets	25
Company owned outlets:	No information supplied
Franchised:	No information supplied
Pilot:	No information supplied
1988 franchise target:	No information supplied

Costs
Total	£30,000 to £40,000
Franchise fee:	No information supplied
Other charges:	No information supplied
Min cash excluding bank:	£15,000
Min overdraft required:	No information supplied
Normal bank advance:	£50%
Working capital first 2 months:	No information supplied
Associated banks:	Barclays
Capital items required:	Shopfitting
Associated leasing co:	None

Royalties
No information supplied on royalties

Bank rating No information supplied
Territory No information supplied
Strings Not highly restrictive – a wide range of goods are sold

Training 5 weeks practical and management training

Support No information supplied
Operating Manual No information supplied
Profit £15,000 to £25,000 depending on site and sales
Risk Competitive area but expanding rapdily
Management only No information supplied

Size and reach
Original company launched:	1964
Overseas connections:	None
UK connections:	None
Viable for whole UK?	Yes
Trade bodies	National Assn of Health Stores, Institute of Health Food Retailing

Franchisor's formula for success
'One of the health food industry's most successful independent companies.'

Good Franchise Guide comment: The information on this franchise is available only through The Franchise Shop who have declined to supply further information.

Number of franchisee addresses provided by franchisor: 00

⇨ Sovereign Services

39 Osborne Road, Eastbourne, East Sussex BN20 8JJ
Phone: 0293 547932

A private ambulance franchise at this address has been listed in some reference books and magazines.
A spokesperson for the company has informed us that the company is not a franchise, despite the claim in one publication that the company has 11 franchised outlets. Letters from private individuals seeking information on the 'franchise' are not answered.

Spar Eight Till Late Convenience Stores

⇨ Spar Eight Till Late Convenience Stores
AF Blakemore & Son Ltd, Long Acres Industrial Estate, Rosehill, Willenhall, West Midlands WV13 2JP

Spar inform us that they do not operate a full franchise scheme, but an underlease arrangement with the store tied to Spar. Stores are available for purchase and while the capital required varies considerably a capital sum of approximately £40,000 would be necessary.

We have no further details of the underleasing system, and how it differs from franchising in the case of Spar.

⇨ Specpoint
4 Hawthorn Grove, Wilmslow, Cheshire SK9 5DE
Phone: 0625 525055

Information available from Saffery Champness Consultancy Services, Fairfax House, Fulwood Place, Gray's Inn, London WC1V 6UB
Phone: 01-405 2828

This franchise has been listed in some reference books and magazines. We received no reply to our questionnaires. Our would-be franchisee was sent a handwritten note on headed paper which gave no proprietor's name (contrary to the Companies Act) but which stated that the company was involved in 'classified advertising on computer'. The franchisor declined to supply information but asked the enquirer to indicate his interest, and the source of the Specpoint address.

A little later our would-be franchisee received a note from Saffery Champness, who act as consultants to this firm and Institute of Tukido (qv). The consultants offered to supply information, but first asked the applicant for details of himself – in particular where the applicant first heard of Specpoint, why was he asking about more than one franchise, if he was acting as a spy for another consultancy, and why he was not on the phone. (This last was in fact untrue – he was on the phone but had refrained from putting his number on the letter.)

The editors decided to take up the matter, and following a full reply from ourselves explaining our situation and supplying yet more questionnaires for the clients of the consultant a more friendly reply was received explaining the problems this consultant was having with another, much larger and well known firm of franchise consultants. We were told the forms had now been sent on to Specpoint, although we have still not received any information. But at least this consultant talked to us openly – which is more than most did.

⇨ Sperrings Convenience Stores
Previously at: Sentosa, Chilworth Road, Southampton S01 7JT

Sperrings has now been bought out by Circle K. We have been unable to obtain further information, but anyone specifically interested in Sperrings should contact Circle K at:

Fareham Point, Wickham Road, Fareham, Hants PO16 7BU
Phone: 0329 822666

⇨ Spud U Like Ltd

34 – 38 Standard Road, Park Royal, London NW10 6EU
Phone: 01-965 0182

Fast food outlet offering a hot baked potato with butter and a choice of fillings.

Outlets

Number of outlets
Company owned outlets: 06
Franchised: 34
Pilot: 04 started 1974
1988 franchise target: Approx 50
Current reach:

South	06	South west	05	South east	15
Midlands	03	East Anglia	01	North east	00
North west	05	Scotland	04	Wales	01
N Ireland	00	Rep Ireland	00	I of Man/CI	00

Costs

Total: No information supplied
Franchise fee: £5,000
Other charges: No information supplied
Min cash excluding bank: £15,000 to £20,000
Min overdraft required: £5,000
Normal bank advance: 66%
Working capital first 2 months: £5,000
Associated banks: Nat West
Capital items required: Fixtures, fittings, equipment
Associated leasing co: Lombard Leisure

Royalties

Total:
5.0% of turnover
3.0% accounts service
0.0% for advertising fund
8.0% monthly sales

No standing royalty independent of turnover

Bank rating — Some problems reported in getting finance

Territory — 1 unit per 45,000 population
Franchisees report: If anything area is too big

Strings — Replies varied from suggesting that there are lots of ties to the franchisor, to a view that 'once you start you are on your own'.

Training —
7 days practical training
7 days management training
Cost: Nil – included in franchise fee except accommodation
Training value: Adequate

Support — Opinion varied from very good to very poor

Operating Manual — Opinion varied from good to 'rubbish'

Profit — As projected (even when franchisee held franchisor in poor esteem)

Risk — This is a high street outlet competing with all the other restaurants. This franchise is different from pizzas and burgers, which may increase or decrease risk, depending on public opinion.

Management only — Potentially good return on investment for a manager with proven ability

Stained Glass Overlay

Size and reach
Original company launched:	1974 – part of BSM Holdings from 1982
Overseas connections:	None
UK connections:	Part of BSM Holdings
Viable for whole UK?	All major towns
Trade bodies	None

Franchisor's formula for success
We believe that Spud U Like is unique in that it is the only fast food operation to major in baked potatoes, which are becoming increasingly popular as potential users become more knowledgeable about healthy eating and the need to adopt a balanced diet.

Inside story from the franchisees
Only two franchisees responded, and their opinions were in many cases contradictory. However, even the negative franchisee was making a profit as expected, and the negative opinion may be explained by a mismatch of expectations and reality in this case.

Insider tips
Beware of the manual – it needs updating

Moans and groans
Both respondents complained that the royalties were too high – but this is not by any means a complaint just reserved for this franchise. 80% of franchisees complain about royalties.

Number of franchisee addresses provided by franchisor: 34

⇨ Stained Glass Overlay
23 Hurricane Way, Norwich NR6 6HE
Phone: 0603 485454

Production and selling of designs on glass

Outlets
Number of outlets
Company owned outlets:	01
Franchised:	03
Pilot:	01 started 1986
1988 franchise target:	15 approx

Current reach:

South	01	South west	00	South east	01
Midlands	00	East Anglia	01	North east	00
North west	00	Scotland	01	Wales	00
N Ireland	00	Rep Ireland	00	I of Man/CI	00

Costs
Total	No information supplied
Franchise fee:	£13,000
Other charges:	£12,000
Min cash excluding bank:	No information supplied
Min overdraft required:	No information supplied
Normal bank advance:	No information supplied
Working capital first 2 months:	£2,500
Associated banks:	None as yet
Capital items required:	Premises as required
Associated leasing co:	GMAC

Royalties
	7.5% of turnover
	0.0% accounts service
	2.5% for advertising fund
Total	10.0% monthly sales
	No standing royalty independent of turnover

StarGull (Sales) Ltd

Bank rating	No information supplied, but this is a new franchise and banks will not yet have a track record on which to base their offers.
Territory	County boundaries
Strings	No information supplied
Training	4 to 5 days practical training 3 to 4 days management training Cost: £3,800 – included in franchise fee Training value: No information supplied
Support	No information supplied
Operating Manual	No information supplied
Profit	No projections provided in brochure
Risk	Depends how good a salesman you are
Management only	Reasonable return for owner with management ability

Size and reach

Original company launched:	1986
Overseas connections:	Part of SGO network worldwide, over 300 franchises
UK connections:	Wholly owned subsidiary of Anglian Windows Ltd and part of the BET group
Viable for whole UK?	Yes
Trade bodies	GGF

Franchisor's formula for success

When stained glass windows are assembled with cut glass many individual pieces of coloured glass are leaded and glued together to form the finished product. Using this method can result in air infiltration, possible water leakage and loss of heated or cooled air. Dealing with these problems is annoying, costly and a major problem for contractors, builders etc. When the overlay method is used coloured film and lead are bonded to a single piece of glass. The finished product is seamless, airtight, waterproof, fade resistant, and contains ultraviolet inhibitors.

Good Franchise Guide comment: The franchisor felt that as theirs is such a new franchise with only three franchisees at present they did not want us to contact the franchisees just yet. They did, however, provide the phone number of one franchisee – but we felt a single telephone interview could provide misleading information. But the franchisor was communicative and co-operative, which augurs well for the future of the franchise.

Number of franchisee addresses provided by franchisor: 00

⇨ StarGull (Sales) Ltd

Unit 9, Rocky Lane Industrial Estate, William Henry Street, Aston, Birmingham B7 5ER
Phone: 021-359 8272

In our opinion this is not a franchise but a distributorship from a company marketing a range of products presented on display cards and selling to a general range of retail outlets. The product range is made up of 60 lines ranging from needles to combs, from toys to shoe laces, selling into corner shops, garages, chemists and small stores. The company claims that it offers many of the advantages of franchising but without the setting-up costs and management charges.

Distributors get the sole rights to existing territory, an established bank of customers and assistance with initial training, plus back-up. Sales are expected to rise rapidly to £1,000 per week with a 40% gross profit.

Good Franchise Guide comment: We welcome the fact that this firm openly says that it is not a franchise and explains why its approach is felt to be best. Everything depends on the products, the outlets, and the distributors' ability to sell. Certainly the fact that the company has no minimum order is a benefit in itself.

⇨ Startrack Satellite TV Reception Equipment
15a Gordon Road, Windsor, Berks SL4 3RG

A franchise at this address has been listed in some reference books and magazines. Mail sent to this address is accepted, but we have been unable to obtain information either in response to general requests from would-be franchisees or specifically for this publication. In the light of this experience we suggest a certain amount of caution may be in order if the franchise does eventually reappear.

⇨ Stayview Ltd
10 Southgate, Manchester M3 2RA

A franchise at this name and address has been listed in some reference books and magazines. Mail sent to this address is accepted, but we have been unable to obtain information either in response to general requests from would-be franchisees or specifically for this publication. In the light of this experience we suggest a certain amount of caution may be in order if the franchise does eventually reappear.

⇨ Stockcheck
The Courtyard, Harewood Estate, Leeds LS17 9LF
Phone: 0532 886565

A tried and tested computerised service designed specifically for liquor stocktaking operated by professional catering people with many years' experience in the hotel, public house, restaurant and leisure industries.

Outlets
Number of outlets
Company owned outlets: 00
Franchised: 12
Pilot: 02 started 1982
1988 franchise target: 20
Current reach:

South	01	South west	01	South east	03
Midlands	01	East Anglia	01	North east	03
North west	02	Scotland	00	Wales	00
N Ireland	00	Rep Ireland	00	I of Man/CI	00

Costs
Total: No information supplied
Franchise fee: £4,500
Other charges: £4,500
Min cash excluding bank: No information supplied
Min overdraft required: No information supplied
Normal bank advance: No information supplied
Working capital first 2 months: £7,000
Associated banks: None
Capital items required: None
Associated leasing co: Lombard

Royalties

Total
7.5% of turnover
2.5% marketing service
0.0% for advertising fund
10.0% monthly sales

No standing royalty independent of turnover

Stop Thief (UK) Ltd

Bank rating	'Not very helpful'
Territory	Population and radius
	Franchisees report: Just right
Strings	Some ties but lots of freedom too
Training	5 days practical training
	10 days management training
	Cost: Nil – included in franchise fee
	Training value: Excellent
Support	Good
Operating Manual	Good
Profit	As expected, or better than expected
Risk	Some competition – you will need to convince potential clients that this system works.
Management only	Ranging from one-man-band operation upwards depending on size.

Size and reach

Original company launched:	1983
Overseas connections:	None
UK connections:	Wholly owned subsidiary of John Gilpin Ltd
Viable for whole UK?	England only
Trade bodies	None

Franchisor's formula for success

Just one stocktaker, using a hand-held computer can conduct quick, regular, on-the-spot checks, to give you stock valuations, profit margins, surpluses and deficits, stock life, and so on, with simultaneous on-site print-out of a complete analysis sheet. Essential information for fast effective management decisions – whatever the size of establishment.

Inside story from the franchisees

'Not a get rich quick franchise, but a good steady business'

Insider tips

Make sure that market research concerning the competition is carried out.

Moans and groans

None

Number of franchisee addresses provided by franchisor: 11

⇨ Stop Thief (UK) Ltd

Unit 9 Avenue One, Business Park, Letchworth, Herts SG6 2BB
Phone: 0462 670555

In 1986 Gamma Electronics combined with Stop-A-Thief to form Stop Thief UK Ltd developing a network of 120 mobile fitting agents to retail, fleet and trade customers. The Gamma range includes vehicle alarms, radio control alarms, central locking kits, sirens and add-on accessories.

Outlets

Number of outlets

Company owned outlets:	03
Franchised:	25
Pilot:	01 started 1983
1988 franchise target:	50

Current reach:

South	04	South west	00	South east	06
Midlands	08	East Anglia	00	North east	01
North west	05	Scotland	01	Wales	00
N Ireland	00	Rep Ireland	00	I of Man/CI	00

Strachan Studio

Costs

Total	£10,000
Franchise fee:	£5,000
Other charges:	Nil
Min cash excluding bank:	£20,000
Min overdraft required:	No information supplied
Normal bank advance:	50%
Working capital first 2 months:	£2,000
Associated banks:	Barclays
Capital items required:	Renault Extra Van
Associated leasing co:	Yes – no details supplied

Royalties

	0.0% of turnover
	0.0% accounts service
	0.0% for advertising fund
Total	0.0% monthly sales
	£25 per week royalty independent of turnover

Bank rating No information supplied
Territory 500,000 population
Franchisees report: Just right
Strings Very strong ties for product
Training 3 to 4 days practical training
2 to 3 days management training
Cost: Nil – included in franchise fee
Training value: Adequate

Support Good
Operating Manual No manual, but instructions for each system
Profit Better than expected
Risk Not a high risk area; everyone is growing more security conscious, which can only benefit franchisees
Management only One-man-band operation

Size and reach

Original company launched:	1979
Overseas connections:	None
UK connections:	Subsidiary of Gamma Electronics
Viable for whole UK?	Yes
Trade bodies	None

Franchisor's formula for success
Previous experience in auto electrics, while an advantage is not a necessity as full training is given. Sales or business experience is helpful especially if it has been gained in the automotive market place.

Inside story from the franchisees
'Franchisee works very hard (and succeeds eventually)'

Insider tips
'Dedication is the word'

Moans and groans
Some problems (which job in this field doesn't have?) but a lot of job satisfaction too.

Number of franchisee addresses provided by franchisor: 10

⇨ **Strachan Studio**
See George Strachan & Co Ltd

Subway Sandwiches and Salads

⇨ Strikes Restaurants
289 Oxford Street, London W1R 2AD
Phone: 01-370 6964

A franchise at this address has been listed in some reference books and magazines. Mail sent to this address is accepted, but we have been unable to obtain information either in response to general requests from would-be franchisees or specifically for this publication. The quoted telephone number rings but we have been unable to obtain a reply. In the light of this experience we suggest a certain amount of caution may be in order if the franchise does eventually reappear.

⇨ Subway Sandwiches and Salads
25 High Street, Milford, CT 06460 USA
Phone: 01-361 9546 (USA 0800 89 1183)

Sandwich bars

Outlets
Number of outlets
Company owned outlets:	10 worldwide				
Franchised:	2200 worldwide				
Pilot:	00				
1988 franchise target:	3000 worldwide				
Current reach:					
South	00	South west	00	South east	01
Midlands	00	East Anglia	00	North east	00
North west	00	Scotland	00	Wales	00
N Ireland	00	Rep Ireland	00	I of Man/CI	00

Costs
Total	£40,000
Franchise fee:	£5,000
Other charges:	No information supplied
Min cash excluding bank:	50%
Min overdraft required:	No information supplied
Normal bank advance:	50%
Working capital first 2 months:	No information supplied
Associated banks:	Lloyds
Capital items required:	Catering equipment
Associated leasing co:	None

Royalties
	8.0% of turnover
	0.0% accounts service
	2.5% for advertising fund
Total	10.5% monthly sales
	No standing royalty independent of turnover

Bank rating	No information supplied
Territory	1 store per 50,000 population
Strings	No information supplied
Training	2 weeks practical training at company's world HQ
	2 weeks management training also at company's HQ
	Cost: Nil – included in franchise fee
	Training value: No information supplied

Summer Air Ltd

Support	No information supplied
Operating Manual	No information supplied
Profit	No information supplied
Risk	Presumably they know what they are doing with over 2000 outlets
Management only	They say 'Proven franchise with good return on investment' but we'd like to see more than one in the UK before making a judgement.

Size and reach

Original company launched:	1965
Overseas connections:	USA company: Subway Sandwiches and Salads (USA) Stores open in 8 countries worldwide
UK connections:	None
Viable for whole UK?	Yes
Trade bodies	None

Good Franchise Guide comment: They are big enough worldwide to be big in the UK, but you never know; the UK is not the States writ smaller.

Number of franchisee addresses provided by franchisor: 00

➪ **Summer Air Ltd**

150 Albert Road, Devonport, Plymouth, Devon PL2 1AW
Phone: 0752 563051

Marketing of dehumidifiers, air cleaners, ionisers, heat exchangers, split systems and air conditioning at competitive prices. Franchisees decide how to exploit the market in their own area via a shop, an in-store facility or a mobile operation.

Outlets

Number of outlets	
Company owned outlets:	01
Franchised:	00
Pilot:	01 started 1987
1988 franchise target:	No information supplied

Costs

Total	£10,500
Franchise fee:	£6,300
Other charges:	£4,200 (stock, van lease, launch)
Min cash excluding bank:	No information supplied
Min overdraft required:	No information supplied
Normal bank advance:	No information supplied
Working capital first 2 months:	No information supplied
Associated banks:	None
Capital items required:	Van
Associated leasing co:	None

Royalties

Total	7.0% of turnover 0.0% accounts service 3.0% for advertising fund 10.0% monthly sales
	No standing royalty independent of turnover
Bank rating	No information supplied
Territory	No information supplied
Strings	Franchisees are tied to the equipment selected by Summer Air

Swinton Insurance Brokers Ltd

Training	5 days practical and management training in Plymouth plus 5 days on site.
	Cost: Nil – included in franchise fee
	Training value: No information supplied
Support	No information supplied
Operating Manual	No information supplied
Profit	No information supplied
Risk	A growing area – be aware of just how many firms there are moving into this area
Management only	Does not appear to be designed as a management-based franchise

Size and reach

Original company launched:	1982
Overseas connections:	None
UK connections:	Owned by Summer Air (Wholesale) Ltd
Viable for whole UK?	Yes
Trade bodies	None

Franchisor's formula for success
The exploitation of the market is largely dependent on the franchisee – but with support from Summer Air. For example, the franchisee may decide to run a small display in a cash and carry or a supermarket. Summer Air will help with a back-up team of demonstrators and sales people if they are needed. A mail-shot to a specifically targeted market is another way.

Good Franchise Guide comment: A new franchise in an expanding area. Everything depends on the quality of the goods supplied.

Number of franchisee addresses provided by franchisor: 00

⇨ Swinton Insurance Brokers Ltd

6 Great Marlborough Street, Manchester M1 5NN
Phone: 061-236 1222

Leading high street insurance broker

Outlets
Number of outlets

Company owned outlets:	170
Franchised:	100
Pilot:	00
1988 franchise target:	350 approx

Current reach:

South	11	South west	00	South east	10
Midlands	63	East Anglia	08	North east	75
North west	93	Scotland	00	Wales	10
N Ireland	00	Rep Ireland	00	I of Man/CI	00

Costs

Total	£19,000
Franchise fee:	£3,450
Other charges:	Nil
Min cash excluding bank:	£7,000
Min overdraft required:	No information supplied
Normal bank advance:	No information supplied
Working capital first 2 months:	£3,000
Associated banks:	None
Capital items required:	None
Associated leasing co:	None

System Consultancy

Royalties

	6.0% of turnover 'guarantee commission'
	0.0% accounts service
	0.0% for advertising fund
Total	6.0% monthly sales
	£100 per quarter standing royalty independent of turnover

Bank rating	No problems encountered
Territory	Franchisees report: 'Just right'
Strings	Lots of ties but some freedom
Training	No information on length of training
	Cost: Nil – included in franchise fee
	Training value: Excellent
Support	Excellent
Operating Manual	Very good
Profit	Better than expected in all cases
Risk	It's a very competitive market, but you must be in the business in order to take up the franchise
Management only	Could be run by manager but with limited profit

Size and reach

Original company launched:	No information supplied
Overseas connections:	None
UK connections:	None
Viable for whole UK?	Yes
Trade bodies	None

Franchisor's formula for success
Swinton's success can be credited to several specific factors – a revolutionary concept in selling insurance; a high degree of professionalism and a carefully planned system.

Inside story from the franchisees
Excellent all the way from top to bottom. An ideal chance to run your own business. 'Excellent back-up'

Insider tips
You must be the 'right type of person'.
'In general I am against franchises unless you have had previous experience in that field, which with Swinton's you have to have had.'
'It is not simply the correct franchise selection that makes a good business but also some blood and thunder.'

Moans and groans
Not a single one

Number of franchisee addresses provided by franchisor: 100

⇨ # System Consultancy

34 Elm Tree Court, King Street, Cottingham, Hull, Humberside
Phone: 0482 843371

A franchise at this address offering information processing systems has been listed in some reference books and magazines. Mail sent to this address is accepted, but we have been unable to obtain information either in response to general requests from would-be franchisees or specifically for this publication.
Our telephone calls were eventually answered with the information that there was a man living at this private address who did have something to do with franchises, but that he had gone away for a while. No information was available on the possible date of his return.
In the light of this experience we suggest a certain amount of caution may be in order if the franchise does eventually reappear.

⇨ System-Text (UK) Ltd

System-Text House, Beavor Lane, Hammersmith, London W6 9BL
Phone: 01-741 7461

Supply of self-adhesive vinyl letters plus logos etc

Outlets
Number of outlets	
Company owned outlets:	01
Franchised:	No information supplied
Pilot:	01 started 1984
1988 franchise target:	No information supplied

Costs
Total	£12,665
Franchise fee:	£3,500
Other charges:	£9,165
Min cash excluding bank:	No information supplied
Min overdraft required:	No information supplied
Normal bank advance:	50%
Working capital first 3 months:	£2,250 (for three months)
Associated banks:	None
Capital items required:	Van on lease (deposit and first rental payment is £615)
Associated leasing co:	None

Royalties
Total	0.0% of turnover
	0.0% accounts service
	0.0% for advertising fund
	0.0% monthly sales
	£125 per month standing royalty independent of turnover in first year rising to £333 per month in subsequent years
Bank rating	No information supplied
Territory	No information supplied
Strings	Standard letters and stripes supplied along with application and laying-up tape plus stationery pack.
Training	2 weeks practical and management training
	Cost: £650 – included in franchise fee
	Training value: No information supplied
Support	No information supplied
Operating Manual	No information supplied
Profit	No information supplied
Risk	age281Difficult to judge without further information
Management only	No information supplied

Size and reach
Original company launched:	1984
Overseas connections:	Parent company is Swedish
UK connections:	None
Viable for whole UK?	Yes
Trade bodies	None

Franchisor's formula for success
System-Text was created in Sweden over 25 years ago as a self-adhesive lettering system and has over the years developed into today's variable sign marking and decoration system. This has made them dominant market leader in their particular field.

Good Franchise Guide comment: A recently started franchise based around a system that has existed for many years. We wonder why the normal percentage royalties have been abandoned in favour of fixed fees.

Number of franchisee addresses provided by franchisor: 00

Taylor Harrison Group Ltd

⇨ Taylor Harrison Group Ltd
See Postal Centres International Ltd

⇨ TC Graphics Ltd (The Compleat Engraver)
Valley House, Needham, Harleston, Norfolk IP20 9LG
Phone: 0379 852168

Glass engraving and colour franchise dealing in crystal tableware, doors, windows, interior screens, mirrors etc for local authorities, exhibitions, breweries, retail outlets, sports and social clubs etc

Outlets
Number of outlets
Company owned outlets:		01				
Franchised:		23				
Pilot:		03 started 1982				
1988 franchise target:		30 plus				
Current reach:						
South	*03	South west	03	South east	*	
Midlands	02	East Anglia	06	North east	03	
North west	00	Scotland	01	Wales	00	
N Ireland	01	Rep Ireland	01	I of Man/CI	00	

* 3 in South and South east
Also 3 in Canada

Costs
Total	£12,575
Franchise fee:	Nil
Other charges:	Nil
Min cash excluding bank:	£12,575
Min overdraft required:	£12,575
Normal bank advance:	£12,575
Working capital first 2 months:	£3,000
Associated banks:	Barclays; Allied Dunbar also offer financial support
Capital items required:	None
Associated leasing co:	None

Royalties
Total	12.5% of turnover
	0.0% accounts service
	0.0% for advertising fund
	12.5% monthly sales
	No standing royalty independent of turnover

Bank rating	No information supplied
Territory	Radius from base and population size
Strings	No information supplied
Training	7 days practical and management training
	Cost: Nil – included in franchise fee
	Training value: No information supplied
Support	No information supplied
Operating Manual	No information supplied
Profit	Nett profit before tax in year one quoted as £10,000
Risk	As an artistic concept it is dependent on fashion and the ability of the artist.
Management only	Could be anything from a one-man-band upwards.

Team Audio Ltd

Size and reach
Original company launched: 1982
Overseas connections: 3 franchises in Canada and 1 in Ireland
UK connections: None
Viable for whole UK? Yes
Trade bodies: None

Franchisor's formula for success
The Compleat Engraver and Colourist is a commercial enterprise with potential for high income and good profitability. It is not a low-production craft-orientated system. It is a low overhead business run from home or a small workshop.

Good Franchise Guide comment: A franchise that to the outsider looks really interesting, but we feel that communication with franchisees is an absolute must for anyone interested, unless they have a lot of experience within this field.

Number of franchisee addresses provided by franchisor: 00

⇨ Team Audio Ltd
Haverscroft Industrial Estate, New Road, Attleborough, Norfolk NR17 1YE
Phone: 0953 454544

A distribution wholesaling franchise, supplying major branded products and accessories to TV, video, electrical and hi-fi retailers and other commercial customers. This home-based operation works from a customised mobile showroom carrying over 1800 different items ranging from video recorders to styli and Team's own brand accessories.

Outlets
Number of outlets
Company owned outlets: 03
Franchised: 13
Pilot: 02 started 1978 and 1982
1988 franchise target: 25
Current reach:

South	03	South west	02	South east	03
Midlands	02	East Anglia	03	North east	02
North west	01	Scotland	00	Wales	00
N Ireland	00	Rep Ireland	00	I of Man/CI	00

Costs
Total: £30,000
Franchise fee: £4,500
Other charges: Nil
Min cash excluding bank: £10,000
Min overdraft required: £20,000
Normal bank advance: £20,000
Working capital first 2 months: 'All Team Franchises must have sufficient capital from day 1'
Associated banks: Most banks
Capital items required: Mobile show room £15,000 finance available
Associated leasing co: Yes, but no details provided

Royalties
4.2% of turnover management service fees
0.0% accounts service
1.2% for advertising fund
Total: 5.4% monthly sales
No standing royalty independent of turnover

Bank rating Very helpful
Territory Allocated by surveyed customer base
Franchisees report: Just right
Strings Strong ties for the product

283

Telephone World (UK) Ltd

Training	8 days practical training
	10 days management training
	Cost: £3,000 – included in franchise fee
	Training value: Excellent
Support	Very good
Operating Manual	Very good
Profit	Most franchisees are doing as projected or better
Risk	No direct competitors that we can see
Management only	One-man-band operation in year 1 with potential to grow

Size and reach

Original company launched:	1978
Overseas connections:	None
UK connections:	None
Viable for whole UK?	UK mainland only
Trade bodies	BFA Registered

Franchisor's formula for success

Team's product range has been finely tuned over the years to ensure quick stock turns with high sales and profit levels. The profit levels you will enjoy are well above those normally associated with the industry. Your objective is always to fulfil the regular needs of the retailer and his customers. Products include vidoes, phones, watches, batteries, audio systems etc.

Inside story from the franchisees

Very good response with franchisees feeling the franchise is well organised and supportive.

Insider tips

'Hard work but very rewarding for the right person'

Moans and groans

'Long long hours'

Number of franchisee addresses provided by franchisor: 07

⇨ Telephone World (UK) Ltd

10 Oxford Court, Bishopsgate, Manchester M2 3WQ

A franchise at this address has been listed in some reference books and magazines. Mail sent to this address is accepted, but we have been unable to obtain information either in response to general requests from would-be franchisees or specifically for this publication. In the light of this experience we suggest a certain amount of caution may be in order if the franchise does eventually reappear.

⇨ Teletone Communication Ltd

Previously at 9 Church Street, Stourbridge, West Midlands

A franchise offering car telephones at this name and address has been listed in some reference books and magazines. Mail sent to this address is now being returned by the Post Office marked 'Gone Away'. The telephone number quoted still gives a ringing tone, but we have been unable to obtain a reply despite repeated attempts.

Enquiries have revealed that no forwarding address has been left, although it is possible that the franchise may have been set up once more in another part of the country. In the light of this experience we suggest a certain amount of caution may be in order.

⇨ Telsell

See Marketing Methods Ltd

J W Thornton Ltd

⇨ Textlite UK Ltd
Concorde House, Concorde, Tyne and Wear NE17 2AS

A franchise at this address has been listed in some reference books and magazines. Mail sent to this address is accepted, but we have been unable to obtain information either in response to general requests from would-be franchisees or specifically for this publication. In the light of this experience we suggest a certain amount of caution may be in order if the franchise does eventually reappear.

⇨ Thermecon
Previously at 3 Aston Road, Aston Fields Industrial Estate, Bromsgrove, Worcs

A franchise at this address has been listed in some reference books and magazines. Mail sent to this address is now being returned by the Post Office marked 'Gone Away' and the quoted phone number is now disconnected. Enquiries have revealed that no forwarding address has been left, although it is possible that the franchise may have been set up once more in another part of the country. In the light of this experience we suggest a certain amount of caution may be in order.

⇨ Thermocrete Chimney Lining Systems Ltd
19 Ottley Road, Shipley, West Yorks BD18 2AN

A franchise at this address has been listed in some reference books and magazines. Mail sent to this address is accepted, but we have been unable to obtain information either in response to general requests from would-be franchisees or specifically for this publication. In the light of this experience we suggest a certain amount of caution may be in order if the franchise does eventually reappear.

⇨ J W Thornton Ltd
Derwent Street, Belper, Derbyshire DE5 1WP
Phone: 077382 4181

Confectionery retailer; the franchises are only available within existing retail outlets selling compatible products such as greetings cards and gifts

Outlets
Number of outlets	
Company owned outlets:	Over 150
Franchised:	Over 80
Pilot:	00
1988 franchise target:	No information supplied

Costs
Total	£14,000
Franchise fee:	£1,000
Other charges:	Fixtures and fittings, as below
Min cash excluding bank:	No information supplied
Min overdraft required:	No information supplied
Normal bank advance:	No information supplied
Working capital first 2 months:	No information supplied
Associated banks:	None
Capital items required:	Fixtures and fittings – £10,000 to £12,000 Scales, tills etc £2,000
Associated leasing co:	None

Thrust Jetstream Marketing

Royalties
No royalties as such; franchisees get 25% to 30% discount on sales lines
Bank rating Should be no problem since most of cost is fixtures
Territory No information supplied
Strings Only JWT branded confectionery goods are sold from the store together with compatible products such as cards

Training Staff are trained in the care and preparation of products
Cost: Nil – included in franchise fee
Training value: No information supplied

Support Franchise adviser visits every 2 to 3 weeks
Operating Manual No information supplied
Profit No information supplied – turnover projected at £45,000
Risk Leaves the franchisee totally tied to one brand of confectionery
Management only Depends on rest of shop

Size and reach
Original company launched: No information supplied
Overseas connections: No information supplied
UK connections: No information supplied
Viable for whole UK? No – only north of line from Minehead to Colchester, excluding Scotland
Trade bodies BFA

Insider tips
Thornton shops seen in many of the major towns and cities of the UK are totally operated by Thornton Retail Division and are not a part of the franchise operation.

Good Franchise Guide comment: If conventional confectionery sales are well catered for in an area, and there is space in a suitable shop this could be a viable proposition if you envisage sufficient sales to redeem the shopfitting costs.

Number of franchisee addresses provided by franchisor: 00

▷ Thrust Jetstream Marketing

PO Buildings, Cardigan Road, Winton, Bournemouth, Dorset BH9 1BJ

A franchise offering to clean buildings has been listed at this name and address in some reference books and magazines. Mail sent to this address is now being returned by the Post Office marked 'Gone Away'. The quoted phone number still rings, but we have been unable to obtain a reply despite repeated attempts. Enquiries have revealed that no forwarding address has been left, although it is possible that the franchise may have been set up once more in another part of the country. In the light of this experience we suggest a certain amount of caution may be in order.

▷ Tie Rack Ltd

Capital Interchange Way, Brentford, Middx TW8 0EX
Phone: 01-995 1344

Retail outlets for ties, handkerchiefs, belts, scarves and the like in key sites selected by the franchisor

Outlets
Number of outlets
Company owned outlets: 18
Franchised: 103
Pilot: 01 started 1981, franchised 1982
1988 franchise target: 00
Current reach: No analysis by areas supplied

Tie Rack Ltd

Costs
Total	from £25,000
Franchise fee:	£5,000
Other charges:	Nil
Min cash excluding bank:	No information supplied
Min overdraft required:	No information supplied
Normal bank advance:	No information supplied
Working capital first 2 months:	Variable
Associated banks:	None – all major banks give support
Capital items required:	Shop equipment supplied by franchisor
Associated leasing co:	None

Royalties

22.5% of turnover which includes rent, rates, service charge
0.0% accounts service
0.0% for advertising fund

Total — 22.5% monthly sales

No standing royalty independent of turnover

Bank rating — No information supplied
Territory — 'Not applicable'
Strings — Franchisor selects and acquires site, sets up shop and supplies stock – very strong ties

Training

2 weeks practical and management training
Cost: Nil – included in franchise fee
Training value: No information supplied

Support — No information supplied
Operating Manual — No information supplied
Profit — No information supplied
Risk — Although it may seem unlikely it must be remembered that the business would fall apart if the fashion for wearing ties suddenly changed!

Management only — Reasonable return for owner with management ability

Size and reach
Original company launched:	1981
Overseas connections:	20 overseas units
UK connections:	None
Viable for whole UK?	Yes
Trade bodies	Full member of BFA

Franchisor's formula for success
A retailing idea hatched six years ago with the words – 'Ties at Sensational Value' displayed in an Oxford Street window, is now a successful chain of shops, which specialises in ties and neckwear for both men and women. The company has experienced phenomenal growth and now boasts a chain of over 100 specialist shops.

Inside story from the franchisees
The franchisor supplies a wide range of testimonials from existing franchisees with its package of information sent to prospective franchisees.

Good Franchise Guide comment: A very well known seemingly successful franchise but with a very high royalty to match; we would have welcomed the chance to talk to franchisees.
It may be significant that growth has been dramatic in the last two years.

Number of franchisee addresses provided by franchisor: 00

Time and Place Marketing Services

⇨ Time and Place Marketing Services
8 Beatrice Road, Worsley, Manchester M28 4TN
Phone: 061-728 1172

'The Advertising Clock'

Outlets
Number of outlets	No information supplied

Costs
Total	£6,000
Franchise fee:	£6,000
Other charges:	Nil
Min cash excluding bank:	No information supplied
Min overdraft required:	No information supplied
Normal bank advance:	No information supplied
Working capital first 2 months:	No information supplied
Associated banks:	None
Capital items required:	None
Associated leasing co:	None

Royalties
	25.0% of turnover
	0.0% accounts service
	0.0% for advertising fund
Total	25.0% monthly sales
	The royalty covers the preparation of artwork, printing etc
	No standing royalty independent of turnover

Bank rating	No information supplied
Territory	No information supplied
Strings	No information supplied
Training	No information supplied
	Cost: Nil – included in franchise fee
	Training value: No information supplied
Support	No information supplied
Operating Manual	No information supplied
Profit	£15,000 per annum selling two spaces a day
Risk	Depends on how good a salesman you are
Management only	One-man-band operation

Size and reach
Original company launched:	Partnership – set up approx 1982
Overseas connections:	None
UK connections:	None
Viable for whole UK?	Yes
Trade bodies	None

Franchisor's formula for success
The clocks are seen on a regular basis because they enjoy the benefit of a captive audience as they are located in places of business and entertainment which are frequented by local inhabitants and business people. Typical locations include public houses, chip shops, cafes, take aways etc. Taxi operators, motor vehicle suppliers, retail shops etc take advertisements on the clock.

Good Franchise Guide comment: A franchise for a salesman – you buy the right to sell a company's product and go out and try and find customers.

Number of franchisee addresses provided by franchisor: 00

⇨ Tioli Glass Engraving
See Calligraphics Ltd

⇨ TNT Parcel Office
TNT House, Long Street, Atherstone, Warwicks CV9 1BS
Phone: 0827 715311

Parcel reception point for forwarding throughout the UK. The franchise exists within an existing business.

Outlets
Number of outlets
Company owned outlets:	00
Franchised:	Over 400
Pilot:	No information supplied
1988 franchise target:	No information supplied
Reach:	No information supplied

Costs
Total	£5,000
	No other financial information supplied
Capital items required:	None
Associated leasing co:	None

Royalties
No royalties – franchisees are paid a commission on revenue generated

Bank rating	Should be no problems
Territory	No information supplied
Strings	None – this is simply an add-on to existing operation
Training	The company states that all necessary training is given but has provided no other information
Support	No information supplied
Operating Manual	No information supplied
Profit	A percentage of turnover
Risk	TNT are in the forefront of the market, and so the high number of competitors may not be as much of a threat as they may at first appear
Management only	Depends on the mainstream business

Size and reach
Original company launched:	1981
Overseas connections:	Numerous
UK connections:	Owned by TNT Roadfreight UK Ltd
Viable for whole UK?	Yes
Trade bodies	BFA

Franchisor's formula for success
A TNT Parcel Office franchise is a unique opportunity. There's no stock requirement to tie up your capital, and all customer invoicing is handled by TNT. As for overheads you can virtually forget them, you are simply utilising existing premises and staff.

Good Franchise Guide comment: If there is no TNT office nearby, and you are on or near a suitable industrial estate or business centre, and if you have the space and the facilities to gain the work then it could be a good add-on to your business. But you will have to promote the parcel service, and that could cut across other existing operations you already have.

Number of franchisee addresses provided by franchisor: 00

Toco Ltd

⇨ Toco Ltd
Previously at Market Street, Llangollen, Clwyd

A franchise at this name and address has been listed in some reference books and magazines. The franchise appears to be related to waterproofing the outside of buildings. Mail sent to this address is now being returned by the Post Office marked 'Gone Away'. Enquiries have revealed that no forwarding address has been left, and the most likely explanation is that this idea for a franchise failed to materialise although it is possible that the franchise may have been set up once more in another part of the country. In the light of this experience we suggest a certain amount of caution may be in order.

⇨ Tonibell Manufacturing Co Ltd
Glacier House, Brook Green, London W6

A franchise at this name and address has been listed in some reference books and magazines as a fast food restaurant chain. Enquiries have revealed that the company left some time ago without leaving a forwarding address or phone number. The phone number quoted in some reference material has been taken over by the new occupiers of the premises.

The name Tonibell is also used by Lyons Maid for soft ice cream, as part of its ice cream distributorships, but there seems to be no connection.

⇨ Trafalgar Cleaning Chemicals
Unit 4, Gillmans Industrial Estate, Billinghurst, West Sussex RH14 9EZ
Phone: 0403 814466

Developers and suppliers of car cleaning products to the motor trade

Outlets
Number of outlets
Company owned outlets: 00
Franchised: 20
Pilot: 05 started 1984
1988 franchise target: 45
Current reach:

South	11	South west	01	South east	03
Midlands	01	East Anglia	03	North east	00
North west	00	Scotland	00	Wales	01
N Ireland	00	Rep Ireland	00	I of Man/CI	00

Costs
Total	£4,900
Franchise fee:	£4,900
Other charges:	Nil
Min cash excluding bank:	£3,000
Min overdraft required:	£4,000 to £5,000
Normal bank advance:	66%
Working capital first 2 months:	Nil
Associated banks:	Royal Bank of Scotland, Lloyds
Capital items required:	Van – first payment incuded in franchise fee
Associated leasing co:	Franchise Finance

Royalties
	2.0% of turnover
	0.0% accounts service
	2.0% (reclaimable) for promotional items on achievement of £850 turnover per week
Total	2.0% monthly sales
	No standing royalty independent of turnover

Tramlines (Sports) Ltd

Bank rating	Helpful
Territory	Each area has 750,000 population; car population and local knowledge taken into account; allocated by post code
	Franchisees report: Most franchisees are happy but some would like a larger area
Strings	Very strong ties for materials
Training	4 days practical training
	4 days management training
	Cost: Nil – included in franchise fee
	Training value: Excellent
Support	Very good
Operating Manual	Good
Profit	Mostly as projected, several better, just one worse
Risk	Competitive area, although these profess to be the market leaders
Management only	Initially designed for owner operator with potential for further vans after one or two years.

Size and reach

Original company launched:	1978
Overseas connections:	None
UK connections:	Trafalgar Ltd owns a 75% stake
Viable for whole UK?	Yes
Trade bodies	Applying for BFA Associate membership

Franchisor's formula for success
Trafalgar has been established for the past 8 years supplying specialist products to the motor trades. These activities led us into the car cleaning side of the industry, which we found to be under served. Research showed a large regular demand for cleaning products. Trafalgar was born. The aims of Trafalgar are to become the largest and most efficient company in the chosen market place by offering first class service, the best range of quality prodcts and competitive prices.

Inside story from the franchisees
Everyone sees this franchise as very helpful and fair

Insider tips
'Check out the competition'
'Keep an eye on the cash flow as most garages want accounts'

Moans and groans
None

Number of franchisee addresses provided by franchisor: 20

⇨ Tramlines (Sports) Ltd
1 East Street, Tonbridge, Kent TN9 1HP

A franchise at this address has been listed in some reference books and magazines. Mail sent to this address is accepted, but we have been unable to obtain information either in response to general requests from would-be franchisees or specifically for this publication. It would appear that the original plan was to set up a chain of retail sports shops, and it may be that the plan has either been aborted or postponed.
In the light of this experience we suggest a certain amount of caution may be in order if the franchise does eventually reappear.

Tramps Trucking

⇨ Tramps Trucking
Formerly at 105 Saltley Trading Estate, Saltley, Birmingham

A franchise at this name and address has been listed in some reference books and magazines. Mail sent to this address is now being returned by the Post Office marked 'Gone Away'. Enquiries have revealed that no forwarding address has been left, although it is possible that the franchise may have been set up once more in another part of the country. In the light of this experience we suggest a certain amount of caution may be in order.

⇨ Trust Parts Ltd
Unit 7, Groundwell Industrial Estate, Crompton Road, Swindon, Wilts SN2 5AY
Phone: 0793 723749

Van-based sales service to the motor and allied trades offering workshop consumables and quality tools to garages, plant hire companies, haulage contractors, council workshops, factories, farms, hospitals etc

Outlets
Number of outlets
Company owned outlets:	65				
Franchised:	05				
Pilot:	Existing sales force served as pilot in 1979				
1988 franchise target:	82				
Current reach:					
South	04	South west	07	South east	08
Midlands	12	East Anglia	07	North east	10
North west	13	Scotland	05	Wales	04
N Ireland	00	Rep Ireland	00	I of Man/CI	00

Costs
Total	£12,250
Franchise fee:	£5,250
Other charges:	£7,000 stock
Min cash excluding bank:	£6,000
Min overdraft required:	£4,000
Normal bank advance:	66%
Working capital first 2 months:	£4,000
Associated banks:	Barclays, Lloyds, Nat West, Midland, Royal Bank of Scotland
Capital items required:	Stock only, vehicles leased
Associated leasing co:	Yes – no details provided

Royalties
	5.0% of turnover after initial £15,000
	0.0% accounts service
	0.0% for advertising fund
Total	5.0% monthly sales
	No standing royalty independent of turnover

Bank rating	Very helpful
Territory	Radius from franchisees base
	Franchisees report: Just right
Strings	Lots of ties but some freedom too
Training	3 days practical training
	2 days management training
	Cost: £1,500 – included in franchise fee
	Training value: Adequate

Tumble Tots (UK) Ltd

Support	Excellent
Operating Manual	Good
Profit	As projected
Risk	A lot of competition in this field. Ensure that you feel this is the best company in the market place. If you don't believe it, will your customers?
Management only	One-man-band operation
Size and reach	
Original company launched:	1979
Overseas connections:	None
UK connections:	None
Viable for whole UK?	Yes
Trade bodies	BFA Associate

Franchisor's formula for success

We are the market leader in direct sales of engineering workshop consumables and tools, sold direct from a mobile sales vehicle. There are 800-plus leading brand products, free weekly delivery of stock, national accounts, comprehensive training programme etc, all built into our franchise package. No premises are required, no need to employ staff. The most successful one man operated franchise in the UK

Inside story from the franchisees
'Franchise is good, but not as easy as made out.'

Insider tips
'Hard at first, but it soon gets better.'

Moans and groans
'The manual was not too comprehensive at first but has been amended'.

Number of franchisee addresses provided by franchisor: 5

⇨ Tuff-Kote Dinol

Conduit Place, 100 Ock Street, Abingdon, Oxon OX14 5DH

A franchise at this name and address has been listed in some reference books and magazines. The company concerned, who are involved in rust proofing cars, have informed us that they are not a franchise. Mail from individuals seeking information on the 'franchise' is not answered.

⇨ Tumble Tots (UK) Ltd

Cannons Sports Club, Cousin Lane, London EC4R 3TE
Phone: 01-621 0904

An active physical play programme for pre-school children designed to stimulate the development of physical skills and encourage early socialisation. Trained leaders join with parents and with specialised equipment promote the development of sensory motor skills.

Outlets
Number of outlets
Company owned outlets:	03
Franchised:	77
Pilot:	40 company centres between 1983 and 1984
1988 franchise target:	90

Current reach:

South	14	South west	05	South east	16
Midlands	18	East Anglia	06	North east	06
North west	10	Scotland	02	Wales	01
N Ireland	02	Rep Ireland	00	I of Man/CI	00

Tumble Tots (UK) Ltd

Costs
Note: Tumble Tots has two agreements:

1. Licence Agreement (duration one year)
Licence fee   £1,860
Insurance   £276 pa
Equipment   £2,000 (one-off payment)

2. Franchise (duration ten years)
Franchise fee   £5,000
Insurance   £276 pa
Royalty   5% of gross turnover
Equipment   £2,000 (one-off payment)

The following details relate to the licence as Tumble Tots does not offer a franchise until the second year.

Total	£4,356
Franchise fee:	£1,860 pa
Other charges:	£2,000 equipment, £276 insurance
Min cash excluding bank:	No information supplied
Min overdraft required:	No information supplied
Normal bank advance:	No information supplied
Working capital first 2 months:	£750
Associated banks:	None
Capital items required:	A trailer or van
Associated leasing co:	None

Royalties

	0.0% of turnover
	0.0% accounts service
	0.0% for advertising fund
Total	0.0% monthly sales

Note: Franchise fee is payable yearly independent of turnover

Bank rating	Helpful all round
Territory	Population
	Franchisees report: 'Not a wide enough area'
Strings	Strong ties but some parts of the operation not controlled
Training	2 days practical training
	2/3 days management training
	Cost: £200 – included in 'total fee' above
	Training value: Adequate
Support	Good
Operating Manual	Very good
Profit	Better than expected
Risk	No competition save local play groups who are very unlikely to be as well organised as a franchisee
Management only	One-man-band operation

Size and reach

Original company launched:	1980
Overseas connections:	Jack Chin Group of Companies (1986 assets $268,460,000)
UK connections:	None
Viable for whole UK?	Yes
Trade bodies	Fair Play for Children, Down's Syndrome Assn

Franchisor's formula for success
This franchise is ideal for people who wish to fit a small business around other commitments (such as a family) as profits depend on the amount of time put in. If done full time a good return on investment can be achieved.

The UK School of Motoring Ltd

Inside story from the franchisees
'Would encourage others with school age children to take up the franchise.'
'Franchisee back-up is improving almost monthly as the organisation grows.'

Insider tips
'You must realise that it takes long hours to make this successful'

Moans and groans
'Good manual but it needs to be updated'

Number of franchisee addresses provided by franchisor: 02

⇨ Tyre & Rubber Co Ltd
Mill Lane, Alton, Hants GU34 2QG

A franchise at this address has been listed in some reference books and magazines. Mail sent to this address is accepted, but we have been unable to obtain information either in response to general requests from would-be franchisees or specifically for this publication. In the light of this experience we suggest a certain amount of caution may be in order if the franchise does eventually reappear.

⇨ The UK School of Motoring Ltd
14 Birmingham Road, Cowes, Isle of Wight PO31 7BH
Phone: 0983 527788

Driving school

Outlets
Number of outlets
Company owned outlets: 02
Franchised: 03
Pilot: 01 started 1986
1988 franchise target: 54
Current reach:

South	02	South west	00	South east	00
Midlands	01	East Anglia	01	North east	00
North west	00	Scotland	01	Wales	00
N Ireland	00	Rep Ireland	00	I of Man/CI	00

Costs
Total	£6,000
Franchise fee:	£6,000
Other charges:	Nil
Min cash excluding bank:	'To suit'
Min overdraft required:	'To suit'
Normal bank advance:	'Unknown'
Working capital first 2 months:	£2,000
Associated banks:	Yes – no details given
Capital items required:	Vehicle insurance
Associated leasing co:	Yes – no details given

Royalties

	0.0% of turnover
	0.0% accounts service
	0.0% for advertising fund
Total	0.0% monthly sales
	£15 per week per vehicle operated standing royalty independent of turnover

Unigate Dairies Ltd

Bank rating	Franchisees felt the need to shop around
Territory	70,000 to 100,000 population
	Franchisees report: Just right
Strings	Lots of ties but some freedom
Training	4 days practical training
	4 days management training
	Cost: Nil – included in franchise fee
	Training value: Responses varied from 'not enough' to 'just right'
Support	Responses varied from 'not too good' to 'excellent'
Operating Manual	Responses varied from 'still being written' to 'excellent'
Profit	Responses varied from 'as projected' to far better than expected
Risk	Lots of competition, but an endless need for training
Management only	Little salary to spare for a manager

Size and reach

Original company launched:	1986
Overseas connections:	None
UK connections:	None
Viable for whole UK?	Yes
Trade bodies	Driving Instructors Assn, National Driving Instructors Assn

Franchisor's formula for success
The UK School of Motoring is offering individuals of the right calibre a franchise that, while requiring low capital investment, will enable them to rapidly establish a thriving and highly profitable business within the field of driving tuition and driving services.

Inside story from the franchisees
Highly variable and no comments can be selected as typical, but one franchisee did say 'most of our problems stem from the newness and inexperience of the franchisor'.

Insider tips
'There's a lot of hard work and worries in running your own business.'

Moans and groans
'When buying a franchise one expects a guaranteed marketing formula'.

Good Franchise Guide comment: As can be seen responses from franchisees varied dramatically, although all were making a reasonable living. This variance is not unusual in a new franchise, and the problems experienced by the one franchisee who complained of the lack of a guaranteed marketing formula may soon be overcome.

Number of franchisee addresses provided by franchisor: 03

⇨ Unigate Dairies Ltd
14 – 40 Victoria Road, Aldershot, Hants
Phone: 0252 24522

Milk round

Outlets	No information supplied

Costs

Total	£4,000
Franchise fee:	£3,000 *
Other charges:	£1,000 to purchase outstanding accounts

No further information supplied

* of which £2,000 is a returnable deposit

Royalties

A royalty is payable but no information supplied

Uticolor (Great Britain) Ltd

Bank rating	Should be no trouble
Territory	No information supplied
Strings	All products must be obtained from franchisor
Training	No information supplied
Support	No information supplied
Operating Manual	No information supplied
Profit	£12,000 to £13,000
Risk	Very low
Management only	One-man-band operation

Size and reach

Original company launched:	No information supplied
Overseas connections:	None disclosed
UK connections:	Part of Unigate
Viable for whole UK?	No information supplied
Trade bodies	BFA

Franchisor's formula for success

The basic qualities that we require of a potential Unigate franchisee are, current driving licence, physical fitness, numeracy, smart appearance, capable of early morning starts, happy to work in inclement weather, prepared to work Monday to Saturday inclusively, ability to deal with and sell to the public, have the complete support of your family.

Number of franchisee addresses provided by franchisor: 00

⇨ United Air Specialists (UK) Ltd

Cranford, Blackdown, Leamington Spa, Warwicks CV32 6RG

UAS is a wholly owned subsidiary of UAS Inc of Cincinnati, USA, selling Smokeeter electronic air cleaners via distributors who are required to invest £5,000 in the firm to cover working stock. Commissions of 40 per cent to 50 per cent are paid on sales.

⇨ Uniweld Ltd

Lower Quay, Fareham, Hants PO16 0RA

A franchise at this name and address has been listed in some reference books and magazines. Mail sent to this address is accepted, but we have been unable to obtain information either in response to general requests from would-be franchisees or specifically for this publication. In the light of this experience we suggest a certain amount of caution may be in order if the franchise does eventually reappear.

⇨ Uticolor (Great Britain) Ltd

Sheraton House, 35-37 North Street, York YO1 1JD
Phone: 0904 37798

The Uticolor process repairs holes and tears in most vinyl and leather materials with particular application to seating, saving 50 per cent in costs compared to recovering the units with new material.

Outlets

Number of outlets	
Company owned outlets:	01
Franchised:	36
Pilot:	00
1988 franchise target:	42

Uticolor (Great Britain) Ltd

Current reach:

South	03	South west	03	South east	08
Midlands	06	East Anglia	03	North east	05
North west	02	Scotland	02	Wales	02
N Ireland	01	Rep Ireland	00	I of Man/CI	01

Costs
Total	£5,000
Franchise fee:	£3,500
Other charges:	£1,500
Min cash excluding bank:	£5,000
Min overdraft required:	No information supplied
Normal bank advance:	No information supplied
Working capital first 2 months:	£1,000
Associated banks:	None but recognised by all majors
Capital items required:	Vehicle
Associated leasing co:	None

Royalties

	10.0% administration fee
	0.0% accounts service
	0.0% for advertising fund
Total	10.0% monthly sales
	£800 minimum royalty independent of turnover

Bank rating	Not too helpful – some searching around needed
Territory	County areas/population
	Franchisees report: Just right
Strings	Lots of ties but a lot of freedom too
Training	15 days practical training
	1 day management training
	Cost: £350 not included in franchise fee
	Training value: Adequate
Support	Good
Operating Manual	Good
Profit	As projected in most cases
Risk	Limited competition which serves to reduce risk
Management only	'Not applicable'

Size and reach
Original company launched:	1977
Overseas connections:	1 franchise with more pending
UK connections:	Subsidiary of Sheraton House Ltd
Viable for whole UK?	Yes
Trade bodies	BFA

Franchisor's formula for success
This is a low cost franchise producing an early return on initial capital but with considerable growth potential.

Inside story from the franchisees
Good response from franchisees who were happy with the franchise in almost every case.

Insider tips
'Helpful to have some trade experience as well as business knowledge before you start'

Moans and groans
Manual needs updating in some areas – especially when covering sales.

Number of franchisee addresses provided by franchisor: 10

Vandervells Business Transfer Centre Ltd

⇨ Vandervells Business Transfer Centre Ltd

Vandervell House, 72 London Road, Southampton SO1 2AJ
Phone: 0703 229271

Business estate agency

Outlets
Number of outlets
Company owned outlets:	01
Franchised:	05 (approx)
Pilot:	No information supplied
1988 franchise target:	No information supplied

Costs
Total	£15,000
Franchise fee:	£4,500
Other charges:	£5,000 stationery, canvassing cost
Min cash excluding bank:	No information supplied
Min overdraft required:	No information supplied
Normal bank advance:	No information supplied
Working capital first 2 months:	£7,500
Associated banks:	None
Capital items required:	£2,000 office equipment
Associated leasing co:	None

Royalties
	10.0% of turnover
	0.0% accounts service
	0.0% for advertising fund
Total	10.0% monthly sales
	No standing royalty independent of turnover

Bank rating	No information supplied
Territory	No information supplied
Strings	No information supplied
Training	No information supplied
Support	No information supplied
Operating Manual	No information supplied
Profit	£12,450 projected for first year
Risk	Growing number of firms in this market
Management only	Little salary to spare for a manager

Size and reach
Original company launched:	1962
Overseas connections:	None
UK connections:	None
Viable for whole UK?	Yes
Trade bodies	None

Franchisor's formula for success
Fees are earned in commissions on sales, plus from stocktaking, loan arrangement and insurance commissions.

Good Franchise Guide comment: The brochure for this franchise wins the all-time prize for incomprehensibility. It opens with an 87-word sentence, the meaning of which is obscure to say the least.

Number of franchisee addresses provided by franchisor: 00

⇨ VDU Services Franchising Ltd
VDU House, Brook Road, Wormley, Surrey GU8 5UR
Phone: 042 879 3733

Specialist computer cleaning company

Outlets
Number of outlets
Company owned outlets: 01
Franchised: 04
Pilot: 01 started 1984
1988 franchise target: 15
Current reach:

South	00	South west	00	South east	04
Midlands	00	East Anglia	00	North east	00
North west	00	Scotland	00	Wales	00
N Ireland	00	Rep Ireland	00	I of Man/CI	00

Costs
Total: £8,350
Franchise fee: No information supplied
Other charges: No information supplied
Min cash excluding bank: £8,350
Min overdraft required: £2,000
Normal bank advance: 66%
Working capital first 2 months: £500
Associated banks: 'Main clearing banks'
Capital items required: Car
Associated leasing co: Yes for cars – no information supplied

Royalties
Total:
10.0% of turnover
0.0% accounts service
0.0% for advertising fund
10.0% monthly sales

No standing royalty independent of turnover
NB Chemicals are supplied free in year one; subsequently 1% of turnover

Bank rating No information supplied
Territory Post codes and computer population
Strings Tied to franchisor for chemicals etc

Training
2 days practical training
4 days management training
Cost: Nil – included in franchise fee
Training value: No information supplied

Support No information supplied
Operating Manual No information supplied
Profit No information supplied
Risk Gross profit projected as £19,520 in year 1
Management only Could be run by manager but with limited profit

Size and reach
Original company launched: 1984
Overseas connections: None
UK connections: None
Viable for whole UK? Yes
Trade bodies None

Ventrolla Ltd

Franchisor's formula for success
The company keep personal computers, micros, minis and ancillary equipment in pristine condition. Clients range from small organisations to large multi-nationals. Uninformed cleaning can cause damage. It must be done knowledgeably. VDU Services have that knowledge.

Inside story from the franchisees
At the time of writing the company has its first 4 franchises assigned and about to start operating. The franchisor felt it too early for us to ask them for their comments.

Good Franchise Guide comment: A highly specialist operation; only those involved will really know how well it works. Our suggestion is that prospective franchisees must persuade the franchisor to divulge the names and addresses of existing franchisees – something we have failed to do!

Number of franchisee addresses provided by franchisor: 00

⇨ Ventrolla Ltd

51 Tower Street, Harrogate, North Yorks HG1 1HS
Phone: 0423 67004

Draft proofing franchise: 'The realistic alternative to double glazing'

Outlets
Number of outlets   No information supplied

Costs
Total   £16,595
Franchise fee: £7,500
Other charges: £1,000 initial order book commission
Min cash excluding bank: £10,500
Min overdraft required: £10,500
Normal bank advance: Up to 50%
Working capital first 2 months: £5,000
Associated banks: None
Capital items required: Tools – £2,785. No premises save a room, and a garage or a shed for storage.
Associated leasing co: None

Royalties

Total
10.0% of turnover
0.0% accounts service
0.0% for advertising fund
10.0% monthly sales

No standing royalty independent of turnover

Note: Sabre kit rental £60 per month; van rental £250 per month

Bank rating   No information supplied
Territory   Several counties
Strings   No information supplied
Training   20 days practical training
                   10 days management training
                   Cost: Nil – included in franchise fee
                   Training value: No information supplied

Vidcam

Support	No information supplied
Operating Manual	No information supplied
Profit	First year net profit £5,000 to £10,000
Risk	A unique system; difficult to evaluate without talking to franchisees.
Management only	It is envisaged that a franchisee will operate two two-man teams by the second year of business. The team leader must be a qualified joiner experienced in the replacement of joinery.

Size and reach

Original company launched:	1983
Overseas connections:	None
UK connections:	An associate company of the Laird Group plc
Viable for whole UK?	Yes
Trade bodies	BFA register

Franchisor's formula for success
Double glazing is the world's most expensive form of draught proofing. Ventrolla developed a unique range of permanent high performance sealing systems suitable for existing doors and windows and equipment with which to install them.

Good Franchise Guide comment: Probably the most comprehensive set of data for franchisees that we have seen.

Number of franchisee addresses provided by franchisor: 00

⇨ Vidcam

Unit 6 Cecil Street, Blackpool FY1 2RA

A franchise at this name and address has been listed in some reference books and magazines. Mail sent to this address is accepted, but we have been unable to obtain information either in response to general requests from would-be franchisees or specifically for this publication.

⇨ Video Cafe

8 Argyll Street, London W1V 1AD

A franchise at this address has been listed in some reference books and magazines. Mail sent to this address is accepted, but we have been unable to obtain information either in response to general requests from would-be franchisees or specifically for this publication. In the light of this experience we suggest a certain amount of caution may be in order if the franchise does eventually reappear.

⇨ Video Events

12 Harley House, London NW1 4PR
Phone: 01-935 4430

A franchise at this name and address has been listed in some reference books and magazines. An advertisement in the *UK Franchise Directory* quoted the company as offering 'a nationwide franchise operation that provides professional quality video programme-making at High Street prices and offers the entrepreneur a unique opportunity to share in one of Britain's major growth markets'. Reports elsewhere suggest that an investment of up to £15,000 is required and that three outlets are currently in operation. Mail sent to this address is accepted, but we have been unable to obtain information either in response to general requests from would-be franchisees or specifically for this publication. In the light of this experience we suggest a certain amount of caution may be in order if the franchise does reappear.

Video Film Franchise

(also known as Premier Videos franchise)
408 Manchester Road, Heaton Chapel, Stockport, Cheshire
Phone: 061-431 5138

Video rental from high street shops, with additional income from sales of cassettes, blank tapes etc

Outlets
Number of outlets   No information supplied

Costs
Total	£45,000
Franchise fee:	£4,950
Other charges:	£21,000 stock
Min cash excluding bank:	No information supplied
Min overdraft required:	No information supplied
Normal bank advance:	66%
Working capital first 2 months:	No information supplied
Associated banks:	Lloyds, Royal Bank of Scotland, Nat West, Barclays
Capital items required:	Videos, shopfitting
Associated leasing co:	None

Royalties
	10.0% of turnover
	0.0% accounts service
	0.0% for advertising fund
Total	10.0% monthly sales

No standing royalty independent of turnover

Bank rating	No information supplied
Territory	No information supplied
Strings	Franchisor supplies videos and stationery (NB an exchange system is operated for old videos)
Training	14 days practical and management training Cost: No information supplied Training value: No information supplied
Support	No information supplied
Operating Manual	No information supplied
Profit	No information supplied
Risk	Video rental is a highly competitive area, highly susceptible to changes in leisure tastes, and vulnerable to decisions by manufacturers to release tapes at such low costs that people prefer to buy. Watch out also for the addition of new cable and satellite TV stations which will reduce the attractiveness of video rental.
Management only	No information supplied
Size and reach	No information supplied

Good Franchise Guide comment: A new franchise in a highly competitive area; a quick review of any high street shows that the video shops that were there have now gone. Is it time for more? Our advice is to wait and see.

Number of franchisee addresses provided by franchisor: 00

Video Genie Network Ltd

➪ Video Genie Network Ltd
Previously at Avon Video Warehouse, Cherington Road, London W7

A franchise offering a video rental franchise from this name and address has been listed in some reference books and magazines. Mail sent to this address is now being returned by the Post Office marked 'Gone Away' and the quoted phone number has been disconnected. Enquiries have revealed that no forwarding address has been left, although it is possible that the franchise may have been set up once more in another part of the country. In the light of this experience we suggest a certain amount of caution may be in order.

➪ Vinyl Master (UK) Ltd
Unit 2a, Vulcan Works, 205 Leckhampton Road, Cheltenham, Glos GL53 0AL
Phone: 0242 584511

International specialists in invisible vinyl repairs and vinyl coatings

Outlets
Number of outlets	
Company owned outlets and franchised outlets	13
Pilot:	No information supplied
1988 franchise target:	No information supplied

Costs
Total	No information supplied
Franchise fee:	£4,500

No other information supplied on costs

Royalties
Total	0.0% of turnover
	0.0% accounts service
	0.0% for advertising fund
	0.0% monthly sales
	£1,000 per annum standing royalty independent of turnover

Bank rating	No information supplied
Territory	No information supplied
Strings	No information supplied
Training	2 weeks practical and management training
	Cost: Nil – included in franchise fee
	Training value: No information supplied
Support	No information supplied
Operating Manual	No information supplied
Profit	No information supplied
Risk	Looks like a low risk area
Management only	No information supplied

Size and reach
Original company launched:	No information supplied
Overseas connections:	Company calls itself 'international'
UK connections:	None
Viable for whole UK?	Yes
Trade bodies	None

Franchisor's formula for success

Repairing cuts, tears and cigarette burns in vinyl material, especially upholstery, has always been an expensive problem, usually necessitating complete removal and recovering of the article concerned. The Vinyl Master process however overcomes this problem, making virtually invisible vinyl repairs a relatively inexpensive and efficient process. The service can be carried out on the spot, wherever vinyl coverings are used. Our vinyl repair service is approved by ICI for use on their Ambla and Vynide range of vinyls and the process is promoted in their sales literature.

Good Franchise Guide comment: A lot of detail on the process and on training, but not much on costs from this franchise.

Number of franchisee addresses provided by franchisor: 00

⇨ Wallspan Bedrooms Ltd

Industrial Estate, Maulden Road, Flitwick, Beds MK45 5BW

Manufacturers and suppliers of fitted bedrooms

A franchise at this address has been listed in some reference books and magazines. They were last reported (1986) to have 45 franchised outlets and 33 company owned outlets. However although mail sent to this address is accepted, we have been unable to obtain information either in response to general requests from would-be franchisees or specifically for this publication.

⇨ Warmawall Insulation Services Ltd

221 Old Christchurch Road, Bournemouth, Dorset BH1 1PG

A franchise at this address has been listed in some reference books and magazines. Mail sent to this address is accepted, but we have been unable to obtain information either in response to general requests from would-be franchisees or specifically for this publication. In the light of this experience we suggest a certain amount of caution may be in order if the franchise does eventually reappear.

⇨ Wash'n'Wax

19 Ainslie Place, Edinburgh EH3 6AU
Phone: 031-226 2823

Complete car valeting service for company cars on contract basis

Outlets
Number of outlets
Company owned outlets: 01
Franchised: 12
Pilot: 02 started 1979
1988 franchise target: 50
Current reach:

South	01	South west	00	South east	01
Midlands	04	East Anglia	00	North east	00
North west	00	Scotland	07	Wales	00
N Ireland	00	Rep Ireland	00	I of Man/CI	00

Costs
Total   £6,000
Franchise fee: £1,500
Other charges: Nil
Min cash excluding bank: £3,000
Min overdraft required: £1,000
Normal bank advance: 60%
Working capital first 2 months: £800
Associated banks: Bank of Scotland
Capital items required: 15cwt van
Associated leasing co: None

Watertite Ltd

Royalties

	10.0% of turnover
	0.0% accounts service
	0.0% for advertising fund
Total	10.0% monthly sales
	No standing royalty independent of turnover
Bank rating	No information supplied
Territory	About 50,000 vehicles
Strings	No information supplied
Training	2 days practical training
	2 days management training
	Cost: Nil – included in franchise fee
	Training value: No information supplied
Support	No information supplied
Operating Manual	No information supplied
Profit	No information supplied
Risk	An area that is becoming increasingly competitive with the advent of new franchises, although the gaining of long-term contracts will help reduce the risk.
Management only	Could be run by manager but with limited profit

Size and reach

Original company launched:	1985
Overseas connections:	None
UK connections:	None
Viable for whole UK?	Yes
Trade bodies	None

Franchisor's formula for success
Wash'n'Wax specialise in offering a complete valeting service to the business car owner on a contract basis, enabling the franchisee to establish a long-term customer base within his protected territory.

Good Franchise Guide comment: We are hampered by a lack of information on this franchise. It certainly looks like a good idea.

Number of franchisee addresses provided by franchisor: 00

⇨ Watertite Ltd
Unit 4, Wall End Close, Leamore, Walsall, W Midlands WS2 7PH

A franchise supplying guttering operating out of this address has been listed in some reference books and magazines. Mail sent to this address is now being returned by the Post Office marked 'Gone Away' and the quoted phone number has been withddrawn by BT. Enquiries have revealed that no forwarding address has been left, although it is possible that the franchise may have been set up once more in another part of the country. In the light of this experience we suggest a certain amount of caution may be in order.

Weider Health and Fitness
Craven House, Station Road, Godalming, Surrey GU7 1JD
Phone: 0483 426226

Retailer of health and fitness equipment, clothes, food etc

Outlets
Number of outlets
Company owned outlets: 03
Franchised: 05
Pilot: 00
1988 franchise target: 15
Current reach:

South	00	South west	01	South east	02
Midlands	01	East Anglia	00	North east	02
North west	01	Scotland	01	Wales	00
N Ireland	00	Rep Ireland	00	I of Man/CI	00

Costs
Total	No information supplied
Franchise fee:	£3,000
Other charges:	Nil
Min cash excluding bank:	£10,000
Min overdraft required:	£20,000
Normal bank advance:	£20,000
Working capital first 2 months:	£5,000
Associated banks:	Nat West
Capital items required:	Shopfittings
Associated leasing co:	None

Royalties
	7.5% of turnover
	0.0% accounts service
	2.5% for advertising fund
Total	10.0% monthly sales
	No standing royalty independent of turnover

Bank rating	No information supplied
Territory	Postal areas
Strings	No information supplied
Training	14 days practical training
	7 days management training
	Cost: Nil – included in franchise fee
	Training value: No information supplied
Support	No information supplied
Operating Manual	No information supplied
Profit	No information supplied
Risk	The health industry continues to grow; fitness may eventually prove to be a fad, but if so it will be a very long term fad.
Management only	Reasonable return for owner with management ability

Size and reach
Original company launched:	1975
Overseas connections:	Weider USA – $100 million company
UK connections:	None
Viable for whole UK?	Yes – all large UK towns
Trade bodies	None

Franchisor's formula for success
A Weider franchise will take advantage of the further growth in the health and fitness boom and will be part of the largest company in the world in this field.

Weigh & Save Ltd

Inside story from the franchisees
The franchisor supplied us with the addresses of four of his five franchisees, but none were willing to give their views of the franchise to us.

Good Franchise Guide comment: The lack of response is disappointing, but it should be remembered that most franchisors with a small number of franchisees have not been willing even to supply the addresses – one up to this franchisor! What's more, the four franchisees are all fairly new to the business, and it takes time to talk to the likes of us; the zero response should not be seen to weigh against what may well prove to be an excellent franchise.

Number of franchisee addresses provided by franchisor: 04

⇨ Weigh & Save Ltd
Unit 4/5, Cromwell Trading Estate, Cromwell Road, Bredbury, Stockport SK6 2RF
Phone: 061-430 8210

Bulk food retailing

Outlets
Number of outlets
Company owned outlets: 25
Franchised: 52
Pilot (company showroom): 01 started 1984
1988 franchise target: 250
Current reach:

South	21	South west	01	South east	00
Midlands	06	East Anglia	13	North east	03
North west	22	Scotland	01	Wales	00
N Ireland	00	Rep Ireland	00	I of Man/CI	00

Costs
Total: £25,000 to £50,000
Franchise fee: £5,000
Other charges: No information supplied
Min cash excluding bank: 'A third of the total cost'
Min overdraft required: No information supplied
Normal bank advance: 66%
Working capital first 2 months: No information supplied
Associated banks: Royal Bank of Scotland
Capital items required: None
Associated leasing co: None

Royalties
Total:
0.0% of turnover
0.0% accounts service
0.0% for advertising fund
0.0% monthly sales

No standing royalty independent of turnover

Bank rating — No information supplied
Territory — 'We do not allocate a territory; it would not be sensible to open one shop near to another'
Strings — No information supplied
Training — 2 weeks practical and management training
Cost: Nil – included in franchise fee
Training value: No information supplied

WeightGuard

Support	No information supplied
Operating Manual	No information supplied
Profit	No information supplied
Risk	Strong identity – mostly against Fine Fare
Management only	'We generally discourage anyone wishing to take a franchise who expects a manager to operate it'

Size and reach

Original company launched:	1984
Overseas connections:	Overseas agencies a possibility
UK connections:	None
Viable for whole UK?	Yes
Trade bodies	Applied for membership of BFA

Franchisor's formula for success

Weigh and Save has four key factors in its success
(1) Impeccably clean, presentable, well-positioned shops
(2) High standard of products
(3) The right marketing and backup
(4) Old fashioned friendly service

Good Franchise Guide comment: We wrote to 10 franchisees but none replied which is most unusual. We are unsure about the lack of a guaranteed territory – it removes one of the securities that franchisees traditionally look for.

Number of franchisee addresses provided by franchisor: 40

➪ WeightGuard

Henlow Grange Health Farm, Henlow, Beds SG16 6DP
Phone: 0462 811111

Slimming club

Outlets

Number of outlets	
Company owned outlets:	No information supplied
Franchised:	No information supplied
Pilot:	No information supplied
1988 franchise target:	No information supplied

Costs

Total	£1,500
Franchise fee:	£1,300
Other charges:	Hotel fees during training
Min cash excluding bank:	£500
Min overdraft required:	Nil
Normal bank advance:	66%
Working capital first 2 months:	No information supplied
Associated banks:	Lloyds, Nat West
Capital items required:	None
Associated leasing co:	None

Royalties

	15.0% of turnover
	0.0% accounts service
	2.0% for advertising fund
Total	17.0% monthly sales
	£12 pa standing insurance charge independent of turnover

Bank rating	No information supplied
Territory	No information supplied
Strings	No information supplied

Wendy's

Training	3 days practical and management training Cost: Nil – included in franchise fee Training value: No information supplied
Support	No information supplied
Operating Manual	No information supplied
Profit	Net profit year 1 projected as £1,305
Risk	No information supplied
Management only	Can be operated on a part-time basis only

Size and reach

Original company launched:	1970
Overseas connections:	None
UK connections:	None
Viable for whole UK?	Yes
Trade bodies	None

Franchisor's formula for success

WeightGuard has played a leading role in the improvement of health and the quality of life since 1970. WeightGuard formulated an inexpensive diet plan which is well-balanced and easy to follow with proven weight losses. Today with the backing and support of Henlow Grange – Britain's leading health farm – WeightGuard Slimming Clubs have thriving branches in the Midlands and South East England and are now expanding nationwide through franchising.

Good Franchise Guide comment: Franchise lasts only 3 years; starting costs low; royalty high – but it is a most modest franchise. We'd like to talk to anyone who has run one, especially to talk about the 17% royalty.

Number of franchisee addresses provided by franchisor: 00

⇨ Wendy's

140a Gloucester Mansions, Cambridge Circus, London WC2H 8HD

A franchise at this name and address has been listed in some reference books and magazines. Mail sent to this address is accepted, but we have been unable to obtain information either in response to general requests from would-be franchisees or specifically for this publication. In the light of this experience we suggest a certain amount of caution may be in order if the franchise does eventually reappear.

⇨ West Coast Video Enterprises

74 – 76 Water Lane, Wilmslow, Cheshire
Phone: None given in literature, but our enquiries suggest Wilmslow 537297 is the correct number

Video rental shops

Outlets

Number of outlets

Company owned outlets:	01 UK; 50 USA
Franchised:	190 USA – about to launch UK
Pilot:	Starting UK 1988
1988 franchise target:	15

Current reach:

South	00	South west	00	South east	00
Midlands	00	East Anglia	00	North east	00
North west	01	Scotland	00	Wales	00
N Ireland	00	Rep Ireland	00	I of Man/CI	00

West Coast Video Enterprises

Costs
Total	No information supplied
Franchise fee:	£4,000
Other charges:	Stock – no price given
Min cash excluding bank:	£40,000
Min overdraft required:	Subject to each franchisee
Normal bank advance:	66%
Working capital first 2 months:	£20,000
Associated banks:	All banks
Capital items required:	Shopfitting
Associated leasing co:	None

Royalties

Total
5.0% of turnover
0.0% accounts service
2.0% for advertising fund
7.0% monthly sales

No standing royalty independent of turnover

Bank rating	No information supplied
Territory	Size of population
Strings	No information supplied
Training	14 days in-store practical training
	7 days management training
	Cost: Nil – included in franchise fee
	Training value: No information supplied
Support	No information supplied
Operating Manual	No information supplied
Profit	No information supplied
Risk	We think there are several uncertainties – see comment below.
Management only	Franchisor suggests that this will be a 'Proven franchise with good return on investment'.

Size and reach
Original company launched:	1983 – USA
Overseas connections:	4th largest video company in USA
UK connections:	None
Viable for whole UK?	Yes
Trade bodies	IFA, VTA

Franchisor's formula for success
In the UK we have almost 50% of homes with VCR compared with the USA only being in the region of 30%. However, in America because of the higher professional image of the video retailer the customer hires more products than the equivalent in the UK. Therefore there is an opportunity to considerably increase the UK video rental market by improved opportuniies for the retail public to hire videos.

Good Franchise Guide comment: Fast rising American firm ready to bring American methods to the image of the UK video shop. The one factor that is different is the quality of what is on TV. Will that make a difference? Our feeling is that this franchise will either be a very fast riser indeed or fade without trace. The mass of information provided even before the first franchise is offered contrasts notably with most franchises.

Number of franchisee addresses provided by franchisor: 00

Wetherby Training Services

⇨ Wetherby Training Services
15 Victoria Street, Wetherby LS22 4RE
Phone: 0937 63940

Secretarial and computer training centre using a self-teaching cassette with workbook system operating from small offices near town centres

Outlets
Number of outlets
Company owned outlets: 01
Franchised: 119
Pilot: 01 started 1977
1988 franchise target: 130
Current reach:

South	30	South west	06	South east	17
Midlands	30	East Anglia	07	North east	02
North west	15	Scotland	09	Wales	01
N Ireland	00	Rep Ireland	01	I of Man/CI	02

Costs
Total: £6,000
Franchise fee: £1,850
Other charges: Annual licence fee (below)
Min cash excluding bank: £2,000
Min overdraft required: £1,000
Normal bank advance: 66%
Working capital first 2 months: No information supplied
Associated banks: None. '66% of total franchise cost available from many major banks'
Capital items required: Largest is set of manual typewriters
Associated leasing co: None

Royalties

Total:
0.0% of turnover
0.0% accounts service
0.0% for advertising fund
0.0% monthly sales
£350 annual licence fee independent of turnover

Bank rating — No problem with raising money for some, difficulties for others

Territory — Radius of centre, or post codes (London)
Franchisees report: Not wide enough

Strings — Lots of ties but lots of freedom

Training
1 day practical training
2 days management training
Cost: £300 – included in franchise fee
Training value: 'Not enough'

Support — Opinions vary from good to poor
Operating Manual — No manual
Profit — Better than expected
Risk — Nothing else quite like it that we have seen
Management only — Could be run by manager but with limited profit

Size and reach
Original company launched: 1977
Overseas connections: 18 outlets overseas
UK connections: Parent company: 'Reach-A-Teacha Ltd'
Viable for whole UK? Yes
Trade bodies: BFA

Inside story from the franchisees
'A good franchise with a fair return for a small outlay. It is not an instant seller, and I would not encourage anyone to take it up if they need a quick return.'
'We are all doing well'

Insider tips
One respondent had the franchise withdrawn – look out for how or why this might happen.

Moans and groans
'More advice on the practical side of running a business would be helpful'
'Was never given a manual – simply recommended to review material'

Number of franchisee addresses provided by franchisor: 119

⇨ What's Cooking

14–16 Grosvenor Street, Chester CH1 2DD
Phone: 051-342 1966

American style restaurant and bar serving hamburgers plus British, Continental and American seafood, pizza, cheeses, chillis, moussakas and mushrooms

Outlets
Number of outlets
Company owned outlets: 04
Franchised: 00
Pilot: 01 started 1984
1988 franchise target: 15
Current reach:

South	00	South west	00	South east	00
Midlands	00	East Anglia	00	North east	00
North west	05	Scotland	00	Wales	00
N Ireland	00	Rep Ireland	00	I of Man/CI	00

Costs
Total: No information supplied
Franchise fee: £5,000
Other charges: Nil
Min cash excluding bank: £30,000
Min overdraft required: Nil
Normal bank advance: £70,000
Working capital first 2 months: £3,000
Associated banks: 'Terms being negotiated'
Capital items required: Catering, equipment, fixtures and fittings
Associated leasing co: None

Royalties

Total:
5.0% of turnover
0.0% accounts service
0.0% for advertising fund
5.0% monthly sales

No standing royalty independent of turnover

Bank rating No information supplied
Territory Radius from franchisees base
Strings No information supplied

Training
300 hours practical training
300 hours management training
Cost: Nil – included in franchise fee
Training value: No information supplied

Wheeler's of St James

Support	No information supplied
Operating Manual	No information supplied
Profit	No information supplied
Risk	They say it is not just another restaurant, and that is the key – new chains really do have to be different to survive.
Management only	Reasonable return for owner with management ability

Size and reach

Original company launched:	1978
Overseas connections:	None
UK connections:	None
Viable for whole UK?	Yes
Trade bodies	None

Franchisor's formula for success

What's Cooking is not just another hamburger joint. Hamburgers *are* high on the customers choice list but experience has shown that palates from Manhattan to Mandalay are catered for. The choice of menu ranges from American, British, Continental and beyond. Steaks compete with seafoods, pineapples with pizzas . . .

Good Franchise Guide comment: We note that in 1987 there were no franchises – just the pilot running from 1985, and yet by the end of 1988 15 franchises were due to open. This may be possible, but it may also put a strain on the resources of the franchisor in sorting out all the inevitable moans and groans which new franchisees bring.

Number of franchisee addresses provided by franchisor: 00

⇨ Wheeler's of St James

103 – 109 Wardour Street, London W1V 3TD
Phone: 01-434 1993

Upper crust fish and seafood restaurant

Outlets
Number of outlets

Company owned outlets:	05 (estimated)
Franchised:	20 plus
Pilot:	Original restaurants opened long before franchising was invented
1988 franchise target:	No information supplied
Current reach:	
	No information supplied

Costs

Total	£170,000 to £250,000 or more
Franchise fee:	£10,000
Other charges:	£40,000 to £50,000 equipment package
Min cash excluding bank:	No information supplied
Min overdraft required:	No information supplied
Normal bank advance:	No information supplied
Working capital first 2 months:	No information supplied
Associated banks:	No information supplied
Capital items required:	Freehold cost, conversion, fittings etc
Associated leasing co:	None

Royalties

	6.0% of turnover
	0.0% accounts service
	1.0% for marketing fund
Total	7.0% monthly sales
	No standing royalty independent of turnover

Wildcat Jeans

Bank rating	No information supplied
Territory	No information supplied
Strings	'The franchisee may only use suppliers which have been approved by Wheeler's as being competent to supply to the specifications and at the price which meet Wheeler's standards.'
Training	No information supplied
Support	No information supplied
Operating Manual	No information supplied
Profit	Return on investment quoted as between 6% and 53% depending on size of restaurant and weekly seat usage
Risk	Highly distinctive restaurant, its only problem is the possible spread to the UK of the growing dislike of seafood in Europe following an increase in pollution awareness.
Management only	No information supplied

Size and reach

Original company launched:	1856
Overseas connections:	None
UK connections:	None
Viable for whole UK?	Yes
Trade bodies	None

Franchisor's formula for success

By 1929 Wheeler's had become a familiar name in London initially as wholesale fishmonger, and later as a fashionable fish restaurant. Additional London restaurants followed providing a unique combination of the highest quality fresh fish, expertly cooked to classic recipes and served in the familiar dark green and gold surroundings.

Good Franchise Guide comment: A long established up-market venture; only for those with a love of seafood and experience of retaurant work.

Number of franchisee addresses provided by franchisor: 00

⇨ Wildcat Jeans

19/21 Overgate, Dundee DD1 1UE
Phone: 0382 21347

Retail outlets selling Wildcat range of denims and casual wear, plus full range of branded garments

Outlets

Number of outlets	No information supplied on outlets

Costs

Total	£23,000
Franchise fee:	£3,000
Other charges:	No information supplied
Min cash excluding bank:	No information supplied
Min overdraft required:	No information supplied
Normal bank advance:	No information supplied
Working capital first 2 months:	£3,000
Associated banks:	None
Capital items required:	Fixtures and fittings – approx £2,500
Associated leasing co:	None

Royalties

	2.75% of turnover
	0.0% accounts service
	0.0% for advertising fund
Total	0.0% monthly sales
	£1,000 pa standing royalty independent of turnover

Wilson's of Cricklewood

Bank rating	No information supplied
Territory	No information supplied
Strings	No information supplied
Training	'All new franchisees will undergo a period of training during which time they will be shown how to implement the standard shop systems and receive full training in all aspects of modern retailing practice.' Cost: Nil – included in franchise fee Training value: No information supplied
Support	No information supplied
Operating Manual	No information supplied
Profit	7.5% of turnover should be profit by year 2.
Risk	A constant demand for new clothes, but the style must be right.
Management only	No information supplied

Size and reach

Original company launched:	No information supplied
Overseas connections:	None
UK connections:	Wildcat is the trading name of Skillerground Ltd
Viable for whole UK?	Yes
Trade bodies	No information supplied

Franchisor's formula for success
The company has developed a strong company image which is reflected in its garments, point of sale materials and packaging. Each franchisee is encouraged to promote his outlet within his/her own chosen catchment area and we are able to provide a selection of useful advertising aids at a reasonable cost when these are available.

Good Franchise Guide comment: A recently established franchise in the highly competitive denim retail arena. The company reveals very, very little about itself and its history in its documentation provided to potential franchisees. Without further information we would suggest potential franchisees hold back pending results from other outlets.

Number of franchisee addresses provided by franchisor: 00

⇨ Wilson's of Cricklewood
208 – 212 Cricklewood Broadway, Cricklewood, London NW2 3DU

A franchise at this address has been listed in some reference books and magazines. Mail sent to this address is accepted, but we have been unable to obtain information either in response to general requests from would-be franchisees or specifically for this publication. In the light of this experience we suggest a certain amount of caution may be in order if the franchise does eventually reappear.

⇨ Wimpy International Ltd
10 Windmill Road, London W4 1SD
Phone: 01-994 6454

Fast food restaurant chain

Outlets
Number of outlets

Company owned outlets:	No information supplied; believed to be about 30
Franchised:	370 (estimated figure)
Pilot:	01 started 1958 (Counter service first introduced in 1980)
1988 franchise target:	No information supplied
Current reach:	
	No regional information supplied

Wimpy International Ltd

Costs
Total	£500,000
Franchise fee:	£10,000
Other charges:	No information supplied
Min cash excluding bank:	No information supplied
Min overdraft required:	No information supplied
Normal bank advance:	60%
Working capital first 2 months:	No information supplied
Associated banks:	No information supplied
Capital items required:	Restaurant fittings
Associated leasing co:	None

Royalties
	8.5% of turnover
	0.0% accounts service
	0.0% for advertising fund
Total	8.5% monthly sales
	No standing royalty independent of turnover

Bank rating	Should be no problem with such a famous name
Territory	No information supplied
Strings	Strong; United Biscuits Ltd own the lease of the premises the franchisee owning the underlease. The franchisee obviously sells the standard Wimpy fare without local variation or addition.
Training	No information supplied
Support	No information supplied
Operating Manual	No information supplied
Profit	'A restaurant will generate an operating profit of approximately 25% prior to rent, rates, tax and depreciation.'
Risk	Wimpy is so well known that the existence of the many other burger outlets will not threaten unless there is a continuing move towards health food, and/or a deterioration in the Wimpy image
Management only	Variable but the largest outlets should be seen as offering a good return on investment

Size and reach
Original company launched:	1956
Overseas connections:	145 outlets in 20 countries
UK connections:	Part of United Biscuits (UK) Ltd
Viable for whole UK?	Yes
Trade bodies	BFA

Franchisor's formula for success
The most successful franchise in the UK, trading for over 30 years. In response to changes in the high street Wimpy have developed counter service restaurants, of which there are more than 120 trading in the UK. All new franchised restaurants will be of the counter service type.

Good Franchise Guide comment: The number of franchised outlets has declined recently, a decline only partially compensated for by the rise in the number of company owned outlets. Wimpy may suffer from the problem of an 'old-fashioned' image as opposed to the more youthful McDonald's image in the UK. But it is a well proved franchise, if you can find a location which Wimpy does not already cover.

Number of franchisee addresses provided by franchisor: 00

Wordplex Ltd

⇨ Wordplex Ltd
Previously at Excel House, 49 De Montfort Road, Reading, Berks

A franchise at this name and address offering wordprocessing services and supplies has been listed in some reference books and magazines. Mail sent to this address is now being returned by the Post Office marked 'Gone Away' and the quoted phone number disconnected. Enquiries have revealed that no forwarding address has been left, although it is possible that the franchise may have been set up once more in another part of the country. In the light of this experience we suggest a certain amount of caution may be in order.

⇨ Wreck a Rent
Bourne House, 7 High Street, Sedgley, Dudley, West Midlands DY3 1RL
Phone: 090 73 64185

Car rental based on second hand car stock

Outlets
Number of outlets	No information supplied

Costs
Total	£8,500*
Franchise fee:	£5,500
Other charges:	£25,000 running costs first year
Min cash excluding bank:	'Up to 100% finance available to the right applicant'
Min overdraft required:	No information supplied
Normal bank advance:	No information supplied
Working capital first 2 months:	No information supplied
Associated banks:	None
Capital items required:	None
Associated leasing co:	None

* Based on £3,000 to purchase 10 used cars. The franchisor expects franchisees to have 25 vehicles on the road after one year.

Royalties
	No information supplied
Bank rating	Must be good to gain 100% finance, but see our comment below
Territory	No information supplied
Strings	Franchisor supplies office equipment and stationery
	Also offers to purchase rental fleet
Training	'Full training given'; the training programme is 'personalised' and is usually completed in 4 to 5 days. Cost: Nil – included in franchise fee Training value: No information supplied
Risk	Competition comes from other second hand rental franchises (such as Practical Used Car Rental) and independent garage owners and second hand car dealers rather than Avis and Budget. Much will depend on the firm's national advertising.

Franchisor's formula for success
  Wreck a Rent doesn't aim to compete with the big national rental firms; it is aimed at low-budget small businesses and the man in the street who is between cars or whose car is in the workshop for repair.

Good Franchise Guide comment: Wreck a Rent is a company that gives out very little information about itself, its history and its franchisees. It is a limited company (registration number 1939647) and prospective franchisees may wish to undertake a company search to find out more. We are not happy with the prospect of 100% finance – everyone should put something into their own business.

Number of franchisee addresses provided by franchisor: 00

⇨ Young's Franchise Ltd
70–78 York Way, London N1 9AG
Phone: 01-278 0343

Outlet for a wide range of formal morning and evening wear

Outlets
Number of outlets
Company owned outlets: 18
Franchised: 50
Pilot: 00
1988 franchise target: 73
Current reach:

South	10	South west	05	South east	03
Midlands	*24	East Anglia	04	North east	02
North west	10	Scotland	06	Wales	02
N Ireland	01	Rep Ireland	01	I of Man/CI	00

*Midland figure includes Midlands and North (excluding North east and North west).

Costs
Total	£50,000 to £120,000
Franchise fee:	£12,000 to £17,000
Other charges:	Nil
Min cash excluding bank:	£30,000 to £60,000
Min overdraft required:	£20,000 to £60,000
Normal bank advance:	66%
Working capital first 2 months:	£10,000
Associated banks:	None
Capital items required:	Shopfitting £25,000 to £50,000
Associated leasing co:	None

Royalties
Total
10.0% of turnover
0.0% accounts service
0.0% for advertising fund
10.0% monthly sales

No standing royalty independent of turnover

Bank rating No information supplied
Territory Either a county or conurbation using post code areas
Strings No information supplied

Training 24 days practical and management training in a company shop
Cost: Nil – included in franchise fee
Training value: No information supplied

Support No information supplied
Operating Manual No information supplied
Profit No information supplied
Risk See comment below
Management only Reasonable return for owner with management ability

Size and reach
Original company launched:	Pronuptia in 1977, Young's in 1948
Overseas connections:	Pronuptia is a French company formed 1958
UK connections:	Master franchise agreement with Pronuptia de Paris SA
Viable for whole UK?	Yes
Trade bodies	BFA

Yves Rocher (London) Ltd

Franchisor's formula for success
At Young's we recognise that formal wear today should be as personal and individually appropriate as day wear, not the look-alike uniform that others provide. Consequently we carry the widest range of morning and evening wear anywhere in the UK – including our special mix and match collection of versatile wedding wear co-ordinates.

Good Franchise Guide comment: Young's franchise group, which went into receivership in 1985, was bought shortly after. The new owners disposed of La Mama (qv) and have continued with Young's Formal Wear and Pronuptia (qv). It is most likely that the new owners have resolved the problems that beset the previous regime, but nevertheless we would have welcomed the chance to talk with franchisees to gauge their feelings following this turbulent past.

Number of franchisee addresses provided by franchisor: 00

⇨ Yves Rocher (London) Ltd

664 Victoria Road, South Ruislip, Middx HA4 0NY
Phone: 01-845 1222

The company has informed us that due to recent decisions made between the parent company in France the the UK subsidiary, it has been decided that no more shops will be opened. This decision will be reviewed at the end of 1988.

⇨ Ziebart UK

3 Downsbrook Trading Estate, Southdownview Way, Worthing, Sussex BN14 8NQ
Phone: 0903 212467

Ziebart UK, operating 'vehicle improvement' services under licence from Ziebart International Corporation, have informed us that they are no longer seeking franchisees in the UK.

⇨ Late entry

⇨ Panic Link (Nationwide Next Day)

St Marys House, 1-7 St Marys Road, Market Harborough, Leics LE16 7PS
Phone: 0858 33334

Transport service

Outlets
Number of outlets
Company owned outlets: 05
Franchised: 54
Pilot: 01 started 1986
1988 franchise target: 80
Current reach:

South	04	South west	07	South east	08
Midlands	12	East Anglia	03	North east	06
North west	07	Scotland	07	Wales	05
N Ireland	00	Rep Ireland	00	I of Man/CI	00

Panic Link (Nationwide Next Day)

Costs
Total	£15,000 average (depends on area)
Franchise fee:	£15,000
Other charges:	£250
Min cash excluding bank:	50%
Min overdraft required:	£5,000
Normal bank advance:	50%
Working capital first 2 months:	£1,000
Associated banks:	Midland
Capital items required:	Small depot, telephone and vehicle
Associated leasing co:	Lombard

Royalties

	0.0% of turnover
	0.0% accounts service
	0.0% for advertising fund
Total	0.0% monthly sales
	No standing royalty independent of turnover

Bank rating	No information supplied
Territory	By post code area
Strings	No information supplied
Training	3 to 4 days practical training
	1 day management training
	Cost: Nil – included in franchise fee
	Training value: No information supplied
Support	No information supplied
Operating Manual	No information supplied
Profit	'Most areas profitable within 3 months'
Risk	Very competitive area indeed
Management only	'Good return on investment with good management'

Size and reach
Original company launched:	1985
Overseas connections:	'Worldwide via associate company'
UK connections:	None
Viable for whole UK?	Yes
Trade bodies	FTA

Franchisor's formula for success
The company is opening a new freehold sortation centre in June 88 and expanding its trunking fleet by eight vehicles, representing a total investment in excess of one million pounds this year, with a similar investment forecast for 1989.

Good Franchise Guide comment: We only found Panic a few days before typesetting of the guide began and hence there was no chance to contact franchisees. But this franchisor fell over himself offering us information which augers very well for the future. It is one of the most competitive markets at present, but if the franchisor's attitude towards us is spread through the operation there is a fair chance this firm will survive and do well while others go to the wall.

Number of franchisee addresses provided by franchisor: List offered by franchisor, but not taken up by ourselves due to the impending deadline.

Broadcasting Franchises

Franchises for broadcasting radio and television programmes are issued by government appointed agencies, such as the Independent Broadcasting Authority. The various categories are dealt with below.

Television

1. Broadcast television

Number of franchises	16
Controlling body	IBA, 70 Brompton Road, London SW3 1EY Phone: 01-584 7011
Costs	Very high, but not so high as to dent profits
Profit	The term 'A licence to print money' was coined in relation to TV franchises, and still applies. There is, however, a government levy.
Ties	Very strong restrictions on how much advertising per hour can be sold, what can be advertised, and which programmes can be shown when.
Risk	Growing competition from satellite TV, an increasingly popular BBC 1 service, and video.

2. Satellite television

Number of franchises	1 (awarded to BSB, due to start 1990)
Controlling body	IBA
Costs	Astronomic
Profit	No one yet knows how profitable this may be
Ties	Some, but less than broadcast television
Risk	Very high, especially if there is a technical fault

3. Cable television

Number of franchises	Growing continuously, no limit set
Controlling body	Cable Authority, Gillingham House, 38 – 44 Gillingham Street, London SW1V 1HU Phone: 01-821 6161
Costs	Laying cables is very cost intensive, although thereafter its not an expensive operation
Profit	None so far – some companies are having problems
Ties	Slight – you have 25 channels to play with
Risk	Very high, this was a high profile industry that seems to have lost its way

Radio

1. National commercial radio

Number of franchises	3, to be offered in 1989
Controlling body	Radio Authority soon to be set up by government
Costs	Bound to be high for a national service
Profit	Looks promising
Ties	Government insists on a 'balanced' service
Risk	A leap into the unknown. Franchises are going to the highest bidder

Broadcasting Franchises

2. Regional radio (originally known as Independent Local Radio)

Number of franchises	46
Controlling body	IBA – in 1989 to be Radio Authority
Costs	High due to very high engineering standards required by IBA
Profit	Highly variable. Big stations such as Capital and Clyde have done well. Central (Leicester) went into liquidation.
Ties	Strong; IBA requires a balanced service and restricted advertising. May reduce ties under new authority.
Risk	Very large – some stations never even got on air, others were forced to amalgamate to survive.

3. Community radio

Number of franchises	Almost unlimited
Controlling body	Radio Authority to be set up in 1989
Costs	Should be very low – next to nothing in some cases
Profit	Impossible to say; some will make a loss, others will just survive on volunteer workers
Ties	Government promises very few ties, so stations are free to serve one particular interest
Risk	Deregulated countries such as Italy and France have found a small number of companies taking over most stations, leaving the enthusiasts to operate fringe stations on a shoestring.

4. Radio text

Number of franchises	2 at present, in London. Could be more
Controlling body	IBA
Costs	Low – text is transmitted on existing radio frequencies
Profit	Unproven – depends on the service
Ties	Virtually none
Risk	An unknown medium – no clear indication that people want this type of electronic information. One company awarded a franchise failed to get on air at all.

Postscript

We have failed thus far to contact or verify the situation regarding the following possible franchises:

Bundles
Business Post
CB (UK)
The Coca-Cola Export Corporation
Computer Estates
Davenports Brewery plc
Herbs and Things
Holiday Breaks
Home Conveyancer
Homesellers
Knitwit
Nationwide Food Systems Ltd
Quest Appointments
Rivington
Rodier Paris
Scotchcare Services
Thompson Jewitt International

In addition a small number of franchises have appeared in a directory put out by a firm of consultants in Norwich, which we have not found elsewhere during our research. The consultants have informed us that in their view the addresses of these franchises are copyright, and we have therefore been unable to contact these franchises. However, the fact that such franchises have not advertised or appeared elsewhere suggests that they are at best operating only in a small way.

Index of Franchisors

A1 Damproofing (UK) Ltd   1
Accounting Centre   2
Air-serv   3
Alfred Marks Ltd   4
Allied Dunbar   5
Alpine   6
Amtrak Express Parcels Ltd   7
Anaco Ltd   8
ANC-The British Parcel Service   9
Anicare Group Services
   (Veterinary) Ltd   10
AP Autela   11
Apex Interiors   11
Apollo Window Blinds   12
Applied Fastenings and
   Components Ltd   14
Ashcombe Distributors Ltd   15
At Computer World   15
Athena   15
Auto-Smart Ltd   17
Autosheen Car Valeting Services
   (UK) Ltd   17
Avis Rent a Car Ltd   18

Badenoch and Clark   19
Badgeman Ltd   19
Balloon Paris   20
Bally Group (UK) Ltd   20
Balmforth and Partners
   (Franchises)   20
Banaman   22
Baskin-Robbins International Co   23
Bath Doctor   24
Bath Transformations Ltd   25
BDP Ltd (t/a British Damp
   Proofing)   25
Beardsley Theobalds Businesses   26
Beck and Call   27
Belgian Chocolates   28
Bellina, see Belgian Chocolates
Benetton (UK) Ltd   28
Better Business Agents   28
Big Apple Health Studios Ltd   28
Big Orange Promotions Ltd   28
A F Blakemore & Sons Ltd   29
Bob's Tiles   29
Body Reform Shops, see Natural
   Beauty Products Ltd
The Body Shop International Ltd   29
Bolos Sobre Cesped SA   29

Bread Roll Company   29
Brewer & Turnbull Ltd   31
Brick-Tie Services Ltd   32
Britannia Business Sales Ltd   33
Britannia Towing Centre   33
Britannic Corporation   33
British Business Consultants   34
British Damp Proofing, see BDP Ltd
British School of Motoring   35
Broadcasting Franchises   322
Bruce and Company   32
Budget Rent a Car International
   Inc   36
Bumpsadaisy   38
Bundles   324
Burger King UK Ltd   38
Burgerhouse   39
Burgerpark   40
Business Post   324
Business Transfer Consultants
   (Franchise) Ltd   40
Buyers World Ltd   41

Calligraphics Ltd   41
Can Can Computers
   (Franchising) Ltd   42
Canterbury of New Zealand
   (UK) Ltd   43
Capstan Careers Centres   44
Car Brokers   44
Car Market Holdings   45
Carpet Master Ltd   46
Carryfast Ltd   47
Cartons Boulangeries   48
Castle Fairs Ltd   49
CB (UK)   324
Ceil Clean   50
Central Office of Publishing   51
Chapter and Verse Bookshop   52
Chemical Express Ltd   53
Churchtown   55
Cico Chimney Linings   55
Circle C Stores Ltd   56
City Link Transport Holdings Ltd   57
Clarks Shoes   58
Clubsun Ltd   59
Cobblestone Paving (UK) Ltd   59
Coca-Cola Export Corporation   324
Coffeeman Management Ltd   60
Coffilta Coffee Services Ltd   62

325

Colour Counsellors 63
Command Performance
 International 64
Compleat Cookshop 65
Compleat Engraver,
 see TC Graphics Ltd
Complete Weed Control Ltd 67
Computa Tune 68
Computer Estates 324
ComputerLand 69
Concorde One Hour Photo Labs 70
Conder Products 71
Contemporary Aluminium Ltd 71
Cookie Coach Company Ltd 72
Copygirl, *see* Gestetner Ltd
Country Properties 72
Countrywide Business Transfer
 Consultants 73
Countrywide Garden
 Maintenance Services 74
Cover Rite 76
Coversure Insurance Services 76
Cranford Conservatories 78
Crimecure/30 Ltd 78
Crown Electrical Appliances 79
Crown Eyeglass plc 79
Culligans Water Softeners 80

Dampco (UK) Ltd 81
Dampcure/30 Ltd 82
Damptechnik UK 83
Dash Ltd 84
Data Maid Ltd 85
Davenports Brewery plc 324
Dayvilles 87
Decorative Fine Arts Ltd 88
Deep Pan Pizza Company 88
Descamps Ltd 88
Dial a Char Ltd 88
Dinol-Protectol Ltd 90
Direct Salon Services Ltd 90
Dirtsearchers 91
DISC Ltd 91
Diversey Ltd 91
Don Millers Hot Bread
 Kitchens Ltd 91
Doran Products 92
Draincure/30 Ltd 92
Drainmasters (London) Ltd 93
Dutch Pancake Houses Ltd 93
Dyno-Electrics 93
Dyno-Plumbing 94

Dyno-Rod plc 95

Electricure/30 Ltd 96
Electron Glaze 97
English Rose Franchises 97
Entre Computer Centres Ltd 98
ESC Ltd 98
Estate Express 99
Euroclean 99
Eurodance Ltd 100
Everett Masson & Furby Ltd 100
J Evershed & Son Ltd 101
Exchange Travel 101
Exide Batteries 103
Express Dairy Ltd 104
Express Hoses Ltd 104

4th Dimension Computer
 Systems Ltd 104
Fastframe Franchises Ltd 104
Fatso's Pasta Joint 106
Fersina International 106
Financial Consultants Ltd 107
Fire Technology Ltd 108
Fires and Things 109
Fixit Tools Ltd 110
Flash Trash 111
Foto-Inn 112
Fotofast 113
Frame Express 114
The Frame Factory Franchise Ltd 116
Frameorama 117
Franchise Development
 Services Ltd 117
Free-Room (UK) Ltd 118
Freezavan Ltd 119
Fudge Kitchen (UK) Ltd 121
FuelBoss Ltd 121

G and T Video Services 122
Garage Door Company 123
Garden Building Centre Ltd 123
George Strachan & Co Ltd 124
Gestetner Ltd 125
Giltsharp Ltd 126
GKD 126
Global Cleaning Contracts 126
Gold Car Ltd 127
Gold Vault Ltd 127
Goldprint 128
Goldstrike Products 129
Graffiti Management 129

Great Adventure Game   130
Greenbank Finance Ltd   132
Group 4 Securities   132
Guarantee System UK Ltd   132
Gun Point Ltd   132

Hairdressing Franchises Ltd,
    see Lady K Salon Services Ltd
Handy Sam Ltd   134
Hayden Timber Ltd   134
Herbal World   134
Herbs and Things   324
Highway Windscreens Ltd   135
Hire Technicians Group Ltd   136
Holiday Breaks   324
Holiday Inn International
    Hotels   136
Holland and Barrett   137
Home Choose Carpets   137
Home Conveyancer   324
Homesellers   324
Home Tune Ltd   138
Hot Wheels   139
House of Regency   139
House of Skinner (UK) Ltd   139
House of Something Different
    Group Ltd   139
House of Wetherby   140
H Plan Manufacturing Co Ltd   141
HPR   142
Hughes, David and Partners   142
Hyde-Barker Travel   143
Hydrosoft Ltd   144

Ideal Showers   144
Identicar   145
In Business Systems Ltd   145
Independent Gas Heating   145
Infopoint Ltd   146
Instagram   147
Institute of Psychology and
    Para Psychology Ltd   147
Institute of Tukido   147
Insurance Management Services   148
Intacab Ltd   148
Interface Network   148
Interlink Express Parcels Ltd   148
International Promotions   148
Intoto Ltd   149
Isodan (UK) Ltd   150

Janus Introduction Bureaux   151

Kall-Kwik Printing (UK) Ltd   151
Keith Hall Hairdressing   153
Kemmytex   153
Kentucky Fried Chicken   154
Kimberleys   154
Kis Services   154
Kitchen Design and Advice   155
Kitchen Gear Ltd   155
Knight Guard Ltd   155
Knitwit   324
Knobs & Knockers Franchising
    Ltd   156
KVC Franchise UK   157
Kwik Silver Print   158
Kwik Strip (UK) Ltd   159

La Mama Ltd   160
Lady K Salon Services Ltd   160
Lamacrest Ltd   161
Late Late Supershop   161
Learning Point   162
Lomax Designs Ltd   162
London Stone   163
Lyons Maid Ltd   163

M & B Marquees Ltd   163
Magic Windshields Ltd   165
Magna-Dry   166
Maids, The, Ltd   166
Mainly Marines   167
Management Selection Services   167
Manns Norwich Brewery Co Ltd   168
Marketing Methods Ltd   169
Massor UK Ltd   170
Mast Midlands   170
Master Thatchers Ltd   171
MBC Distributorships   172
McDonalds   172
Med-Ped SA   172
Metro Express   173
Metro Rod Franchising Ltd   174
MGN Consultants Ltd   175
Micrex Microfilm Express Ltd   176
Micro Management (ECS) Ltd   177
Microlec   177
Midas (Great Britain) Ltd   179
Midas Identicar, see Identicar
Midland Magazines Ltd   180
Midland Waterlife Franchising
    Ltd   180
Millie's Cookies (UK) Ltd   181
Mister Donut UK   182

327

Mister Softee   183
Mixamate Concrete (Mixamate Holdings Ltd)   183
Mobiletuning Ltd   185
Modular Marquees Ltd   186
Molly Maid   187
Morley's   188
Motabitz (Franchising) Ltd   189
Motoplas Ltd   190
Mr Big (UK) Ltd   191
Mr Boilerserviceman   191
Mr Clutch Franchising Ltd   192
Mr Cod Ltd   193
Mr Fish on Wheels   193
Mr Lift Ltd   194
Mr Slade Dry Cleaning   195
Mr Slot   195
MTR Training Centre   195

National Security   196
National Slimming Centres   197
National Vacuum Cleaner Services   197
Nationwide Food Systems Ltd   324
Nationwide Investigations   199
Natural Beauty Products Ltd   199
Natural Life Health Foods   200
Nectar Cosmetics   201
New Moves   203
Newlook Bath Services   203
Northern Dairies Ltd   203
Novus Windscreen Repair   204
Nulon Products Ltd   205
Nurse-Call   206

Oasis Trading   207
O'Corrain Heraldry   208
Olivers UK Ltd   209
Opportunity Exchange   209
Original Art Shops Ltd   210
Original Kitchen Company Ltd   211

Panarama Sunroofs   212
Pancake Place   212
Panic Link (Nationwide Next Day)   320
Paper Place   214
Paramount Syndications   215
Party Rentals   215
Pass & Co Ltd   216
Pava Products   217
PDC Copyprint (Franchise) Ltd   217

Peak Insulation Ltd   218
Perfect Pizza   220
Phildar (UK) Ltd   221
Phone-In UK Ltd   221
Photomaid Ltd   223
Photomarkets (UK) Ltd   224
Pickwicks of England   224
PIP Printing (Franprint Ltd)   225
Pizza Hut   226
PizzaExpress   226
PJs Drive In Ltd   228
Plastercure/30 Ltd   229
Plumbingcure/30 Ltd   229
PMR Dental, *see* The Gold Vault Ltd
Polymer Protection Ltd   229
Ponderosa Inc   229
Poppies UK Ltd   230
Poppy's Body Centre Ltd   232
Portico Canopies   232
Posh Wash   233
Postal Centres International Ltd   233
Potholes Ltd   233
PPG Industries (UK) Ltd   235
Practical Used Car Rental   235
PRB Self Drive Hire   236
Premier Videos, *see* Video Film Franchise
Primetime Video Centre Ltd   238
Prodata   239
Professional Appearance Services (PAS) Ltd   240
The Progressive Conveyancing Company   241
Prontaprint plc   242
Pronuptia de Paris Bridalwear   244
Prospectglen Ltd   245
Protoplas   246
PSJ Business Consultants   246

Quest Appointments   324
Quest Estates International   246
Quikframe   247

Rainbow Insurances   248
Red Baron   248
Regional Business Services Ltd   249
Reliant Security System   250
Renubath Services Ltd   250
Response Communications   250
Restor Antique Restoration Ltd   251
Revolution Oil   252
Riviera Plant Interiors Ltd   253

Rivington   324
Rodier Paris   324
Rotary Space Creators (North) Ltd   253
RSH Consultants Ltd   253
Ryman Ltd   253

Safeclean International   254
Satinstyle Ltd   255
Scan (Franchising) Ltd   256
Scotchcare Services   324
Securicor Carphones   256
Seekers (Thornganby) Ltd   256
Serviceman Franchise plc   257
ServiceMaster Ltd   258
Servotomic Ltd   260
The Shooting Box   260
Signtalk Ltd   260
Silver Shield Windscreens Ltd   260
Singer Consumer Products   261
Sketchley Franchises Ltd   262
Skirmish Ltd   263
Slim Gym   264
Small Business Advisory Centres   264
Snap On Tools Ltd   265
Snappy Snaps   266
Snappy Tomato Pizza   267
The Sock Shop   268
Southern Health Food Stores   269
Sovereign Services   269
Spar Eight Till Late Convenience Stores   270
Specpoint   270
Sperrings Convenience Stores   270
Spud U Like Ltd   271
Stained Glass Overlay   272
StarGull (Sales) Ltd   273
Startrack Stellite TV Reception Equipment   274
Stayview Ltd   274
Stockcheck   274
Stop Thief (UK) Ltd   275
Strachan Studio, *see* George Strachan & Co Ltd
Strikes Restaurants   277
Subway Sandwiches and Salads   277
Summer Air Ltd   278
Swinton Insurance Brokers Ltd   279
System Consultancy   280
System-Text (UK) Ltd   281

TC Graphics Ltd   282

Taylor Harrison Group, *see* Postal Centres International Ltd
Team Audio Ltd   283
Telephone World Ltd   284
Teletone Communication Ltd   284
Telsell, *see* Marketing Methods Ltd
Textlite UK Ltd   285
Thermecon   285
Thermocrete Chimney Lining Systems Ltd   285
Thompson Jewitt International   324
JW Thornton Ltd   285
Thrust Jetstream Marketing   286
Tie Rack Ltd   286
Time and Place Marketing Services   288
Tioli Glass Engraving, *see* Calligraphics Ltd
TNT Parcel Office   289
Toco Ltd   290
Tonibell Manufacturing Co Ltd   290
Trafalgar Cleaning Chemicals   290
Tramlines (Sports) Ltd   291
Tramps Trucking   292
Trust Parts Ltd   292
Tuff-Kote Dinol   293
Tumble Tots (UK) Ltd   293
Tyre & Rubber Co Ltd   295

UK School of Motoring Ltd   295
Unigate Dairies Ltd   296
United Air Specialists (UK) Ltd   297
Uniweld Ltd   297
Uticolor (Great Britain) Ltd   297

Vandervells Business Transfer Centres Ltd   299
VDU Services Franchising Ltd   300
Ventrolla Ltd   301
Vidcam   302
Video Cafe   302
Video Events   302
Video Film Franchise   303
Video Genie Network Ltd   304
Vinyl Master (UK) Ltd   304

Wallspan Bedrooms Ltd   305
Warmawall Insulation Services Ltd   305
Wash 'n' Wax   305
Watertite Ltd   306
Weider Health and Fitness   307

329

Weigh & Save Ltd   308
WeightGuard   309
Wendy's   310
West Coast Video Enterprises   310
Wetherby Training Services   312
What's Cooking   313
Wheeler's of St James   314
Wildcat Jeans   315
Wilson's of Cricklewood   316

Wimpy International Ltd   318
Wordplex Ltd   318
Wreck a Rent   318

Young's Franchise Ltd   319
Yves Rocher Ltd   320

Ziebart UK   320

Franchises by Trade Category

BOOKS AND PUBLISHING
Central Office of Publishing   51
Chapter and Verse Bookshop   52

BUILDING TRADES
A1 Damproofing (UK) Ltd   1
Bath Doctor   24
Bath Transformations Ltd   25
BDP Ltd   25
Brick-Tie Services Ltd   32
Cico Chimney Linings   55
Cobblestone Paving (UK) Ltd   59
Dampco (UK) Ltd   81
Dampcure/30 Ltd   82
Damptechnik UK   83
Dyno-Electrics   93
Dyno-Plumbing   94
Dyno-Rod plc   95
Fersina International   106
Fire Technology   108
Fixit Tools Ltd   110
FuelBoss   121
Gun-Point   132
House of Something Different   139
House of Wetherby   140
Isodan (UK) Ltd   150
Kemmytex   153
Kwik Strip (UK) Ltd   159
Metro Rod Franchising Ltd   174
Microlec   177
Mixamate Concrete   183
Pass and Co Ltd   216
Peak Insulation Ltd   218
Potholes Ltd   233
Ventrolla Ltd   301

BUSINESS SERVICES
Accounting Centre   2

Alfred Marks Ltd   4
Allied Dunbar   5
Badgeman Ltd   19
Banaman   22
British Business Consultants   34
Franchise Development Services
 Ltd   117
Free-Room (UK) Ltd   118
In Business Systems Ltd   145
Marketing Methods Ltd   169
Motabitz (Franchising) Ltd   189
Mr Lift Ltd   194
National Vacuum Cleaner
 Services   197
Portico Canopies   232
Prodata   239
Prospectglen Ltd   245
Regional Business Services Ltd   249
Small Business Advisory Centres   264
Stockcheck   274
System-Text (UK) Ltd   281
TC Graphics Ltd   282
Team Audio   293
Time and Place Marketing
 Services   288

BUSINESS TRANSFER
Beardsley Theobalds Businesses   26
Bruce and Company   35
Business Transfer Consultants   40
Countrywide Business Transfer
 Consultants   73
Everett Masson & Furby Ltd   100
Hughes, David and Partners   142
Master Thatchers Ltd   171
Quest Estates International   246
Vendervells Business Transfer
 Centres Ltd   299

330

CAR RENTAL
Avis Rent a Car Ltd 18
Budget Rent a Car International Inc 36
Practical Used Car Rental 235
PRB Self Drive Hire 236
Wreck a Rent 318

CHEMICALS
Anaco Ltd 8
Chemical Express Ltd 53
Tralfalgar Cleaning Chemicals 290

CLEANING
Ceil Clean 50
Dial a Char Ltd 88
Euroclean 99
Global Cleaning Contracts 126
Maids, The, Ltd 166
Molly Maid 187
Poppies UK Ltd 230
Professional Appearance Services (PAS) Ltd 240
Safeclean International 254
ServiceMaster Ltd 258
Sketchley Franchises Ltd 262

CLOTHES HIRE
Bumpsadaisy 38
Pronuptia de Paris Bridalwear 244
Young's Franchise Ltd 319

COFFEE
Coffeeman Management Ltd 60
Coffilta Coffee Services Ltd 62

COMPUTERS
Can Can Computers (Franchising) Ltd 42
ComputerLand 69
VDU Services Franchising Ltd 300

EDUCATION AND TRAINING
UK School of Motoring Ltd 295
Wetherby Training Services 312

ENVIRONMENTAL CONTROL
Crimecure/30 Ltd 78
Graffiti Management 129
Knight Guard Ltd 155
National Security 196
Stop Thief (UK) Ltd 275

ESTATE AGENCIES AND CONVEYANCING
Balmforth and Partners (Franchise) 20
Country Properties 72
MGN Consultants Ltd 175
Progressive Conveyancing Company 241
Seekers (Thornganby) Ltd 256

FITTINGS AND FURNITURE
Applied Fastenings and Components Ltd 14
English Rose Franchises 97
George Strachan and Co Ltd 124
H Plan Manufacturing Co Ltd 141
Intoto Ltd 149
Knobs and Knockers Franchising Ltd 156
Original Kitchen Company Ltd 211

FOOD AND HOTELS
Bread Roll Company 29
Burger King UK Ltd 38
Cartons Boulangeries 48
Don Millers Hot Bread Kitchens Ltd 91
Holiday Inn International Hotels 136
Millies Cookies (UK) Ltd 181
Mister Donut UK 182
Morley's 188
Mr Fish on Wheels 193
Olivers UK Ltd 208
Pancake Place, The 212
Perfect Pizza 220
PizzaExpress 226
PJs Drive In Ltd 228
Ponderosa Inc 229
Snappy Tomato Pizza 267
Southern Health Food Stores 269
Spud U Like Ltd 271
Subway Sandwiches and Salads 277
What's Cooking 313
Wheeler's of St James 314
Wimpey International Ltd 316

GAMES AND PHYSICAL FITNESS
Great Adventure Game 130
Skirmish Ltd 263
Tumble Tots (UK) Ltd 293
Weider Health and Fitness 307
Weight Guard 309

GARDENING
Complete Weed Control Ltd   67
Countrywide Garden Maintenance
   Services   74
Garden Building Centres Ltd   123
Midland Waterlife Franchising
   Ltd   180

HAIR
Command Performance
   International   64
Direct Salon Services Ltd   90
Lady K Salon Services Ltd   160

HEALTH MATTERS
Anicare Group Services
   (Veterinary) Ltd   9
Crown Eyeglass plc   79
Gold Vault Ltd   127
Nurse-Call   206

ICE CREAM
Baskin-Robbins International Co   23
Dayvilles   87
Lyons Maid Ltd   163

INTERIOR DESIGN (including
pictures and framing)
Apex Interiors   11
Apollo Window Blinds   12
Athena   15
Colour Counsellors   63
Fastframe Franchises Ltd   104
Frame Express   114
The Frame Factory Franchise Ltd   116
Original Art Shops Ltd   210
Quikframe   247

INSURANCE
Coversure Insurance Services   76
Swintons Insurance Brokers Ltd   279

MOTOR TRADE
AIR-serv   3
AP Autela   11
Autosheen Car Valeting Services
   (UK) Ltd   17
Car Brokers   44
Computa Tune   68
Data Maid Ltd   85
Exide Batteries   103
Highway Windscreens Ltd   135

KVC Franchise UK   157
Magic Windshields Ltd   165
Med-Ped SA   172
Midas (Great Britain) Ltd   179
Mobiletuning Ltd   185
Motoplas Ltd   190
Mr Clutch Franchising Ltd   192
Novus Windscreen Repair   204
Nulon Products   205
Panarama Sunroofs Ltd   212
Revolution Oil   252
Serviceman Franchise plc   257
Snap on Tools Ltd   265
Trust Parts Ltd   292
Wash'n'Wax   305

PHOTOGRAPHIC AND MICROFILM
Concorde One Hour Photo Labs   70
Foto-Inn   112
Fotofast   113
Kwik Silver Print   158
Micrex Microfilm Express Ltd   176
Photomaid Ltd   223
Snappy Snaps   266

PRINTING
Kall-Kwik Printing (UK) Ltd   151
PDC Copyprint (Franchise) Ltd   217
PIP Printing (Franprint Ltd)   225
Prontoprint plc   242

REPAIRS
Uticolor (Great Britain) Ltd   297
Vinyl Master (UK) Ltd   304

RETAIL
Alpine   6
Canterbury of New Zealand
   (UK) Ltd   43
Carpet Master Ltd   46
Circle C Stores Ltd   56
Clarks Shoes   58
Compleat Cookshop   65
Fires and Things   109
Flash Trash   111
Freezavan Ltd   119
Herbal World   134
Home Choose Carpets   137
Late Late Supershop   161
Manns Norwich Brewery Co Ltd   168
Natural Beauty Products Ltd   199
Natural Life Health Foods   200

Nectar Cosmetics   201
Northern Dairies   203
Oasis Trading   207
Paper Place   214
Paramount Syndications   215
Phone-In UK Ltd   221
Poppy's Body Centre Ltd   232
Response Communications   250
Ryman Ltd   253
Singer Consumer Products   261
Stained Glass Overlay   272
Summer Air Ltd   278
JW Thornton Ltd   285
Tie Rack Ltd   286
Unigate Dairies Ltd   296
Weigh & Save Ltd   308
Wildcat Jeans   315

SOCIAL FUNCTIONS
Castle Fairs Ltd   49
M & B Marquees Ltd   163
Modular Marquees Ltd   186
Party Rentals   215
Red Baron   248

TRANSPORT
Amtrak Express Parcels Ltd   7
ANC - The British Parcel Service   9
Brewer & Turnbull Ltd   31
Carryfast Ltd   47
City Link Transport Holdings Ltd   57
Panic Link (Nationwide
   Next Day)   320
TNT Parcel Office   289

TRAVEL AGENTS AND TOURIST
SERVICES
Exchange Travel   101
Hyde-Barker Travel   143
Infopoint Ltd   146

VIDEO
G and T Video Services   122
Primetime Video Centre Ltd   238
Video Film Franchise   303
West Coast Video Enterprises   310

Further Reading from Kogan Page

Kogan Page publish an extensive list of books for business. A full list is available from the publishers.

Be Your Own Company Secretary, A J Scrine, 1987
Be Your Own PR Man, 2nd edition, Michael Bland, 1987
Business Rip-Offs and How to Avoid Them, Tony Attwood, 1987
Buying for Business: How to Get the Best Deal from your Suppliers, Tony Attwood, 1988
Choosing and Using Professional Advisers, ed Paul Chaplin, 1986
Customer Service, Malcolm Peel, 1987
Debt Collection Made Easy, Peter Buckland, 1987
Do Your Own Market Research, Paul N Hague and Peter Jackson, 1987
Expenses and Benefits of Directors and Higher Paid Employees, John F Staddon, annual
Financial Management for the Small Business: a Daily Telegraph Guide, 2nd edition, Colin Barrow, 1988
The First-Time Manager, M J Morris, 1988
How to Make Meetings Work, Malcolm Peel, 1988
Make Every Minute Count, Marion E Haynes, 1988
Profits from Improved Productivity, Fiona Halse and John Humphrey, 1988
The Practice of Successful Business Management, Kenneth Winckles, 1986
Taking Up a Franchise, 4th edition, Colin Barrow and Godfrey Golzen, 1987